License to Drive

License to Drive

Alliance for Safe Driving
Santa Monica, California

Africa • Australia • Canada • Denmark • Japan • Mexico • New Zealand • Philippines
Puerto Rico • Singapore • Spain • United Kingdom • United States

NOTICE TO THE READER

Publisher and author do not warrant or guarantee any of the products described herein. Publisher and author do not perform any independent analysis in connection with any or the product information contained herein. Publisher and author do not assume, and expressly disclaim, any obligation to obtain and include information other than that provided to it by the manufacturer.

The reader is expressly warned to consider and adopt all safety precautions that might be indicated by the activities herein and to avoid all potential hazards. By following the instructions contained herein, the reader willingly assumes all risks in connection with such instructions.

The publisher and author make no representations or warranties of any kind, whether express or implied, including but not limited to, the warranties of fitness for particular purpose or merchantability, nor are any such representations implied with respect to the material set forth herein, its reliability, completeness, correctness, accuracy, legality, practicality or operativeness and the publisher and author do not take any responsibility with respect to such material. The publisher and author shall not be liable for any special, consequential, or exemplary damages resulting, in whole or part, from the readers' use of, interpretation of, application or reliance upon, this material. The material contained herein does not in any way constitute and is not intended to be legal advice, or any promise, guarantee or binding statement of the state of the law.

Delmar Staff:
Business Unit Director: Susan L. Simpfenderfer
Executive Editor: Marlene McHugh Pratt
Developmental Editor: Melissa Riveglia
Executive Marketing Manager: Donna J. Lewis
Executive Production Manager: Wendy A. Troeger
Production Editor: Carolyn Miller
Cover Image: Alliance for Safe Driving
Cover Design: Carolyn Miller

For more information, contact:
Delmar, 3 Columbia Circle, P.O. Box 15015, Albany, New York 12212-0515;
or find us on the World Wide Web at http://www.delmar.com

Library of Congress Cataloging-in-Publication Data

License to drive / Alliance for Safe Driving, Santa Monica,
  California.
      p.   cm.
    Includes index.
    ISBN 0-7668-0302-3
    1. Automobile driving.   I. Alliance for Safe Driving (U.S.)
  TL152.5.L46   1998   98-38549
  629.28'3—dc21   CIP

Figure 21-5 copyright by and courtesy of GeoSystems Global Corporation

This book is dedicated to the memory of Rick Price,
whose life was tragically cut short at the young age of 23 by a drunk driver.
He never had a chance to fulfill his dreams.

About the Authors

The Alliance for Safe Driving is a driving and traffic safety organization dedicated to improving the education of drivers in all jurisdictions. Through many years of educating drivers on behalf of departments of motor vehicles, municipal courts, and traffic courts across North America, the Alliance for Safe Driving has developed a successful, reality-based, interactive learning system that comprises textbooks, workbooks, videotapes, and computerized educational products, including www. licensetodrive.com. The Alliance for Safe Driving's driver safety and traffic education professionals have all contributed to the development of this unique and innovative *License to Drive* driver education course of study.

Contents

Special Boxes

AUTO ACCESSORIES

ROAD WEIRDNESS

Foreword

New drivers are painfully aware of their driving records. But frequently the knowledge and advice offered them is not relevant to their perception of the driving task. *License to Drive* will both appeal and satisfy this need through innovative and pedagogically sound techniques.

The goal of most driver education students is acquiring adequate preparation for passing the tests required to obtain a license. These students already have considerable background with motor vehicles, having been passengers and observers of drivers from infancy. Therefore, it is imperative that new drivers be considered as adults when learning driving skills.

The objectives of this text are stated in behavioral, measurable terms. The text deals with real-world situations and offers suggestions to avoid common driving hazards. Actual police-recorded collisions are analyzed, with emphasis on determining responsibility. Students are encouraged to think about specific driving situations outside of the classroom. Such analysis emphasizes the multiple-cause theory of collisions, searching for all contributory causes.

New drivers need to develop certain driving skills and understand the reasons for rules of the road. Emphasis in this text is made to identify active steps to keep out of harm's way, rather than react to an impending collision. Students are made aware of the rationale for motor-vehicle regulations and potential penalties.

The format has consistency, with sequencing and flow of text in a logical order, and not split up unnecessarily.

License to Drive is designed to be student-centered, with the teacher being a facilitator, using interactive exercises. The text includes critical thinking questions, allowing students to analyze complicated driving situations. Suggested projects are designed for use in group or individual settings, later to be shared in class.

Learning activities include games on an Activity Disk, a computerized test bank, videotapes, and the wide use of visuals. Inviting guest speakers is encouraged. The authors use simple and plain sentence structure, with stress on explaining terminology and concepts.

The benefits of driving involvement are explained, including supervised driving practice and the use of contracts. Emphasis is placed on hands-on training, applying abstract concepts to the realities of actual driving. The involvement of all student observers during driving instruction is encouraged and explained.

The text uses the concept of defensive driving throughout, with advanced driving skills for various environments and situations. An interesting facet of this book is relating appropriate driving incidents of well-known celebrities, again emphasizing real-world relationships.

License to Drive will be an excellent foundation to any basic driver education program. Students and teachers alike will find this text to be both interesting and informative.

Donald L. Smith, Ph.D.
Professor Emeritus
Highway Traffic Safety Program
Michigan State University
Lansing, Michigan

Preface

The object of *License to Drive* is to present you, the beginning driver, with a practical and realistic guide to the fundamentals of driving and the rules of the road. Unlike other textbooks, this book speaks *to* you, not *at* you. It focuses on situations that you are likely to encounter in the real world and offers useful suggestions on how to avoid common driving hazards. *License to Drive* takes you step by step from the basics of vehicle control to the specific dangers of different driving environments to the responsibilities of vehicle ownership. This book also highlights the motor-vehicle regulations and potential penalties that all drivers in North America face when they get behind the wheel.

You are no doubt anxious to start driving as soon as possible. You have waited a long time for the opportunity to go where you want to, when you want to. In fact, if you are like many students, your only goal in taking a driver education course is to pass the driving test in your jurisdiction. However, you must learn how to be a safe driver first. Safety, in all forms—from defensive driving to auto accessories—is thoroughly discussed in this book to provide you with the skills and knowledge you need when on the road. This book teaches you not only what you can and cannot do on the road, but why. By thinking creatively about the driving experience, you will reduce the risks of being involved in a collision.

The guiding philosophy of Alliance for Safe Driving, and of *License to Drive*, is that by driving defensively you can avoid most, if not all, dangerous situations on the roadway. Rather than *react* to an impending collision or road hazard, you *actively* take steps to keep out of harm's way. This book presents a simple defensive-driving technique called SAFE that is easy to remember and apply. By constantly *scanning* ahead, *assessing* road and weather conditions, *finding* an "out" or escape route, and *executing* the best option available, you can become a safer driver. By becoming a safer driver, you will feel more comfortable and confident behind the wheel and will be able to enjoy more of the wonderful rewards that driving a motor vehicle can bring to your life.

License to Drive includes several features to make the subject informative, interesting, and fun. Throughout the margins of the text are Factoids that present surprising statistics and facts. Yellow defensive-driving boxes provide helpful driving tips, debunk common myths, and describe real-life situations that can get you in trouble. Most chapters include a red box on a collision or driving-related incident involving a celebrity, demonstrating that famous actors, sports figures, and artists face the same dangers that you do. Various auto accessories are keyed to the text in blue boxes. Because driving is not *all* work, the book includes amusing Bumper Sticker Sightings, Crazy Auto Laws, and examples of Road Weirdness in green boxes. If you cannot Guess the Vanity Plate or identify the Wild Wheels in each chapter, you can find the answers after Chapter 21.

To make the text accessible to students throughout North America, metric equivalents are provided in parentheses after all units of measure. These are rounded off to avoid awkward numbers, fractions, or decimals. For example, the actual metric equivalent of 30 miles per hour is 48.28041 kilometers per hour, but in the text, it is presented as "(50 km/h)."

To focus your reading and prompt you to think about the material, *License to Drive* offers a wide array of study aids. Chapter Objectives and Key Terms are listed at the front of each chapter. The Key Terms also appear in color in the text and are defined in the glossary at the back of this book. Chapters 2 through 17 include special Who's at Fault? boxes that challenge you to analyze an actual collision taken from real police records and determine who is responsible. Beginning with Chapter 2, each chapter has a comprehensive Self-Test, including two Critical Thinking questions that ask you what to do in a complex driving situation. Finally, two Projects that can be done individually or as classroom activities are provided to translate what you read in the chapter to the real world. All of these activities are designed to start you thinking about and preparing for your time on the road, which we hope will be rewarding.

Alliance for Safe Driving

Acknowledgments

The authors gratefully acknowledge the following individuals for their assistance in the development of this book:

Lt. Barry I. Beck
Former Deputy Director, Traffic
    Control Section
Delaware State Police
Dover, Delaware

Ricardo Cerna
Executive Secretary
Association of Driver Educators
    for the Disabled
Edgerton, Wisconsin

Richard Coleman
Visual Information Specialist
U.S. Department of Transportation
Federal Highway Administration
Washington, D.C.

Arthur G. Ericson
Chief of Driver Services,
    Division of Motor Vehicles
Delaware Division of Motor
    Vehicles
Dover, Delaware

Wayne Hurder
Director, Driver License Section,
    Division of Motor Vehicles
North Carolina Department
    of Transportation
Raleigh, North Carolina

Penny Martucci
Assistant Division Director,
    Commercial Licensing Program,
    Motor Vehicle Division
Arizona Department of
    Transportation
Phoenix, Arizona

Margaret R. Mink
Washington Department
    of Licensing
Olympia, Washington

Jamie Morrison
Registrar of Motor Vehicles,
    Motor Vehicle Branch
Department of Transportation
Fredericton, New Brunswick

Mark A. Patrick
Curator, National Automotive
    History Collection
Detroit Public Library
Detroit, Michigan

Sandy Saunders
Museum Services Manager
National Automotive Museum
The Harrah Collection
Reno, Nevada

Dr. Donald L. Smith
Professor Emeritus, Highway
    Traffic Safety Program
Michigan State University
Lansing, Michigan

Sergeant Robert P. Stein
Arizona Department of Public
    Safety
Phoenix, Arizona

Alliance for Safe Driving and Delmar Publishers wish to express their appreciation to a dedicated group of professionals who reviewed and provided commentary at various stages. Their insights, suggestions, and attention to detail were very important in guiding the development of this textbook.

Lou Autry
Senior Consultant
Region 10, Education Service
    Center
Richardson, Texas

Mackey D. Ervin
Coordinator, Driver Education
Region IV Education Service
    Center
Houston, Texas

Terry Barnett
Driver Education Instructor
McClintock High School
Tempe, Arizona

Derek J. Ewing
Instructor/Manager
E&E Defensive Driving Associates
Loudonville, New York

James A. Brooks
Supervisor, Driver and Safety Education
Mississippi Department of Education
Jackson, Mississippi

Dr. Frank J. Gruber, IV
Associate Professor, Technology
    and Safety Studies
Northern Illinois University
DeKalb, Illinois

Alice Ann Klakos
Principal, Driver Education Instructor
Oak Glen High School
New Cumberland, West Virginia

Robert E. Lambert
Driver Education Instructor
Cabell Midland High School
Ona, West Virginia

Richard A. Mossey
Co-Owner
Defensive Driving School, Inc.
Seattle, Washington

John Papa
President, Illinois High School and College Driver Education Association
Lake Park High School
Roselle, Illinois

Sharon Postigo
President
D&D Driving School, Inc.
Kettering, Ohio

John R. Sawyer
Coordinator, Driver Education Services
Wellsville Local Schools
Wellsville, Ohio

Craig Westfall
Driver Education Instructor
Santa Rita High School
Tucson, Arizona

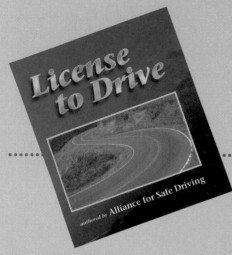

How to Use *License to Drive*

License to Drive is designed to help you learn to drive defensively, responsibly, and safely. The text has many unique features that also make learning how to drive interesting and fun.

1 Unit Openers

Each unit opener includes a photograph relating to the unit topic and a list of the chapters within that unit.

2 Chapter Openers

Each chapter opener includes a photograph for discussion that captures the theme of the chapter, a brief introduction to the chapter content, a list of Chapter Objectives tied to each section within the chapter, and a list of Key Terms in the order in which they appear in the chapter.

3 Chapter Objectives

Chapter Objectives identify key information to be gained from the chapters. Use these objectives, together with the Your Turn questions, to reinforce your understanding of the chapter's content.

4 Key Terms

Important terms to know are listed at the beginning of each chapter and appear in red the first time they are used in text.

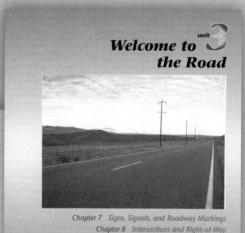

Welcome to the Road unit 3

Chapter 7 *Signs, Signals, and Roadway Markings*
Chapter 8 *Intersections and Right-of-Way*
Chapter 9 *Turning*

chapter 3

The Condition of the Driver

Your ability to drive safely is determined by both your physical condition and your emotional well-being. The quality of your eyesight and hearing, whether you have an illness or disability, and even your size and height are factors that you must consider when you get behind the wheel. Your mental state is equally important. It takes a good attitude to be courteous to other drivers and to drive defensively. A negative attitude, overconfidence or underconfidence, and any other feelings that affect your driving do not belong in the car. Anger, stress, anxiety, and other emotions can and do lead to crashes.

CHAPTER OBJECTIVES

Upon completion of this chapter, you should be able to:

3–1 The Physical Condition of the Driver
1. Describe permanent physical conditions that can limit your ability to drive safely.
2. Describe the four main components of vision.
3. Describe temporary physical conditions that can limit your ability to drive safely.
4. Understand how you can prevent carbon monoxide poisoning.

3–2 The Mental Condition of the Driver
5. Understand how your mental condition impacts your ability to drive safely.
6. Understand how to avoid becoming a victim of road rage.
7. Describe activities you should avoid while driving.

KEY TERMS

visual acuity	depth perception	carbon monoxide
field of vision	color vision	road rage
central vision	color blindness	rubbernecking
peripheral vision	fatigue	

5 Color Photographs and Illustrations

Throughout the text, there are many visual images and detailed captions to aid in the explanation and understanding of the subject matter. Color photographs provide realistic examples of the content described. Full-color illustrations depict "real-life" driving scenarios and driving instructions, and reinforce chapter material.

186 ◆ UNIT 3 *Welcome to the Road*

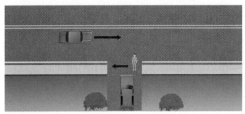

Figure 8–14 Alleys and private roads

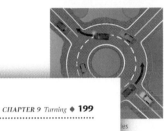

motor-vehicle department to find out exactly what the rules are.

If you are making a left turn, all approaching vehicles have the right-of-way. Wait until the road is clear of oncoming traffic to make your turn. If you are in an intersection when your light turns yellow, wait until oncoming traffic has stopped, then proceed. If the light turns red while you are waiting to make your left turn, stay calm and proceed cautiously only when oncoming traffic has stopped. Cross

CHAPTER 9 Turning ◆ **199**

Figure 9–1 At some intersections, you may turn only when you have a green arrow.

9–1 BASICS

A **protected turn** is one made from a turn lane posted with signs, road marked with arrows, and accompanied by a traffic signal arrow. A green arrow or special green light for your lane allows you to turn while traffic from the oncoming lane(s) is halted with a red light. If the signal allows you to make a turn only when you have a green ar-

row (the green arrow turns to a red arrow or red light), it is a **fully protected turn**.

A **semiprotected turn** is one made from a turn lane but *not* accompanied by a special traffic signal light that directs your turn with a green arrow or a special green light. You are allowed to make such a turn either while you have a regular solid green light or when there is no light and a sufficient gap in traffic occurs.

Figure 9–2 When making a semiprotected turn, you may turn on a solid green light once a sufficient gap in traffic exists.

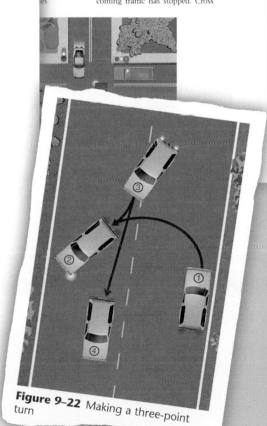

Figure 9–22 Making a three-point turn

Special Features

License to Drive includes many text boxes and marginal text features that provide advice, facts, and entertaining samples related to the driving experience.

- Celebrity scenarios are presented in red-shaded boxes throughout the text. The celebrity boxes convey the details of a collision or driving-related incident involving a famous artist, athlete, or musician.

- Fun items are presented in green-shaded boxes and marginal text. They include Auto Slang, Bumper Sticker Sightings, Guess the Vanity Plate, Crazy Auto Laws, and Wild Wheels.

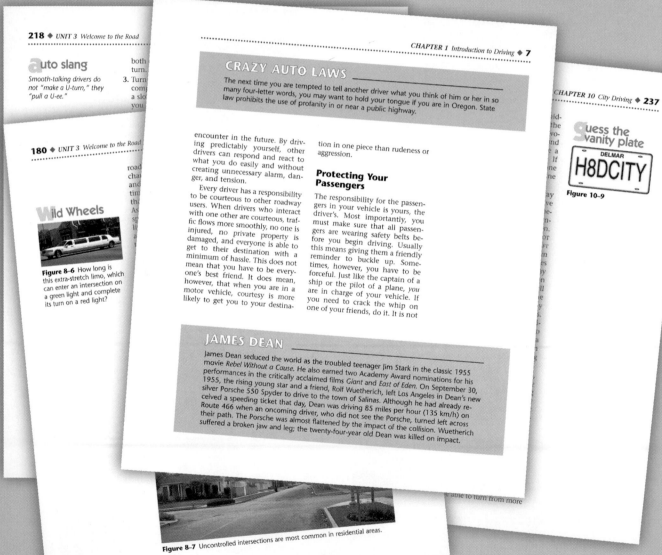

218 ◆ UNIT 3 *Welcome to the Road*

auto slang

Smooth-talking drivers do not "make a U-turn," they "pull a U-ee."

180 ◆ UNIT 3 *Welcome to the Road*

Wild Wheels

Figure 8–6 How long is this extra-stretch limo, which can enter an intersection on a green light and complete its turn on a red light?

CHAPTER 1 *Introduction to Driving* ◆ **7**

CRAZY AUTO LAWS

The next time you are tempted to tell another driver what you think of him or her in so many four-letter words, you may want to hold your tongue if you are in Oregon. State law prohibits the use of profanity in or near a public highway.

encounter in the future. By driving predictably yourself, other drivers can respond and react to what you do easily and without creating unnecessary alarm, danger, and tension.

Every driver has a responsibility to be courteous to other roadway users. When drivers who interact with one other are courteous, traffic flows more smoothly, no one is injured, no private property is damaged, and everyone is able to get to their destination with a minimum of hassle. This does not mean that you have to be everyone's best friend. It does mean, however, that when you are in a motor vehicle, courtesy is more likely to get you to your destina-

tion in one piece than rudeness or aggression.

Protecting Your Passengers

The responsibility for the passengers in your vehicle is yours, the driver's. Most importantly, you must make sure that all passengers are wearing safety belts before you begin driving. Usually this means giving them a friendly reminder to buckle up. Sometimes, however, you have to be forceful. Just like the captain of a ship or the pilot of a plane, *you* are in charge of your vehicle. If you need to crack the whip on one of your friends, do it. It is not

JAMES DEAN

James Dean seduced the world as the troubled teenager Jim Stark in the classic 1955 movie *Rebel Without a Cause*. He also earned two Academy Award nominations for his performances in the critically acclaimed films *Giant* and *East of Eden*. On September 30, 1955, the rising young star and a friend, Rolf Wuetherich, left Los Angeles in Dean's new silver Porsche 550 Spyder to drive to the town of Salinas. Although he had already received a speeding ticket that day, Dean was driving 85 miles per hour (135 km/h) on Route 466 when an oncoming driver, who did not see the Porsche, turned left across their path. The Porsche was almost flattened by the impact of the collision. Wuetherich suffered a broken jaw and leg; the twenty-four-year old Dean was killed on impact.

Figure 8–7 Uncontrolled intersections are most common in residential areas.

CHAPTER 10 *City Driving* ◆ **237**

Guess the vanity plate

DELMAR
H8DCITY

Figure 10–9

- Defensive-driving features are presented in three types of yellow-shaded boxes and marginal text: Driving Tips, Reality Check, and Driving Myths.

- Factual information appears in blue-shaded boxes and marginal text. Factoids present interesting data that reinforce points made in the text. Auto Accessories boxes provide examples of optional equipment available for vehicles.

---

208 ◆ UNIT 3 *Welcome to the Road*

USING SAFE "Stealing" Left Turns

You are stopped at a red light at an intersection. Two left-turning drivers in oncoming traffic have just completed their turns, and your light changes to green. You accelerate into the intersection and nearly collide with a third driver trying to "steal" a left across your path. This is an all-too-common situation that you can avoid by using the SAFE process. While waiting at the light, use the opportunity to thoroughly *scan* the intersection. Note whether left turns are protected or semiprotected and if there are DO NOT BLOCK INTERSECTION signs. *Assess* whether there are any drivers who may try to sneak a left. Is traffic heavy, causing impatient drivers to take risks rather than wait for the next light? Are oncoming drivers queued up in the left-turn lane, displaying signs of nervousness, anxiety, or frustration? Are they creeping forward into the intersection? Are drivers in lanes adjoining yours showing signs of racing into the intersection, leading to a collision that could spill over into your lane? *Find* an "out" by checking the lanes on either side of you and the distance between your vehicle and oncoming left-turn drivers. *Execute* your decision to avoid a potential crash by starting your forward movement slowly and being prepared to tap your brakes to communicate the danger to drivers behind you.

left. You can get to the same point of your intended left turn by going up a block, making a right, turning right at the next intersection, and then making a right to get back to the original street where you intended to make your left. This may sound like a lot of trouble, but in the end, you will actually get where you want to go faster and more safely.

Heavy Traffic Situations

Turning left in the middle of a block to enter a driveway or alley in heavy traffic can be tricky. Because there are no intersection lines for the opposite traffic to stop behind, there is nothing to help create a gap in traffic to allow you to turn left. This situation calls for using the "Four C's": *crawling, communication, confidence, and caution.*

DRIVING TIPS Hesitant Left-Turners

Everyone is familiar with the driver who is afraid to move toward the center of an intersection to prepare for a left turn. In heavy traffic, this failure to "move up" will probably mean that you will miss your chance to turn left, making you wait for the next green light. Be patient. Whatever you do, do not pressure the driver to move by honking your horn, flashing your lights, or gesturing in any way. It is not worth scaring the driver and causing a collision. Wait until you can safely advance into the intersection and then make your turn.

---

190 ◆ UNIT 3 *Welcome to the Road*

◆factoid

A motorist is forty times more likely to die in a collision with a train than with another car.

◆factoid

Texas, Illinois, Indiana, and Cali... together account... third of all highw... crossing crashes... United States.

REALITY CHECK Playing "Chicke...

If you live in a rural area where weekend nights are... you and your friends might be tempted to head for... play an old and dangerous car game of "chicken." ... until the last minute before you hit the gas and try... fore the train hits your car. Sounds fun, right? The... look cool in front of your friends you have forgott... a piece of metal weighing 6,000 times more than... against you! Playing chicken with another driver... with a train is certain suicide.

...nals, and Roadway Markings ◆ **163**

...tions.

...a lane
...d and
...rection
...reduce

...com-
...at traf-
...es oth-
... traffic.
... on one
...onfused
...tention
...on colli-
...ous just
...esignated
...rsed.
...ccupancy
...iamond"
...e special

AUTO ACCESSORIES Fog Lights

Having fog lights on your vehicle can dramatically increase your ability to see roadway markings and lanes at night or in bad weather. Because roads in areas that receive severe weather do not usually have lane dividers, fog lights can provide that extra margin of safety to keep you on the road and in your lane.

7 Who's at Fault?

Chapters 2 through 17 each include an account of two collisions taken from actual police records. Based on your knowledge of the chapter content, you determine who is at fault.

8 Your Turn

Use these questions, which mirror the Chapter Objectives, to test your understanding of the chapter content.

YOUR TURN

2–1 Defensive-Driving Skills

1. What is defensive driving?
2. What are the essential skills you need to driv

2–2 Managing Time, Space, and Visibilit

3. Why is following distance important?
4. What is the 3-second rule?
5. How large should your space cushion be?
6. How can you deal with tailgaters?
7. How can you make yourself known to ot

2–3 The SAFE Method

8. What does "SAFE" stand for?
9. What is the sequence of the orderly vi
10. What is the purpose of each step in th

SELF-TEST

Multiple Choice

1. Ideally, a space cushion should be _____ vehicle space(s) to either s
   a. two
   b. one
2. Gradually reducing your speed ca
   a. large trucks
   b. buses
3. You should honk your horn:
   a. to greet a friend.
   b. at another driver's error.
   d. to warn a ___ path.
4. On a freeway at high speeds, you should be scanning about _____ ahead.
   a. ¼ mile (400 m)
   b. 500 feet (150 m)
   c. ⅓ mile (500 m)
   d. 200 feet (60 m)

CHAPTER 10 *City Driving* ◆ **245**

WHO'S AT FAULT?

1. Driver 1 was proceeding eastbound on a residential street at approximately 20 miles per hour (30 km/h). Driver 3 had just completed parallel parking on the eastbound side of the street ahead of Driver 1. Driver 2 was traveling westbound and had slowed to approximately 15 miles per hour (25 km/h). She had moved well toward the center of the street to avoid the parked cars on the north side of the street. Driver 1, estimating that he had adequate space to maneuver between Driver 2 and Driver 3, continued eastbound in the only lane available and was unable to stop when Driver 3 opened the door to exit his vehicle. Driver 1 applied his brakes but still knocked Driver 3's left front door completely off. *Who's at fault?*

2. Driver 1 was proceeding northbound on Central Avenue approaching a signal-controlled intersection at approximately 35 miles per hour (55 km/h) in the number 2 lane. Drivers 3 and 4 were stopped at the red light ahead. Driver 2, who was northbound in the number 1 lane immediately next to Driver 1, was slowing in preparation to stop. Driver 1 had just purchased a hamburger at a fast food restaurant and was eating as he drove. While approaching the intersection he took a bite out of his burger, being careful not to spill it on his clothes. As he looked up, Driver 1 realized he was about to rear-end Driver 3. He simultaneously swerved to his left and stomped on the brake. Driver 1 managed to avoid hitting either Driver 3 or 4, but he slammed into Driver 2, who collided with the center median. *Who's at fault?*

9 Self-Test

Every chapter, with the exception of Chapter 1, includes a test with five components (Multiple Choice, Sentence Completion, Matching, Short Answer, and Critical Thinking). Complete the Self-Test to be sure that you understand the chapter material.

10 Projects

Each chapter following Chapter 1 includes two Projects that you can complete outside of class individually or in groups. Also, ask the instructor about the Activity Disk and how to access the website **www.licensetodrive.com**. Each offers you additional games, exercises, and resources for learning.

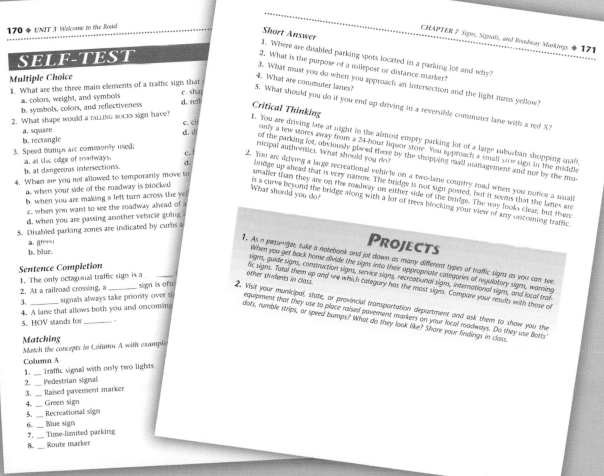

170 ◆ UNIT 3 *Welcome to the Road*

SELF-TEST

Multiple Choice

1. What are the three main elements of a traffic sign that
   a. colors, weight, and symbols   c. shap
   b. symbols, colors, and reflectiveness   d. refl
2. What shape would a FALLING ROCKS sign have?
   a. square   c. cir
   b. rectangle   d. di
3. Speed bumps are commonly used:
   a. at the edge of roadways.   c.
   b. at dangerous intersections.   d.
4. When are you *not* allowed to temporarily move to
   a. when your side of the roadway is blocked
   b. when you are making a left turn across the yel
   c. when you want to see the roadway ahead of a
   d. when you are passing another vehicle going
5. Disabled parking zones are indicated by curbs a
   a. green
   b. blue.

Sentence Completion

1. The only octagonal traffic sign is a _____
2. At a railroad crossing, a _____ sign is ofte
3. _____ signals always take priority over si
4. A lane that allows both you and oncoming
5. HOV stands for _____ .

Matching
Match the concepts in Column A with example

Column A
1. __ Traffic signal with only two lights
2. __ Pedestrian signal
3. __ Raised pavement marker
4. __ Green sign
5. __ Recreational sign
6. __ Blue sign
7. __ Time-limited parking
8. __ Route marker

CHAPTER 7 *Signs, Signals, and Roadway Markings* ◆ **171**

Short Answer
1. Where are disabled parking spots located in a parking lot and why?
2. What is the purpose of a milepost or distance marker?
3. What must you do when you approach an intersection and the light turns yellow?
4. What are commuter lanes?
5. What should you do if you end up driving in a reversible commuter lane with a red X?

Critical Thinking
1. You are driving late at night in the almost empty parking lot of a large suburban shopping mall, only a few stores away from a 24-hour liquor store. You approach a small STOP sign in the middle of the parking lot, obviously placed there by the shopping mall management and not by the municipal authorities. What should you do?
2. You are driving a large recreational vehicle on a two-lane country road when you notice a small bridge up ahead that is very narrow. The bridge is not sign posted, but it seems that the lanes are smaller than they are on the roadway on either side of the bridge. The way looks clear, but there is a curve beyond the bridge along with a lot of trees blocking your view of any oncoming traffic. What should you do?

PROJECTS

1. As a passenger, take a notebook and jot down as many different types of traffic signs as you can see. When you get back home divide the signs into their appropriate categories of regulatory signs, warning signs, guide signs, construction signs, service signs, recreational signs, international signs, and local traffic signs. Total them up and see which category has the most signs. Compare your results with those of other students in class.

2. Visit your municipal, state, or provincial transportation department and ask them to show you the equipment that they use to place raised pavement markers on your local roadways. Do they use Botts' dots, rumble strips, or speed bumps? What do they look like? Share your findings in class.

11 Glossary and Index

An extensive glossary of definitions for all of the Key Terms appears at the back of this book. Use the comprehensive index to easily locate subject areas throughout the text.

Introduction to Driving

You are about to learn how to do something that you have wanted to do for a long time. Perhaps you have an older brother or sister who is already driving or a friend who has already taken driver education and is operating a vehicle with a learner's permit. Whatever the case, now is your chance to finally get behind the wheel! The excitement that you feel now is very positive, and it will put you in the right frame of mind to learn all about driving and traffic safety.

Upon completion of this chapter, you should be able to:

1–1 Driver Education

1. Understand the purpose of driver education.
2. Describe the basic components of a "driver ed" course.

1–2 Driving Is a Privilege

3. Understand why driving is a privilege, not a right.
4. Describe your basic responsibilities as a driver.
5. Understand why it is important for you to be courteous as a driver.
6. Understand the importance of being emotionally, physically, and mentally fit to drive.

1–3 The Highway Transportation System

7. Understand what the Highway Transportation System is.
8. List the three main classifications of roadways.
9. Identify who is responsible for enforcing traffic laws.

KEY TERMS

driver education

Highway Transportation
  System (HTS)

traffic laws

by-laws

law enforcement

1–1 DRIVER EDUCATION

Driver education is designed to help unlicensed drivers become familiar with the basics of vehicle control and the rules of the road so that they can successfully pass the tests required to earn a driver's license. Even though you will be taught many skills and safe driving practices in your driver education course, you should remember that completing the course does not mean the end of your education.

A driver education course, or "driver ed," cannot teach you everything. The world of driving is constantly changing, and you must be prepared to handle new problems that may occur in the future. If you move from one location to another, for example, you will have to cope with driving situations you never experienced before. When crossing any state or provincial boundary, be aware that motor-vehicle laws, safety standards, registration rules, insurance requirements, and the costs of vehicle ownership change. With each new day of driving, you will gain more knowledge and experience that will make you a better and safer driver as time goes on.

Who Takes a Driver Education Course?

Some people cannot wait to begin driving, whatever their age. On the other hand, more people than you think never bother to get a license. The typical driver education student in the United States and Canada is a fifteen- or sixteen-year-old high school sophomore or junior. You, however, may fit into one of the following categories:

- A fourteen-year-old son or daughter of a farmer in a rural jurisdiction that allows you to become licensed to drive farm vehicles to a nearby town

Figure 1–1 "Driver ed" is just the start of your education in driving.

- A twenty-one-year-old recent graduate from college who never needed to drive, but who now has taken a job in a suburban area and needs a car to get there
- A thirty-eight-year-old recent immigrant to North America who never drove before in your country of origin
- A seventy-six-year-old retiree who always depended on a spouse for transportation and so never got around to learning how to drive

Types of Driver Education Courses

Typically, you have three options if you want to enroll in a driver education course. You can take classes at a private or public high school, a community college, or a private driving school. Because of budget cuts, more and more high schools are contracting these courses out to specific private driving schools or suggesting that students pursue training at a private driving school of their choice. Depending on the area and the length of the program, a course at a private school can cost the student or the student's family anywhere from $100 to $500 or more.

Components of a Driver Education Course

The typical driver education course includes both in-class instruction and training behind the wheel. The in-class component usually consists of 30 hours of textbook

instruction, with additional hours of homework and examinations. Driver training usually includes 6 hours of behind-the-wheel instruction, often in a dual-steering-wheeled vehicle. During this training, you will be accompanied at all times by the driving instructor.

Because 6 hours is inadequate behind-the-wheel instruction, you should count on practicing for many more hours with family members, friends, or another professional driving instructor. Practicing as much as you can before you take your driving test will increase your confidence. You also will not have to cope with the pressure of learning everything you will need to know in a mere 6 hours. Driving instructors generally believe that a minimum of 30 hours of training behind the wheel is necessary, and many recommend even more time.

1–2 DRIVING IS A PRIVILEGE

If you learn one thing from this book, always remember that *driving is a privilege, not a right.* There is no "natural" or constitutional right to operate a motor vehicle. Driving is a privilege granted to those who meet certain requirements and obligations. Society has determined that for practical reasons it should be up to the individual provinces and states to decide when and under what conditions a person can drive. Not all jurisdictions agree on what the magic age should be. Some allow you to begin learning how to drive as early as fourteen years of age,

bumper sticker sightings

EVACUATE THE ROAD!!! STUDENT DRIVING!!

whereas others do not let you behind the wheel until you are much older.

Those who wish to drive must demonstrate that they are worthy of a driver's license by passing tests and obeying the law. A license can be restricted, suspended, or even revoked (taken away) for committing various driving offenses. Even if your driver's license is necessary for you to get to work or school every day, this does not mean that the government *has* to give it to you.

Once you obtain your driver's license, you will be treated the same as any adult with a license who is also on the roadways. This includes drivers who have been driving for decades and are much more experienced than you are. Driving is an opportunity that society gives you to be treated like an adult, so take your obligations seriously.

Driving Is a Responsibility

Once your state or province has given you a driver's license, society expects you to give back something in return for your new freedom. Take responsibility for your driving. Your main obligations while driving a motor vehicle are to obey the law, to fulfill the financial obligations associated with a crash you cause, to show courtesy to other roadway users, to protect your passengers, to know and properly maintain your vehicle, and to drive only when you are physically and mentally able.

Your Legal Duties

You have a responsibility to obey the law when you drive. This means that you must not break any of the laws in the state or provincial vehicle code or any municipal laws or ordinances that may be in effect in the area in which you are driving. It also means trying to minimize the chances of colliding with another vehicle. If you think that this is a responsibility that does not need to be taken seriously, think again. You may be found liable or partly liable for causing a collision that

---

REALITY CHECK *Driving with a Fake License* _____

Just because you do not have a driver's license yet does not mean that you are not responsible for your actions if you drive illegally. Many teens obtain fake licenses, or borrow licenses from a relative or friend, just to have "a piece of paper" in case they get pulled over by the police. If you drive without having first received proper instruction and your license, however, you are endangering yourself and everyone else on the road. Driving is a privilege earned through education, practice, and the licensing process. If you drive illegally, you or your parents will be held accountable for whatever deaths, injuries, or property damage you cause.

was not strictly your fault but which you could have avoided.

Your Financial Obligations

When you drive a motor vehicle, you are interacting with countless other people, vehicles, and private property. If you commit an error while driving and injure someone else or damage property, you must pay for these injuries and damages if the accident is determined to be your fault. The primary reason for having automobile insurance is that if such an unfortunate event occurs, your insurance company will cover the costs. Keep in mind, however, that if you do not have enough

insurance to cover the injuries or damage, you are not off the hook. The person or persons who are injured or whose property was damaged can sue you in court for any damages over and above your insurance limits.

Courtesy to Others

If you were the only person on the roadway, driving would be a lot easier than it is. Not only do *you* have to drive safely, but you also have to watch for other drivers and pedestrians. By watching how other drivers or pedestrians react to different situations, you will soon discover that you can make fairly accurate predictions about similar situations you may

Figure 1–2 Do not wait until it is too late to realize your responsibilities as a driver.

CRAZY AUTO LAWS

The next time you are tempted to tell another driver what you think of him or her in so many four-letter words, you may want to hold your tongue if you are in Oregon. State law prohibits the use of profanity in or near a public highway.

encounter in the future. By driving predictably yourself, other drivers can respond and react to what you do easily and without creating unnecessary alarm, danger, and tension.

Every driver has a responsibility to be courteous to other roadway users. When drivers who interact with one other are courteous, traffic flows more smoothly, no one is injured, no private property is damaged, and everyone is able to get to their destination with a minimum of hassle. This does not mean that you have to be everyone's best friend. It does mean, however, that when you are in a motor vehicle, courtesy is more likely to get you to your destination in one piece than rudeness or aggression.

Protecting Your Passengers

The responsibility for the passengers in your vehicle is yours, the driver's. Most importantly, you must make sure that all passengers are wearing safety belts before you begin driving. Usually this means giving them a friendly reminder to buckle up. Sometimes, however, you have to be forceful. Just like the captain of a ship or the pilot of a plane, *you* are in charge of your vehicle. If you need to crack the whip on one of your friends, do it. It is not

JAMES DEAN

James Dean seduced the world as the troubled teenager Jim Stark in the classic 1955 movie *Rebel Without a Cause*. He also earned two Academy Award nominations for his performances in the critically acclaimed films *Giant* and *East of Eden*. On September 30, 1955, the rising young star and a friend, Rolf Wuetherich, left Los Angeles in Dean's new silver Porsche 550 Spyder to drive to the town of Salinas. Although he had already received a speeding ticket that day, Dean was driving 85 miles per hour (135 km/h) on Route 466 when an oncoming driver, who did not see the Porsche, turned left across their path. The Porsche was almost flattened by the impact of the collision. Wuetherich suffered a broken jaw and leg; the twenty-four-year old Dean was killed on impact.

Figure 1–3 It is your responsibility as a driver to ensure that passengers fasten their safety belts.

worth risking the safety of the other occupants and yourself.

Knowing Your Vehicle

Knowing your vehicle's limitations, what it can and cannot do, is crucial to safe driving. A car with a small engine will have some problems keeping up with traffic in the fast lane on a steep hill. A car with low ground clearance will have a problem traversing a rutted dirt road. A car with high ground clearance will have problems negotiating sharp turns at the same speed as a normal passenger sedan. The better you know your vehicle, the more control you will have in an emergency situation and the easier it will be to park or execute potentially dangerous maneuvers such as passing.

For your own safety and comfort, as well as for the safety and comfort of other drivers on the roadways, you have a responsibility to perform regular maintenance on your vehicle. Some of this maintenance, such as adding oil or coolant, inflating your tires, or changing a windshield wiper blade, is basic and can be performed by you. Other tasks are more complicated and should be performed by a certified mechanic. Parts wear down, break, and lose lubrication over time. Day-to-day maintenance and periodic servicing will keep your repair costs to a minimum and reduce the risk of a breakdown.

Because your vehicle is a machine that releases emissions from the burning of fuel, it naturally has effects on the environment, some of which are quite harmful. You have a responsibility as a member of society to understand what kind of fuel emissions your car discharges and what you can do to minimize pollutants. Usually, this means ensuring that any emissions control device on the vehicle, such as a catalytic converter, is performing properly. It also means using public transportation (such as buses or light rail), carpooling, and taking every opportunity to walk or ride a bicycle for short trips.

Being Ready to Drive

Driving with the right attitude—a good attitude—is an important responsibility. Attitude directly affects your driving, which involves constantly making decisions, many of them with life-or-death implications. To make good decisions, you need to think clearly and not be burdened by your emotions. All of us have a "bad day" once in awhile, but if you have just broken up with someone, failed a test, or lost your job, you must either put these problems behind you or

avoid driving. Having the right attitude means not being overconfident and cocky, which can also lead to poor decision making.

You are also responsible for being in good physical shape when you drive. This does not mean that you have to have the physique of a body builder or the stamina of a marathon runner. It does mean that you need to have the physical ability to perform all of the tasks associated with driving, such as steering, braking, and shifting gears. It also means that your vision, hearing, and hand-eye coordination (with or without the use of special equipment) must be adequate. Finally, it means that you should avoid driving when you are sick, under the influence of alcohol or other drugs, have an injury, or are taking medications that interfere with driving skills.

Driving is a mental, as well as an emotional and physical, exercise. Because all the vehicle's systems are controlled by the driver, your brain must constantly assess what systems are in use, how they are being used, and to what extent

DRIVING TIPS *Behind-the-Wheel Jitters*

It is natural to be nervous the first time you are guiding a huge piece of machinery that weighs a couple of thousand pounds down streets, around corners, and into parking spaces. Driving it at high speeds with other, more experienced drivers flying past you or honking at you can literally cause you to shake. Remember that a healthy fear of the dangers of driving is a good thing, but if you feel overwhelmed by the requirements of driving your vehicle, pull over in a safe area so that you can calm down. Take a few deep breaths, replay in your mind the instructions for the particular driving task you are practicing, and when you feel ready, re-enter traffic.

their use needs to be modified. Your mind's ability to correctly judge space and time is critical to your ability to negotiate a road and keep clear of other vehicles and obstacles.

Your capacity to memorize things is another aspect of being mentally fit. While you drive, you need to remember how your car functions, what the traffic laws are, and what you have just scanned ahead, to the sides, and to the rear of your vehicle. If an emergency develops or if you need to take immediate evasive action, your memory will help you out. For example, by remembering that a shoulder you scanned seconds earlier is clear of traffic, you know that you have an escape route should an obstacle suddenly appear in your path.

1–3 THE HIGHWAY TRANSPORTATION SYSTEM

The **Highway Transportation System (HTS)** is part of our interconnected North American transportation system, which includes rail, air, sea, underground, and pedestrian traffic, as well as motor vehicle transportation. It covers Canada, the United States, and parts of the Caribbean and Pacific Islands. By far, the most important component of the system, as it impacts our daily lives, is motor vehicles. As individuals we are likely to spend more of our time in a motor vehicle than in any other form of transportation. The purpose of the HTS is to move people and goods in a safe, efficient, and timely manner across state, provincial, and in-

Figure 1–4 The Highway Transportation System includes roadways, vehicles, and the people who use them.

ternational boundaries with a minimum of bother. This facilitation of travel and movement contributes significantly to the dynamic economy of North America.

As population increases in North America and society becomes more mobile, the HTS is getting more crowded and indispensable. Think for a moment where we would be without it. How would we get to our relative's house halfway across the state or province? How would food get to your local supermarket? How would an injured person get to a hospital? With very few exceptions, almost everyone on the continent depends on motor vehicles for transportation. Places where the motor vehicle is secondary in importance to subways, trains, ferries, and even airplanes—New York and Boston (subways); Chicago, San Francisco, and Washington, D.C. (subway/light rail); rural Alaska (small airplanes); and Puget Sound, Washington (ferries)—are rare. Even in urban commuting situations in which people depend on public transportation to go back and forth to work, most either maintain or have access to a motor vehicle for their non-commuting needs.

The motor vehicle has become such an important aspect of our lives over the past century that the way our cities, towns, shopping malls, and other public places look has a lot to do with the automobile. The suburb, which is so common to cities in the United States and Canada, is largely a creation of the automobile, because with-

out it, commuting back and forth to jobs in urban centers would have been impossible.

Of course, the HTS would not be what it is were it not for the people who make it function day in and day out. Many people depend on the HTS for their livelihood, and many jobs would be impossible without its existence. Truck drivers, car salespeople, autoworkers, law-enforcement officials, and auto mechanics are just some of the people who rely on the HTS to make a living.

How You Relate to the HTS

The HTS is a large grid or network much like the communication systems that connect people's telephones and computers to one another. In both cases, the overall system is made up of many smaller grids or networks. For example, each geographic region has its own telephone system and "area" code, but they are all linked together so that people in different regions can communicate. Similarly, your neighborhood is its own small grid connected to the larger HTS grid.

You have walked the sidewalks and streets in your neighborhood countless times, perhaps on a newspaper delivery route. Or perhaps you have ridden your bicycle or skateboard down to the local shopping mall. Undoubtedly, you have been a passenger in an adult's car while being driven out of town on a freeway.

In each case, you were actively playing a part in the HTS. When

Only about 60% of the nearly 4 million miles of roadway in the United States are paved.

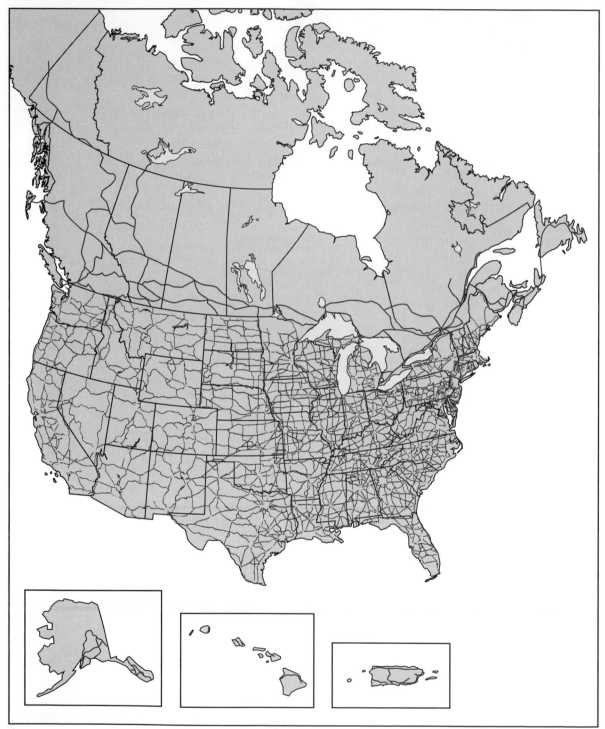

Figure 1–5 The Highway Transportation System links all of North America.

you delivered newspapers in the morning, you met the delivery truck that distributed a large bundle of papers to your driveway from the printing press at the other side of town. You then used the streets designed and built by road construction companies to deliver the newspapers on your bicycle. When you rode your bicycle to the shopping mall, you had to leave the neighborhood and ride down a busy main street to get to the mall, interacting with cars, motorcycles, buses, and trucks on your way. When you were a passenger in an adult's car, you left the neighborhood and the main street behind when you entered the freeway on-ramp and joined thousands of other vehicles on the high-speed thoroughfare that connects your local main street to the rest of North America.

Many people use several different parts of the HTS daily. Consider the person who drives his or her car through residential streets to the vanpool parking lot, commutes into the city on the freeway via vanpool to a central drop-off point, takes a bus from the drop-off point to the block where he or she works, walks the rest of the way down the sidewalk to the office building, and then takes a bike ride during the lunch hour for physical exercise. This person has used five different types of transportation; has covered three types of roadway; has been a driver, passenger, pedestrian, and rider; and has interacted with countless other HTS users—all in one day!

Each time that you use the HTS, you will inevitably face conflict of some kind. Not to worry, this conflict is almost always resolved, thanks to the way the HTS is maintained and ordered. Conflict is created between two or more users of the HTS when their goals or desires are different from one another. For example, when you are driving a car and you desire to proceed forward on a straight road, the fact that a pedestrian has begun to cross the street in a crosswalk in front of you leads to conflict. You want to continue straight on your way. The pedestrian wants to cross the street. Your goals and desires are in conflict. The HTS has rules about who has priority to use the road at any one given point in time and place, and these rules tell you that you need to stop for the pedestrian. The conflict is resolved.

Roadways

The three main components of the HTS are roadways, vehicles, and people. There are almost as many types of roadway in North America as you can imagine. Whether it is an eight-lane interstate freeway or a small dirt access road, each has its own purpose and type of traffic. Roadways can be classified by condition, such as dirt roads, gravel roads, paved roads, and roads under construction. They can also be classified by function. Some of the basic function classifications are interstate freeways and expressways, auto routes (Canada), major divided highways (United States, state, and Canadian provincial), secondary highways, and local roadways (county roads, municipal roads, and streets). Finally, roadways can be classified by whether they are free or whether you must pay a usage fee, or toll, each time you use that road.

Vehicles

The HTS also includes many types of vehicles, ranging from lightweight children's bicycles to large tractor-trailer rigs weighing more than 100,000 pounds (45,000 kg). They share the HTS every day, usually using different parts of the system at the same time, but not always. For example, when a tractor-trailer truck moves a suburban family from one house to another, it must begin and end its journey in the same residential neighborhood that a child uses to ride his or her bike. When operators of vehicles in the HTS do not share space intelligently, the sometimes massive disproportion in weight between the vehicles can and does cause serious injury and death.

Although trucks, buses, and motorcycles all transport drivers and passengers, the most commonly used vehicles for passenger travel in North America are cars, pickup trucks, sport utility vehicles, and vans. Because of the variety of vehicles using the roadway, it is always advisable to be aware of which vehicles are around you at any given time. A car will take longer to stop than a bicycle. A truck will need more room to turn than a car. A sports car can accelerate faster than a sedan. A motorcycle behind you is harder to spot than a bus. Because you must share the roadway with so many kinds of vehicles, you must learn their different limitations, characteristics, and capabilities to become a safe driver.

People

All types of people use the HTS. They may be young or old, tall or short, mature or immature. They may have quick reflexes or be slow to react. They may have excellent or poor vision. They may be sober or under the influence of alcohol or other drugs. They may be healthy or sick, injured, or disabled. They may be seasoned truckers or bus drivers who operate a vehicle for a living, or they may use the car once a month to make a shopping trip. The point is that you cannot rely on sharing the road with others who have your own strengths and weaknesses. Although you can easily learn to distinguish between different types of vehicles, it is much more difficult to identify different types of drivers. To be a safe driver, you must be a defensive driver.

Order in the HTS

Order in the HTS is maintained by a complex system of laws, rules, and regulations. These are necessary to help drivers predict what others will do, help preserve a smooth traffic flow, and act as a basis for the police and courts to determine who is and who is not contributing to order in the HTS. As a member of society, you are expected to know the motor-vehicle laws. *Ignorance of the law is no excuse.*

factoid

Nearly 220 million vehicles are registered in North America.

Wild Wheels

Figure 1–6 How long has this vehicle been roaming the HTS?

Figure 1–7 Many types of people and vehicles share the HTS.

The federal governments in both Canada and the United States have established laws that create standards and structures that govern the roadways and those who use them. However, these federal governments by and large let the states and provinces determine their own laws and procedures within these structures. Apart from a few federal traffic laws in Canada regarding dangerous driving, driving while under the influence of alcohol or other drugs, and vehicular negligence, almost all other laws regarding motor vehicles and drivers in both countries are state and provincial laws.

The state or provincial vehicle code is the single most important source of **traffic laws** within a jurisdiction. It covers the licensing of drivers, registering and titling of vehicles, financial responsibility laws, minimum safety equipment of vehicles, the various traffic and vehicle laws, and infractions and penalties. Local and municipal governments pass some traffic laws, also called **by-laws** in Canada, including parking rules, certain speed limits, and prohibited turns, but their influence is minimal. State and provincial governments are working more closely together in several areas with the goal of increasing safety in the HTS. They are coordinating their efforts with regard to drivers who have outstanding moving violations, drivers with suspended or revoked licenses, and drivers who have failed to properly register their vehicles.

Designing, Building, and Maintaining the HTS

All levels of government participate in the design and building of the roadways of the HTS. The federal government plays a large role in financing roadway construction and maintenance in addition to building and maintaining certain exclusively federal roads (such as those in national parks). State and provincial governments build and maintain their own roadway systems, and counties and municipal-ities build and maintain local roads.

The main elements of building a roadway are design, engineering, and construction, whether the roadway is new or an old or unsafe roadway that is being improved. Modern technologies and engineering studies are used to make roads safer than they were in the past. Some improvements that have been applied to freeways and higher-speed highways in recent years are banked curves, breakaway signs and poles, carpool lanes, and widened traffic lanes. On urban streets, special turn lanes have been added at intersections to separate turning traffic from through traffic, while signs prohibiting parking in certain places or turning onto side streets help make traffic flow more smoothly. On certain residential and rural streets, STOP signs and traffic signals have been added to intersections that did not have them before, and speed bumps have been installed in residential areas to improve safety.

Figure 1–8 Roadway construction and maintenance are funded by all levels of government.

ROAD WEIRDNESS *Roads to Nowhere* _____

The builders of Amstutz highway in Waukegan, Illinois, had grand plans for two connecting highways. They built one, but they ran out of money for the second, making the Amstutz highway a true "dead end route." Not be outdone, the builders of Clark's Ford Canyon Road in Wyoming constructed 12 miles (20 km) of highway before changing their minds and just stopping.

Federal, state/provincial, and local maintenance crews maintain the roadways by keeping them clean; setting up warning signs, signals, and message boards; removing snow and ice; repairing potholes, broken guardrails, and signs; cleaning up after a collision; and removing obstacles and obstructions such as auto parts that have fallen from vehicles.

Enforcement of Traffic Laws

The traffic laws that govern conduct of users of the HTS are enforced by a wide range of **law-enforcement** agencies, depending on the road and location. The role of the police who patrol the HTS is to apply the laws in a uniform manner, resolve conflicts, act as a deterrent to potential lawbreakers, and catch offenders who make driving less predictable for the rest of the users. This gives every driver a sense of security and stability, and it allows a system that functions smoothly. If we could not predict what we can and cannot do legally when we drive, the result would be total confusion on the roadways.

We are all familiar with law-enforcement officials from their role as "traffic cops" who issue moving violations. Sometimes a peace officer stops a driver and issues a ticket after witnessing the

William Phelps Engo, known as the "Father of Traffic Safety" for originating modern traffic regulations, never drove a car.

Figure 1–9 Without law-enforcement agencies, chaos would rule on the roadways.

violation. In other cases, the offense was seen by a police spotter airplane, radar, photo radar, or other device used to detect drivers exceeding the speed limit or breaking other traffic laws. Law enforcement also does its part to remove problems from the HTS, such as drivers under the influence of alcohol or other drugs and those operating substandard vehicles that do not comply with the minimum safety standards. The police also help drivers who are stranded on the side of the road because of a mechanical breakdown or other emergency, and they assist at collision scenes.

Because there are so many different law-enforcement agencies operating at any one time in the HTS, order is maintained by a system of "jurisdiction" in which certain agencies have primary enforcement responsibility over a given geographic area. The state and provincial police and highway patrols normally have primary jurisdiction on local, state, and interstate roadways within their state or province.

In the United States, park police and other federal law-enforcement agencies have primary jurisdiction on federally owned roadways. In Canada, federal police such as the Royal Canadian Mounted Police have authority not only on federal roadways but also on most roadways in provinces without their own police forces. Local and regional police forces such as county sheriff departments often have primary jurisdiction on local roadways. Parking enforcement officers, also known as "by-law enforcement officers" in Canada, are usually local police who enforce municipal parking regulations.

Breakdowns in the HTS

Sometimes the HTS breaks down, resulting in traffic jams, delays, and road closures. Drivers create most of the problems in the HTS when they block traffic because of a mechanical failure or collision. Those who fail to show courtesy to other drivers or who violate the law often end up causing collisions. Drivers who never bother to perform routine maintenance on their vehicles will inevitably have breakdowns.

Occasionally, the HTS breaks down because of failures in the system itself. When urban planners fail to construct enough lanes on a freeway or offer alternative forms of public transportation, the result can be rush-hour gridlock. Sometimes roads must be closed for construction, repair, or snow or ice removal. In general, the United States and Canada have one of the best and most efficient roadway systems in the world. The next time you complain about a detour or traffic jam that causes you to be late to your destination, remember that drivers in other parts of the world would gladly trade places with you.

Figure 1–10

YOUR TURN

1–1 Driver Education

1. What is the purpose of driver education?

2. What are the basic components of a "driver ed" course?

1–2 Driving Is a Privilege

3. Why is driving a privilege, not a right?

4. What are your basic responsibilities as a driver?

5. Why is it important for you to be courteous as a driver?

6. What is the importance of being emotionally, physically, and mentally fit to drive?

1–3 The Highway Transportation System

7. What is the Highway Transportation System?

8. What are the three main classifications of roadways?

9. Who is responsible for enforcing traffic laws?

The Driver and the Driving Task

Defensive Driving

Defensive driving is a method of driving that emphasizes anticipating and avoiding danger on the roadway. By staying alert and being prepared for the worst, you will be able to manage almost any hazardous situation with confidence and control. Defensive drivers actively observe, analyze, and plan. They evaluate road and traffic conditions, assess what other drivers and pedestrians will do, weigh their options, and decide on the best solution *before* they act. They do not blindly react to whatever happens around them.

CHAPTER OBJECTIVES ....

Upon completion of this chapter, you should be able to:

2–1 Defensive-Driving Skills

1. Understand what defensive driving is.
2. Describe the essential skills you need for defensive driving.

2–2 Managing Time, Space, and Visibility

3. Understand the importance of following distance and space cushioning.
4. Describe the 3-second rule.
5. Describe how large your space cushion should be.
6. Describe ways to deal with tailgaters.
7. Describe ways to make yourself known to others on the roadway.

2–3 The SAFE Method

8. Explain what "SAFE" stands for.
9. List the sequence of the orderly visual search pattern.
10. Describe the purpose of each step in the SAFE process.

KEY TERMS

defensive driving	tailgate	orderly visual search (OVS)
following distance	hand signals	assess
3-second rule	SAFE	find
space cushion	scan	execute

2–1 DEFENSIVE-DRIVING SKILLS

Defensive driving does not come naturally. You must train yourself to stay alert while monitoring the driving scene. Because of the large amount of information you must process, it is easy to become distracted. Once you lose your concentration, you become at risk for a collision. A driver who is tired, lazy, or unfocused is a dangerous driver. Therefore, it is important to develop sound habits early on so that defensive driving becomes a routine rather than a chore.

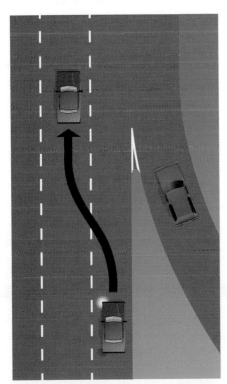

Figure 2–1 A defensive driver *actively* avoids potentially dangerous situations.

Knowledge

Defensive driving relies on several skills. To be able to safely maneuver your car or truck in various situations, you must have a thorough working knowledge of all its operating devices and controls. If you are thinking about how to steer or shift gears while driving, you are not watching the road.

Figure 2–2 To obey traffic laws and controls, you must understand them.

Knowledge of traffic laws, signs, signals, and roadway markings is also essential to defensive driving. To obey traffic laws and controls, you must first understand them. Although you cannot be expected to memorize your jurisdiction's vehicle code, which may be hundreds of pages long depending on where you live, you have a responsibility to become as informed as possible. The more you know about the rules of the road, the fewer tickets you will receive and the less chance you will have of getting involved in a collision. You will also experience less stress behind the wheel.

Preparation

Your safety depends on your being prepared to drive. You must be not only physically and mentally ready, but also able to respond when things do not go as planned. What if your car breaks down on the road? What if you are on an unfamiliar freeway and miss your exit? What if the weather changes for the worse? Asking "what if?" questions prepares you for possible emergencies and helps you avoid them entirely.

For example, by asking "What if my car breaks down?" you will remind yourself that your vehicle has needs beyond gas. When was the last time you checked your oil or antifreeze? Have you had your brake pads checked recently? You will also be forced to rethink your driving schedule and route. Is today the best day to drive across the desert? Are there service stations along the road you are taking? If your car's timing belt blows out far from a service station on Sunday night, you will have no one to blame but yourself because you failed to plan properly.

Awareness

Awareness is essential to defensive driving. Being aware of what is happening around you allows you to spot potentially dangerous situations early. If you see a line of parked cars on the road, for example, you should be ready for surprise door openings. Brake lights on cars ahead tell you to prepare for sudden stops or changes in speed. If you encounter a road construction detour, you should expect confused or frustrated drivers to dart in and out of lanes. By remaining aware of the driving environment, you can detect even the smallest indications of trouble before it occurs.

Anticipation

No matter where you are driving or what the road conditions are, you should always "expect the unexpected." The ability to anticipate problems before they happen is fundamental to developing an overall defensive-driver attitude. Make a habit of anticipating what drivers and pedestrians around you are about to do and how your car will respond in both normal and emergency situations. No matter what driving decision you make, always have in mind an alternative you can implement if you get into trouble.

Good Judgment

Good judgment in driving situations involves choosing the safest and most effective option available to you. For example, you must decide when to start applying your brakes, how early you should signal, whether you have enough room to pass, and how close you should follow another vehicle. You must consider a number of factors when determining how to avoid potential hazards:

- *The type of road you are on:* Is it a smooth, straight, and well-marked city street with

Figure 2–3 Driving on rain-slick or icy roads calls for good judgment.

clearly painted lines and helpful signs or a poorly lit, narrow country road with soft shoulders and potholes?

- *The weather:* Is it a warm day with a clear, blue sky and good visibility or is rain coming down in sheets too thick for your windshield wipers to handle? Is fog obscuring the road ahead? Is wind whipping your vehicle dangerously close to the guardrail? Are freezing temperatures transforming gentle bends in the road into icy, hairpin turns?

- *Visibility:* Maybe you have 20/20 vision, but what about the driver about to make the left turn in front of you? Is that driver someone who could not see the "E" at the top of the vision test chart even with glasses—which, by the way, the driver is not wearing right now! Can that driver on your right who is about to move into your lane see your car through the mud-caked windows?

- *Vehicle condition:* Are you driving a brand-new car outfitted with the latest antilock brakes or an old, hand-me-down "junkmobile" that needs new tires and a brake job? What about the cars around you?

- *Traffic conditions:* Are you on a six-lane interstate highway with few cars in sight or a four-lane freeway with bumper-to-bumper, rush-hour traffic?

- *Other drivers:* Are other drivers around you courteous and law-abiding or are they drunk, careless, rude, or angry at the world and ready to prove a point at your expense?

Practicing Defensive Driving

You have likely heard the expression, "practice makes perfect." Although practicing driving will not necessarily make you a perfect driver, it will definitely make you a safer driver. The more you practice, the faster you will gain confidence behind the wheel. The best way

Experience Counts _____

Compared with the average driver, young drivers have superior physical skills. They are generally in excellent health and have both good eyesight and fast reflexes. However, most people involved in motor-vehicle collisions are teenagers. In fact, traffic-related injuries are the leading cause of death among people between the ages of 15 and 19. Why? Teenagers have less experience, maturity, and motor-vehicle training than most adults. Some feel uncomfortable behind the wheel and drive in constant fear of getting into a collision or being pulled over by the police. Teenagers also have a more difficult time analyzing different variables at once and can easily become distracted. They are more likely to drink, use drugs, and engage in reckless behavior because of peer pressure. For all of these reasons, it is especially important for teens to drive defensively.

to develop your driving skills is to practice them in a low-density, low-stress environment like an empty parking lot or on quiet suburban streets. Once you master the basics, you will have the self-confidence to move to more challenging environments where your alertness and concentration are even more critical.

Defensive driving means developing the ability to perform evasive driving maneuvers. To safely execute such a maneuver, you must be comfortable with using all of your car's controls. You have to be "in synch" with your vehicle's limits and capabilities. In most cases, you can resolve a problem with basic actions like braking, stopping, turning, flashing your headlights, or tapping your horn. In more complex situations, however, you may have to use a combination of well-timed and smoothly coordinated maneuvers to move your vehicle out of harm's way or to minimize an impending impact. The only way to be good at executing such maneuvers is to practice, practice, practice!

2–2 MANAGING TIME, SPACE, AND VISIBILITY

Defensive driving involves managing time, space, and visibility as much as possible. You can never completely control these factors in a particular driving situation, but the better you manage them, the more flexibility you will have in choosing a course of action.

Following Distance

One of the greatest errors committed by drivers is following the vehicle ahead too closely. By increasing your **following distance**, the distance between your vehicle and the vehicle directly ahead of you, you can significantly reduce the chance of becoming involved in a collision. A long following distance allows you to scan farther ahead, makes it easier for drivers ahead to see you in their mirrors, gives you more time to react if the vehicle in front of you suddenly comes to a stop, and provides you with an escape path if another vehicle is about to rear-end your own car. Because rear-end collisions are one of the most common types of motor-vehicle collisions, increasing your following distance is critical to defensive driving.

In ideal low-speed driving conditions, with little traffic congestion and good visibility, you should maintain a minimum following distance of 3 seconds behind another vehicle. Because at higher speeds your car travels farther in the same amount of time and it takes longer to stop, you should increase our following distance the faster you travel. As a rule of thumb, maintain at least a 4-second following distance at speeds between 40 and 60 miles per hour (65 to 100 km/h) and a 5-second following distance at speeds greater than 60 miles per hour (100 km/h).

There are a couple of easy tests that you can perform to check your following distance. The simplest test to use for low-speed

Figure 2–4 Maintaining a safe following distance increases your options in an emergency.

BESSIE SMITH

Born in Chattanooga, Tennessee, in 1894, Bessie Smith reached the peak of her fame as a blues singer in the 1920s. Her style influenced other artists such as Billie Holiday, LaVern Baker, and Janis Joplin. After the huge success of her first record, "Downhearted Blues," she was dubbed "The Queen of the Blues." On September 26, 1937, Smith was badly injured when her car, driven by her friend Richard Morgan, crashed into the back of a truck on Route 61 near Clarksdale, Mississippi. Smith suffered a shattered left elbow, crushed ribs, and internal injuries. While they were waiting for an ambulance, another driver, not seeing the collision scene, crashed into the rear of Smith's car and injured her further. Despite the best efforts of a doctor at the scene and at a nearby hospital, Smith died from shock several hours later. By increasing your following distance from vehicles ahead of you and giving yourself an escape route, you can avoid rear-end collisions like the one that killed Bessie Smith. By scanning ahead down the roadway, you will be able to spot a collision scene or other hazard far enough in advance to allow you to stop or drive around it safely.

driving is the **3-second rule.** To check your following distance, pick a fixed object ahead, such as a tree, sign, or telephone pole. Count the number of seconds that pass between the time that the car ahead of you passes this object and the time that you pass it. Use *full* seconds: "one thousand and one . . . one thousand and two . . . one thousand and three." If you reach the landmark before you count to three, you are driving too closely to the vehicle ahead of you.

A second way to gauge your proper following distance is to maintain a space between you and the vehicle in front of you equal to one car length for every 10 miles per hour (15 km/h) that you are traveling. This method works well for all speeds that you are driving. For example, if you are driving 30 miles per hour (50 km/h), you should be at least three car lengths behind the vehicle in front of you. If you are on a freeway traveling 65 miles per hour (100 km/h), you should be six and a half car lengths back.

In certain low-speed driving situations, you should increase your following distance to 4, 5, or even 6 seconds:

- If you are a new driver
- When driving in severe weather
- If traction is poor
- When driving at night or anytime visibility is reduced
- If your view ahead is blocked by a large vehicle such as a truck or bus
- When following a motorcycle
- When following an obviously unsafe vehicle
- When following vehicles with license plates from another jurisdiction
- When traveling on unfamiliar roadways

"One thousand and one ..."

"... one thousand and two ..."

"... one thousand and three."

Figure 2–5 Use full seconds when testing your following distance to vehicles ahead of you.

Figure 2–6 Space cushioning increases visibility and leaves you potential escape routes.

- When a driver ahead of you is driving erratically or unsafely
- When a driver behind you is following too closely
- When pulling a trailer or a heavy load
- When driving downhill
- When you are stopped in traffic going uphill
- When you sense trouble ahead
- If you feel sick or tired

Space Cushioning

As you drive, try to surround all sides of your vehicle with a **space cushion**, an empty space between you and the cars and other objects on the roadway around you. This unoccupied space helps you in two important ways. First, it allows you to have a better view of your driving environment so that you can recognize potential problems early. Second, space cushioning provides escape routes that you can use to avoid a potential hazard.

Ideally, a space cushion should be at least one vehicle space to either side of you and at least three to seven vehicle lengths ahead of you and behind you. Often, as the driver, you must *create* a space cushion around your vehicle by increasing and decreasing your

Figure 2–7

Wild Wheels

Figure 2–8 What was the name of this 1948 "Flying Car" designed to create the ultimate space cushion for drivers?

The biggest complaint drivers have against others on the road is tailgating.

speed or switching lanes to change your vehicle's position relative to the cars traveling around you. This requires communicating your intentions to other drivers by using your turn signals, headlights, brake lights, horn, body movements—whatever it takes.

In heavy traffic, it can be nearly impossible to maintain a large space cushion. However, this does not mean you are completely helpless. In these situations, you can still increase your following distance. At the very least, you will be able to maintain a cushion in front of you, even if you are hemmed in from the rear and sides by other drivers.

Tailgating

Drivers who follow other cars too closely pose one of the most common and dangerous challenges to maintaining a proper space cushion around your car. Fortunately, there are ways to deal with those who **tailgate.** Increase your own following distance from the vehicle in front of you to 6 seconds or more. If the driver ahead has to stop quickly, you will have more time to gradually apply your own brakes and reduce the chance of the tailgater hitting you. Move to the right side of your lane to give the tailgater a better view of the road ahead so that if he wants to pass you he can do so safely. Plan an escape route in the next lane or on the road shoulder in case you have to swerve to avoid being rear-ended.

If a tailgater cannot or will not pass you, politely signal him to "back off" by tapping gently on

your brakes to flash your brake lights. Do *not* slam on your brakes—this can easily cause a collision or provoke an angry response from the driver behind you. If this is ineffective, try very gradually reducing your speed to encourage the tailgater to move into another lane. If this still does not work, change lanes yourself at the first opportunity. Finally, if you think that the tailgater is a real threat to you or other drivers on the road, pull over as soon as it is safe to do so to let the driver get by you.

Making Yourself Known

Always remember that you must be visible to other drivers. When positioning yourself on the road, consider *their* field of vision. It is just as important that you can be seen at all times as it is for you to see what is happening around you. Many collisions can be avoided simply by making your presence known to other drivers. When your view is blocked and you are not sure if others are aware of you, or when you see another vehicle but are not sure if the other driver sees you, use all available means to *make yourself known!* Other drivers will be able to respond appropriately to your actions if they know exactly what you are doing.

Communicating Your Intentions

Use your turn signals to let other drivers know that you are turning, changing lanes, merging onto or exiting a roadway, parking, or pulling into or out of a driveway.

Signal far enough ahead of time that drivers near you can respond to your change of direction and speed. Signaling just as you turn is too late. On the other hand, if you signal too early the driver behind you may misinterpret your intentions. For example, suppose you activate your left-turn signal two blocks ahead of the cross street you plan to turn onto. The driver behind you will expect you to turn at the first intersection and may not slow down when you actually turn because he or she no longer trusts the meaning of your signal.

Use your brake lights to signal your intention to stop. Drivers behind you may not be paying close attention to the road ahead or cannot see what you can. Do not simply hit your brakes when you have to stop. Instead, tap your brake pedal to warn other drivers that you are slowing down.

Hand signals, sometimes called arm signals, are another way to inform other drivers and pedestrians that you intend to turn, abruptly slow down, or stop. You might use hand signals in addition to turn indicators and brakes when bright sunlight

DRIVING TIPS *To Honk or Not to Honk?* _____

Your horn is a valuable safety feature that is both overlooked and overused as a communication tool.

- Honk when approaching blind or narrow curves or when exiting a narrow alley to alert approaching drivers of your presence.
- Use a light tap on your horn to get the attention of another driver or a pedestrian who cannot see you.
- Use your horn, loudly if necessary, to avoid a collision. Use a sharp blast when a pedestrian or bicyclist is about to walk or ride into the street in front of you, or when another vehicle is in danger of hitting you.
- Use your horn when you lose control of your vehicle and are moving toward someone or another vehicle. This may give the other person enough warning to get out of the way.
- Do *not* use your horn to encourage someone to drive faster.
- Do *not* honk if you can avoid entering into a blind spot by speeding up or slowing down.
- Do *not* use your horn to greet friends.
- Do *not* use your horn if a blind pedestrian enters the road, even against traffic signals. Stop and allow the person to cross.
- Do *not* honk if you can make eye contact with the other driver or communicate with a hand gesture.

Check the laws in your jurisdiction regarding the use of horns. Some cities (for example, New York City) prohibit the use of horns in many situations.

Figure 2–9 Use hand signals to help communicate your intention to turn, stop, or slow down.

decreases the visibility of your rear lights or if you think the driver behind you is not paying enough attention to the road. Hand signals should not be used instead of your vehicle's mechanical indicators, but as an extra warning or in case your "blinkers" or brake lights malfunction.

When using hand signals, make sure that you begin to signal at least 100 feet (30 m) before turning, stopping, or suddenly decreasing in speed. To signal a left turn, extend your left hand and arm straight horizontally out the window of the vehicle. To signal a right turn, extend your left arm out the window and bend it at the elbow so that your left hand points skyward at a 90-degree angle. To signal a stop or abrupt slowing, extend your left hand and arm out the window and bend it at the elbow so that your left hand points downward at a right angle.

The position of your vehicle also communicates your inten-

tions to other drivers. Moving to the right side of the lane, for example, may indicate that you are preparing to turn right or park by the curb. Moving to the left of the lane may signal your desire to pass a driver ahead of you.

Make eye contact with other drivers or pedestrians when possible. Although you should never depend on eye contact alone to communicate your intentions, it may help reduce the risk of conflict. You can use body movements such as waving to tell a pedestrian to cross. You can also motion clearly with your arm or hand to other drivers, indicating to them to proceed before you or to wait.

Increasing Your Visibility

Your headlights improve your view of the road, but they also help others see you. You should always use your headlights at dawn, dusk, and in bad weather conditions such as rain, snow, or fog, as well as at night. In some jurisdictions, you are required to

Figure 2–10 Where you position your vehicle tells other drivers what you intend to do.

turn on your headlights when you turn on your windshield wipers. As an added measure of safety, use your headlights during regular daytime hours. "Flash" your high beams when approaching a blind or narrow curve at night to alert drivers approaching from the opposite direction who might turn wide into your lane of travel. As a gesture of courtesy, you might also briefly flick on your "brights" at oncoming drivers who have forgotten to turn on their headlights at night or when visibility is poor.

Use your emergency flashers to tell other drivers that your vehicle cannot move or is moving very slowly. This will encourage them to give you extra space on the road and be patient while you get your vehicle to a safe stopping point. Once you are stopped, your emergency flashers will help other drivers see you on the side of the road, especially at night. They will also make it easier for the police, emergency vehicles, and tow trucks to find you if you need help.

2–3 THE "SAFE" METHOD

SAFE is an innovative defensive-driving strategy that you can use to evade potential danger on the roadway. By helping you to manage time, space, and visibility in a manner that is simple and easy to remember, it prevents conflicts and makes for safer, less stressful driving. The SAFE method builds on the defensive-driving skills de-

scribed at the beginning of this chapter. The more knowledge, preparation, awareness, anticipation, and good judgment you have, the more effective it will be.

SAFE stands for *scan, assess, find,* and *execute.* Following this four-step sequence gives you an organized way to gather, interpret, and act on information about the driving environment. When driving you should constantly scan for clues, assess what others are likely to do and what your options are, find a solution or "out," and execute any necessary driving maneuvers successfully. In some situations, you might repeat this process dozens of times. With practice, the SAFE system will help you avoid risky situations and escape from sudden and unexpected dangers.

Scan

The first principle of SAFE is that you **scan** ahead to gather as much information as possible about the complete driving scene. Your eyes are your best tool to identify traffic situations and road conditions. You want to be aware of other vehicles, pedestrians, bicycles, and possible hazards around you as soon as possible. By scanning ahead, you give yourself time to slow down gradually and to change lanes smoothly while avoiding unnecessary braking. When you eliminate the need to stop or turn suddenly, you are less likely to be involved in a collision.

Look far ahead down the road to spot potential problems. This

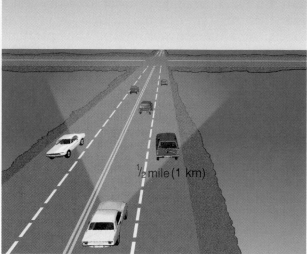

Figure 2–11 Your speed determines how far ahead you should look.

allows you to analyze traffic situations and road conditions and to predict what might happen long before a driving conflict arises. As a general rule, you should look between 20 and 30 seconds ahead of you. In urban driving, in which you are typically moving from 25 to 30 miles per hour (40 to 50 km/h), this is equivalent to 1½ to 2 average city blocks. On highways and freeways, when you are moving anywhere from 50 to 70 miles per hour (80 to 110 km/h), you should look between ⅓ and ½ mile (500 m to 1 km) down the road.

Identifying traffic controls is one of the essential purposes of scanning. Traffic signals and signs may be located overhead, in the center of the road, or off to the side. Look for anything unusual such as temporary detour signs, orange road-construction cones, or flashing lights that can alert you to an upcoming change in traffic flow. It is especially important to identify and interpret traffic controls that are hard to read or see because they are located in a shady area, are covered by natural growth, or are reflecting bright sunlight.

Figure 2–12 Not all traffic controls are easy to identify.

As you scan with your eyes, make sure that you get the "big picture" of what is ahead of you. Search the whole scene, not just part of it. Try to gain a sense of what vehicles and pedestrians in *all* directions are doing. Never gaze straight ahead or "fixate" on an object for too long. When scanning the areas near your vehicle, look to the sides of the driving lanes for hazards such as pedestrians stepping into the street or cars pulling away from the curb. Alternate glances ahead and to the sides with checks of your vehicle's mirrors and dashboard instrument panel. If you are

constantly scanning, you should be able to pick up the movement of hard-to-see vehicles such as bicycles and motorcycles. Once you have identified someone outside your normal field of vision, keep track of him or her until the person turns off your path of travel. Occasionally scan at ground level to check the orientation of other vehicles' tires to determine which way a driver is going to turn.

One way to make sure that you scan in all directions is to make an **orderly visual search (OVS)** of the scene around you. In the late 1950s, Howard L. Smith of the Ford Motor Company developed a

It takes only one-tenth of a second for a collision to occur, half the time it takes just to blink your eyes.

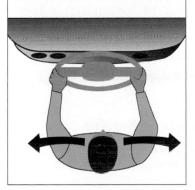

Figure 2–13 The OVS pattern is an effective scanning technique.

systematic technique that requires using selective glances in a constantly repeating pattern to monitor all the different areas around your vehicle:

1. Look at the road near you.
2. Look ahead in the distance.
3. Alternate glances at each of the following with looking ahead down the road:
   - To your right
   - To your left
   - At your rearview mirror
   - At the driver sideview mirror
   - At the passenger sideview mirror
   - At the instrument panel

By repeating this sequence as you drive and by remaining alert, you will spot most changing road conditions and potential dangers quickly. You can then adjust your speed and position in plenty of time. Whether you use the OVS pattern or create your own system, remember to *always keep your eyes moving.*

Assess

The next step in the SAFE process is to **assess** potential threats on the roadway. The ability to predict problems before they happen is fundamental to defensive driving. Once you are able to consistently and accurately anticipate what others are going to do in a dangerous situation, the options available to you, the probable consequences of your actions, and how your vehicle will respond, you can make informed decisions to prevent a collision.

The knowledge needed to make good predictions partly comes from the study of traffic laws, the experiences of friends and family, and common sense. There is no substitute, however, for personal experience. The more time you spend behind the wheel, the bet-

Figure 2–14 The condition of other vehicles on the road, as well as your own, may affect what you decide to do in a hazardous situation.

DRIVING MYTHS   *Do Not Judge a Driver by His or Her Car*

Just because someone drives a vehicle with a high safety rating does not mean he or she is a safe driver. Always watch others on the road equally closely, no matter what they are driving.

Figure 2–15 Clues can help you predict whether this driver is entering or pulling out of the parking space.

ter you will be at predicting which hazard is the most critical to avoid. As time goes by, your ability to forecast outcomes will improve with the level of your experience.

Threats come in many forms. Other vehicles may suddenly enter your lane of travel and cause you to maneuver around them or stop suddenly. An oncoming car may unexpectedly turn left in front of you. A pedestrian may ignore a flashing DON'T WALK sign and step off the curb right in front of you. By looking for certain clues, you can anticipate the actions of others on the roadway. For example, if you identify a car at the curbside with its left-turn signal on, the wheels turned toward the street, and smoke coming out of the exhaust pipe, the driver may be preparing to pull away from the curb into your path of travel. A driver on a cross street who is looking at *your* signal may try to "get a jump" on

the light and enter the intersection too early. Be on the lookout for drivers who speed, change lanes often to get ahead of normal traffic flow, or drive slowly because they are lost and confused. Assess whether drivers using cellular phones, drinking coffee, or doing something else distracting are possible threats.

The dangers you face largely depend on your driving environment. On city streets, for example, pedestrians and bicyclists, vehicles pulling in and out of parking spaces, and double-parked cars or delivery vehicles that may block your lane of travel are common hazards. In residential or suburban neighborhoods, you must watch for children playing, pets, and cars backing out of driveways. On rural roads, dangers include hidden intersections, downed tree limbs, and wild or domestic animals. On freeways, you have to keep track of multiple vehicles in several lanes, as well as those entering and exiting the roadway, to maintain a safe space cushion.

As you travel, roadway conditions constantly change. You must determine which of these changing conditions might affect your position on the road or pose a danger. Look for information that will help you identify upcoming intersections or changes in the width of your lane. If you are approaching a construction zone or a bridge on a rural road, for example, you should expect less space for your vehicle to pass oncoming traffic.

When driving in heavy rain, at night or in conditions of reduced visibility, or on very hilly or curving roads that restrict your ability to scan far ahead, you must assess possible hazards as early as possible. Sometimes the road surface itself is a problem. A street that is slick because of the weather or is poorly maintained will affect how your vehicle handles. If you skid on a slippery road or hit a large pothole, you can lose control of your vehicle and cause a collision. By evaluating how standing water, patches of snow or ice, leaves, potholes, debris, and warning signs and signals affect *other* drivers, you can adjust your driving in time to avoid a problem.

Find

Once you have identified a potential danger and assessed your options, you must **find** an "out." An out is an escape route that you have identified as the best means of avoiding a conflict on the road. Always position your vehicle so

that there is a margin of space around it to provide a cushion between you and other vehicles. Constantly adjust your position in changing traffic conditions to keep that space cushion around your car. This will give you the extra time needed to stop suddenly or to move to the side to avoid a hazard.

Do not assume that others on the road will always take the correct evasive action in a driving conflict. Consider all the possible paths that other drivers may take

Figure 2–16 Change your position to leave yourself as many "outs" as possible.

Do Not Let the Pressure Get to You _____

As a new driver, you may drive more slowly or need extra time to decide when it is safe to make a difficult driving maneuver, such as taking a left turn in front of oncoming traffic. If other drivers honk their horns at you or express impatience in other ways, do not let them pressure you into taking a risk. You should execute a difficult maneuver only when *you* know it is safe to do so.

Figure 2–17 Many roadways offer limited room to find an out.

and think of how you might respond to each one. Look for escape routes in each of the possible outcomes. Try to predict when and where another vehicle will intrude on your space cushion, cross your path, or make contact with your vehicle. Not every emergency has a perfect out. Your only options may be a rear-end collision or being sideswiped by a car in an adjoining lane. If you see no clear way of avoiding a crash, do not panic and throw in the towel. Accept the situation and find the safest alternative.

Execute

The final step in the SAFE method is to **execute**, or carry out, your decision to avoid an upcoming conflict. You always have at least two options if you encounter danger on the road. You can change your speed, and you can change your direction. In most cases, if you change your speed you will choose to slow down or stop. If you have maintained a safe following distance, you should have plenty of room to slow down before hitting the vehicle ahead of you. If another car is about to rear-end you or hit you from the side, however, it may be to your advantage to speed up if the road ahead of you is clear of other vehicles and pedestrians.

In some situations, you may decide to change direction if you cannot stop in time and there is an escape path to either side of your vehicle. By swerving or making a sharp right or left turn, you may be able to avoid a hazard with less risk to yourself or others.

WHO'S AT FAULT?

1. Driver 1 did not notice the sign that read RIGHT LANE ENDS 1,000 FEET and continued driving in the right lane. At the last moment, he was forced to swerve into the middle lane. This in turn caused Driver 2 to swerve into the left lane, and he hit Driver 3. *Who's at fault?*

2. Driver 1 was approaching the end of an entrance ramp to a freeway. Driver 2 was coming down the ramp right behind him. Driver 3 was approaching in the right lane of the freeway. Just as Driver 1 was about to merge with freeway traffic, she noticed that Driver 3 was too close, so she stopped to let Driver 3 pass. Driver 2 thought that Driver 1 was going to enter the freeway without stopping. He turned his head to check traffic on the freeway. When he turned back and saw that Driver 1 had stopped, he slammed on his brakes but could not stop in time and rear-ended Driver 1. *Who's at fault?*

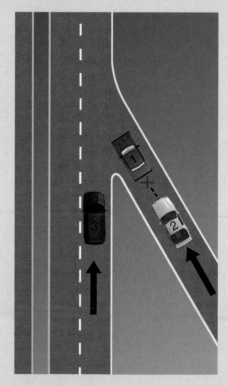

YOUR TURN

2–1 *Defensive-Driving Skills*

1. What is defensive driving?

2. What are the essential skills you need to drive defensively?

2–2 *Managing Time, Space, and Visibility*

3. Why is following distance important?

4. What is the 3-second rule?

5. How large should your space cushion be?

6. How can you deal with tailgaters?

7. How can you make yourself known to others on the roadway?

2–3 *The SAFE Method*

8. What does "SAFE" stand for?

9. What is the sequence of the orderly visual search pattern?

10. What is the purpose of each step in the SAFE process?

SELF-TEST

Multiple Choice

1. Ideally, a space cushion should be at least three to seven vehicle lengths ahead of you and _____ vehicle space(s) to either side.
   - **a.** two
   - **b.** one
   - **c.** zero
   - **d.** three

2. Gradually reducing your speed can encourage _____ to move into another lane.
   - **a.** large trucks
   - **b.** buses
   - **c.** tailgaters
   - **d.** police cars

3. You should honk your horn:
   - **a.** to greet a friend.
   - **b.** at another driver's error.
   - **c.** to avoid a collision.
   - **d.** to warn a blind pedestrian who is in your path.

4. On a freeway at high speeds, you should be scanning about _____ ahead.
   - **a.** ¼ mile (400 m)
   - **b.** 500 feet (150 m)
   - **c.** ⅓ mile (500 m)
   - **d.** 200 feet (60 m)

5. If you are traveling on a highway at 50 miles per hour (80 km/h), allow a following distance of at least _____ car lengths.

   a. three   **c.** five

   b. four and a half   **d.** seven

Sentence Completion

1. You will spot most changing road conditions and potential dangers quickly by constantly repeating an _____ sequence.

2. Increasing your _____ significantly reduces the chances of rear-ending the vehicle in front of you.

3. A _____ allows a better view of your surroundings so that you can predict problems early and provides you with an escape route.

4. An _____ is an escape path that you have identified as the best means of avoiding a conflict on the road.

5. SAFE stands for _____, _____, _____, and _____.

Matching

Match the concepts in Column A with the examples of the concepts in Column B.

Column A

1. __ Assess
2. __ Keep your eyes moving
3. __ Find
4. __ Communicate your intentions
5. __ Increase your following distance
6. __ Scan ahead
7. __ Create a space cushion
8. __ Make yourself known

Column B

a. Escape path
b. Orderly visual search
c. Look two city blocks ahead
d. When being followed by a tailgater
e. Flash high beams on blind curves at night
f. Double-parked car
g. Decrease your speed
h. Tap brake lights before stopping

Short Answer

1. What two choices do you always have when you encounter a road hazard?

2. How does asking "what if?" questions help you?

3. Describe a situation in which your vehicle position communicates your intention to another driver.

4. What does scanning ahead allow you to do?

5. What is meant by the phrase, "Not every emergency has a perfect out"?

Critical Thinking

1. You are driving on a two-lane road and want to make a left turn into a local shopping center. You notice, however, that there is a large truck blocking the driveway as it tries to exit. Just as the truck pulls out to make a left turn, you observe the car behind you trying to pass you on the right. What should you do?

2. You are in the right lane of a four-lane highway driving 55 miles per hour (90 km/h). As you approach a sharp curve, you observe a speed reduction warning sign and slow to 35 miles per hour (55 km/h). Rounding the curve, you notice that traffic is backed up nearly to the end of the curve because of a collision farther down the road. The driver in a car behind you appears to have ignored the speed reduction sign and is coming on fast without being aware of the danger ahead. What should you do?

PROJECTS

1. As a passenger in a motor vehicle, watch how other drivers communicate with one another. Based on what you see, predict what different drivers will do. Did you predict correctly? Note how many vehicles turn, pull out of parking spots, change lanes, and execute other maneuvers without signaling properly. Were you able to correctly predict their intentions using such clues such as wheel direction, lane position, and so on?

2. As a passenger, observe how the following distance and space cushion around the vehicle you are in changes. As you move into various situations, determine what your best escape route would be if you were the driver.

3

The Condition of the Driver

Your ability to drive safely is determined by both your physical condition and your emotional well-being. The quality of your eyesight and hearing, whether you have an illness or disability, and even your size and height are factors that you must consider when you get behind the wheel. Your mental state is equally important. It takes a good attitude to be courteous to other drivers and to drive defensively. A negative attitude, overconfidence or underconfidence, and any other feelings that affect your driving do not belong in the car. Anger, stress, anxiety, and other emotions can and do lead to crashes.

Upon completion of this chapter, you should be able to:

3–1 The Physical Condition of the Driver

1. Describe permanent physical conditions that can limit your ability to drive safely.
2. Describe the four main components of vision.
3. Describe temporary physical conditions that can limit your ability to drive safely.
4. Understand how you can prevent carbon monoxide poisoning.

3–2 The Mental Condition of the Driver

5. Understand how your mental condition impacts your ability to drive safely.
6. Understand how to avoid becoming a victim of road rage.
7. Describe activities you should avoid while driving.

KEY TERMS

visual acuity	depth perception	carbon monoxide
field of vision	color vision	road rage
central vision	color blindness	rubbernecking
peripheral vision	fatigue	

3–1 THE PHYSICAL CONDITION OF THE DRIVER

Your individual makeup, the natural process of aging, and chronic illness or disability can all impose physical limitations on your driving skills. Although you can correct for poor vision or compensate for deficiencies in hearing, you must always take such permanent conditions into consideration when you make choices behind the wheel. Other physical conditions such as fatigue or injury may only temporarily affect your ability to drive safely, but they are equally deadly if ignored.

Vision

Because so many of your decisions as a driver are based on what you see and when you see it, good vision is one of the most important physical qualities necessary for driving. You need to see far enough ahead to clearly read traffic signals and signs and to allow you to make adjustments in speed and direction to avoid potential hazards. If you have vision problems, you should get your eyes checked at least every two years to make sure that you have the best prescription to provide clear vision. *If you need corrective lenses to pass the driver's license eye exam, you must wear them while driving.*

Visual Acuity

Every jurisdiction requires that you meet a minimum vision standard to obtain a driver's license. **Visual acuity** is the ability to see objects both near and far. Normal visual acuity is 20/20, which means that you can clearly read letters ⅜ of an inch (1 cm) high from a distance of 20 feet (6 m) away. The typical minimum standard is a correctable visual acuity of at least 20/40. Someone with 20/40 vision needs to be twice as close as someone with 20/20 vision—that is, 10 feet (3 m) away— to read the same letters. An eye exam will determine your visual acuity and whether you need corrective glasses or contact lenses to drive.

Field of Vision

Your **field of vision** includes the area you can see directly in front of you, to the sides, and when looking straight ahead. The area directly in front of you where everything is clear is your **central vision**. This area is only about 3 degrees wide. To give you an idea of how narrow that is, sit in a chair and fix your eyes on a point straight ahead of you. Take a pencil and hold it at arm's length directly in front of your eyes. The pencil will look very clear, and you should be able to read the brand name and number of the pencil. Keeping your eyes fixed straight ahead, begin to move the pencil slightly to the right or left. Almost immediately you can no longer see details of the pencil—just its general shape, color, and location. As you move the pencil farther to the sides, it will become less visible. When your arm is even with your shoul-

driving tips

If you wear glasses or contact lenses, keep a spare pair of glasses in your vehicle in case your regular glasses are lost or broken, or if you need to remove your contact lenses.

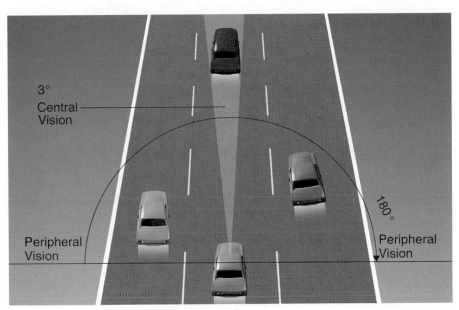

Figure 3–1 Your central vision is extremely narrow.

der you will barely be able to see it at all, even if you wiggle it back and forth.

The unfocused areas to the sides of your central vision form your **peripheral vision**, which extends to 180 degrees. Although objects to the sides of your peripheral vision are not focused, you will still be able to detect them. The faster you drive, the harder it is to see to the sides. At 30 miles per hour (50 km/h), peripheral vision may be reduced by 25%, whereas at 60 miles per hour (100 km/h) it can be reduced by 90%. Because your field of vision narrows while driving, it is essential to move your head *constantly* to see what is happening around you.

Depth Perception

Depth perception is the ability to judge the distance between two objects. We can perceive depth well because we have binocular vision that combines the two separate images from our two eyes into a three-dimensional image. When driving, you use depth perception to evaluate the distance between you and other objects. It is important to keep in mind that depth is more difficult to judge when you are moving than when you are stationary.

Depth perception is also used to judge your following distance behind other vehicles and to evaluate your stopping distance. Those with impaired depth perception should increase their following distance behind other vehicles and drive more slowly than those with normal depth perception. In some jurisdictions, you must pass a depth perception test before you can obtain a driver's license.

Color Vision

Drivers use **color vision**, or the ability to see color, to help determine the meaning of various signs and traffic signals. The colors used most often in signs and signals are red, green, and yellow. Some jurisdictions require you to take a test for color blindness when applying for a driver's license. **Color blindness** is an inability to differentiate between certain colors such as red and green, the most common form of color blindness. If you are color blind, you can still drive, but you must interpret signs and signals by memorizing their shape and meaning. For example, a color-blind person can identify a red traffic light by knowing that it is either at the top of a vertical signal or at the far left of a horizontal signal.

Age

Age is another physical condition that can have an impact on a person's driving abilities. Older drivers generally are better at detecting and avoiding potential hazards than younger drivers. However, they also tend to have decreased reaction time, weaker eyesight, and poorer hearing. To compensate for such limitations, older drivers may reduce their speed and try to avoid situations that require quicker reflexes, such as driving on heavily congested streets or in the fast lane of a freeway.

Coordination

Your coordination is determined by how quickly and efficiently your nervous and muscular systems work together. When driving you must constantly interpret what you see and make adjustments. Coordination affects how quickly and efficiently you synchronize your hands and feet for various tasks such as steering, manually shifting gears, and pressing the accelerator, brake pedal, and clutch with your foot.

Some people are naturally more coordinated than others, but even those with average coordination can develop good driving skills. If you are not very coordinated, you can compensate by staying more focused and attentive. Increase your space cushioning and following distance if necessary. With experience, your ability to smoothly work your vehicle's controls in response to hazardous situations will improve.

Hearing

Hearing greatly increases your awareness while driving. Your ears detect sounds of potential hazards outside the car such as horns, sirens, train whistles, nearby vehicles you cannot see, trucks, pedestrians, and bicycles. Hearing tells you when to shift gears on a manual transmission. Sounds may warn you of an impending engine breakdown or a flat tire on your own or another driver's vehicle. Screeching brakes can warn you that someone is about to rear-end you. The information you obtain by hearing can be crucial in some of the split-second decisions you have to make while driving. Drivers who are hearing impaired can

factoid

Deaf drivers are among the safest on the road because they develop better visual skills to compensate for their loss of hearing.

Figure 3–2 Drivers with hearing problems must compensate for their impairment by scanning ahead and using their mirrors more often.

still drive safely with the help of hearing aids.

Size and Height

Size and height may limit a driver's ability to comfortably or safely operate a motor vehicle. A tall or obese person may feel too restricted in a subcompact. A short driver may be unable to see the road well from the seat of a very large sedan. When you get behind the wheel, take a minute to adjust your seat and mirrors so that you can easily reach the controls while maintaining good visibility of the road. You might need to obtain special equipment for your car to enable you to see clearly over the dashboard and out the windows, or to allow you to reach all the foot pedals without stretching.

Chronic Illness and Disability

Many drivers with chronic illnesses or permanent disabilities are able to drive because of medical and technological advances. Those with an illness such as diabetes, asthma, epilepsy, and heart disease can regulate their symptoms with medication. Drivers have a responsibility to carefully monitor their own medical condition and refrain from driving if they experience side effects, such

Figure 3–3 Do not drive a vehicle if you cannot comfortably see out the windows or reach the pedals.

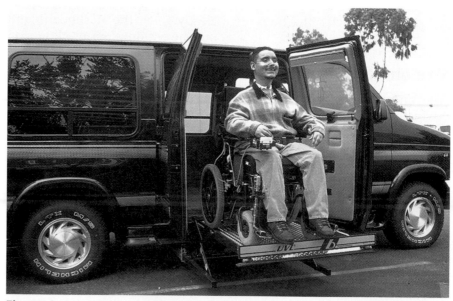

Figure 3–4 Specially modified vans allow wheelchair-bound people to drive.

as dizziness or fatigue, that adversely affect their ability to drive.

People who have permanent physical disabilities that limit their use of arms, legs, or hands can drive vehicles adapted with special equipment such as hand-operated foot pedals and steering wheel "spinners." Although certain disabilities can prevent you from getting a driver's license, most jurisdictions decide whether to grant licenses to people with permanent disabilities on a case-by-case basis.

Fatigue

Not all physical limitations are the result of permanent conditions. **Fatigue** severely affects your reaction time and decision-making abilities. Driving while fatigued greatly increases your chances of having a collision. Fatigue is most likely to set in on long trips, but it may be caused by a number of factors, such as boredom, eyestrain from driving too long or from sun glare, poor ventilation, and eating or drinking too much. Because teenagers generally need more sleep than older drivers, they are especially at risk, accounting for more than half of all collisions caused by a driver falling asleep.

Fatigue can set in slowly. Some physical symptoms of fatigue are drowsiness, blurred or double vision, slowed reactions, lack of co-ordination, and problems judging distance and speed. Emotional indications include irritability and inattentiveness. Because most people are programmed to sleep when it is dark, it is not surprising that most fatigue-related collisions occur between 1 AM and 6 AM.

If you feel tired or sleepy, stop in a safe place and get out of your

factoid

The young man awarded "America's Safest Teen Driver" in 1990 later was killed in a collision when he fell asleep behind the wheel.

DRIVING TIPS **Preventing Fatigue** _____

You can do a lot to prevent fatigue before even getting behind the wheel:
- Always get a good night's sleep so you are well rested before driving.
- Try not to drive during your normal sleeping hours.
- Do not drink alcohol, which will make you more tired.
- Avoid eating large, heavy meals before driving.
- If you feel tired after school or work, walk around and relax for a while before driving.

To prevent fatigue while you are driving:
- Make sure you have lots of fresh air.
- Talk to a passenger or listen to the radio to keep you alert.
- Do not set the heater or air conditioner too high because extreme temperatures can make you groggy.
- Wear sunglasses if there is too much glare.

vehicle. Use the opportunity to splash cold water on your face, walk around, stretch, and clear your head. Eat something light. Beware of drinking too much coffee or soda containing caffeine and/or sugar. It may perk you up for a short while, but excessive caffeine or sugar intake can actually make you more tired than before when the effects of the stimulant wear off. If you have passengers who are licensed drivers, allow someone else to drive for a while so that you can rest.

If you pull over to get some sleep, park your vehicle in a crowded, well-lit area, turn off the engine, lock the doors, and crack the windows open. After taking a nap, make sure you are fully awake before getting back on the road.

Illness

Avoid driving when you are sick. Cold, allergy, and flu symptoms can slow your reactions and make you uncomfortable, drowsy, and inattentive. Serious symptoms such as dizziness, sneezing, or constant coughing may even cause you to lose control of your vehicle. If it is absolutely necessary for you to drive, concentrate fully on your driving, keep your speed lower than normal, and stay clear of heavy traffic and high-speed roadways.

Injury

If you are injured, you may or may not be able to drive, depend-ing on the location and extent of your injury. A broken hand, a severe sprain to the right foot, or an eye injury, for example, could all make it difficult, if not impossible, to drive. Before you drive, evaluate how much mobility or strength you may have lost, whether your senses are impaired, and how much pain and discomfort you are feeling because of the injury.

You must also consider what kind of vehicle you are driving. If you have a moderately sprained left ankle, you should have little trouble driving a car with an automatic transmission. However, with the same injury you might not be able to safely operate the clutch on a car with manual transmission. If an injury seriously affects your abilities, do not risk a collision. Ask someone else to drive you, take a bus, or call a taxi.

Carbon Monoxide Poisoning

Exhaust fumes from all gasoline engines contain **carbon monoxide,** a colorless, odorless, tasteless gas that under certain circumstances can seep undetected into the passenger compartment of a vehicle. If the levels become high enough, you can develop carbon monoxide poisoning and not know until it is too late. Carbon monoxide poisoning can have a number of causes:

- A damaged exhaust system
- Driving in an area with insufficient ventilation such as

Figure 3–5 Do not try to drive if an injury prevents you from safely operating a motor vehicle.

enclosed parking garages and tunnels

- Starting a vehicle in a garage with the garage door closed
- Driving a sport utility vehicle, van, hatchback, or station wagon in heavy traffic with only the back window open
- Smoking with the windows closed

Some recognizable early warning signs of carbon monoxide poisoning are headaches, nausea, drowsiness, confusion, and/or loss of strength. Ignoring these symptoms and neglecting to do something about them can ultimately lead to unconsciousness and even death.

Always try to keep your car windows open, at least slightly, when the engine is running. If your heater or air conditioner is on, keep your distance from vehicles in front of you while you are in heavy traffic to prevent their exhaust from entering your ventilation system. Remember to turn off the engine when you are motionless in an enclosed area. It is a good idea to have your exhaust system checked regularly for leaks, especially if at any time you feel any of the symptoms described above. When you suspect high levels of carbon monoxide, get out of any confined space as soon as possible and ventilate your car with fresh air.

Wild Wheels

Figure 3–6 What is the name of this car, which pushed the physical and mental limits of its American driving team in the 1908 Round-the-World Race, logging 12,427 miles (20,000 km) in 170 days?

3–2 THE MENTAL CONDITION OF THE DRIVER

Your emotional state is a very important factor in your ability to drive well. When you are angry, excited, or depressed, you cannot allow your emotions to distract you. Giving in to powerful emotions while driving diminishes your coordination, concentration, and reaction time, all of which are fundamental driving tools. If you are upset by a personal issue or something that happens on the road, remind yourself to focus on the driving task. Wait to deal with the problem affecting you once you have arrived safely at your destination. Do not abandon good judgment and take risks that you would normally avoid.

Figure 3–7 Strong emotions and driving do not mix.

Anger

One of the most powerful emotions that can affect driving is anger. You may become angry at another driver who performs unexpected, illegal, or dangerous maneuvers. Your temper might flare at drivers who follow your vehicle too closely, drive too slowly ahead of you, fail to go forward as fast as you think they should at a green light, or "cut you off" by suddenly turning into your lane without signaling. If you are under stress, tired, or irritated in any way, threats to your safety and peace of mind may cause you to respond more angrily than you would otherwise. If you are in the wrong frame of mind, just getting stuck in traffic can cause you to blow your stack.

Dealing with Anger

Do not be tempted to take out your aggression on the road. If you are angry, cool down before you get in your car. Compose yourself by talking to friends or taking a walk and thinking things out. When you are driving, *expect* others to exhibit poor judgment. If another driver makes an error, swears at you, or just gets under your skin, remain calm and patient. By simply increasing your space cushioning and following distance, you will go a long way toward avoiding situations that can lead to anger. If you are tempted to act on your anger by driving recklessly yourself, take a deep breath and ask yourself, "Is it worth it?" The answer is no!

Road Rage

The phrase **road rage** is used to describe the increasingly com-

guess the vanity plate

DELMAR

MADABTU

Figure 3–8

mon phenomenon of aggressive driving. Examples of road rage include deliberate tailgating, yelling at other drivers, using obscene gestures, purposely blocking other drivers' paths, and in extreme cases, assaulting others. Road rage is often set off by a minor event, such as an argument over a parking space, that acts as a "final straw" for a motorist already under stress. It is often aggravated by hot temperatures and overcrowding on the roadways. Although most "road ragers" are young males, usually with histories of emotional problems and drug or alcohol use, anyone can lose their cool under the right circumstances.

There are things you can do to avoid becoming a victim of road rage. Avoid the urge to honk your horn or flash your "brights" at other drivers out of anger or frustration. Do not tailgate, block the passing lane or merging lane, blare your music out of open windows, or switch lanes without first signaling. When parking, make sure that you do not take up more than one spot and that you do not hit the car parked next to you when opening your door. Do not use bumper stickers or vanity plates that may offend others. Always give other drivers the benefit of the doubt if a conflict develops.

If you find yourself the "target" of an extremely aggressive driver, do not allow the incident to escalate. Avoid making eye contact with angry drivers, gesturing, or participating in challenges of any kind. If you recognize that the other driver is getting violent, either seek help or protect yourself as best you can. Drive to a police station or an area crowded with people. If you cannot drive your

An average of 1,500 people are injured or killed annually in the United States because of aggressive driving.

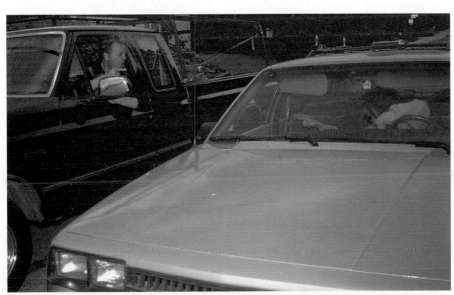

Figure 3–9 Do not risk a confrontation with other drivers.

JACK NICHOLSON

A two-time Oscar winner for Best Actor, Jack Nicholson has starred in a number of popular films over the course of his career. His uncanny ability to portray emotionally disturbed characters has made him an icon of American cinema, perhaps best symbolized by his role as the murderous hotel caretaker Jack Torrance in *The Shining*. On February 8, 1994, Nicholson gave another chilling performance, in real life this time, in the role of a driver suffering from road rage. Nicholson stepped out of his car at a red light in North Hollywood and, with a golf club, repeatedly struck the windshield of the car behind him, the driver of which he believed had cut him off. After the attack, Nicholson returned to his car and drove away. The victim of the attack was injured by flying glass from the windshield and feared for his life. Nicholson, who was easily identified by witnesses at the scene, was charged with misdemeanor vandalism and assault. Never drive if you are angry or upset in any way. As a defensive driver, you should expect other drivers to make mistakes or break road rules, and you should be as prepared as possible to react to these errors to protect your own safety. However, no matter what other drivers have done, you do not have the right to verbally or physically assault them or their property.

car to safety, make sure your doors are locked and your windows are rolled up.

Stress

If you have a busy schedule with a lot to accomplish in a limited amount of time, you are acquainted with stress. Extreme stress from being too busy, not getting enough sleep, or personal problems at home, work, or school can seriously impact your physical and emotional state. Stress can cause adrenaline "rushes," muscle tension, increased breathing and heart rates, sweaty palms, headaches, and extreme fatigue. All of these can make it difficult for you to perform the physical action of driving. You should avoid getting behind the wheel when you are

under enormous stress. If you have to drive, keep your thoughts on your driving and not what is causing you stress. Increase your space cushioning and decrease your speed.

Because certain driving experiences themselves can provoke stressful reactions, try to plan ahead to reduce their stress factor. For example, allow extra time during rush hour and bad weather, map out your route before traveling to unfamiliar areas, and call ahead if you are going to be late for an appointment so you will not be rushing to get there.

Anxiety, Excitement, and Depression

A major source of anxiety is driving in unfamiliar surroundings. If you get lost you may panic or get

Figure 3–10 To reduce stress when traveling to an unfamiliar place, allow extra time to reach your destination.

confused, causing you to overlook critical information or potentially threatening situations. Once panic sets in, it is easy to become indecisive or miss the signals of other vehicles. If you are too preoccupied looking for a street address, for example, you might rear-end the car in front of you because you did not notice its brake lights. Being overly excited can also affect driving by decreasing your attentiveness and increasing your willingness to take risks. Depression, or feelings of hopelessness and despair, can likewise diminish your concentration and coordination.

If you are coping with anxiety, excitement, or depression, try to have another licensed driver drive for you. If you must drive, make an extra effort to concentrate on the road, not on your emotions.

Stay away from heavy traffic. If you are overwhelmed, pull over and try to relax until you feel able to concentrate again.

Distractions

There is no substitute for a mentally alert driver who is aware of the surroundings and can react quickly and clearly to every driving situation encountered. Anything that takes your attention away from driving can cause you to make poor decisions and impair your reactions at a crucial moment. Trying to simultaneously drive and perform unrelated tasks reduces your concentration and may cause you to take your eyes off the road. Activities you should avoid while driving include eating, retrieving and replacing drinks in cup holders, searching

driving tips

Wearing headphones while driving is extremely dangerous and, in many jurisdictions, illegal.

for objects or pocket change for tolls, reading maps or directions, looking at yourself in the rearview mirror, putting on makeup, shaving, or brushing your teeth.

Figure 3–11 When you are behind the wheel, avoid distracting tasks unrelated to driving.

If you have a passenger, ask him or her to help you with any necessary tasks such as pulling out money for tolls or reading maps. Allow time to eat your meals and get ready before you get in your car, or plan to do other tasks once you arrive at your destination. If something draws your attention either inside or outside the vehicle, quickly assess whether it is a hazard and return your attention to the road.

Car Stereos

Music or talk radio can help you pass the time and stay relaxed and alert on long trips or in slow traffic. In addition to being good entertainment, your car stereo is a great means to get information about local traffic conditions and weather reports. However, under certain conditions, your stereo can become a distraction. If you play music too loudly, you may not hear approaching emergency vehicles or warning sounds such as horns or screeching brakes. You may also irritate your neighboring drivers to the point of anger. Fumbling with tapes or CDs or looking down at the radio and not at the road can cause you to crash or veer out of your lane even at slow speeds.

You can listen to music while driving, but make sure it is not so loud that you cannot hear the sounds of your car or what is happening around you. If your radio has preset buttons, set them on your favorite stations before you start driving. Change CDs or tapes before you drive or only when safely stopped, and do not try to pull them out of hard-to-reach places like the back seat! It is not worth the risk. Listen to what is already on the stereo, or turn it off and focus on your driving.

Cellular Phones

Speaking on a cellular mobile phone, or "cell phone," while

REALITY CHECK
"Flirting" with Danger _____

As a passenger, you can indulge yourself by smiling at every good-looking person you see out of the car windows. However, as a driver, every second you spend making eyes at your new love is a second when you might miss some crucial information about what is happening around you. Keep your eyes on the road, and do not flirt with danger.

REALITY CHECK   *Deadly Decibels*

Many drivers insist on playing their stereos at maximum volume. Their cars are like speakers on wheels, blaring music so loudly that it can be heard several blocks away. These drivers can go right through an intersection without having any idea that an emergency vehicle is approaching along a cross street. When they are at a stop light, everyone else has to hear their music whether they like it or not. This kind of behavior is both dangerous and irritating to other drivers. It is also illegal to exceed specified noise limits in many communities.

driving can increase the chances of a collision by as much as four times. Talking on a cellular phone is distracting in general because your attention is divided between two separate tasks. You might have to take your eyes off the road when dialing, for example, which can cause you to weave or erratically vary your speed. Handheld cellular phones are particularly dangerous be cause you will have only one hand on the steering wheel while calling and talking. It is always best to make calls only when stopped and parked. If you must talk while driving, it is safest to use a speaker phone system, which allows your hands to be free to drive.

Figure 3–12 You should use a car phone only when you are stopped or parked.

Passengers and Kids

Passengers can be a great support, especially on long trips, by helping with tasks such as tuning the radio, giving you directions, or keeping you alert. Passengers, however, can also be distracting, especially "back seat drivers" who try to influence your driving decisions. Even passengers who do not address you directly can distract you by talking too loudly to one another or by "roughhousing" with one another, hanging out of windows, or blocking your rear visibility. Small children can also get noisy and excitable, making it hard to concentrate on the road.

When you are behind the wheel, *you* must take full responsibility for driving safely. Even though it is natural and polite to look at people when talking to them, you should avoid taking your eyes off the road when conversing with passengers. Calmly ignore back seat drivers. If passengers are getting out of control, pull over to the side of the road and ask them to settle down or get out. To prevent arguments with children while driving, establish a firm set of "car rules"

bumper sticker sightings

HANG UP AND DRIVE!

Figure 3–13 Out-of-control children can be a major distraction to driving.

In Norman, Oklahoma, it is illegal to drive an auto while reading a comic book.

and try to consistently follow them.

Smoking

Smoking is one of the most distracting things you can do while driving. Because you have less use of your hands, smoking decreases your ability to coordinate controls. Lighting cigarettes or cigars causes you to look away from the road while handling an open flame or a hot cigarette lighter. There is also the constant danger of dropping a lit cigarette or match in your lap or somewhere else in the car. Cigarettes discarded out of a front window can make their way into the back of the car through an open rear window.

Try to avoid smoking while driving. If you feel the need for a smoke, use the car lighter, which requires only one hand, rather than a match to light up. Always discard your cigarettes in the ashtray, first making sure that they are no longer burning. If you often smoke in your car, film from the smoke can build up on the interior of your windows and obscure your view. You should regularly clean the windows of your vehicle before this layer of film affects your visibility.

Pets

Pets should always be secured in a carrier that is well made and the right size, either inside the car or in the open bed of a truck. Specially designed harnesses are available to secure medium- and large-sized dogs. Do not put an animal in the back of a pickup with an unventilated camper shell—you may be putting the animal at risk for carbon monoxide poisoning. If you do not have a carrier or harness, and it is urgent to transport your pet, have a passenger hold and watch the animal. Never let a pet sit on your lap or wander around your vehicle where it may interfere with your driving in some other way.

Figure 3–14 Rubbernecking causes traffic congestion and can lead to other accidents.

Rubbernecking

Do not slow down to observe a crash site. So-called **rubbernecking** is a dangerous habit that contributes to traffic congestion on both sides of a roadway and often leads to further collisions. If you pass the scene of a crash, keep your attention focused on driving.

Other Distractions

Driving in unfamiliar areas can be distracting because you are taking in a great deal of information for the first time, but you can be equally distracted in your own neighborhood or town. For instance, if you run into a friend or neighbor on your way to school or when running an errand, you may become concerned with getting their attention and not be attentive to your driving. If you want to get a pedestrian's attention, pull over and park before you call out to him or her. If you are talking to friends in another vehicle, make sure that you both move into a parking spot or to the side of the road and that you are not blocking traffic.

Observing scenery rather than paying attention to the road can be extremely dangerous. Stay focused on driving and save any sightseeing for a rest stop or specially designated scenic "lookouts." If you can, switch drivers periodically so that one person can focus on driving while the others can enjoy the sights.

WHO'S AT FAULT?

1. Driver 1 was driving late at night in the left-hand lane of a straight, flat highway. He fell asleep and began to drift across the right-hand lane in front of Driver 2 and off the side of the road. Driver 2 thought that Driver 1 was pulling off the roadway. She slowed down but did not change lanes as she went past Driver 1. At that moment, Driver 1 woke up and veered suddenly to the left, back onto the roadway, colliding with Driver 2. *Who's at fault?*

2. Driver 1 thought Driver 2 had cut him off. He became angry and decided to give Driver 2 a taste of his own medicine. He accelerated alongside Driver 2 and cut in front of him. Driver 2 slammed on his brakes but could not stop in time and crashed into Driver 1. *Who's at fault?*

YOUR TURN

3–1 *The Physical Condition of the Driver*

1. What permanent physical conditions can limit your ability to drive safely?

2. What are the four main components of vision?

3. What temporary physical conditions can limit your ability to drive safely?

4. How can you prevent carbon monoxide poisoning?

3–2 *The Mental Condition of the Driver*

5. How does your mental condition impact your ability to drive safely?

6. How can you avoid becoming a victim of road rage?

7. What activities should you avoid while driving?

SELF-TEST

Multiple Choice

1. Road rage is a common form of what type of driving?
   a. beneficial
   b. aggressive
   c. safe
   d. defensive

2. Your central vision is typically how wide?
   a. 45 degrees
   b. 90 degrees
   c. 10 degrees
   d. 3 degrees

3. Visual acuity is the ability to:
   a. drive only in daylight.
   b. distinguish colors of road signs.
   c. see objects close and far away.
   d. drive only at night.

4. If you are driving, the best way to deal with a back seat driver is to:
   a. pull off the road and let the person drive.
   b. ignore the person.
   c. ask the person to sit in the passenger's seat.
   d. stop the car and wait for the person to finish his or her thoughts.

5. Normal 20/20 visual acuity is the ability to:
   a. read letters 1 inch (2½ cm) high from a distance of 20 feet (6 m).
   b. read letters ⅜ inch (1 cm) high from a distance of 20 feet (6 m).
   c. read at least twenty letters of the alphabet from a distance of 20 feet (6 m).
   d. read letters ¾ inch (2 cm) high from a distance of 20 feet (6 m).

Sentence Completion

1. The ability to judge distance between two objects is called _____ .

2. Boredom, eye strain, and poor ventilation all contribute to _____ .

3. Your _____ is determined by the quickness and efficiency that your nervous and muscular systems work together.

4. If you are unable to distinguish between red and green, you will have to depend on the _____ and meaning of road signs to drive safely.

5. Smoking with the windows closed can cause _____ .

Matching

Match the concepts in Column A with examples of the concepts in Column B.

Column A	Column B
1. __ Road rage	**a.** Distance between two objects
2. __ Carbon monoxide	**b.** Eating, shaving, reading
3. __ Fatigue	**c.** Extends 180 degrees
4. __ Preventing fatigue	**d.** Odorless, colorless, tasteless
5. __ Central vision	**e.** Talk to a passenger
6. __ Distractions	**f.** Area directly ahead
7. __ Peripheral vision	**g.** Temporary impairment
8. __ Depth perception	**h.** Deliberate tailgating

Short Answer

1. What are some of the early signs of carbon monoxide poisoning?

2. What should you do if another driver becomes aggressive toward you?

3. How can car stereos be distracting to driving?

4. What can you do to prevent fatigue while driving?

5. How does driving affect peripheral vision and depth perception?

Critical Thinking

1. You are driving down a busy street when the door of a parked vehicle immediately ahead of you flies open. You swerve quickly to the left side of your lane to avoid hitting the door, but a driver just behind you in the left lane is angered that you nearly cut him off. He pulls up next to you honking his horn and making gestures at you, then cuts in front of you and slows down. What should you do?

2. At the last STOP sign, an elderly woman driving a white sedan just in front of you turned left. You made a left turn into the same side street behind her. It is dark, and you are in an unfamiliar neighborhood looking for a friend's house that you are pretty sure is coming up on your left. The woman is driving very slowly and you are late for dinner. You want to pass her, but you notice that her left-turn signal is still on. What should you do?

PROJECTS

1. *Your sight is your most valuable sense when driving, but other senses such as your hearing help you know what is happening around your vehicle. The next time that you are riding as a passenger in a vehicle, close your eyes and listen for sounds that clue you in to what other vehicles are doing on the road. Do you hear horns, an accelerating engine, emergency sirens, or the squeal of a truck's brakes as it comes to a stop beside you?*

2. *As a passenger, observe the drivers of other vehicles and take note of how many people are doing other distracting things while driving such as eating, drinking, looking at their passengers rather than the roadway, smoking a cigarette, and talking on the phone. Share your results with the rest of your class.*

Driving Fundamentals

unit **2**

Preparing to Drive

The first step in learning how to drive defensively is to understand the various instruments, operating devices, and controls of your car. When you are behind the wheel, you have the ability to change everything from your speed to the angle of your mirrors to the temperature inside the passenger compartment. Over time, the use of this equipment will become second nature, but until then you must gradually familiarize yourself with each component.

Upon completion of this chapter, you should be able to:

4–1 Vehicle Instrumentation

1. Identify the gauges and warning lights on a typical instrument panel.
2. Understand what might cause the temperature and oil-pressure warning lights to come on.
3. Understand what an alternator does.

4–2 Operating Devices

4. Describe the different types of exterior lights found on most motor vehicles.
5. Identify the three settings on a typical headlight switch.
6. Know how to properly adjust mirrors.
7. Know what blind spots are and why they exist.

4–3 Vehicle Controls

8. Understand why seat position is important to driving.
9. Identify the controls found on both automatic- and manual-transmission vehicles.

KEY TERMS

gauge	running lights	accelerator
warning lights	parking lights	power brakes
speedometer	turn-signal lights	brake lights
tachometer	hazard lights	parking brake
odometer	rearview mirror	gearshift
alternator	sideview mirrors	clutch
headlights	blind spots	cruise control
taillights	steering wheel	
back-up lights	ignition	

4–1 VEHICLE INSTRUMENTATION

Various gauges and warning lights are arranged on the dashboard within easy view of the driver's position behind the wheel to provide you with accurate and important information about the status of your vehicle. The exact layout varies by vehicle type and model, but these instruments serve the same functions in every car.

Figure 4–1 The instrument panel contains gauges and warning lights.

A **gauge** has a scale with an indicator needle or numerical marker that keeps track of a changing condition like fuel level or speed. **Warning lights**, which are usually red or yellow to attract your attention, indicate a more serious problem or safety concern. At night, the dashboard instruments are usually backlit to help you see them better. Some vehicles have a feature called a "rheostat" that allows you to regulate the intensity of backlighting in the instrument panel to the level most visible and comfortable for you.

The **speedometer** is a gauge that indicates how fast your vehi-

cle is traveling, usually in both miles and kilometers per hour. A **tachometer** is a gauge that measures your engine in revolutions per minute (rpm). The higher the rpm, the faster your engine is "turning" and the harder it is working. Tachometers are useful to help you determine when to shift gears if you have a manual transmission. The red zone on the tachometer specifies an unsafe range of rpms for your vehicle's engine. If your gauge is in the red area, you should either slow down or shift to a higher gear.

The **odometer** is a meter that displays the total number of miles a vehicle has been driven since it was manufactured. Because this gauge is an important measure of the wear and tear on a vehicle, it is strictly illegal to alter it. The odometer is useful for calculating fuel consumption and trip mileage, and for keeping track of your vehicle's maintenance schedule. Most cars also have a separate "trip odometer" that can be set back to zero at any time with the press of a button.

The fuel gauge displays the amount of fuel in the fuel tank. The fuel gauge in some vehicles displays the fuel level whether the engine is on or off. In other cars, you must turn on the ignition to activate the gauge. Consult your owner's manual to find out how many gallons or liters your vehicle's tank holds. The fuel gauge usually has at least five levels of fuel indicated: empty, $\frac{1}{4}$ of a tank, $\frac{1}{2}$ of a tank, $\frac{3}{4}$ of a tank, and full.

Running out of gas is a common mistake for new drivers. As a

factoid

The first car with computerized digital instrumentation appeared in 1976.

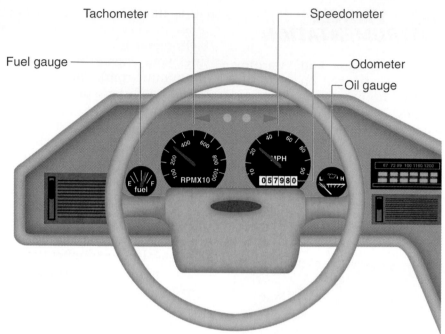

Figure 4–2 Gauges

road
weirdness

*Make sure you have a full
tank before heading out on
sparsely populated U.S.
Highway 50 in Nevada,
known as "The Loneliest
Highway in America."*

rule of thumb, it is best to not let your tank get below one-quarter full. In cold weather, you should try to keep the tank at least half full. This will help prevent "fuel-line freeze" caused by moisture that condenses and freezes inside the tank and fuel line, forming ice particles that can block the fuel line.

The temperature warning light goes on if the engine temperature is too high or if coolant in the radiator is getting too hot. Other reasons this light may go on include a loss of coolant, a clogged radiator, a slipping or broken belt, a defective thermostat, the need for oil in the crankcase, or an unusual strain on the engine. On some vehicles, a gauge is used instead of a warning light. The gauge will read "hot" or the needle will be in the red zone if the

REALITY CHECK *Know Your Nozzles*

When you refuel, do not get distracted and put the wrong fuel in your car. It is unlikely that you would put leaded fuel in the tank of a vehicle that runs on unleaded fuel because the nozzle for leaded gas is too big to fit in the opening of most unleaded tanks. However, you must be very careful never to put diesel fuel in an unleaded fuel tank because the nozzles are closer in size. Diesel fuel can destroy an unleaded engine.

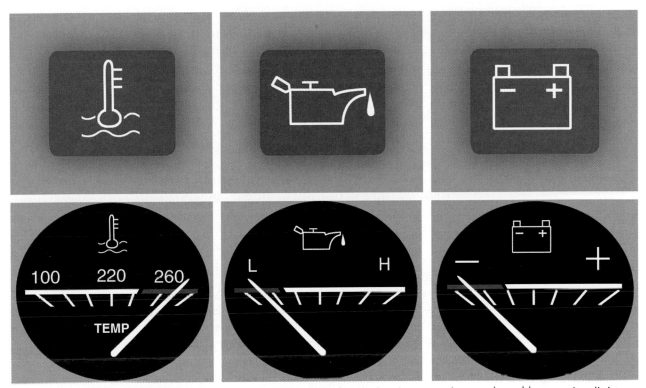

Figure 4–3 Engine temperature, oil pressure, and the car's electrical system may be monitored by warning lights and/or gauges, depending on your vehicle.

car is overheating. If you have a gauge indicator, learn where the needle normally points so that you can recognize when the engine is getting too hot.

The oil-pressure warning light or gauge warns you when the engine oil is not circulating at the right pressure. If the warning light goes on or the gauge reads "low," stop immediately. Because oil is needed to reduce friction between engine parts, losing oil pressure can seriously damage your engine. Oil pressure loss may be caused by a slow leak, a puncture of the oil pan, or natural burning as your car gets older. It is your responsibility to check your oil level regularly,

using the dipstick located under the hood.

The oil-pressure light will go on briefly when the ignition is turned to the "on" position to show that it is working and will go off again once the car is started. If the light does not go on, or remains on, check for problems as soon as possible. The oil pressure should be zero when the engine is at rest, and it may remain low when the engine is idling.

In most vehicles, there is a red light labeled "alt" for "alternator" or "gen" for "generator" on the instrument panel. The **alternator** is a generator that produces electricity to power the car's electrical system. Everything that uses electricity in the car, including the ignition system, lights, and accessories such as the stereo, runs off of the alternator. When the alternator warning light is on, it indicates trouble in the car's electrical system. If the alternator is not putting out enough electricity to run the car, the engine must use stored electricity from the battery. This will eventually drain the battery, and once that happens the car can no longer run at all.

Some vehicles have a gauge rather than a warning light. Usually the gauge has a scale marked by a positive sign (+) at one end and a negative sign (−) or the word "discharge" at the other end. If the indicator on the gauge moves to the (−)/"discharge" side of the gauge, shut off all nonessential equipment such as the radio and go to the nearest service station to have your electrical system checked.

Figure 4–4 If you see this light and your parking brake is not on, have your braking system checked immediately.

Many cars have a braking system warning light that serves two functions. First, it reminds you to release the parking brake before moving the vehicle. Second, it indicates that part or all of the braking system is not working properly or that your brake fluid may be low or leaking. If this light goes on while your foot is pressing the brake pedal, have the brake system checked out by a mechanic right away.

4–2 OPERATING DEVICES

Motor vehicles are equipped with many devices that must be operated by the driver. Some are required for the safety of the driver and passengers, whereas others are designed to increase comfort and convenience. Most of these devices are within easy reach of the driver's seat: on the steering wheel column, on the dashboard, on the console or "hump" between the front seats, on the driver's door, and near the floor to the driver's left.

Lights

Making yourself visible to others is an essential part of driving defensively. All vehicles are required to have two **headlights** giving off white light, one on each side of the front of the vehicle. High beams must be capable of illuminating objects within 350 feet (100 m), and low beams must be strong enough to reveal objects within 100 feet (30 m). Headlights must be lit from sunset to

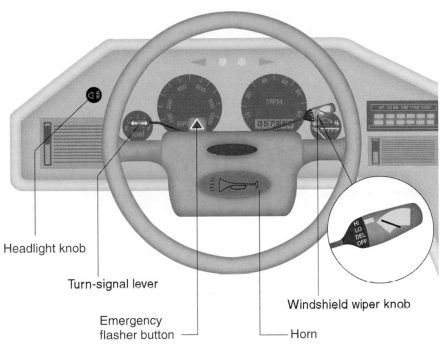

Figure 4–5 Operating devices

Headlight knob

Turn-signal lever

Emergency
flasher button

Windshield wiper knob

Horn

sunrise or at any other time when your visibility is limited such as in rain or snow. Law enforcement takes driving without headlights very seriously, and you will be cited if your headlights are not functioning properly. All vehicles are also required to have two **taillights** giving off red light that can be seen from a distance of

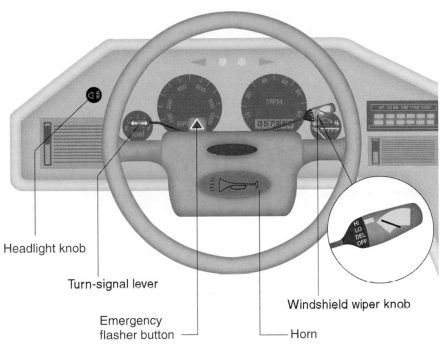

Figure 4–6 You can be cited for driving with a burned-out headlight.

500 feet (150 m). Taillights come on whenever you turn on your headlights.

Vehicles may have no more than two white or amber **back-up lights.** These lights are activated when the transmission is set to RE-VERSE, indicating your intention to back up.

Daytime **running lights** have been installed on many vehicles manufactured after 1989. These lights are on the front of a vehicle and automatically illuminate upon ignition. They can be a dimmer setting of your headlights or a separate set of lights located next to your headlights. **Parking lights** are white or amber-colored on the front of the vehicle, and red on the rear of the vehicle. All parking lights must be visible from 500 feet

Crazy
auto laws

In Berea, Kentucky, any animals on the streets after dark must prominently display a red "tail" light.

The first electric "winker" turn indicators were offered by Buick in 1939.

(150 m) away and must be used only for parking purposes. *Never use your parking lights as an alternative to headlights and taillights while driving your vehicle.*

The headlight switch is usually a knob at the end of the turn-signal lever. It may also be located on the dashboard instrument panel to the left of the driver. When you turn your headlights on, your instrument panel and license plate should light up as well.

No matter where it is located on your vehicle, the headlight switch usually has three settings. The first turns on only the parking and side-marker lights, the second turns on your low-beam headlights, and the third turns on your high beams. If your headlight switch is on the steering column, you may also be able to activate your high beams by pulling the lever toward you. Pull it again to click the high beams off. To "flash" your high beams at another driver as a warning, pull the lever back slightly and release it. In some older cars, the high-beam switch may be a foot-activated button on the floor to the far left of the pedals.

When your high beams are on, a blue indicator light appears on the instrument panel of most vehicles. High beams generally allow you to see twice as far as low beams, but with less clarity immediately in front of your vehicle. Their use should be restricted to very dark, uncrowded, or unfamiliar roadways. Always "dim" your high beams back to the normal low-beam setting when you see an oncoming vehicle or are following another vehicle in traffic to prevent blinding the other driver.

Turn Signals

Your vehicle must have **turn-signal lights** on all four corners of the vehicle. These lights must be visible from at least 100 feet (30 m) away in daylight. They normally cast off white or amber light in front, and red or amber light in the rear. Turn signals usually appear as two green arrow-shaped lights on the instrument panel that flash to indicate the direction of your turn. These lights are synchronized with the signal lights on the exterior of your vehicle.

DRIVING TIPS *"Reading" by the Light of Your Turn Signals*

Whenever it is dark and you are searching for an address on a poorly lit residential street, take advantage of address numbers painted in white or fluorescent paint on the side of the curb. When you approach a residence to find out its number, pull out of traffic safely and approach the number on the curb. Park slightly behind it, and keep your turn signal on. The signal will cast a glow against the curb and illuminate the number so that you can read it.

Figure 4–7 Turn signals are located at the front and rear of the vehicle.

The turn-signal lever is almost always located on the left side of the steering column. You move the lever up to signal a right turn and down to signal a left turn. When you push the lever up or down far enough, you will feel it click into place. Both the exterior and dashboard turn-signal lights are designed to stop automatically after a turn is made. However, sometimes if you are changing lanes, merging, or making a very wide turn, the sensor may

not detect the "turn" and you must cancel the signal manually.

Hazard lights, also called emergency flashers, are used to indicate that you are experiencing an emergency situation or to warn other drivers that your vehicle is not functioning properly. The emergency-flasher switch or button activates all four exterior turn-signal lights at once and may be located on the steering column, on the dashboard, or even on the console. On most vehicles, the emergency flashers are indicated on the dashboard by both turn-signal lights flashing at the same time. Some cars have a hazard-light indicator independent of the dashboard turn-signal indicators.

Windshield Wipers

You must have windshield wipers to remove rain, snow, and other moisture from the windshield to see clearly while driving. Windshield wipers are activated by a lever on the right side of the steering column or a switch located either on the dashboard or on the turn-signal lever. They can usually be set at one of several variable speeds, according to the severity of the weather. Some cars have rear-window wipers that

DRIVING TIPS *Safe Signaling*

For lane changes, lightly hold the turn-signal lever up or down with one finger until the lane change is complete, then release it back to the standard position. This will allow you to keep both hands on the wheel.

No Rain in the Forecast _____

On a clear, sunny day, just when you least expect it, a blinding spray of water smacks your windshield. This "rain" is not from the sky but rather from the vehicle ahead of you whose driver decided to wash the windshield while the car was moving. If this happens, do not panic. Slow down and clear your view with your windshield wipers. The next time *you* feel the urge to squirt your windshield while you are driving, think of the person behind you and wait until you are safely stopped at a light or a STOP sign.

may be activated by another setting on the windshield-wiper lever or by a separate switch on the dashboard instrument panel. The windshield-wiper switch or lever can also be used to dispense washer fluid for cleaning the windshield when necessary.

Horn

A working horn that can be heard at a distance of 200 feet (60 m) is required by law and can be used to warn others of your presence or an impending collision. The horn is usually located on the steering wheel, but on some vehicles it is found on the turn-signal lever. This allows you to honk without taking your hands completely off the wheel. Make sure that you know where the horn is located in your vehicle and how much pressure it takes to activate it.

Mirrors

To drive defensively, you must be aware of what is happening around you at all times. By revealing what you cannot see out of your front windows, your mirrors help you respond to traffic events quickly and safely. Most vehicles have two types of mirrors. The interior **rearview mirror** is a wide, rectangular mirror either suspended from the roof or attached to the windshield that allows you to see directly behind you. Exterior **sideview mirrors** mounted on the doors allow you to see along the sides of your vehicle and neighboring lanes of traffic.

Every time you get into your vehicle, you should make sure that all of your mirrors are properly adjusted. If someone else used your car, he or she may have shifted the mirror settings. You or a passenger may have knocked the rearview mirror out of alignment getting out. A person walking past your car may have knocked a sideview mirror out of place.

To adjust your rearview mirror, sit as you would to drive. Without moving your head, grasp the mirror by the frame and adjust its position so that you can see out of the rear window with the right edge of the mirror aligned with the right edge of the rear window. You should use only your eyes to properly align the rearview mirror. Adjust the sideview mirrors so that you can barely see the sides of your car from the driving posi-

crazy auto laws

In the early days of the automobile, a bell was used rather than a horn on some vehicles, such as fire trucks. Some jurisdictions today still have laws specifying that individually owned motor vehicles are prohibited from using bells as a warning device.

Figure 4–9 Always adjust your sideview mirrors before driving.

tion. The right sideview mirror often takes a little more effort because you must lean over to adjust it (unless you have electric controls). The important thing to remember is that vehicles passing you should be in your sideview mirrors before they leave your rearview mirrors and in your peripheral vision before they leave your sideview mirrors.

Most rearview mirrors have a day/night lever on the back that allows you to switch the angle of the mirror to reduce glare when driving at night or if the sun is directly behind you. Always make

sure your mirror is set for the time of day you are driving to ensure maximum visibility.

Blind Spots

The areas *not* reflected in your mirrors are called **blind spots.** The size of a blind spot varies with the design of the vehicle and the physical characteristics of the driver. A driver who is short and drives a huge sedan, for example, will have larger blind spots than a tall driver in a compact. The two main blind spots on a car extend from just behind the driver's normal field of forward vision to the right and left sides of the vehicle. Proper mirror adjustment will help reduce the size of blind

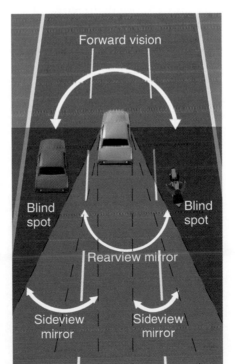

Figure 4–11 Your mirrors cannot reveal what is in your blind spots.

Figure 4–10 Your rearview mirror can be adjusted for both daytime and nighttime driving.

Figure 4–8 What is the name of this American vehicle, built in 1911, that was the first car to have a rearview mirror?

spots, but it will not completely eliminate them. *Never trust only your mirrors. Always turn your head and look before you change your position!*

As a defensive driver, you have the responsibility not only to drive outside of other vehicles' blind spots but also not to allow other drivers to stray into *your* blind spots. If you pay attention to the traffic patterns to your sides, you will know when a car approaching from the rear or slowing down in front of you is moving into your blind spot. When this happens, use gentle increases and decreases of speed by momentarily taking your foot off the gas pedal or by lightly applying some pressure to the brakes to position yourself so that these cars are no longer in your blind spots.

Other Operating Devices

Seat adjustment controls allow you to move your seat to the best and most comfortable driving position. For vehicles with electrically adjustable seats, a series of switches usually located on the left side of the driver's seat allows you to move your seat up or down, and forward or backward, as needed. For most cars with manually adjustable seats, you must slide and hold a lever under the front edge of the seat as you use your weight to push the seat forward and backward. Always make sure that your seat is securely locked into place before you start driving. On the door

side of the front seats near the floor are levers that control the angle of the seats.

Door locks protect your car from theft or unauthorized entry, and they prevent doors from opening in a collision. To prevent drivers from accidentally locking themselves out of their cars, the driver's door on many vehicles can typically be locked only from the outside. Most door locks can be unlocked only with a key, but some vehicles have electronic locks. Door locks are operated from the inside of the vehicle either manually or electronically.

Windows are controlled from the inside of the vehicle either manually or electronically, depending on the vehicle. Manual window controls are cranks that you turn counterclockwise to "roll down," or open, and clockwise to "roll up," or close. On cars with electric, or "power," windows, the controls for each door are located on the door handles.

Sun visors are hinged panels located at the top of the windshield over the head of the driver and front-seat passenger. When the sun is directly in your eyes, you can lower the sun visor to help cut glare. Most sun visors can also be rotated to the side to shield you from sun glare entering through the side windows. Position the visor in such a way that it effectively blocks the sun without interfering with your view of the roadway.

The heater, air conditioner, and defroster controls are usually located in the center of the dashboard to be within easy reach of both the driver and front-seat passenger. The "defrost" setting is used in cold or rainy weather to remove condensation from the inside of the windshield, which can partially or completely block your view outside. Some vehicles also have a "defrost" setting or switch for the rear window.

Your vehicle also includes devices that provide access to the engine, trunk, and fuel tank. Check your owner's manual to see where they are located.

4–3   VEHICLE CONTROLS

The five basic controls found on all cars are the steering wheel, ignition, accelerator, brakes, and gear shift. Vehicles with manual transmissions also have a clutch. These controls are simple to use with experience, but it takes practice to learn to smoothly coordinate their movements. When driving a car for the first time, always take the time to get a "feel" for the controls. Each vehicle is different, and the controls of one car may be more or less sensitive than the same controls on another car.

When driving, sit in a comfortable, erect position squarely behind the steering wheel with your back firmly against the seat. Make sure that you are sitting high enough to see over the steering wheel and the hood. The top of the steering wheel should never be more than 1 inch (2½ cm) higher than the top of your shoulder. If you cannot see the road within 12 feet (3½ m) of your car, even at your seat's highest setting, get a firm wedge-shaped seat cushion to raise you higher. If necessary, adjust your headrest to reach the middle of the back of your head.

If your seat is positioned properly, you should be able to easily reach all of the vehicle's controls. Your right heel should rest on the floor at the base of the accelerator. You should be able to pivot your right foot from the accelerator to the brake pedal without lifting your heel from the floor. Your left foot should rest on the floor to the left of the brake pedal if you have an automatic transmission, or at the base of the clutch if you have a manual transmission. Your legs should be slightly bent, not stretched out as far as they will go. If your legs are straight, you will not be able to push the brake pedal down all the way if necessary. If you cannot reach the pedals comfortably after your seat is adjusted to the right height, you may need to buy extensions for the pedals.

Steering Wheel

The **steering wheel** controls the front wheels of the vehicle, and turning the wheel determines the direction the vehicle will take. Some cars have an adjustable steering wheel, or "tilt-wheel," for better comfort and control. Most vehicles today have a power steering system that mechanically assists the driver so that turning the wheel requires a minimum of

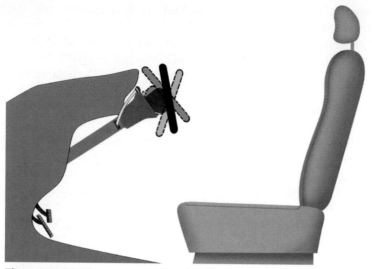

Figure 4–12 The angle of "tilt-wheel" steering wheels can be adjusted.

physical effort. If your vehicle has power steering and your steering wheel is extremely hard to turn, you should have the steering system checked by a mechanic.

Ignition

The **ignition**, where you insert your key to start the engine, is usually located on the right side of the steering column. The ignition has at least three positions. When the transmission is in "park" and the engine is off, the ignition is in the "lock," or "off," position. Insert your key and turn it clockwise one notch to the "on" position. The dashboard instruments should come on to show that they are working properly. Turn the key one more notch to the "start" position to start the engine. To turn the engine off, turn the key back to the original "lock"/"off" position. To remove the key in some vehicles, you must push the ignition in before

turning it all the way off, or press a button located right next to the ignition. These safety catches prevent you from removing the key accidentally while driving.

You can lock your steering wheel when the ignition is off and the key is out by turning the wheel to one side until you feel it lock. To unlock the wheel, you usually insert the key and turn it to the "on" position and then turn the wheel to release it. Locking your steering wheel is a deterrent to theft and will keep your tires pointed in the right direction when parked on a hill.

Some vehicles have an additional "accessory" position on the ignition that activates the electrical system, allowing you to operate the radio and other electrical equipment without starting the engine. This position is usually one notch away from "off" in the clockwise direction. Be careful not to use the accessory setting for too

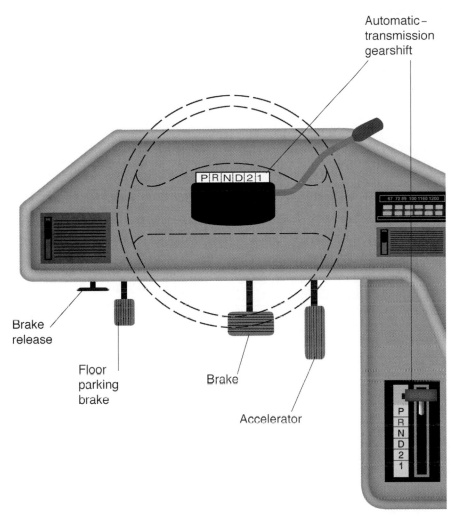

Figure 4–13 Typical vehicle with automatic transmission

long. Depending on which accessories you are running and the condition of your battery, you might drain the battery.

Accelerator

The **accelerator**, also called the gas pedal, is the far-right foot pedal. The accelerator controls the amount of fuel your car's car- buretor or fuel injectors feed to the engine. You operate the accelerator with your right foot. Resting your heel on the floor, gradually depress the gas pedal to increase speed and let up on the gas pedal to let the car slow down on its own. Because vehicles accelerate differently, you must develop a sensitivity to your own accelerator.

The floor-mounted accelerator was developed in 1899.

Brakes

The brake pedal, which allows you to slow or stop your car, is the pedal located just to the left of the accelerator. Like the accelerator, you operate the brake pedal with your right foot. Keeping your heel on the floor, exert pressure on the pedal with the ball of your foot to activate your car's braking system.

Your vehicle may have standard brakes or power-assisted brakes. If you have standard brakes, the pedal will move a couple of inches/centimeters until it meets resistance. **Power brakes** require less foot pressure to operate than standard brakes, but they do *not* shorten the distance needed to stop the car. When driving a car with power brakes for the first time, you should depress the pedal gradually and gently to get a feel for how much pressure is needed to bring the vehicle to a smooth stop. If you apply pressure too suddenly, you may stop so abruptly as to cause a driver behind you to rear-end your vehicle. If the power-brake system fails or your engine stalls, you will still be able to stop the car but you will have to put heavy pressure on the brake pedal.

Your brakes are also a very important communication device. When you step on the brake pedal, you activate your **brake lights**. In some vehicles, the taillights also function as brake lights by getting brighter when the brakes are applied. Most jurisdictions require that brake lights be visible from a minimum of 100

uess the vanity plate

DELMAR

STOPN10

Figure 4–14

feet (30 m) away in daylight. If you see that traffic ahead of you is slowing or stopping, you can warn other drivers behind you to prepare to slow or stop by tapping lightly on your brakes a few times.

A feature required on all passenger cars manufactured since 1985, and on all light-duty trucks, vans, and sport utility vehicles manufactured since 1993, is the center high-mounted rear brake light. This "extra" brake light is highly effective in reducing rear-end collisions because drivers are less likely to confuse it with the taillights of the vehicle. If you have a vehicle made before 1985, you should consider having a center high-mounted brake light installed.

The **parking brake** keeps your vehicle in place when parked. It can also be used to stop your car in emergency situations in which the normal brakes fail. In most vehicles, the parking brake is a large handle located on the console. To set the brake, pull the handle up until it feels tight and locked into place. To release the brake, push the button at the tip of the handle with your thumb and lower it down as far as it will go.

In some cars and trucks, you must activate the parking brake using a foot pedal. Usually this pedal is smaller than the other foot pedals and is located on the far-left side. Push the pedal down as far as you can to set the brake. This type of parking brake is usually released by pulling a lever or handle located on the driver's

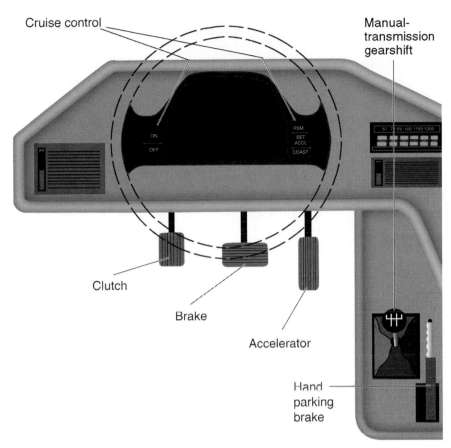

Figure 4–15 Typical vehicle with manual transmission

left side, just under the bottom edge of the instrument panel. Driving with the parking brake engaged, even partially, can damage the brake lining, so always check to make sure that the parking brake is released before you start moving.

Gearshift

The **gearshift** is mounted either on the console or on the right side of the steering column, and it is attached to the transmission, allowing the driver to either drive for-

ward, reverse, or remain in neutral. In automatic-transmission vehicles, if the gearshift is on the console, you must move the handle backward and forward to switch from one gear to another. If the gearshift is on the steering column, you must pull the handle toward you and then slide it to engage the gear you want.

In vehicles with a manual transmission, the stick shift, or "stick," is a handle with a knob on top that rests on the console. To switch to different gears, you must learn to coordinate moving

DRIVING TIPS *"Preflight" Checks* _____

Aircraft pilots conduct a preflight check before takeoff, and so should you when you get behind the wheel of an automobile. Driver and passenger safety depends on what you do before driving, including making proper adjustments to your seat and mirrors, using safety belts, checking outside your vehicle for obstacles, and securing items in and on the vehicle. It is important to develop a sequence of predriving checks to run through your mind each time you drive.

auto slang

The expression "four on the floor" refers to a gearshift, which in older cars usually had four gears.

the gearshift handle with operating the clutch pedal.

Clutch

The **clutch** is a pedal found only on cars with a manual transmission and is located to the left of the brake pedal. The clutch must be pressed each time you shift gears. To operate the clutch, rest the heel of your left foot on the floor of the car and use the ball of the foot to depress and release the pedal each time you change gears.

Cruise Control

Cruise control is a device that allows you to regulate your vehicle's speed for highway or freeway driving without using the accelerator. It is usually activated by a button on the end of the turn-signal lever or on the steering wheel. To set most cruise controls, accelerate to the speed desired and then allow the speed of the vehicle to decrease by 2 to 3 miles per hour (3 to 5 km/h). Push the "set cruise control" button. Usually a light on your instrument panel will indicate that cruise control is on. Remove your foot from the accelerator. Your speed will stay constant. To cancel cruise control at any time, turn the control switch off or lightly tap the brake pedal.

Exercise caution when using the cruise control feature because it reduces the amount of control you have over your speed. You will not be able to quickly slow down by easing up on the accelerator, or you may skid if you hit the brake to disengage the control while on a slick surface. You also risk developing a false sense of security and becoming less alert. If you get into a situation in which you have to brake quickly, you may not be able to react fast enough because you are too relaxed or your foot is too far from the brake pedal. Even when cruise control is on, keep your right foot on the floor at the base of the accelerator, ready to either engage the accelerator or pivot to the brake pedal instantly.

WHO'S AT FAULT?

1. Driver 1 neglected to adjust his mirrors when he got into the car after his mother, who is much shorter, had been driving it. Because of the position of the mirrors, his blind spots were larger than usual. As he was changing lanes on the freeway, he checked his mirrors but did not look over his shoulder. Driver 2 was in the next lane and swerved to avoid Driver 1. She in turn crashed into Driver 3, who hit the center concrete divider. *Who's at fault?*

2. Driver 1 was heading home after a day in the city. Her brake warning light went on, but she ignored it and proceeded into the tunnel she had to take to reach her house on the other side of the river. As she was descending into the tunnel, her brakes failed. Unable to stop, and with no escape route, she rear-ended Driver 2, who crashed into Driver 3. Driver 4 was just behind Driver 1 but could not stop in time and rear-ended her. *Who's at fault?*

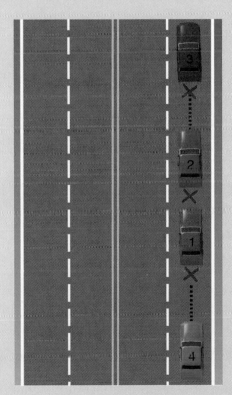

YOUR TURN

4–1 Vehicle Instrumentation

1. What gauges and warning lights are found on a typical instrument panel?

2. What might cause your temperature and oil-pressure warning lights to come on?

3. What does an alternator do?

4–2 Operating Devices

4. What are the different types of exterior lights found on most motor vehicles?

5. What are the three settings on a typical headlight switch?

6. What is the proper way to adjust mirrors?

7. What are blind spots and why do they exist?

4–3 Vehicle Controls

8. How is seat position important to driving?

9. What controls are found on all automatic-transmission vehicles? manual-transmission vehicles?

SELF-TEST

Multiple Choice

1. A tachometer measures:
   a. the total number of miles/kilometers on your car.
   b. oil pressure.
   c. gasoline level.
   d. engine revolutions per minute.

2. What is the main purpose of the alternator?
   a. to regulate the speed of the car
   b. to keep the engine cool
   c. to maintain constant oil pressure
   d. to power the car's electrical system

3. From how far away must turn signals be visible in daylight?
   a. 100 feet (30 m)
   b. 25 feet (7½ m)
   c. 10 feet (3 m)
   d. They do not have to be visible in daylight.

4. Blind spots are those areas not reflected in your:
   a. sideview mirrors.
   b. rearview mirror.
   c. rearview and sideview mirrors.
   d. sun visor vanity mirror.

5. Power brakes:
   a. require less foot pressure to operate than standard brakes.
   b. increase the distance needed to stop the car.
   c. keep your vehicle in place when parked.
   d. have been required on all passenger cars manufactured since 1985.

Sentence Completion

1. The _____ shows the total number of miles/kilometers that a car has been driven since it was new.
2. _____ are on the front of a vehicle and automatically illuminate upon ignition.
3. The _____ controls the amount of fuel that the carburetor or fuel injectors supply to the engine.
4. The _____ setting is used in cold or rainy weather to remove condensation from the inside of the windshield.
5. The _____ is effective at reducing rear-end collisions because they are less likely to be confused with the taillights of a vehicle.

Matching

Match the concepts in Column A with examples of the concepts in Column B.

Column A

1. __ Kilometers per hour
2. __ Reduce blind spots
3. __ Ignition
4. __ Alternator
5. __ Maintain a constant speed
6. __ Reduce glare
7. __ High beams
8. __ Communication device

Column B

a. Speedometer
b. Adjust mirrors
c. "Discharge"
d. "Lock," "On," "Start"
e. Sun visor
f. Brake lights
g. "Set cruise control"
h. Blue indicator light

Short Answer

1. Why is it illegal to alter the odometer on a vehicle?
2. How do you "flash" your high beams?
3. What affects the size of blind spots?
4. Why is it a good idea to lock your doors while driving?
5. What are the chief advantages of power brakes over standard brakes?

Critical Thinking

1. You start your car and begin to pull out of a parking space. After leaving the space, you notice that the brake light on your instrument panel is still on. What should you do?
2. Come up with your own "preflight" check before driving a car. Briefly describe the importance of each step.

PROJECTS

1. *Make a diagram of the instrument panel of your car to help you remember the location of all the gauges and warning lights. Study it for a day or two and then put it away. Take a blank piece of paper and draw the panel again from memory. How did you do?*

2. *Sit in the driver's seat of your vehicle while parked in your driveway or an empty parking lot. Adjust your mirrors so that you can see the maximum area behind you and to the sides. Ask a friend to move around the vehicle one step at a time and, with a piece of chalk, mark your blind spots. Switch places and repeat the same exercise. How do your blind spots compare with your friend's?*

Vehicle Operation Basics

There is more to driving a car than getting behind the wheel and hitting the gas. If you have been around cars your entire life, you might think that steering, changing gears, parking, and other basic operations will come quickly to you. In fact, many adult drivers do not know how to engage a manual transmission, and even experienced drivers can have trouble parking. Before you are ready to handle the more difficult challenges that face today's drivers, you must master the fundamental skills of operating a vehicle.

CHAPTER OBJECTIVES

Upon completion of this chapter, you should be able to:

5–1 *Starting the Engine and Engaging the Transmission*

1. Identify the different gears on an automatic and manual transmission.
2. Describe how to engage an automatic and manual transmission.
3. Describe how to shift gears on a manual transmission.
4. Understand what precautions you should take when putting your vehicle in motion on a hill.

5–2 *Steering*

5. Understand how steering is different from turning.
6. Describe the two basic steering methods.

5–3 *Backing up*

7. Describe the proper procedure for backing up.
8. Understand what precautions you should take when backing up to the left or right.

5–4 *Parking*

9. Identify the four main types of parking.
10. Describe the proper procedure for entering and exiting a parallel parking space.
11. Understand how you should turn your wheels when parking on hills.

KEY TERMS

choke	tracking	curb parking
flooded engine	hand-over-hand method	parallel parking
friction point	push-pull method	angled parking
downshift	double parking	perpendicular parking
steer		

5–1 STARTING THE ENGINE AND ENGAGING THE TRANSMISSION

The steps you take to start the engine depend on whether your vehicle has an automatic or manual transmission. Although manual transmissions require more effort and skill from a driver, they give you more choice in gear selection, require less maintenance, have better gas mileage, and put less wear and tear on the brakes.

Take time to familiarize yourself with the gear configuration of your vehicle. The main difference between automatic and manual transmissions is the number of driving gears. Lower gears deliver more power, and higher gears allow you to maintain higher speeds using less power on level roads. Keep in mind that all engines are different, and your transmission may have different optimal speeds for each gear.

Starting the Engine

To start the engine, first confirm that the parking brake is set. If you have an automatic transmission, shift to PARK. If you have a manual transmission, fully depress the clutch with your left foot while pressing the brake with your right foot, and shift into NEUTRAL. On some vehicles, you do not have to depress the clutch while starting the engine.

If the engine is cold and you do not have a fuel-injected car, press and release the accelerator once to set the automatic **choke**, a device that controls the amount of air that enters the carburetor. If your vehicle has fuel injection, you do not need to press the accelerator.

Turn the key to start the engine, and release it as soon as the

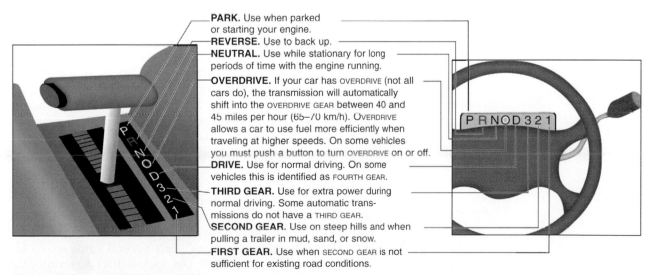

PARK. Use when parked or starting your engine.

REVERSE. Use to back up.

NEUTRAL. Use while stationary for long periods of time with the engine running.

OVERDRIVE. If your car has OVERDRIVE (not all cars do), the transmission will automatically shift into the OVERDRIVE GEAR between 40 and 45 miles per hour (65–70 km/h). OVERDRIVE allows a car to use fuel more efficiently when traveling at higher speeds. On some vehicles you must push a button to turn OVERDRIVE on or off.

DRIVE. Use for normal driving. On some vehicles this is identified as FOURTH GEAR.

THIRD GEAR. Use for extra power during normal driving. Some automatic transmissions do not have a THIRD GEAR.

SECOND GEAR. Use on steep hills and when pulling a trailer in mud, sand, or snow.

FIRST GEAR. Use when SECOND GEAR is not sufficient for existing road conditions.

Figure 5–1 Automatic transmission

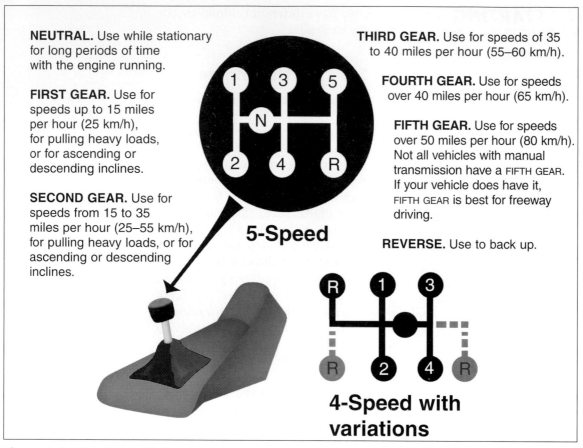

NEUTRAL. Use while stationary for long periods of time with the engine running.

FIRST GEAR. Use for speeds up to 15 miles per hour (25 km/h), for pulling heavy loads, or for ascending or descending inclines.

SECOND GEAR. Use for speeds from 15 to 35 miles per hour (25–55 km/h), for pulling heavy loads, or for ascending or descending inclines.

5-Speed

THIRD GEAR. Use for speeds of 35 to 40 miles per hour (55–60 km/h).

FOURTH GEAR. Use for speeds over 40 miles per hour (65 km/h).

FIFTH GEAR. Use for speeds over 50 miles per hour (80 km/h). Not all vehicles with manual transmission have a FIFTH GEAR. If your vehicle does have it, FIFTH GEAR is best for freeway driving.

REVERSE. Use to back up.

4-Speed with variations

Figure 5–2 Manual transmission

engine starts. If you continue to turn the key after the engine has started, you may damage the starter. In some vehicles, you must first push the key and then turn it to start the engine. If you are driving an older car with a manual choke, pull the choke out before turning the key in the ignition and push it in after the engine has started. When the car is idling smoothly, release the choke. If you have a manual transmission, release the clutch after the engine has started.

If you turn the ignition key and can hear the starter clicking but the car does not start, the engine may be **flooded.** Flooding occurs when there is too much gasoline in the engine, which can be caused by depressing the accelerator too many times before starting the car. If you think your engine is flooded, press down continuously on the accelerator as you turn the key in the ignition for about 10 seconds, making sure to let off the accelerator if the car begins to start. If this does not work, wait several minutes to allow the excess fuel to evaporate and then try starting the engine again.

Putting the Vehicle in Motion

Once you start your vehicle and the engine is running, you must engage the transmission to put the car in motion. The procedure you follow depends on what type of transmission you have.

Automatic Transmission

If you are a new driver, many instructors recommend that you first drive a vehicle with an automatic transmission. Automatic transmissions are designed to be "user friendly." Because they have no clutch, less coordination of hands and feet is required to operate the vehicle. In addition, gears change automatically during normal driving, so you can concentrate more on the driving task. To engage an automatic transmission, first press firmly on the brake pedal. Shift to either DRIVE, FIRST gear, or REVERSE, depending on which way you want to go. Release the parking brake. Check for traffic in your mirrors, and look over your shoulder to make sure that your blind spots are clear. If you are driving forward, use your turn indicator to signal to others

which direction you want to move. When your intended path is clear, remove your foot from the brake and apply gradual pressure to the gas pedal, accelerating smoothly into traffic.

Manual Transmission

Manual transmissions are more complicated to operate than automatic transmissions. You must coordinate the clutch, gearshift, and accelerator to engage the gears. Depending on driving conditions, you may have to change gears often. In heavy traffic, on city streets, and on windy roads, for example, you have to shift gears constantly. Although anybody can learn to use a stick shift with practice, it takes time to do it so that you can shift gears in one fluid motion without having to think about what you are doing.

To engage a manual transmission, follow these steps and refer to Figure 5–3:

1. While pressing on the brake pedal, fully depress the clutch.
2. Shift into FIRST gear or REVERSE, depending on which way you want to go. To shift into

factoid

The first production car with an automatic transmission, called Dynaflow, was offered by Buick in 1948.

DRIVING MYTHS *The Runaway Vehicle* _____

Some people believe that if you have an automatic transmission and you take your foot off the brake while the vehicle is idling in DRIVE, it will begin to move and continue to increase in speed automatically on its own. In fact, if you are on level ground and you take your foot off the brake while the automatic transmission is in DRIVE, the car may begin to creep forward but it will not exceed more than a few miles/kilometers per hour. The speed at which it will move depends on the setting for the engine idle and varies among vehicles, but it will not *increase* until you actually press the accelerator.

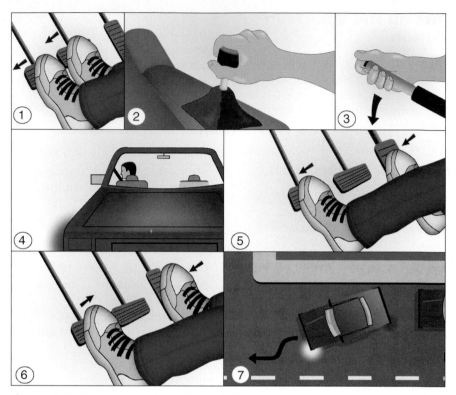

Figure 5–3 Engaging a manual transmission

REVERSE, you may have to use extra effort to engage the gear. Most manual transmissions have a safeguard to prevent accidental shifting into REVERSE from a driving gear, and to engage REVERSE you may have to push the gearshift down first.

3. Release the parking brake.
4. Check for traffic in your mirrors and by looking over your shoulder. Make sure that your blind spots are clear. If driving forward, use your turn indicator to signal to others in which direction you intend to move. Get ready to accelerate.

5. Lightly press the accelerator and hold.
6. With your eyes on the road, slowly release the clutch until it reaches the **friction point**, the point at which the engine begins to engage the transmission. At first you may find this difficult, but in time you will recognize the friction point through the "feel" of the clutch pedal and the sound of the motor.
7. Once you have reached the friction point, continue to slowly release the clutch while gently accelerating. Accelerating too quickly might cause

the wheels to spin, and cause you to lose control if the car moves forward too quickly.

If the car jerks when you try to engage the transmission, try releasing the clutch more slowly or putting less pressure on the accelerator. However, the engine will stall if you do not give it enough gas. A stall may also occur if you do not fully depress the clutch. Remember that every clutch is different. If you learn how to drive a manual transmission on one car, it may take time to get used to the clutch on another car.

Shifting to Higher Gears. As you accelerate, you must engage higher gears to efficiently transfer power from the engine to the transmission. Each gear has a maximum speed, which varies by vehicle, and to reach a higher speed you must switch to a higher gear. If you are driving in a gear that is too low, your engine will "rev" too high—that is, it will operate at too many revolutions per minute (rpm).

If you are driving a vehicle with an automatic transmission, the gears will shift automatically for you. Although you may want to manually shift to a higher gear—for example, from "1" to "2" to "D"—under certain conditions, you normally do not have to "shift" to a higher gear if you stay in "D."

To shift to a higher gear in a vehicle with a manual transmission, release the accelerator and fully depress the clutch. Briefly pausing in NEUTRAL, shift to the next gear.

You should always shift up one gear at a time in sequence—from 1 to 2, from 3 to 4, and so on. Gradually release the clutch while slowly accelerating. Avoid "riding the clutch," or driving with your foot continuously resting on the clutch. Once you have released the clutch, lift your left foot completely off the pedal.

In addition to the feel of the clutch and the sound of the engine, you can refer to your speedometer and the tachometer to help you decide when to change gears. Just as it takes experience to recognize the friction point when first engaging the transmission, it will take time to learn when to switch gears.

Downshifting. To downshift means to shift from higher to lower gears. There are a number of reasons for downshifting: to slow down or prepare to stop, to gain more power from the engine, or to gain more control—for example, on curves and downward slopes.

For normal driving, you do not need to downshift an automatic transmission. To get more power—for example, during passing—you need only press the accelerator further. You will feel and hear the gears "kick in." If conditions require you to manually downshift, be careful to do so at low speeds. Slow down by either easing off the accelerator or braking to around 30 to 40 miles per hour (40 to 65 km/h) if you are switching to SECOND gear, and even slower if you are switching to FIRST gear.

auto slang

To "pop the clutch" is to release it too fast.

If you are driving a vehicle with a manual transmission, downshifting is an integral part of driving at all speeds. When you are traveling at higher speeds in higher gears, for example, downshifting can help you slow down without using your brakes, which will extend the life of your brake pads. To downshift, release the accelerator, fully depress the clutch, shift to the best gear for the speed at which you are traveling, slowly release the clutch pedal to the friction point, and press the accelerator as necessary.

You do not always have to shift to the next lowest gear when downshifting. For example, you can downshift from FIFTH to THIRD gear, or from FOURTH to SECOND gear, as long as the gear you shift into is consistent with your speed. The most difficult downshift to make is from SECOND to FIRST gear because it requires the vehicle to be slowing down rapidly.

Putting Your Vehicle in Motion on a Hill

If you have an automatic transmission, starting a vehicle and putting it in motion on a hill is virtually the same as it is on a level surface. Remember to keep your foot firmly on the brake as you shift into DRIVE and release the parking brake with your hand. Once the vehicle is in DRIVE, you can safely move your right foot to the accelerator without danger of the car rolling backwards.

Starting a vehicle with a manual transmission and putting it in

Figure 5–4 When starting your vehicle on a hill, make sure the parking brake is on first.

motion on a hill can be tricky if you are facing uphill. If there is another vehicle parked behind you, be aware of how much space is behind you before you get inside your car and start the engine. Because you need your right foot for the accelerator, you will not always be able to use the brake while starting on a hill, so *make absolutely sure the parking brake is securely set.*

Fully depress the clutch while firmly pressing the brake pedal, and shift into NEUTRAL. After starting the engine, press the clutch and shift into FIRST gear. Slowly begin to release the clutch until you reach the friction point, and then fully release the parking brake and apply pressure to the accelerator. Accelerate as evenly as possible to minimize the distance you might roll back downhill and to move forward steadily without jerking or stalling.

5–2 STEERING

Once you have put your vehicle in motion, you must control your direction, as well as your speed.

DRIVING TIPS **Dry Steering**

You should turn the steering wheel only while the car is in motion. "Dry steering," or turning the steering wheel when the car is stopped, can prematurely wear out your tires.

To direct, or **steer**, your automobile, you must use the steering wheel. Steering is not exactly the same thing as turning, which means to change directions. However, you still do "steer" through a turn. Even if you are driving on a straight road and your tires are perfectly aligned, your vehicle may veer in one direction or another because of engine torque, uneven pavement, wind, and other factors. Therefore, you should always steer with both hands on the wheel.

Figure 5–5 Driving with one hand is dangerous because you have less control if you have to react quickly to a hazardous situation.

Hand Position

The safest and most practical position for your hands on the steering wheel is at opposite sides of the wheel. Generally, the left hand should be placed at the 9 o'clock position on the wheel, and the right hand should be placed at 3 o'clock. Make sure you are sitting at a comfortable distance from the wheel and that your arms are relaxed and free to move. This will also allow you to turn at higher speeds without taking your hands off the wheel. Grip the wheel with your fingers rather than your palms, and keep your thumbs pointing up along the face of the steering wheel.

Tracking

Steering requires constant adjustments of the steering wheel to maintain a smooth and steady course. **Tracking** is a method of steering that allows you to keep your vehicle on the intended path of travel whether you are traveling on straight or curving roads. To track, look toward the center of the lane ahead of you, making only the slightest of movements with the steering wheel to adjust your course. When driving in a straight line, it is important to steer toward the center of your path of travel. If you do this, you should have to make only minor adjustments to keep your vehicle in your lane

Figure 5–6 Keep your "sight" focused on the center of the road to maintain a smooth and steady course.

and on the correct path. Looking continuously to either side of the road, rather than toward the center, while driving straight can cause you to drift outside of your lane.

Steering Methods for Turns

There are two basic ways to steer during a turn. Each method has its own advantages, and you should experiment with both to deter-

KELSEY GRAMMER

Actor Kelsey Grammer first gained recognition as the neurotic psychologist Frasier Crane on the hit TV series *Cheers*. In 1993, he first appeared in his own television comedy, *Frasier*, based on the same character. Still running strong, *Frasier* has earned dozens of awards, including multiple consecutive Emmys for Outstanding Comedy. On the night of September 21, 1996, Grammer was driving on Cornell Road in the Malibu Lake area near Los Angeles when he allowed his Dodge Viper to drift to the right shoulder of the roadway. Trying to correct his steering, he swerved across the road, hit a dirt embankment, and flipped his sports car. Grammer was lucky to suffer only minor abrasions, but his Viper had major damage. Even experienced drivers can make a costly mistake if they do not remain attentive to the road and smoothly adjust their steering in response to changing road conditions.

mine which is best for you in different situations.

Hand-over-Hand Method

The **hand-over-hand method** requires you to have only one hand on the wheel at times, so you must always be attentive to keeping control of the car. This method is generally more comfortable, especially on wide, slow turns, and allows you to keep your shoulders straight. To steer hand-over-hand, you use one hand to push the steering wheel around and down as the other hand crosses over to pull the wheel even further down. For example, to execute a left turn you would do the following (see Figure 5–7):

1. With your hands positioned at 9 o'clock and 3 o'clock, begin turning the wheel toward the left with both hands.

2. With your right hand, continue pushing the wheel past the top and then down to the left. Release your left hand.

3. Cross your left hand over your right arm, grabbing the far side of the wheel.

4. Once you are sure you have a firm grasp of the far side of the wheel with the left hand, release your right hand and bring it back to the right side of the wheel while at the same time pulling the wheel to the left past the top and then down to the left.

5. Return to the 9 o'clock and 3 o'clock position or repeat

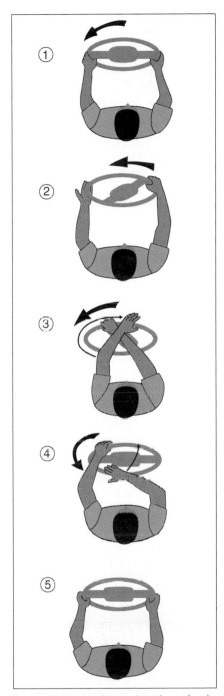

Figure 5–7 Hand-over-hand method

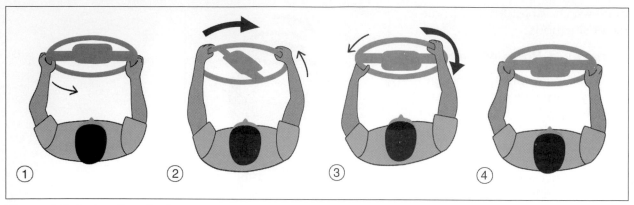

Figure 5–8 Push-pull method

steps 1 to 4 as necessary until the turn is complete.

Push-Pull Method

The advantage of the **push-pull method** of turning is that it allows you to make sharp turns quickly while keeping both hands on the wheel. To use this method to make a sharp right turn, you would do the following (see Figure 5–8):

1. Slide your left hand to the 7 o'clock position and firmly grip the wheel.
2. With your left hand, push the wheel up to the 11 o'clock position, and slide your right hand along the wheel back to 1 o'clock.
3. Pull the wheel down with your right hand. As you do so, allow your left hand to slide over the wheel back to 9 o'clock.
4. From the 9 o'clock and 3 o'clock position, repeat steps 1 to 3 as necessary until

the turn is complete. On most turns, you will only need to complete the push-pull cycle once to make the turn.

Straightening Out

After any turn, make sure that you straighten out the wheel yourself by reversing either the hand-over-hand method or the push-pull method. Letting the wheel straighten itself out by completely letting go of the wheel or letting it "slip through your fingers" as you accelerate could cause you to lose control of the car. When you are back on course, remember to adjust your hands back to their usual position on the steering wheel.

5–3 BACKING UP

When backing up, or driving in REVERSE, it is important to realize that your visibility through the back window is limited. Your vision might also be restricted by headrests, passengers, and child

Figure 5–9

seats. Be careful to keep control of the steering wheel and back up slowly, while constantly being aware of what is around you. You must be prepared at all times to brake if someone or something enters your path. Never back up out of a driveway or on a street unless you are sure that the road you are backing into is clear of traffic.

Before entering your vehicle, inspect the surrounding area for pedestrians, signposts, trash cans, parked cars, gardening tools, and other potential obstacles. Make sure nothing is behind your vehicle that you cannot see through your rear window. Follow these steps to back up straight (see Figure 5–11):

1. Once inside your vehicle, turn your head and look behind you to make sure that your path of travel is clear. Also, look to each side for anything that may enter your intended path.

2. Depress the brake and shift into REVERSE. If you have a manual transmission, remember to depress the clutch before shifting into REVERSE.

3. Turn your body to the right, and with your right arm over the back of the passenger seat or headrest, look through the back window, and identify where you intend to move. *Never use only the rearview mirror while backing up.* Place your left hand at the 12 o'clock position of the steering wheel.

4. Back up slowly. If you have an automatic transmission, you can usually idle backwards without using the accelerator. Ease up on the brake until the car slowly begins to move, keeping your foot over the brake pedal in case you need to stop to avoid hitting someone or something. If you have a manual transmission, release the brake and ease up on the clutch until you reach the friction point. Maintain the clutch at the friction point to slowly back up, and keep your foot over the brake if you can back up without using the accelerator. Otherwise, lightly press the accelerator and carefully release the clutch a little at a time. Fully releasing the clutch all at once can cause the car to jerk backwards or stall.

5. Turn away from anything you get too close to by making slight steering adjustments. Continue looking out the back window, while periodically checking in all other directions.

6. Once you have finished backing up, come to a complete stop by braking smoothly. If you have a manual transmission, remember to fully depress the clutch first.

When backing up, keep in mind that the turning radius of the front of the vehicle is wider than that of the rear. As a result, the front wheels swing out farther

driving tips

Always keep a window open while backing up to hear any warning yells from other drivers or pedestrians.

Wild Wheels

Figure 5–10 What was the name of this 1903 car that used a handle instead of a steering wheel to turn and that could be operated from either the left or right seat?

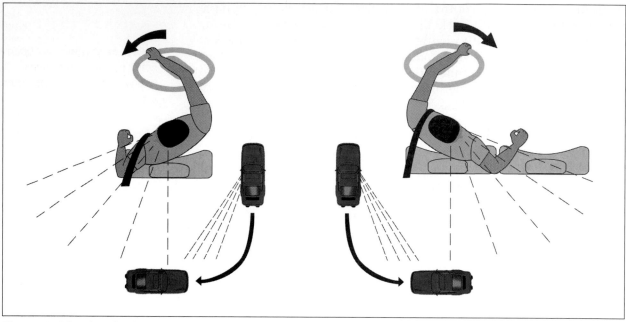

Figure 5–11 When backing up, always turn and look over your shoulder to make sure that your intended path is clear.

than the rear wheels do. When backing up to the left, you must leave extra space for the car to swing right. When backing up to the right, you must leave extra space for your car to swing left. By anticipating the room you will need to back up, you will avoid accidentally striking pedestrians, other vehicles, and stationary objects.

When backing up to the left or right, turn your wheel in the direction you are backing. In other words, if you are backing up to the left, turn the wheel to the left. If you are backing up to the right, turn your wheel to the right. Until you gain more experience, avoid backing up around corners or sharp turns. Try to approach the space you are moving into head-on, even if this means driving around the block to position yourself properly.

5–4   PARKING

Parking is a difficult skill to master. You need to be able to steer accurately into spaces that are often tight and narrow. You must be aware of the space around your car at all times so that you can judge the distance from curbs you cannot see up close, other parked cars, and passing traffic. You must be on the lookout for pedestrians and other vehicles that may get in your path. No matter how experienced a driver you are, you should always enter and exit parking spaces slowly. Do not be pressured into pulling out too quickly or racing to a space to beat someone else to it.

Figure 5–12 It takes practice to determine how much space you need to park your vehicle.

Before you park, ask yourself if there are any parking restrictions. Are there curb or roadway markings, prohibited parking signs, or posted time limits? Make sure that there is enough space on all sides of your car to enter and exit the space and that you have enough time to park in the space given the speed of traffic.

When parking, always remember to set the parking brake when

DRIVING TIPS *Prohibited Parking*

Parking prohibitions are different in every jurisdiction, but in general, you should never park in the following places:

- On the roadway side of another parked or stopped vehicle—this is called **double parking**
- More than 18 inches (45 cm) from the curb
- Within or near an intersection, railway crossing, or crosswalk
- In any designated fire lane or near a fire hydrant
- In front of driveways
- On sidewalks or bicycle paths
- In tunnels or on bridges
- In any zone or space where parking is specifically prohibited
- In bus zones or loading zones
- In a lane or any other paved portion of a highway

You should also never park in such a way that you are creating a hazard for other motorists.

you park and release it before you exit a parking space. Put the gear in PARK if you have an automatic transmission, or in FIRST or REVERSE if you have a stick shift. Park so that other drivers can both see and avoid hitting your vehicle. Check that your headlights, radio, heater, and any other devices are turned off. Finally, remember to lock your doors and take the keys with you.

Entering and Exiting Parking Spaces

As you approach a parking space, always check traffic ahead of you and then behind you by using your rearview and sideview mirrors to make sure that your path is clear. Signal your intention to park using your turn signal. Tap your brakes to warn drivers behind you that you will be slowing down. Watch for vehicles behind you as you gradually reduce your speed, and keep an eye out for parked vehicles that may be exiting nearby spaces. Before turning out of traffic, check your mirrors again and look over your shoulder to make sure that your blind spots are clear. After parking, remember to cancel your turn signal.

When exiting a parking space, first check for traffic in your rearview and sideview mirrors. Turn your head to make sure that your blind spots are clear. Warn other drivers that you are preparing to exit the parking space by signaling with your turn indicator. When it is clear and safe to move, slowly pull away from the curb and into the nearest lane on the street. Gradually accelerate to a normal driving speed and cancel your turn signal.

Curb Parking

There are four basic types of parking. The easiest is **curb parking**, which involves parking alongside a curb where there are no other surrounding vehicles. You have more room to maneuver, and unless another driver parks ahead of you or you are parked at the end of a curb, you do not have to back up to exit the space. Park as close to the curb as possible so that other vehicles will not hit you.

Parallel Parking

Parallel parking involves parking alongside a curb between two previously parked vehicles and can be extremely difficult even for seasoned drivers. You must back up into traffic, which can be danger-

AUTO ACCESSORIES *Curb Feelers*

Curb feelers are flexible metal rods that attach easily to your vehicle near the tires and act as "whiskers" to let you know when you are close to the curb. This product is especially helpful if you are driving a station wagon, pickup, camper, van, or other large vehicle in which it is difficult to see the curb or judge your distance from it.

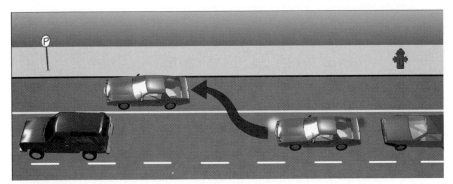

Figure 5–13 If you can, park on a curb without surrounding vehicles.

ous and frustrating if there is congestion. It takes time and practice to develop the ability to judge space and distance accurately enough to be able to parallel park correctly. Good steering and speed control skills are also essential.

It is your responsibility to avoid collisions while entering and exiting a parallel parking space. To reduce the risk of a collision, choose a parallel parking space that is at least 6 feet (20 m) longer than your vehicle to allow enough room for you to maneuver. Be aware of passing traffic and of how far the front of your car is projecting out into the nearest lane.

Follow these steps to parallel park in a space on the right side of the street (see Figure 5–14):

1. Pull up alongside the vehicle in front of the empty space so that the right side of your car is about 3 feet (1 m) away from the left side of the parked car. Stop when your rear bumper is even with that of the parked car.

2. As you look over your right shoulder, slowly back into the space while sharply turning the steering wheel to the right. You should aim the rear of your car for the rear right corner of the parking space. *As you back up, always be prepared to stop suddenly for passing vehicles, bicyclists, and pedestrians.*

3. When your steering wheel is even with the front vehicle's rear bumper, straighten out. Keep looking behind you, but make repeated glances ahead to make sure that your front bumper clears the vehicle in front of you.

4. Make a sharp left turn when the front end of your bumper is even with the rear bumper of the front vehicle.

5. Slowly back up until your vehicle is parallel to the curb. Straighten the steering wheel. Be sure to stop before your rear bumper hits the vehicle behind you. Drive forward slowly to center your car within the parking space.

If you misjudge the distance between your car and the front car or if you make your turns too

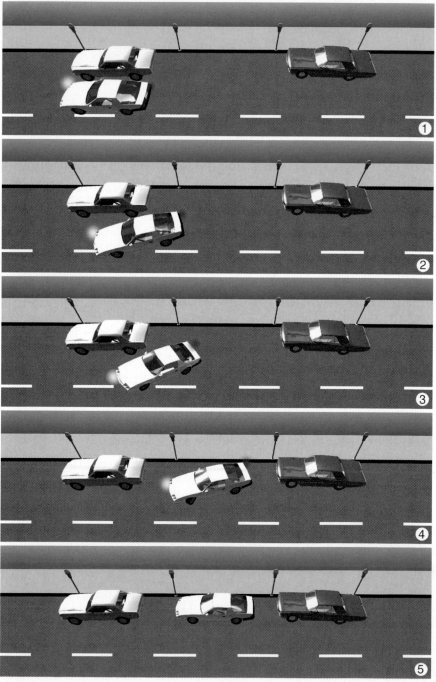

Figure 5–14 Entering a parallel parking space

early or too late, you may not be able to enter the parking space all the way. If this happens, pull out of the spot completely and start over again. If you try to make adjustments when you are partially or incorrectly positioned in a space, you risk hitting the other parked vehicles or confusing approaching traffic and causing a collision.

Follow these steps to exit a parallel parking space on the right side of the street (see Figure 5–15):

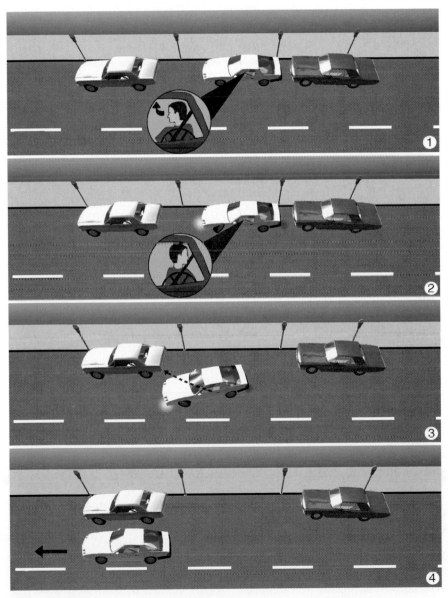

Figure 5–15 Leaving a parallel parking space

DRIVING TIPS *Getting Out of a Parked Car* _____

When curb or parallel parking, *always look before you open the door!* Watch out for approaching vehicles, pedestrians, and bicyclists. In some jurisdictions, you can be held liable for causing a collision by opening the door of a parked vehicle without first exercising caution. Do not assume that it is up to other drivers to make room for you. You also risk getting hit by passing cars if you stand in an open doorway next to traffic to get a jacket, backpack, or anything else out of your vehicle. Instead, retrieve your belongings from the sidewalk side of your car.

1. Turn your body to the right, and with your right arm over the back of the passenger seat or headrest, look through the back window and make sure there is nothing between your vehicle and the vehicle behind you. Slowly back up straight until your rear bumper is close to the other car.

2. Sharply turn the steering wheel to the left as you stop.

3. When it is clear, slowly move forward while repeatedly checking your right front bumper to make sure you are not in danger of hitting the vehicle in front of you.

4. When your car is halfway out of the space, slowly turn right to center your car in the nearest lane of the street.

Angled and Perpendicular Parking

Angled parking involves parking in a space that is angled to the curb, usually at about 30 degrees. **Perpendicular parking** involves parking at a 90-degree angle from the curb, in which the front or rear of your vehicle is aligned with the curb. Angled and perpendicular parking spaces are most often found in parking lots and garages and on some wide streets. Because spaces can be narrow, you will need to keep precise control of your steering and an awareness of the space around your vehicle. This is especially true if your vehicle is large and has a wide turning radius.

To avoid hitting other parked vehicles, you should choose an empty parking space with as much room as possible between the neighboring vehicles. You should also be aware of how the cars on either side of an empty space are parked. Are they parked to one side or the other of their own space? Are they parked at a crooked angle within their own space? Both of these factors will affect how you will have to maneuver your vehicle.

If it is an angled space, leave about 5 feet ($1\frac{1}{2}$ m) between your vehicle and the parked car to your right to allow sufficient steering space and visibility. When you

Figure 5–16 Why should you not park in this space?

can see the left side of the vehicle parked on the right side of the space you want to pull into, make a hard right. If it is a perpendicular space, approach the empty space as far to the left in your lane as possible and slowly brake. When your front bumper passes the back of the vehicle just before the open space, make a hard right.

As you repeatedly check your clearance on the left and right side with quick glances, slowly pull into the space. Make sure your right rear bumper does not hit the vehicle to your right, especially in a perpendicular parking space. Straighten your wheel once you are in the center of the space, and brake just short of the curb or painted line.

When exiting an angled or perpendicular parking space, position yourself so that you can look back over your right shoul-

der while constantly checking to the sides for pedestrians or oncoming traffic. When the area behind you is clear and it is safe to do so, slowly back up straight. Other vehicles may restrict your visibility as you back up, so be ready to brake for passing cars. *Always give the right-of-way to oncoming traffic.* Turn the steering wheel to the right when the front of your vehicle begins to pass the rear bumper of the vehicle parked to your left. As you back into the nearest lane of traffic, straighten out your wheels and come to a complete stop before accelerating into traffic.

Parking on Hills

If you park on a hill, you have to take special precautions to prevent your vehicle from rolling away. Whether you park uphill or downhill, make extra sure that the vehicle is in FIRST gear or

The world's first parking meter was introduced in Oklahoma City in 1935.

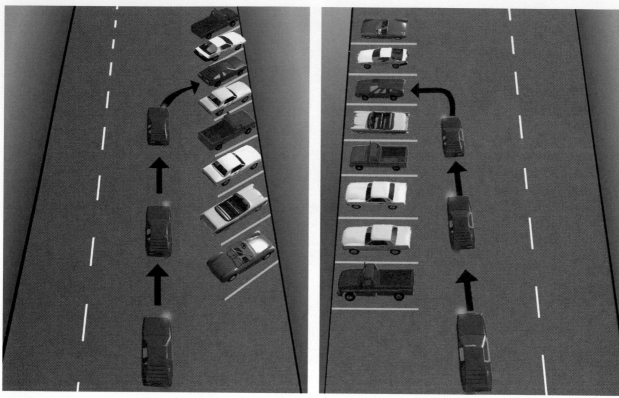

Figure 5–17 You need to steer precisely when navigating into narrow angled and perpendicular spaces.

REVERSE for manual transmissions, or in PARK for automatic transmissions, and that the parking brake is engaged.

When parking with your vehicle facing downhill, turn the front wheels *toward the curb* or sidewalk. If the parking brake fails, the curb will prevent the car from rolling downhill. If there is no curb, turn the front wheels in the same direction—away from the road—to prevent the vehicle from coasting into the street if your parking brake fails.

When parking with your vehicle facing uphill, turn the front wheels *away from the curb* or sidewalk. If the parking brake fails, the car will roll backwards into the curb and not into the street. If there is no curb, turn the front wheels the other away—away from the road—to prevent the vehicle from coasting backward into the street if your parking brake fails.

Parking Lots and Garages

Parking lots and garages usually have restricted maneuvering space. Visibility can also be limited, especially in dark parking garages.

Figure 5–18 When parking on a hill, make sure your wheels are turned in the proper direction.

Drivers preparing to back out of parking spaces may not see you approaching. Other cars may surprise you coming around blind corners. A space that appears to be empty may have a small car, motorcycle, or shopping cart in it that you do not discover until you have already started to pull in. Always drive slowly and watch constantly for vehicles backing out of spaces and pedestrians walking to and from their vehicles, especially children. Observe all traffic arrows and signs, and stay to the right. Do not be tempted to cut across a row of empty spaces to get to a space or get out of a lot.

Figure 5–19 Drive slowly in parking garages, where visibility is poor and there is little room to maneuver.

actoid

The world's largest parking lot, located at the West Edmonton Mall in Alberta, Canada, can accommodate 30,000 cars.

Airport Parking

Parking can be an inconvenience at major airports. At terminals there are loading zones where you can pull over for a brief period to load and unload passengers and their luggage. Because of problems with traffic congestion in many airports, loading zone rules are usually strictly enforced. Do not leave your car unattended in these areas or your car may be quickly towed. If you want to leave your vehicle at the airport during a trip or if you want to greet guests at the airplane gate, short- and long-term parking is usually available nearby.

WHO'S *AT FAULT?*

1. Driver 1 pulled away from a parking spot at the curb just as Driver 2 approached at a legal speed of 45 miles per hour (70 km/h). To avoid hitting Driver 1, Driver 2 swerved across the center line and hit Driver 3 head-on. Driver 3 had just turned right at the intersection. *Who's at fault?*

2. Driver 1 was in the center lane of a three-lane road traveling 20 miles per hour (30 km/h). She was watching two drivers in the far-right lane who were arguing over a fender bender. Without realizing it, Driver 1 drifted left into the far-left lane, causing Driver 2, who was traveling at 35 miles per hour (55 km/h), to abruptly hit his brakes. Driver 2 was not able to stop in time to avoid clipping the side of Driver 1's car. *Who's at fault?*

YOUR TURN

5–1 Starting the Engine and Engaging the Transmission

1. What are the gears on an automatic and manual transmission?

2. How do you engage an automatic and manual transmission?

3. How do you shift gears on a manual transmission?

4. What precautions should you take when putting your vehicle in motion on a hill?

5–2 Steering

5. How is steering different from turning?

6. What are the two basic steering methods?

5–3 Backing up

7. What is the proper procedure for backing up?

8. What precautions should you take when backing up to the left or right?

5–4 Parking

9. What are the four main types of parking?

10. What is the proper procedure for entering and exiting a parallel parking space?

11. How should you turn your wheels when parking on hills?

SELF-TEST

Multiple Choice

1. Engine flooding is an indication that there is:
   a. not enough oil in the car.
   b. rain on the pavement.
   c. too much air in the fuel injector.
   d. too much gasoline in the engine.

2. THIRD gear on a manual transmission is best for:
   a. freeway and highway driving.
   b. backing up.
   c. city driving.
   d. for speeds from 35 to 40 miles per hour (55 to 65 km/h).

3. The push-pull method of driving:
   a. requires you to have only one hand on the wheel at times.
   b. is best on wide, slow turns.
   c. allows you to make sharp turns quickly while keeping both hands on the wheel.
   d. requires you to start with your hands at 12 o'clock and 6 o'clock.

4. Tracking refers to:
   a. monitoring how far you are traveling.
   b. a method of steering.
   c. a method of backing around corners.
   d. changing gears on an automatic transmission.

5. When parking your vehicle facing downhill, keep the front wheels:
   a. turned toward the curb.
   b. straight ahead.
   c. turned away from the curb.
   d. in the original position that you parked the car.

Sentence Completion

1. The _____ is the point at which the engine begins to engage the transmission.
2. You do not always have to shift to the next lower gear when _____.
3. The _____ controls the amount of air entering the carburetor.
4. When backing up to the left, turn your wheel to the _____.
5. _____ parking involves parking between two previously parked vehicles.

Matching

Match the concepts in Column A with examples of the concepts in Column B.

Column A	Column B
1. __ Manual transmission	a. Parking in the roadway
2. __ Parking on a hill	b. Grab the far side of the wheel
3. __ Downshifting	c. Slide your hand along the wheel
4. __ Dry steering	d. Turning wheels toward curb
5. __ Hand-over-hand method	e. Parking lot
6. __ Double parking	f. Requires a stick shift
7. __ Push-pull method	g. Shifting from "4" to "1"
8. __ Perpendicular parking	h. Turning wheels when stopped

Short Answer

1. If you are driving a car with a manual transmission, how can you prevent rolling backwards when leaving an uphill parking space?
2. What should you always do before backing up?
3. What are the advantages and disadvantages of a manual transmission?
4. What makes parallel parking so challenging?
5. What is the proper way to straighten out the wheel?

Critical Thinking

1. You are preparing to back out of a perpendicular parking space in a busy lot. The driver directly behind you, across the aisle, has just entered a parking spot also, but you are not sure if he has seen you. Several drivers are lined up to your right anxiously waiting for an empty spot. What should you do?

2. You have just climbed a very steep hill in a car with a manual transmission and are stopped at a red light at the top. A car pulls up right behind your bumper, and the driver starts "revving" the engine in anticipation of the light turning green. He is so close that you are afraid you will roll back into his car no matter how quickly you engage the transmission. What should you do?

PROJECTS

1. Have two friends park their cars along a curb, leaving a parallel parking space. Measure the distance between the vehicles. Practice entering and exiting the space several times, having your friends move their cars slightly closer together each time to reduce the available space. Drive very slowly when parking and pulling out, and make sure that they stand nearby to caution you if you get too close to either vehicle. Determine the smallest space that you can fit in, and share the results with your class.

2. One of the most challenging places to engage gears in a vehicle with a manual transmission is on a hill. If you cannot engage your transmission smoothly, your car will stall or you will roll back too far, possibly hitting the vehicle behind you. Practice this skill on an incline of a quiet street by having someone stand behind your vehicle on the sidewalk to determine how far back you roll each time.

The Speed Factor: Negotiating Curves and Braking

Although you do not need to be a scientist to drive a car, the more you understand about the basic physical laws acting on you and your vehicle the better you will be able to maintain control under different circumstances and avoid becoming involved in a collision. How long will it take you to stop on a wet road? How much traction will you have going around a sharp curve? What will happen if you accelerate too rapidly? Knowing the answers to these kinds of questions will make you a safer and more skillful driver.

CHAPTER OBJECTIVES ....

Upon completion of this chapter, you should be able to:

6–1 Physical Laws Affecting Driving

1. Understand the importance of gravity as it relates to driving.
2. Describe the factors that affect vehicle traction.
3. Understand the importance of inertia as it relates to driving.
4. Understand why it is better to collide with a soft object than a hard one.

6–2 Negotiating Curves

5. Understand what centrifugal force is.
6. Understand the importance of center of gravity and loading in negotiating curves.
7. Understand the difference between banked and crowned roads.

6–3 Braking

8. Describe the proper way to brake under normal conditions.
9. Understand what an antilock braking system is.
10. Describe the three factors that determine stopping distance.

6–4 Speed Limits

11. Describe the purpose of maximum and minimum speed limits.
12. Know what the basic speed law is.

KEY TERMS

speed	center of gravity	pumping the brakes
acceleration	loading	locking the brakes
gravity	banked road	reaction distance
traction	crowned road	braking distance
torque	oversteering	stopping distance
inertia	understeering	maximum speed
kinetic energy	antilock braking system (ABS)	minimum speed
force of impact		basic speed law
centrifugal force	threshold braking	uniform speed zones

6–1 PHYSICAL LAWS AFFECTING DRIVING

To properly understand the physical laws that play a crucial role in your ability to control your vehicle, you must first become familiar with some of the basic terms used in discussing the science of driving.

Speed and Acceleration

Speed refers to how fast something is moving—that is, how quickly its position is changing over time. In driving terms, speed is measured in miles or kilometers per hour. **Acceleration** measures the rate of change of an object's speed. When you increase your vehicle's speed over a given period, you accelerate. When you reduce your speed, you decrease acceleration or decelerate.

Gravity

Gravity is an invisible force that massive objects like the Earth exert on other objects. This force attracts or "pulls" other objects toward their center. If you stop a car at the top of a steep hill, put the transmission in NEUTRAL, and take your foot off the brake, what will happen? Not only will the car roll down the hill, it will accelerate as it does so.

The force of gravity exerts a strong pull on all objects, including you and your car. It is most noticeable when climbing or descending a grade. As you travel uphill, it takes more power from your engine to maintain or increase speed because you are moving against the force of gravity. Going downhill takes less power, if any, from your engine to maintain or increase speed because you are moving in the direction of the force of gravity.

Traction

Traction is the friction between your vehicle's wheels and the surface of the road. Traction is necessary to move, change direction,

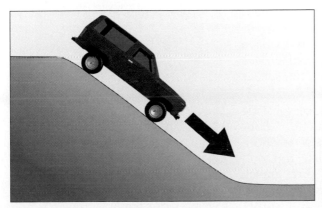

Figure 6–1 Gravity pulls objects toward the center of the Earth.

and stop. Without traction, your car's wheels cannot "grip" the road. If you are already moving and lose traction, your car may skid, and you will lose some or all of your ability to steer. You may also be unable to stop your vehicle, at least where you intend to stop it. Many factors influence how much traction your vehicle has at any given time.

The total weight of your vehicle and its load, as well as the manner in which it is distributed over your tires, affects traction. For example, even though a large truck may be extremely heavy, it could still have poor traction if the vehicle has rear-wheel drive and most of the vehicle's weight is put on the front tires.

New tires with deep treads grip the road better than worn tires. Wider tires have better traction than narrower ones. Specialty tires such as snow tires provide peak performance on packed snow but may not handle as well on dry pavement or ice. Overinflated tires provide less surface area in which to grip the road and therefore have reduced traction. Tires on vehicles with very "tight" suspension, poor wheel alignment, or badly worn shock absorbers have less contact with the road surface as well, especially at higher speeds or on bumpy roads.

Different road surfaces provide varying degrees of traction. Concrete provides the best traction, followed in turn by blacktop, polished concrete, hard dirt, gravel, and sand. Potholes, bumps, cracks, pavement grooves, and other physical alterations on the roadway can adversely affect traction by diminishing the amount of surface in contact with tires. The presence of loose gravel, water, oil, snow, ice, wet leaves, or any other intervening material will reduce traction. The temperature of the road surface will affect traction as well. For example, black asphalt on a hot summer day will become softer and may either increase or decrease traction.

Torque is the ability of a force to cause an object to rotate. As it applies to driving, it is your engine's ability to apply more force to turn the wheels of your car. As

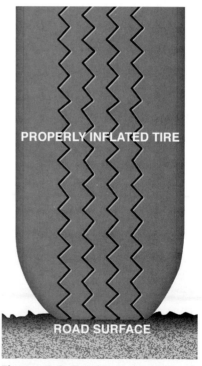

Figure 6–2 Traction is the friction between the surface of the road and your vehicle's tires.

you press down on a car's accelerator, the car's engine applies torque to the transmission. This torque turns the wheels of the car and, provided there is adequate traction, puts the car in motion.

To understand the role that torque plays in affecting traction, you need only be familiar with the term *burning rubber.* When the force applied to turn your vehicle's wheels exceeds the force resisting this motion, the traction between the road and your tires is lost. Your wheels spin more or less freely against the pavement and screech loudly. The resulting rapid rotation of the tires against the road surface produces intense heat. This heat can indeed melt the rubber on the tires of your car, and you can smell the proof.

Inertia

The law of **inertia** states that *an object at rest tends to remain at rest, and an object in motion will continue in motion in a straight line until acted upon by a force.* Anyone who has ever tried to drive a car with a dead battery can confirm the fact that objects at rest tend to remain at rest! Our experience tells us that the more an object weighs, the more difficult it is to move. You have probably experienced the feeling of being pushed back against the seat of an automobile when it is accelerating rapidly. You were merely experiencing your body's tendency to remain at rest—its inertia—even as the car's speed was increasing.

The law of inertia also states that objects in motion tend to remain in motion until acted upon by another force. At first, this may seem to go against what we see in everyday life. If you take your foot off the accelerator, for example, your car will slow down and eventually stop. It will not keep moving endlessly down the road on its own. This is because the force of friction between your car's tires and the road opposes the forward motion of the car.

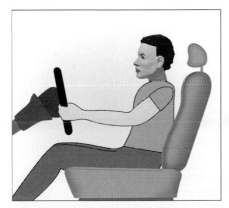 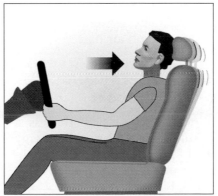

Figure 6–3 The inertia of a passenger at rest "pushes" the passenger back as the car accelerates forward.

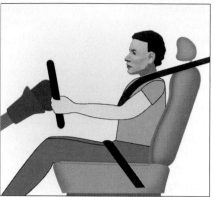 

Figure 6–4 The inertia of a moving passenger makes it seem as if the car is "thrown forward" as it decelerates.

auto accessories

If you have a large trunk or a cargo area in your vehicle, you may want to invest in a trunk organizer, usually made of plastic or canvas, that will hold your supplies and personal items in place when they are subject to the inertia of motion.

The same force that makes our car able to move also means it is necessary to continue to apply the force of the engine to keep it moving!

You experience inertia while driving if you apply the brake forcefully. The car slows, and you are "thrown forward." In fact, your body is merely exhibiting its tendency to stay in motion as the car is slowing. To prevent your body's inertia from taking you straight through your car's windshield during a very sudden stop, vehicles are equipped with occupant restraint systems such as safety belts and air bags.

Kinetic Energy and Force of Impact

All objects in motion possess a measurable quantity of energy called **kinetic energy**. For an object to move, it must acquire kinetic energy. A car's kinetic energy is related directly to its weight and speed.

For a vehicle to stop, it must lose its kinetic energy. This normally happens in one of two ways. The most common method is to apply the vehicle's brakes to reduce its speed. Another is to remove your foot from the accelerator and let the car coast to a stop by allowing the friction of the car's wheels on the roadway to decrease its speed slowly.

A third and much less desirable way for a vehicle to lose kinetic energy is through an impact with a solid object. The less distance over which an object is stopped, the faster it must lose its kinetic energy, and the greater the **force of impact**. The force of impact is determined by both the magnitude of the kinetic energy of the objects colliding and the distance over which the kinetic energy is lost.

Although you can do little to reduce your car's weight, you can reduce its speed. As both common sense and the physics of kinetic energy tell you, decreasing

Figure 6–5 Sand-filled canisters and safety cushions spread out the force of impact.

speed reduces the severity of an impact with any object. Similarly, objects that are softer or have more "give" will spread the force of impact over a greater distance and reduce the severity of the collision. Crashing into a row of bushes will result in much less damage than hitting a concrete wall or telephone pole.

Figure 6–6 The force of impact resulting from a collision with a fixed object can be tremendous.

Precisely for this reason, newly built freeways include steel-beam and cable guardrails to shield objects that cannot be removed

or relocated off the roadway. Safety-shaped concrete barriers separate opposing traffic, and "crash cushions," sand-filled plastic barrels or crushable foam cartridges surrounded by sections of guardrail, are sometimes placed at bridge abutments, exit ramp neutral areas, and toll booths. Also, many road signs and light supports have breakable bases or hinge mechanisms that allow them to break when struck by a vehicle.

Not only are today's roadways designed with the force of impact in mind, but so are vehicles. Unlike the interiors of older cars, which were almost entirely made of metal, the dashboards of modern cars are made of plastic or other soft material that will "give" on impact. Bumpers and bodies are designed with "crush zones" to absorb as much of an impact as possible rather than have the car's occupants experience the full brunt of the force.

6–2 NEGOTIATING CURVES

You have undoubtedly experienced the feeling of being "pulled" outward when rounding a curve in a car. The faster the car goes around the curve, the stronger this force is. This mysterious pull, sometimes called **centrifugal force**, is nothing more than the inertia of your body attempting to continue traveling in a straight line as the car's path changes directions. Sharper curves act to change the direction of

Wild Wheels

Figure 6–7 What is the name of this sturdy car, built in 1934, that was able to drive off under its own power after being driven off a 100-foot (30-m) cliff?

 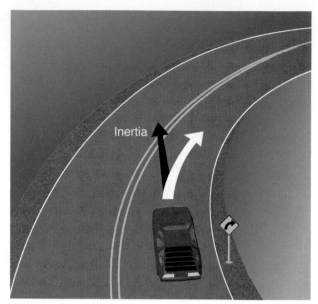

Inertia

Figure 6–8 A car's inertia exerts force to keep it traveling in a straight line.

your car more quickly. At speeds that are high relative to the angle of the turn, your vehicle's inertia will exceed its ability to follow the curve of the roadway. If your car's inertia exceeds the traction force of your tires, your vehicle may swing wide into oncoming traffic, slide off the road, or roll over.

JACKSON POLLOCK

Born in 1912, Jackson Pollock was the leading painter of a group of artists known as the Abstract Expressionists working in the United States after World War II. Pollock became internationally famous for his "action painting," in which he dripped colored paint onto canvases laid on the floor. On the evening of August 11, 1956, Pollock was speeding to his home in Long Island, New York, with two weekend guests in his 1950 Oldsmobile convertible when he lost control of the vehicle at a curve. The car ran off the road, rebounded from an embankment, swerved to the other side of the road, and turned end over end through underbrush until it collided, upside down, with some trees. Pollock was thrown clear, but he died instantly when his head struck a tree. One of the passengers was also thrown clear and survived with severe injuries, but the other died when her neck was broken as she was pushed back into the trunk by the great force of the impact. Pollock's collision is a gruesome example of how a moving vehicle is affected by physical forces. As a driver, you cannot change the laws of physics, but you can always control your speed.

Center of Gravity and Loading

An object's **center of gravity** is the point about which the object's weight is centered. Vehicles that are wide and low have a relatively low center of gravity. Other vehicles, such as jeeps and sport utility vehicles, have a relatively high center of gravity. When vehicles with a high center of gravity make sharp turns, or attempt to round curves at high speeds, they are much more vulnerable to rolling over.

A vehicle's loading can significantly change its center of gravity. **Loading** means adding weight to your vehicle's weight as measured when it is empty. You "load" your vehicle anytime you or any passengers get into it, or when you attach cargo or pack luggage for a trip. Increased loading will make your engine work harder, which will reduce acceleration. Consider this when calculating the safe distance you will need to make a maneuver such as turning left in front of oncoming traffic. Your engine is much more likely to overheat as it works harder, especially if you are driving in hot weather or up steep inclines. Your fuel economy will also be significantly less than normal.

Adding weight increases your car's kinetic energy, making it harder to stop or change the direction of your vehicle. Depending on the amount of weight being added and the physical location of the added weight, your car's center of gravity can also be altered. This is potentially the most dangerous aspect of loading because you may not fully realize the extent to which the loading has been changed until it is too late. Your car might begin to tip when going around a curve at a speed you normally would think of as safe.

Road Slopes

The slope of the road is another important factor in negotiating a curve. Roads may be either level, banked, or crowned. A **banked road** dips down in one direction, so either the left or right side of the road is higher than the other. A banked road that dips in the direction of a curve reduces the risk of rollover. In most cases, roads are banked in the direction of the

---

DRIVING TIPS *Do Not Drive in the Shadow of a Large Load*

Large tractor-trailer trucks often carry loads that can shift, such as tanks containing liquid or propane, large metal pipes, or lumber. Avoid riding next to "big rigs" carrying this kind of load, especially on curves. Depending on the speed of the truck and the road conditions, the load could break loose and land on you, or the tractor-trailer could jackknife and collide with your vehicle. Drop back and allow the truck to take the curve ahead first, maintaining a large following distance in case you need to stop.

Level road

Banked road

Crowned road

Figure 6–9 Roads may be level, banked, or crowned.

curve, but some stretches of rural roadway may actually bank in the wrong direction. This is not done by design, but is often the result of insufficient funding to properly grade lesser-used roads.

Crowned roads are higher in the center than on the sides. Roads are crowned to promote water runoff after rains and to reduce the risk of hydroplaning. The bank of a crowned road can either work with or against you, depending on the direction of travel. If you are going around a right curve, the bank reduces the risk of turnover, but if you are going around a left curve it may ac-tually *increase* the chance of rolling over.

Entering a Curve

Of all the factors that affect negotiating a curve, speed is the only one over which you have a large degree of control. You cannot make a sharp corner less sharp, nor can you change the bank of the curve. You cannot reduce the weight of your vehicle or lower its center of gravity either. The only way to safely negotiate a curve is to reduce your speed *before* entering the curve. Reducing speed by sudden braking or downshifting

USING SAFE *Curves*

As you approach a curve in the roadway, remember to use the SAFE process. *Scanning* ahead is especially important on curves, where objects can appear suddenly because of your limited line of sight. Watch for speed advisory signs and special warning signs, chevrons (yellow markers with V-shaped "arrows" pointing in the direction of the curve), and reflectors posted along the edge of the roadway to help guide you around the curve. *Assess* how your vehicle will react to the curve given your speed, the sharpness of the turn, the weight of your vehicle, the condition of the road, and other factors. *Find* an escape route in case an approaching car is straddling the center line or an unexpected hazard appears suddenly. Be especially careful on two-lane, two-way roads and roads with narrow shoulders and drop-offs. *Execute* the best alternative to negotiate the curve and avoid potential dangers smoothly and safely.

during a turn is extremely dangerous and should be considered a measure of last resort. Reducing speed before entering a curve also allows more time to react should an emergency arise.

Once you have adequately reduced your speed before entering the curve, maintain your lane position by avoiding either oversteering or understeering around the curve. **Oversteering** is turning too sharply into the curve. This can cause your rear wheels to slide out, forcing you into a skid. **Understeering** is not turning sufficiently to round the curve. This can cause you to drift into an outside lane, off the road, or into the opposing lane of travel. By prop-

erly maintaining your lane position, you will retain solid directional control of your vehicle while rounding a curve.

Under normal circumstances, you should gently accelerate into the curve after entering it and resume a safe speed once you have straightened out again. However, if it is raining or snowing or if the roads are icy, accelerate only *after* you have exited the curve.

6–3 BRAKING

By now, you may be wondering exactly how brakes "remove" kinetic energy from a moving car. When brakes slow a car down, where does this invisible energy

Figure 6–10 Reduce speed *before* entering a curve.

actually go? When you apply your brake pedal, the force from your foot is transferred through the hydraulic pressure of your braking system to the brake pads or drums against the brake linings on your wheels. Friction increases greatly as the pad or drum comes into contact with the brake linings on the wheel. The friction opposes the force of the rotating wheels, causing them to slow. As the wheels slow, the friction between the rubber of your tires and the surface of the road also increases. If you brake rapidly, the friction between your tires and the road surface increases to the point where traction is lost, resulting in a skid.

The kinetic energy of the car's motion is transformed into heat as the friction of the brakes resists the motion of the wheels. Your brakes and the rubber on your tires get hot. As you may have experienced at one time or another by smelling "burning" brakes, this heat becomes more intense as the brakes are applied continually for long periods or very hard for short periods.

How to Brake

To prepare for those times when you will have to apply your brakes under less than ideal conditions, you should practice proper braking procedures on a dry, flat, firm surface with properly functioning brakes. In time, you will learn to apply just the right amount of pressure to decrease your speed uniformly so that you avoid either stomping on the brake at the last minute or stopping far short of your intended point.

Always practice with the particular vehicle in which you will be doing the braking. When you drive a new or unfamiliar car, allow yourself time to "get a feel" for the car's brakes. They may be "mushier" or "tighter" than the

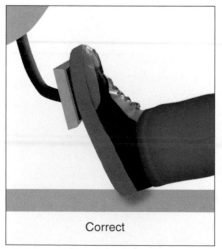
Correct

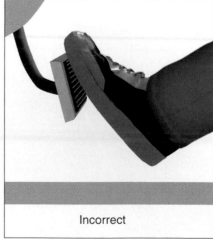
Incorrect

Figure 6–11 Keep your heel on the floor when braking.

ones in the car you are used to driving. Waiting until you are traveling at a high speed approaching a yellow light is the wrong time to learn.

When braking under normal conditions to reduce speed or stop, begin by lifting your right foot from the accelerator while keeping the heel of your foot resting on the floor of the car. Then, without lifting the heel of your foot off the floor of the car, move your foot to the brake pedal and gradually apply pressure against it with your toes. Do not lift your entire foot off the floor or use the ball of your foot to brake. If you lift your entire foot off the floor, you have to use your more powerful thigh muscle, which makes applying pressure to the pedal more difficult to control.

Antilock Braking Systems

Antilock braking systems (ABS) consist of a sensor mounted on each wheel that is capable of determining whether the wheel locks or stops rotating during braking. When this occurs, the sensor sends a signal to the microprocessor that controls the brakes. The microprocessor then instructs the braking system to release just enough pressure on *that particular wheel* to allow it to resume rotation and avoid a skid. As soon as the wheel begins to rotate, the sensor sends a different signal to the microprocessor that the wheel is no longer locked. The microprocessor then increases pressure on the brake once again.

This cycle is repeated many times a second so that the ABS can stop your car in the shortest possible distance while leaving you with full steering control. There are two primary reasons ABS brakes are more effective than standard brakes. First, because antilock braking systems work *independently* on each wheel, they are more efficient and give you more control than non-ABS brakes. Second, antilock braking systems are controlled by a computer chip that can sense a wheel lock, release it, and then reapply the brakes much faster than a person ever could.

For automobiles with antilock braking systems, you can apply your brakes without worrying whether the brakes will "lock." To properly apply ABS brakes, you need only firmly apply the brake pedal. The ABS computer will do all the remaining work for you. A common mistake made by ABS users is to fully apply the brakes but let off pressure when they feel the "pulsing" sensation from the pedal. This sensation, however, is typical of a properly functioning ABS and is *not* a brake malfunction. Antilock braking systems will prevent you from entering a skid even if the brakes are applied suddenly and forcefully.

Emergency Braking

Even when you do your best to drive defensively, there are times when you must reduce your speed as quickly as possible using a full application of the brakes. If you do *not* have ABS brakes, you can use

Antilock braking systems automatically "pump" the brakes at a rate of eighteen times per second.

one of three techniques, depending on how fast you need to stop.

Threshold braking involves using a full and firm application of the brake pedal *up to* the point where the brakes lock and cause the vehicle to enter a skid. When a car begins to skid, the driver loses steering control, making a bad situation worse. When possible, threshold braking should be used to avoid skidding. Skidding not only is dangerous, but also greatly accelerates wear on your tires by burning rubber off them during the skid.

Pumping the brakes involves alternately applying the brakes completely until they lock and then releasing them in rapid succession. In effect, you are attempting to imitate the action of antilock brakes. To avoid losing control of your vehicle if you experience some skidding, you must disengage the vehicle's power train to remove any unbalancing effects it presents. If you are driving a vehicle with an automatic transmission, you disengage the power train by putting the car in NEUTRAL. If you are driving a car with a manual transmission, push and hold in the car's clutch. Because this method involves some degree of skidding, it is a more aggressive technique than threshold braking, but it will also stop your car in a shorter distance.

Never pump the brakes on a vehicle with ABS. This sends false or confusing information to the system's sensors that can actually cause the car to begin skidding.

Figure 6–13 Locking brakes results in a loss of steering control.

Locking the brakes is the most radical braking technique and should be used only when there is no time to react otherwise or use alternative braking methods. To lock your brakes, you firmly press and hold the brake pedal until the vehicle comes to a complete stop. Locking the brakes can stop your car in the shortest possible distance, but you will also go into a skid and lose all or most of your ability to steer.

Stopping Distance

The speed at which you are traveling and the time required for you to stop your vehicle are strongly and directly correlated. Your ability as a driver to stop smoothly, accurately, and rapidly is a function of both reaction distance and braking distance.

Figure 6–12

REALITY CHECK   *Rolling Forward without Motion* _____

A favorite prank among teenagers calls for two drivers to get on either side of a third car while it is stopped at a red light. While waiting for the light to turn green, they both shift into REVERSE at the same time and slowly roll backward, giving the person in the middle the perceptual experience that his or her car is moving forward. Fearing that the car is rolling into the intersection and the path of oncoming traffic, the driver often re-acts by jamming on the brakes. While you might think this is funny, it can be truly frightening for the victim. Never try this on someone else. Not only might you cause a heart attack, but while rolling backwards you are watching the effect of the joke rather than the road behind you. Vehicles approaching from the rear may drive right into your car, not realizing that you are moving in reverse. Rear-end collisions are usually the fault of the driver in the rear, but if you were to cause a collision playing this trick the fault would be yours.

Reaction distance is the distance traveled by your vehicle during the time it takes you to identify the need to stop and re-act to the braking situation. This time translates into actual feet or meters based on the speed of your vehicle, visibility, and on your

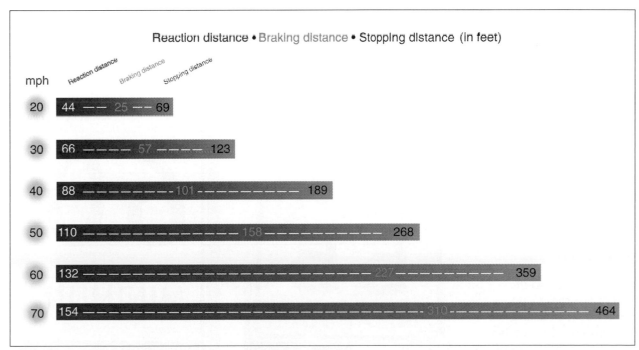

Figure 6–14 The time it takes to come to a complete stop once you recognize the need to apply your brakes in-creases dramatically at higher speeds.

mental and physical state. The faster you are moving and the harder it is to see, the longer it takes to react. Inattention, fatigue, sleepiness, the presence of alcohol or other drugs in your system, and age can also adversely affect your reaction time.

Braking distance is the time needed to come to a complete stop once the brakes have been applied. Brake effectiveness depends on vehicle type and weight, road and weather conditions, type and wear of tires, and the type and physical condition of your brakes.

Together, the reaction distance and braking distance add up to your **stopping distance**, which is the total distance required to stop from the time you first recognize the need to brake to the time your vehicle is no longer moving. The most important determining factor in your ability to brake is your speed. Simply put, the faster you

travel, the longer it takes to stop. Therefore, you should always carefully monitor the one thing over which you have complete control—your speed. Remember that if you ever suspect trouble ahead, slow down!

6–4 SPEED LIMITS

Now that you understand how speed relates to kinetic energy, inertia, traction, force of impact, turning, and braking, you should have a better appreciation for the importance of operating your vehicle at a safe speed. What, exactly, is a "safe" speed? To determine the proper driving speed, you must consider posted speed limits, weather conditions, visibility, the surface condition of the roadway, traffic conditions, lane width, and any special speed laws that might apply to the type of vehicle you are driving.

Figure 6–15 Different speed limits exist to take special circumstances into account.

Posted Speed Limits

Jurisdictions establish certain fixed speed limits for different roadways. Where posted, speed limits indicate the maximum, and sometimes the minimum, legal speed at which to operate your vehicle *under normal conditions*. Posted **maximum speed** limits are not there to *recommend* a driving speed, but to advise you of the maximum legal speed, based on considerations of safety and economy. Factors considered in setting speed limits include road conditions, pedestrian activity, collision statistics, public demand, noise and air pollution restrictions, and parking patterns.

Many jurisdictions also post **minimum speed** limits on some roads to prevent drivers from moving at such a slow speed as to impede or block the normal and reasonable movement of traffic, except when reduced speed is necessary for safe operation or in compliance with the law. Studies have shown that when all vehicles on a roadway are operated at about the same speed, the chance of a collision is less than when one vehicle is being operated at a much slower speed than the others surrounding it.

Basic Speed Law

All jurisdictions have a **basic speed law**. This law says that a driver should always operate his or her vehicle at a speed that is reasonable and prudent for existing conditions. A "reasonable and prudent" speed is one that does not endanger the safety of persons or property. The basic speed law exists to communicate to drivers that they should never blindly drive at the posted limit regardless of the driving situation. In other words, *the posted maximum speed limit may not be legal if factors such as weather, visibility, traffic conditions, and the surface condition of the roadway adversely affect the driving environment.* For example, if there is a coat of "black ice" on the highway, the basic speed law would likely dictate that 50 miles per hour (80 km/h) is too fast even if the posted maximum is 65 miles per hour (105 km/h).

Uniform Speed Zones

Uniform speed zones provide speed limits in commonly encountered locations even where no maximum or minimum speed limits are posted. Common examples of locations with uniform speed zones include school zones, railroad crossings, alleys, business districts, residential districts, open rural highways, and interstate freeways.

Special Speed Laws

Jurisdictions often have their own special speed laws. For example, the far-right lane of steep grades is often reserved for slow-moving traffic. Certain vehicles may have a lower speed limit that applies to them at night. In areas with livestock on the roadway, you may be legally required to reduce your speed. Vehicles hauling trailers

Speed is a factor in one-third of all fatal collisions.

may be limited to lower speeds even though the posted maximum limit is 65 miles per hour (105 km/h) or more. Similar restrictions may apply to trucks or tractors with three or more axles or those that are pulling another vehicle, school buses transporting students, farm labor vehicles transporting people, vehicles carrying explosives, and trailer buses.

Special speed laws may or may not be posted. If you are driving a commercial vehicle or a vehicle other than a passenger car or light truck, save yourself a ticket and check the local laws before you hit the road.

WHO'S AT FAULT?

1. Driver 1 was on his way to college with a hard storage carrier strapped to the roof of his vehicle. He was driving on the interstate in heavy Labor Day traffic when Driver 2 ahead of him had to stop suddenly. Driver 1 was able to stop in time to avoid hitting Driver 2 with his car, but the storage container on his roof broke loose and landed on Driver 2's vehicle, smashing the trunk and breaking the rear window. *Who's at fault?*

2. A pedestrian stepped onto the roadway outside of a crosswalk in front of Driver 1, who was driving a brand-new sport utility vehicle 5 miles per hour (8 km/h) over the posted speed limit. Driver 1 swerved sharply to avoid the pedestrian and overturned the vehicle, which skidded for some distance before hitting a lamp post. *Who's at fault?*

Storage container

YOUR TURN

6–1 *Physical Laws Affecting Driving*

1. What is the importance of gravity as it relates to driving?

2. What are the factors that affect vehicle traction?

3. What is the importance of inertia as it relates to driving?

4. Why is it better to collide with a soft object than a hard one?

6–2 *Negotiating Curves*

5. What is centrifugal force?

6. What is the importance of center of gravity and loading in negotiating curves?

7. What is the difference between banked and crowned roads?

6–3 *Braking*

8. What is the proper way to brake under normal conditions?

9. What is an antilock braking system?

10. What three factors determine stopping distance?

6–4 *Speed Limits*

11. What is the purpose of maximum and minimum speed limits?

12. What is the basic speed law?

SELF-TEST

Multiple Choice

1. Which of the following can significantly change a vehicle's center of gravity?
   - **a.** loading
   - **b.** force of impact
   - **c.** antilock brakes
   - **d.** torque

2. Which of the following statements about antilock braking systems (ABS) is *not* correct?
   - **a.** ABS works on each wheel independently.
   - **b.** ABS works best when you "pump" your brakes.
   - **c.** ABS causes the brake pedal to "pulse."
   - **d.** Motion sensors and a microprocessor are key components of ABS.

3. Where posted, maximum speed limits indicate:
   a. the suggested speed for driving under normal conditions.
   b. the suggested speed for driving under *most* conditions.
   c. the maximum legal speed permitted at *all* times.
   d. the maximum legal speed permitted under normal driving conditions.

4. The proper way to brake in an emergency situation with non-ABS brakes is to:
   a. apply threshold braking.
   b. "pump" the brakes.
   c. lock the brakes.
   d. all of the above

5. If it were not for _____, your car would be unable to move.
   a. centrifugal force and kinetic energy
   b. centrifugal force and gravity
   c. torque and traction
   d. torque and centrifugal force

Sentence Completion

1. _____ measures the rate at which an object's speed is changing.

2. _____ is the force that "pulls" you to the outside while rounding a curve.

3. The _____ says that a driver should always operate his or her vehicle at a speed that is reasonable and prudent for existing conditions.

4. _____ is the force that pushes you back into your seat when your car accelerates.

5. _____ distance is the distance traveled by your vehicle during the time it takes you to identify the need to stop and react to the braking situation.

Matching

Match the concepts in Column A with examples of the concepts in Column B.

Column A	Column B
1. __ Gravity	a. How quickly an object's position changes over time
2. __ Force of impact	b. The friction between your tires and the road
3. __ Inertia	c. Is zero while maintaining a constant speed
4. __ Center of gravity	d. "Pulls" objects toward the Earth
5. __ Acceleration	e. Continuing in motion until acted upon by another force
6. __ Traction	f. The force your engine applies to turn your car's wheels
7. __ Speed	g. Point at which an object's weight is centered
8. __ Torque	h. Varies with the distance over which kinetic energy is lost when objects collide

Short Answer

1. How should you apply the brakes on a vehicle equipped with an antilock braking system?
2. What are the advantages and disadvantages of crowned roads?
3. In terms of the natural laws that act on cars and drivers, what role do safety belts play?
4. What factors should you consider in deciding how fast to drive?
5. What might happen if you understeer going around a curve?

Critical Thinking

1. Your friend, who usually drives a small compact car, takes you on a "test ride" in a large sport utility vehicle that she is considering purchasing. She begins to drive aggressively to "put it to the test." What are some of the risks you both face even if few cars are on the road? What specific risks may be associated with negotiating curves and braking?
2. You have been "elected" to drive several friends back down the mountain after a full day of skiing. It is late in the afternoon when you begin your trip down the steep, treacherous grade. What factors do you need to consider when deciding how closely to follow a large truck in front of you that you are unable to pass?

PROJECTS

1. Using a local street map, draw a circle around your home that extends for 1 mile (1½ km) in all directions. Find all of the speed limit signs that fall within the circled area and indicate their location on a map. Classify the signs according to whether they indicate maximum speed limits, minimum speed limits, uniform speed zones, and special speed limits. Some signs may fall in more than one category. Share your results with the rest of the class.

2. Armed with a pad and pen, visit a nearby amusement park. Select three rides that best demonstrate inertia, the effects of gravity, and centrifugal force. Sketch each and explain to the class how the ride demonstrates one or more of these forces at work.

Welcome to the Road

Signs, Signals, and Roadway Markings

Signs, signals, pavement markings, and painted curbs are all designed to reduce confusion and increase safety on the roadway. Traffic controls ensure an orderly flow of traffic, regulate where you can drive and park, warn you of hazardous areas or conditions ahead, and provide information about nearby places and services. It is important that you familiarize yourself with the different kinds of traffic controls to protect yourself and other users of the roadway.

Upon completion of this chapter, you should be able to:

7–1 Traffic Signs

1. Understand the meaning of different colors in traffic signs.
2. Identify signs that have their own distinctive shapes.

7–2 Traffic Signals

3. Explain what you do at a red light, yellow light, and green light.
4. Understand how signal arrows control traffic.
5. Understand what a metered on-ramp is.

7–3 Roadway Markings, Lanes, and Painted Curbs

6. Understand how white and yellow lines are used on roads to control traffic.
7. Identify special lanes with distinctive roadway markings.
8. Understand how different colors are used to regulate parking at curbs and parking stops.
9. Understand the purpose of raised pavement markers.

KEY TERMS

regulatory sign	international sign	carpool lane
warning sign	reversible lane	bus lane
crossbuck	lane-use signals	bicycle lane
guide sign	on-ramp meter	limit line
construction sign	turn lane	Botts' dots
service sign	center turn lane	rumble strips
recreational sign	commuter lane	speed bump

7–1 TRAFFIC SIGNS

Nothing about a traffic sign's color, size, shape, or location is an accident. There are very strict and detailed requirements about what signs look like and how and where they are posted. Traffic signs tell you which lanes you can use, how fast you can go, what dangers lie ahead, and where and how long you can park. The use of different combinations of colors, shapes, and symbols allows drivers to recognize signs quickly and from a distance.

Regulatory Signs

Regulatory signs tell you what you can or cannot do at certain times and places. They direct traffic to stop, yield, or go in a particular direction. They also control parking and passing, and restrict pedestrians and drivers from doing certain things. Obey regulatory signs wherever you see them. The next time you feel like ignoring a STOP sign in the parking lot of a shopping mall, theme park, or stadium, keep in mind that signs posted on private property may be just as enforceable as signs on the public roadway.

Regulatory signs come in a variety of shapes and colors. The STOP sign is the only octagonal (eight-sided) sign on the road. The YIELD sign is the only sign in the shape of a downward-pointing triangle. Both of these signs usually appear at intersections of all types.

Most other regulatory signs are white squares or rectangles with black letters, words, or symbols. In general, these signs tell you what to do or set limits on what you can do. Red is reserved exclusively for STOP (ARRÊT in the provinces of Quebec and New Brunswick), YIELD, WRONG WAY, and DO NOT ENTER signs and to prohibit certain movements. Some square-shaped

Figure 7–1 There are specific laws about the shape, color, and placement of signs.

Figure 7–2 Regulatory signs

REALITY CHECK   *Sign Vandalism* _____

On a clear night in February, 1996, an 8-ton truck hit a white Camaro at a rural intersection in Tampa, Florida, instantly killing the three teenagers inside. The STOP sign at the intersection had been pulled from the ground and lay face down by the side of the road. Just days earlier, three young friends heading home from a shopping trip had removed several road signs in the area "for a rush," piling them in the back of their pickup. Although they claimed not to have removed the STOP sign at the site of the fatal crash, the trio was arrested and convicted of manslaughter the following year. Although you may think it is fun to knock down signs or have a road sign on your bedroom wall, sign vandalism is a crime, not a prank. As the mother of one of the victims said, "Pranks don't kill."

Figure 7–3 STOP and YIELD signs have their own shapes.

signs have a black symbol—for example, a U-turn or "P" for parking—inside a red circle crossed by a diagonal red slash. This type of sign indicates that the action or vehicle shown is not permitted on the roadway. In Canada, a green circle is used to indicate that the action *is* permitted.

Parking, standing, and loading zone signs are rectangular in shape with black, green, red, or blue colors on a white background. Green letters usually indicate a time restriction, for example, parking is allowed only for 2 hours. Parking, standing, or loading is either not allowed at all or prohibited at certain times or on certain days if the letters are red.

Blue letters usually mean that the area is designated for use by disabled persons. Parking signs for the disabled often display the symbol of a person in a wheelchair and include blue-painted

Figure 7–4 Pay careful attention to signs before you park your vehicle.

curbs or pavement markings. Parking spots for the disabled are located closer to building entrances than are other parking spots. If you illegally park in a space reserved for the disabled, you will pay a very large fine and may get your car towed. More importantly, you will be taking up a space that a disabled person needs much more than you do.

Warning Signs

Warning signs alert you to hazards or possible hazards ahead such as upcoming intersections or changing traffic and road conditions. Most warning signs are diamond shaped, and they normally have a yellow background with

Figure 7–5 Do not be tempted to park in a space designated for the disabled if you are not qualified to use it.

Figure 7–6 Warning signs

Figure 7–7 Yellow signs alert drivers to hazardous conditions.

black symbols or letters. Fluorescent strong yellow-green warning signs are now being used at pedestrian, bicycle, and school crossings. There are dozens of different diamond-shaped warning signs, and depending on where you live or travel, you are unlikely to have seen them all. If you spend most of your time in the city, for example, you may have never seen a TRACTOR CROSSING sign. On the other hand, if you live in a rural area you may not be familiar with some of the warning signs found on complicated freeway interchanges. Many diamond-shaped warning signs reflect specific dangers in local areas, so pay close attention!

Pennant-shaped warning signs indicate no-passing zones. Because your view of the right side of the road is partially blocked while trying to pass another vehicle, they are normally posted on the left side of a two-way road. Sometimes black-and-white rectangular DO NOT PASS signs are also posted on the right side of the road as an extra warning.

A round yellow sign with a large black X and two black R's (for "railroad") warns you that you are approaching a railroad intersection. Additional markings may also appear on the roadway. The crossing itself is often marked with a crossed white sign called a **crossbuck**. It is sometimes mounted over a pair of red lights that flash when a train is coming. There may also be a crossing gate with warning bells.

School zone signs are the only signs that have five sides (a pentagon). These signs are yellow or

Figure 7–8 Railroad crossing signs

At nearly 8,000 kilometers (5,000 miles), the Trans-Canada Highway is the world's longest national highway.

yellow-green in the United States and blue in Canada. One type shows a pair of children and is posted about a block from the school, indicating the beginning of the school zone. A school zone sign showing children in a crosswalk alerts you to an intersection that either is within a school zone or is one used by schoolchildren. In addition to these signs, school zones may include various regulatory signs, roadway markings, warning signals, and crossing guards.

Guide Signs

Guide signs tell you where you are, where you are going, and how to get somewhere. These signs come in a variety of colors, shapes, and sizes. Route markers are used to identify numbered roadways or roadways designated for special purposes. In the United States, these include county routes, state routes, U.S. routes, interstate routes, off-interstate routes (spurs and business loops), forest routes, and routes designated for trucks. In Canada, distinctive route markers exist for the Trans-Canada Highway, provincial highways, autoroutes, and municipal grid roads.

Green-colored square and rectangular signs provide information about destinations and distance. Destination signs tell you where you are, where you are going, or how to get to a particular place from the roadway you are on. These types of signs often include directional arrows to indicate which road, exit, or lane to use. Distance signs indicate the distance in miles or kilometers

Figure 7–9 Guide signs

from certain locations, roadways, or exits ahead of you.

A special type of distance sign, called a milepost in the United States and a distance marker in Canada, is posted at intervals along sections of numbered highways and freeways to indicate your location on the roadway within a jurisdiction. Numbers start at the south end for north–south routes and the west end for east–west routes. For example, if you are driving west on an interstate in the United States and see a MILE 20 sign, you are 20 miles

Figure 7–10 Green signs provide information about where you are and where you are going.

east of the western state boundary line. Numbering for mileposts and distance markers may also start at junctions where routes begin.

Construction Signs

Orange **construction signs** alert you that you are in or about to enter a construction or work area. Cones, drums, reflectors, flares, barricades, flashing warning lights, or other objects may also be used to guide drivers. In many construction zones, special workers with flags or handheld signs assist drivers in getting safely through the area.

Service Signs

Blue **service signs** inform the driver of nearby services, including call boxes, hospitals, rest stops, telephones, restaurants, gasoline stations, and roadside motels. In the case of gas, food, lodging, or camping signs, they may be posted with other signs provided by specific businesses.

Recreational Signs

Brown **recreational signs** are in the shape of a rectangle or trapezoid and tell you about nearby places of cultural interest and public recreation such as historic sites, museums, and national parks. Square-shaped brown signs with symbols tell you where you can find rest rooms, trails, swimming areas, and other facilities located within recreational areas. Recreational signs for privately operated areas, such as theme parks, are usually green or have their own distinctive design.

Figure 7–11 Construction signs

Figure 7–12 Use extra caution when driving through a construction zone.

Figure 7–13 Service signs

Figure 7–14 Blue service signs often include the names of gas stations and other roadside businesses.

Figure 7–15 Recreational signs

International Signs

International signs use symbols instead of words because they are designed to be understood without knowing a particular language. Many of these signs are used in North America, and as international travel increases, you are likely to encounter more of them.

Local Traffic Signs

Cities and towns have their own traffic signs for parks, libraries, bus and subway routes, public beaches, scenic routes, and so on. Local regulatory signs are also found on private roadways. Keep in mind that these signs may have irregular or unfamiliar shapes and color schemes.

Figure 7–16 International signs

7–2 TRAFFIC SIGNALS

Traffic signals are normally found in intersections and other areas where traffic is heavy or there is a high level of risk that different roadway users will cross paths. They are also used to inform users about the roadway that they are approaching or to let them know that they are entering an area with special dangers or restrictions, such as a school zone, construction area, or toll area.

Traffic Lights

Traffic lights have two advantages over signs. First, because they are illuminated and mounted higher than most signs, they are easier to see from a distance, especially if it is dark or the weather is bad. Second, because they are often timed or linked to sensors in the roadway, they can be programmed to adjust to the changing flow of traffic.

Most traffic lights in North America use the same red-yellow-green color sequence, arranged vertically or horizontally, so that drivers who are color blind or who cannot see part of the signal can still observe them. Lights can be solid, flashing, or illuminated arrows.

Red Light

You must come to a *full* stop at a red light. You cannot proceed until the light turns green. A flashing red light works like a STOP sign. Come to a complete stop and then proceed when it is safe or you have the right-of-way.

Yellow Light

A yellow light warns drivers to slow down. When you see a solid yellow light, make a complete stop if you can safely do so within the amount of space between your vehicle and the limit line. If you cannot stop safely, proceed through the yellow light. If the light is flashing yellow, slow down, give the right-of-way to other traffic, and proceed with caution. Flashing yellow lights often appear by themselves in dangerous parts of a roadway or before an upcoming intersection or hazardous area. If you see a light that appears to be orange or amber in color, you should treat it as a yellow light.

Green Light

A green light means to proceed if safe. If you have been stopped at a red light, make sure that you first look to your left and right to check for any vehicles or pedestrians that might still be in the intersection. If you are already moving when you approach a green light, continue to move through it with caution. When you see a green light, especially if you have noticed that it has been green for a while, be prepared for the "stale" green light to turn yellow and then red.

Red Arrow

You cannot go in the direction indicated until the light changes to green.

factoid

Motorists are more likely to be injured in a collision involving running a red light than any other type of crash.

Figure 7–17 Signals regulate traffic more efficiently than signs.

Yellow Arrow

Come to a complete stop if you can do so safely. If the yellow arrow is flashing, slow down, watch for other traffic and hazards, and proceed in the direction indicated with caution.

Green Arrow

Proceed in the direction indicated if it is clear and safe to do so.

Lane-Use Signals

Reversible lanes are designed to allow traffic on high-density commuter roadways to go in one direction at certain times of the day and in the opposite direction at other times of the day. Overhead **lane-use signals** indicate whether it is clear for you to use the lane or whether the lane is open only to oncoming traffic.

RED X
You must never drive in a lane under a RED X signal.

YELLOW X
A steady YELLOW X indicates the driver should safely vacate this lane—because it soon will be controlled by a RED X.

GREEN ARROW
You are permitted to drive in a lane under a GREEN ARROW.

FLASHING YELLOW X
A flashing YELLOW X indicates the lane is to be used, with caution, for left-turn movements only.

Figure 7–18 Lane-use signals

Green Arrow Pointed Downward

You may drive in the lane indicated, which is open to traffic going in your direction.

Yellow X

The lane indicated is about to be opened ahead to oncoming traffic. Move over as soon as you can do so safely to a lane with a downward-pointing green arrow.

Flashing Yellow X

You are permitted to make a left turn at the intersection where the signal is located.

Red X

Stay out of this lane! It is open to oncoming traffic. If you accidentally get stuck in a lane with a red X, put on your hazard lights and pull into an adjoining lane with a yellow X or downward-pointing green arrow as soon as it is safe to do so. If this is impossible and there is an open road or driveway off to the side of the road, turn left and go into it as soon as you can.

Busy sections of some freeways also have lane-use signals to warn drivers of problems ahead, such as merging traffic from on-ramps or lane closings because of a collision or construction. If you see a green signal, usually a downward-pointing arrow or X, it means that the lane is clear ahead. If the signal is red, it means that the lane ends, is blocked or closed, or has heavy traffic merging into it. As soon as it is safe to do so, move over into a clear lane.

On-Ramp Meters

In and around cities where there is a lot of rush-hour traffic, many freeway on-ramps have special signals to control the number of vehicles merging onto the freeway at one time. Similar in appearance to stop lights, **on-ramp meters** usually have red and green lights (some also have yellow) and allow one or more vehicles in each on-ramp lane to proceed at intervals. On-ramp meters operate only at peak traffic hours. Otherwise they are turned off to allow cars direct freeway entry when traffic is light.

auto slang

"Traffic calming" refers to what traffic engineers do to make a roadway safer, such as posting frequent warning signs or preventing drivers from seeing lights regulating cross traffic.

A sign posted with the signal indicates how many vehicles may proceed on each green light.

Figure 7–19 Carefully read signs posted with metered on-ramp signals.

Warning Signals

Special traffic signals are sometimes used at school or construction zones and near fire stations and hospitals. These signals usually flash yellow, but in some cases, they may turn to a steady yellow followed by a steady red when pedestrians or emergency vehicles are passing. Some roadways have permanently flashing yellow lights to warn drivers of an approaching curve or exit, dangerous intersection, dividing freeway, or any other place requiring vehicles to slow down.

Figure 7–20 Flashing yellow lights warn you to slow down for a hazardous area ahead.

Variable Message Signs

Many highways have special electronic signs that provide up-to-date information about lane and

Figure 7–21 Variable message signs provide current information on road conditions.

exit closings, delays, collisions, weather problems, carpooling, and other important items that affect driving conditions. These signs are usually posted in areas with high-density commuter traffic or where bad weather is common. Variable message signs or panels with electronic arrows can also be set up by construction or maintenance crews to help direct traffic or warn drivers of problems on the roadway ahead.

Pedestrian Signals

Pedestrian signals are designed for intersections with heavy pedestrian traffic. Most are mounted just below traffic signals. Pedestrians are allowed to cross when they face a green or white WALK signal or the symbol of a person walking. When they face a flashing orange or red DON'T WALK signal or the symbol of a raised hand, they must wait at the curb if they have not yet started to cross the street, or they should clear the intersection if they are still in it.

Sometimes pedestrian signals must be activated by hand with special buttons. Do not assume that a pedestrian who approaches a green light at an intersection and is too late to activate the WALK signal will stop. Also, be aware that pedestrians may ignore a DON'T WALK signal or not realize it is on and try to cross in front of you.

Hand Signals for Directing Traffic

Sometimes signal lights malfunction or traffic becomes so heavy at an intersection that police or traffic control officers are called in to direct traffic. This is common at sports events, concerts, and theme parks where the parking lot entrances and exits merge into the main roadway. Holding the hand up, palm facing outward, is the signal to stop. Waving one arm forward is the signal to proceed. Hand signals always take priority over signs and traffic signals.

7–3 ROADWAY MARKINGS, LANES, AND PAINTED CURBS

Roadway markings are painted on the pavement and curbs to provide warning and direction. They can be lines, symbols, letters, or words. Roadway markings define where lanes are and how they may be used, regulate traffic and parking, and warn of approaching dangers. Like signs and signals, they have colors that mean different things.

White Traffic Lines

Broken or dotted white lines separate traffic moving in the same direction and may be crossed when changing lanes or merging. Solid white lines are used to separate driving lanes from the shoulder of the road or a bicycle lane, and to mark fixed obstacles such as bridge supports on one-way roads. Special white lines or chevrons indicate the "neutral area" between freeway lanes and on-ramps and off-ramps. Solid white lines should never be crossed.

Figure 7–22 Pedestrian signals

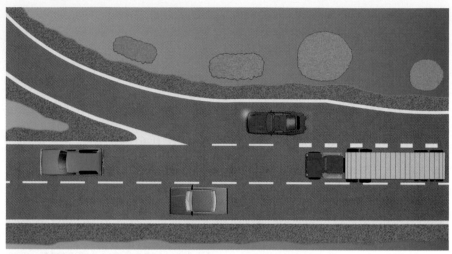

Figure 7–23 White lines may be solid, dashed, or dotted.

Yellow Traffic Lines

Yellow lines separate traffic going in opposite directions on a two-way road. They may be solid or broken, or a combination of solid and broken yellow lines. They may also be single or double lines. If two-way traffic is separated by an island or divider, the left side of the roadway is marked with a single yellow line. Solid yellow lines also mark obstacles in the center of a two-way road.

To avoid driving the wrong way against oncoming traffic, stay to the right of the yellow line(s). You can temporarily move to the left side of a yellow line only under the following circumstances:

- When you are instructed to do so by law enforcement or emergency personnel
- When temporary markers are used to create a detour or to force you to drive in a temporary lane on the other side of the roadway
- When you are passing another vehicle going your direction on a two-lane undivided highway, if passing is allowed
- When the right half of the roadway is closed to traffic

REALITY CHECK   *Old Lane Markings* _____

When roads are repainted or new lanes are added, sometimes the old roadway markings are not completely removed. Watch out for other drivers that move into your lane because they are following the old markings.

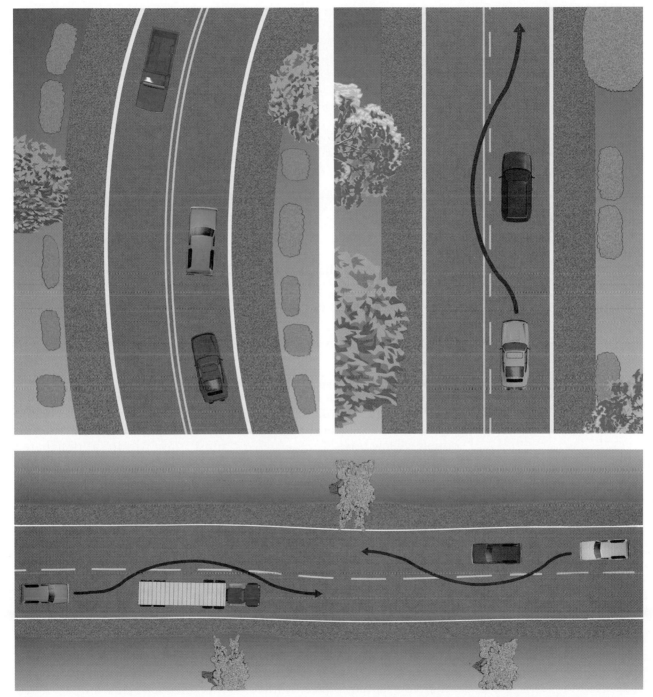

Figure 7–24 The pattern of yellow lines on a roadway determines whether passing is permitted.

RUDY TOMJANOVICH

During his eleven-year career as a player with the Houston Rockets basketball team, Rudy Tomjanovich competed in the NBA playoffs five times, scored 13,000 points, and made five trips to the All-Star Game. Upon his retirement in 1981, the "Rocket Man" became a scout, then assistant coach, and eventually head coach of the Rockets. In July 1994, 3 weeks after his team won the NBA championships, Tomjanovich was arrested on a highway in Houston for crossing a yellow dividing line twice in his jeep. The coach spent the night in jail for this offense, as well as other violations. Straying out of a lane is often an indication of drunk driving, fatigue, or speeding, and is certain to get the attention of law enforcement. If you want to avoid being pulled over by the police, pay close attention to roadway markings and other traffic controls.

because of construction or repair

- When the road is not sufficiently wide
- When you are making a lawful left turn

Some jurisdictions allow you to turn left across double-yellow lines in certain situations, but when in doubt, never turn across double-yellow lines.

The pattern of solid and dashed yellow lines used on a roadway indicates whether passing is permitted. No passing is allowed if there are two solid yellow lines. If a solid and a broken yellow line appear together, passing is allowed if there are no oncoming cars and you are next to the broken line; passing is not allowed if you are next to the solid line. In some jurisdictions, it is legal for you to cross a solid yellow line when passing *if* the line was broken when you started to pass. If there is only one broken yellow line and no oncoming cars, passing is allowed.

Special Lanes

Special roadway markings are used to separate lanes reserved for certain actions or vehicles from the normal lanes of traffic. **Turn lanes** are often added near intersections to separate left- or right-turning traffic from through traffic at an intersection. White arrows, often accompanied by the word "ONLY," indicate that you must stay within a designated lane while turning onto the cross street. Some turn lanes have multiple arrows, allowing you to turn left or right, or even go straight. To discourage drivers from changing lanes near an intersection, turn lanes are often separated from through traffic lanes by solid white lines.

On some roadways, a **center turn lane** between two opposing directions of traffic—also called a "two-way left-turn lane"—is designated for left turns only from either direction. This lane is marked by parallel solid and broken yellow lines, sometimes accompanied by white arrows painted on

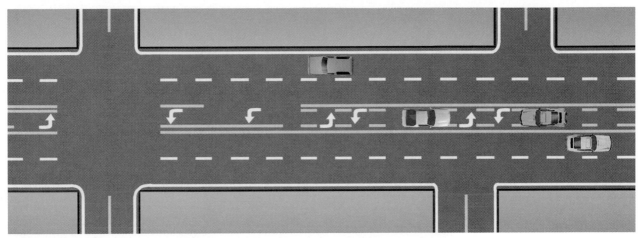

Figure 7–25 Center turn lanes can be used by traffic moving in both directions.

the pavement that alternately point left and right. Vehicles moving in either direction can use these lanes to make left turns into another road or driveway.

Commuter lanes are an efficient way to minimize urban traffic during rush-hour periods. Dedicated reversible commuter lanes are separated by broken double-yellow lines. You can cross these lines only if the overhead signal above the lane you wish to enter has a green X or if a sign permits you to do so. Temporary commuter lanes are sometimes established to create an extra lane of traffic in one direction. Orange cones or other types of dividers

may be used to "borrow" a lane from one side of the road and "lend" this lane to the direction of highest traffic flow to reduce congestion.

When you encounter commuter lanes, remember that traffic will be traveling in lanes otherwise used by opposing traffic. The danger is that a driver on one side of the road may get confused or will not be paying attention and cause a deadly head-on collision. Be especially cautious just before and after the designated times when traffic is reversed.

Often called "high-occupancy vehicle" (HOV) or "diamond" lanes, **carpool lanes** are special

AUTO ACCESSORIES *Fog Lights* _____

Having fog lights on your vehicle can dramatically increase your ability to see roadway markings and lanes at night or in bad weather. Because roads in areas that receive severe weather do not usually have lane dividers, fog lights can provide that extra margin of safety to keep you on the road and in your lane.

Figure 7–27 The direction of travel on reversible lanes depends on the time of day.

lanes designed for buses, motorcycles, and vehicles carrying a minimum of two or sometimes three persons. Carpool lanes have distinctive roadway markings—usually a diamond symbol and words such as "CARPOOL ONLY"—and posted signs. They are usually found on the far-left side of a freeway and are separated from the other lanes by various combinations of white and/or yellow lines and raised roadway markers. If you are pulled over by the police for driving in a carpool lane without having the minimum number of persons in your vehicle, you will pay a large fine.

If you are traveling in a carpool lane or next to one, be aware that HOV lanes often appear, become more than one lane, or disappear suddenly, forcing vehicles in the carpool lane to merge back into

Figure 7–28 Carpool lanes are usually reserved for motorcycles and vehicles with two or more occupants.

Do Not Carpool with a "Dummy" _____

Police are quite good at spotting blow-up dummies used as "passengers" in cars whose drivers are illegally using carpool lanes. Remember, passengers must be human! Odds are the officer who pulls you over will not be amused enough to let you off without a ticket.

regular freeway traffic. Be careful not to stray into a carpool lane if you are not eligible to drive in one, and never cross solid white or yellow lines to enter or leave a carpool lane.

In urban areas where there is a lot of congestion and bus traffic, buses may have their own lanes. This type of lane, which often has "BUS ONLY" roadway markings and/or signs, is usually the far-right lane. In most cases, you cannot enter a **bus lane** unless you are making a right turn.

Many roadways have a special lane for bicycles, which is on the far-right side of a two-way roadway. These **bicycle lanes** are separated from the traffic lanes by a solid white line, which changes to a broken line near intersections. Vehicles are permitted to enter the bicycle lane on a two-way roadway only where the line is broken to make a right turn. Bicycle lanes sometimes have a bicycle symbol and/or the words "BIKE LANE" painted on the roadway inside the lane. Roadways with bicycle lanes

Figure 7–29 Downtown areas of cities may have special lanes for buses.

factoid

Bicycle lanes have been shown to reduce collisions involving vehicles and bicycles at intersections by 50%.

Figure 7–30 Bicycle lanes provide a safe alternative to riding on the shoulder of a roadway.

may also have green BIKE ROUTE or white BIKE LANE signs posted.

Limit Lines

A **limit line** is either a wide white or yellow stop line at an intersection, or the nearer of two crosswalk lines. Crosswalk markings are often connected with diagonal lines, or the crosswalk itself may appear as a series of painted bars or raised markers on the road. Sometimes words such as "STOP" or "X WALK" are also painted on the pavement. When you are required to come to a stop at an intersection by a sign or signal, your vehicle must come to a full stop *behind* the limit line. If there is no limit line, you must stop at a point nearest the intersecting roadway where you have a clear view of traffic.

Painted Curbs

Curbs and parking stops are painted to regulate parking. If a curb is painted any color, it means that there are special parking rules. Although colors may vary somewhat from jurisdiction to jurisdiction, the following markings are what you would normally find in your community.

Yellow

Yellow designates a loading zone. You can stop only to unload or load. If you are driving a non-commercial vehicle, you must remain in your vehicle. City ordinances normally govern the amount of time you may remain in a loading zone.

Red

Red designates areas in which you cannot stop, park, load, or stand. Only buses can stop at these curbs, if the curb is marked allowing them to do so.

Bright White

Bright white designates areas that permit stopping for brief periods only when picking up or dropping off people or mail. You may not leave your vehicle.

Green

Green designates a time-limited parking zone. The length of time you may park is either designated on the curb itself or on a nearby sign.

Blue

Blue designates a parking zone for the disabled. You can park at a blue curb only if you have a special license plate, decal, or properly displayed sign issued by the jurisdiction in which you live.

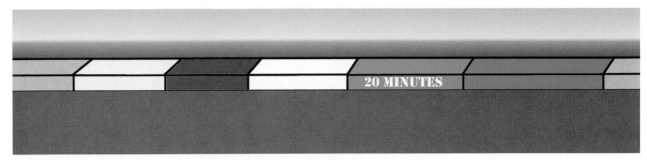

Figure 7–31 What is the meaning of each of these curb colors?

You will be issued a heavy fine and might have your car towed if you park illegally in a parking space designated for the disabled.

Raised Pavement Markers

If you are driving at night or in bad weather, it is often hard to see painted lines on the roadway. It can also be difficult to stay within lines if you are tired or otherwise impaired.

Some roads are equipped with raised buttons or square-shaped reflectors to help drivers stay within lanes. Called **Botts' dots** after their inventor, Elbert Botts, they are commonly placed on or between dividing lines. They may also be used on the edge of roadways, especially those with narrow or soft shoulders or drop-offs. Botts' dots work in two ways. First, the noise and vibration they make when your tire strikes them tells you if you are straying out of your lane or off the road. Second, they reflect the light from your headlights, allowing you to better see the driving lane.

Rumble strips are grooved or raised sections of the roadway commonly found before dangerous

Figure 7–32 (a) Botts' dots help drivers stay within lanes and alert them to dangers ahead; **(b)** Rumble strips are often used to warn drivers traveling at a high rate of speed that they must stop or slow down ahead; **(c)** Speed bumps are an effective way to force drivers to reduce their speed.

factoid

intersections and toll areas and alongside individual lanes or shoulders of highways and freeways. Like Botts' dots, their noise and vibration alert you to possible dangers ahead, warn you to slow down, or let you know that you are straying out of your lane or off the roadway.

Speed bumps are raised slabs of pavement usually found in parking lots, residential neighborhoods, large condominium or apartment complexes, and even on some narrow winding streets with poor visibility. Speed bumps are usually painted or striped white, yellow, or red, and they force you to reduce speed to about 5 miles per hour (8 km/h) for safety. Some speed bumps are very high, and if you travel over them too fast you can seriously damage your vehicle.

WHO'S AT FAULT?

1. Turns at the intersection of First and Main are controlled by arrow signals. Driver 2 was proceeding south on First Street. Observing that the traffic light was yellow, Driver 2 accelerated into the intersection of First and Main. Driver 1 entered the intersection northbound on First and, intending to make a left turn on a solid green light, pulled suddenly into Driver 2's path of travel. Driver 2 was unable to stop and broadsided Driver 1. *Who's at fault?*

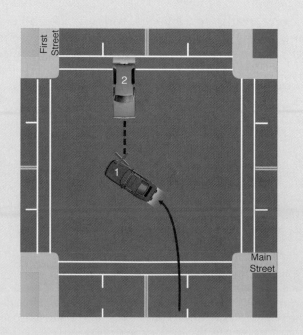

2. Driver 2 was eastbound in the center turn lane for quite some distance in preparation to make a left turn into a driveway. Driver 1 made a left turn out of a strip mall parking lot and also entered the center turn lane to prepare to enter westbound traffic. Driver 2 attempted to veer to his left to avoid impact, but traffic in the westbound lanes prevented him from doing so. Driver 2 then stopped abruptly and was impacted on the front right side by Driver 1, who was apparently unaware of Driver 2's presence in the lane. ***Who's at fault?***

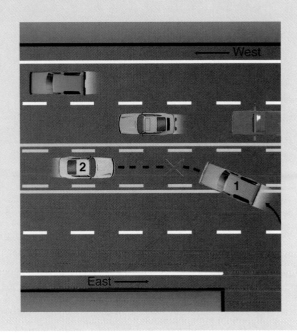

Y O U R   T U R N

7–1 Traffic Signs

1. How are different colors used in traffic signs?
2. Which signs have their own distinctive shapes?

7–2 Traffic Signals

3. What do you do at a red light, yellow light, and green light?
4. How do signal arrows control traffic?
5. What is a metered on-ramp?

7–3 Roadway Markings, Lanes, and Painted Curbs

6. How are white and yellow traffic lines used on roads to control traffic?
7. What special lanes have distinctive roadway markings?
8. How are different colors used to regulate parking on curbs and parking stops?
9. What is the purpose of raised pavement markers?

SELF-TEST

Multiple Choice

1. What are the three main elements of a traffic sign that communicate information?
   a. colors, weight, and symbols
   b. symbols, colors, and reflectiveness
   c. shapes, symbols, and colors
   d. reflectiveness, height, and colors

2. What shape would a FALLING ROCKS sign have?
   a. square
   b. rectangle
   c. circle
   d. diamond

3. Speed bumps are commonly used:
   a. at the edge of roadways.
   b. at dangerous intersections.
   c. between dividing lines.
   d. in parking lots.

4. When are you *not* allowed to temporarily move to the left side of a yellow line?
   a. when your side of the roadway is blocked
   b. when you are making a left turn across the yellow line
   c. when you want to see the roadway ahead of a big truck in front of you
   d. when you are passing another vehicle going in your direction

5. Disabled parking zones are indicated by curbs and parking stops painted:
   a. green.
   b. blue.
   c. bright white.
   d. red.

Sentence Completion

1. The only octagonal traffic sign is a _____ sign.
2. At a railroad crossing, a _____ sign is often accompanied with flashing red lights.
3. _____ signals always take priority over signs and traffic signals.
4. A lane that allows both you and oncoming traffic to make a left turn is called a _____ .
5. HOV stands for _____ .

Matching

Match the concepts in Column A with examples of the concepts in Column B.

Column A	Column B
1. __ Traffic signal with only two lights	a. Disabled parking zone
2. __ Pedestrian signal	b. INTERSTATE 56
3. __ Raised pavement marker	c. MINNEAPOLIS, EXIT 14
4. __ Green sign	d. LOS PADRES NATIONAL FOREST
5. __ Recreational sign	e. On-ramp meter
6. __ Blue sign	f. WALK
7. __ Time-limited parking	g. Botts' dots
8. __ Route marker	h. Green curb

Short Answer

1. Where are disabled parking spots located in a parking lot and why?
2. What is the purpose of a milepost or distance marker?
3. What must you do when you approach an intersection and the light turns yellow?
4. What are commuter lanes?
5. What should you do if you end up driving in a reversible commuter lane with a red X?

Critical Thinking

1. You are driving late at night in the almost empty parking lot of a large suburban shopping mall, only a few stores away from a 24-hour liquor store. You approach a small STOP sign in the middle of the parking lot, obviously placed there by the shopping mall management and not by the municipal authorities. What should you do?
2. You are driving a large recreational vehicle on a two-lane country road when you notice a small bridge up ahead that is very narrow. The bridge is not sign posted, but it seems that the lanes are smaller than they are on the roadway on either side of the bridge. The way looks clear, but there is a curve beyond the bridge along with a lot of trees blocking your view of any oncoming traffic. What should you do?

PROJECTS

1. As a passenger, take a notebook and jot down as many different types of traffic signs as you can see. When you get back home divide the signs into their appropriate categories of regulatory signs, warning signs, guide signs, construction signs, service signs, recreational signs, international signs, and local traffic signs. Total them up and see which category has the most signs. Compare your results with those of other students in class.

2. Visit your municipal, state, or provincial transportation department and ask them to show you the equipment that they use to place raised pavement markers on your local roadways. Do they use Botts' dots, rumble strips, or speed bumps? What do they look like? Share your findings in class.

Intersections and Right-of-Way

Intersections are places where different roadways meet or cross. Because pedestrians and vehicles of different sizes and speeds must cross one another's paths, intersections are extremely dangerous places. Studies indicate that one-third to nearly one-half of all collisions occur in and around intersections. Your chance of having a collision at an intersection is greater than at any other place on the roadway.

Upon completion of this chapter, you should be able to:

8–1 Intersections

1. Understand the difference between a controlled and semicontrolled intersection.
2. Understand the proper way to approach an uncontrolled intersection.
3. Describe some of the hazards associated with alleys, traffic circles, and parking lots.

8–2 Right-of-Way

4. Understand what right-of-way is.
5. Understand what the right-hand rule is.

8–3 Railroad Crossings

6. Understand the difference between a controlled and uncontrolled railroad crossing.
7. Understand the proper procedure for crossing railroad tracks.

KEY TERMS

intersection

controlled intersection

semicontrolled intersection

uncontrolled intersection

"stale" green light

"fresh" green light

traffic circles

right-of-way

right-hand rule

controlled railroad crossing

uncontrolled railroad crossing

Figure 8–1 Traffic controls allow drivers to navigate intersections safely and efficiently.

The first traffic light appeared in Cleveland, Ohio, in 1914.

8–1 INTERSECTIONS

There are three basic types of intersections. **Controlled intersections** use some form of signal, sign, or control device to direct the flow of traffic. Stop lights, STOP and YIELD signs, flashing yellow lights, and railroad crossing gates are all examples of controls found at controlled intersections.

Semicontrolled intersections have either signs or signals on one or several approaches to the intersection, but not on every approach. This type of intersection, which is common in North America, is very dangerous precisely be-

Figure 8–2 What is dangerous about this kind of intersection?

cause it does not tell every driver exactly what to do.

Uncontrolled intersections lack any form of control, such as traffic signs or signals, to regulate traffic. They are typically found in rural and residential areas with little traffic congestion. They are rarely found in urban areas or places with a lot of traffic.

Approaching a Controlled Intersection

As you approach an intersection, scan for signs, signals, and other clues such as bus stop benches, rows of mailboxes, newspaper vending machines, parked cars, and pedestrian activity to help you identify a controlled intersection as soon as possible. Stay far enough behind the vehicles in front of you so that your field of vision is not blocked. The earlier you can spot an intersection, the more time you have to slow down, stop, move into the proper lane, or signal to others that there is a halt in traffic ahead by lightly tapping your brakes.

Many lanes change upon approach to an intersection. For example, a through-traffic lane can quickly turn into a left-turn-only lane, forcing you to go somewhere you do not want to go. Make sure that you leave yourself plenty of time to get in the proper lane before arriving at an intersection. Changes in the number and type of lanes are normally indicated with a sign and/or roadway markings. If you pay attention, you will be able to move out of a lane that does not suit your travel plans well in advance of the intersection, where it will be too late to switch.

Red Lights and STOP Signs

If you are approaching a red light or STOP sign, reduce your speed to stop. Even if it is the middle of

Figure 8–3 Signs rather than signals are used at intersections with a low volume of traffic.

TRINIDAD SILVA, JR. _____

Actor Trinidad Silva, Jr., moved from his native Texas to Los Angeles to pursue his dream. He worked his way up in Hollywood the hard way, winning praise for his work on stage and in independent films. Silva got his big break in 1981 with the role of gang leader-turned-lawyer Jesus Martinez in the TV cop show *Hill Street Blues*. This popular series aired for seven years and won twenty-six Emmy awards. After the last episode in 1987, Silva appeared in several critically praised movies, including *The Milagro Beanfield War* and *Colors,* and formed his own television production company. On July 31, 1988, Silva's promising career abruptly ended when a driver ran a red light and broadsided his pickup at an intersection in Whittier, California. The thirty-eight-year-old Silva was thrown 100 feet (30 m) from his vehicle and died instantly. His wife and two-year-old daughter were also injured. The next time you think about racing through an intersection to "beat" a red light, remember that you are risking other lives, as well as your own.

the night and no cross traffic is in sight, you must make a *full* stop at the crosswalk, stop line, or imaginary line extending from a STOP sign if no actual line is painted on the roadway. Many drivers fail to come to a complete stop at STOP signs or before turning right on a red light. Not only is "rolling" through a stop dangerous, but it also is an easy way to get a ticket.

Some drivers like to play a game with traffic signals to save time by trying to enter the intersection at full speed just as the red light turns green. However, if you guess wrong and the light does not turn green as fast as you think it will, you may be forced to come to a quick stop, or worse, enter the intersection on a red light. Never try to "beat" a red traffic signal by attempting to anticipate the light change. Worse yet, never look out your side window to react to the cross traffic's signal. You do not know the timing of that particular signal, and there may be special

left- or right-turn arrows you are unaware of that will delay the green light you expected.

As you approach a red signal, look for signs indicating turning prohibitions. If you are turning right at the intersection, do you have to wait for a green light or can you go once you have stopped and the path is clear? Even if turning right on a red light is legal in your jurisdiction, it may not be allowed at certain intersections for reasons of safety.

Yellow Lights and YIELD Signs

If the light ahead is solid yellow, the general rule of thumb is to stop safely before entering the intersection. If you are already in the intersection, or cannot stop safely, proceed through it at a constant speed, watching carefully for cross traffic that might enter the intersection before you have cleared it. If you are near the intersection but think that you will be able to stop safely before entering it, check the traffic to your rear at this critical decision point. If it appears that a car behind you is attempting to make it through the intersection on the yellow light, it is better to proceed if you can do so safely rather than risk getting rear-ended.

If you can see one or two lights down the road, you may be able to discover whether the light ahead is a "long" or "short" yellow. In many cases, how long a light stays yellow depends on the time of day or night and the volume of traffic. If you observe that the yellow light is short, you can be better prepared to stop at the intersection rather than have to worry about making a sudden stop. If you know that the yellow light ahead is long, you will be better able to judge whether you can make it through the intersection without having to accelerate at the last second.

If you are approaching a flashing yellow or YIELD sign at an intersection, reduce your speed and scan in both directions of the cross street for oncoming traffic. Look left, right, ahead, and left again. If the way is clear, proceed cautiously through the intersection or turn onto the cross street and gradually increase your speed.

Green Lights

Scanning ahead will help you determine whether a green light is "stale." When you approach an intersection with a **"stale" green light**, a light that has been green for a long time or ever since you first noticed it, anticipate that it will turn yellow and slow down. A flashing red pedestrian DON'T WALK sign is a good indication that a stale green light is about to turn yellow. As you approach a stale green light, keep an eye out for drivers or pedestrians in cross traffic who may try to "get a jump" on the light and proceed before their light turns green.

If the light is a **"fresh" green light**, or has just changed from red to green, proceed when cross traffic has safely cleared. Always remember to look left first because on a two-way road cross traffic will approach you first from this side as you enter the intersection. Then look right, ahead, and left again. Watch for drivers who may have tried to "run" a yellow light just as it was

REALITY CHECK **Red-Light Cameras** _____

In many jurisdictions, high-tech photographic detection systems are used to photograph cars that enter an intersection after the light has turned red. Offenders receive a ticket in the mail along with a photo of the violation. These cameras are hard to spot and are often moved among various sites so that motorists do not know which intersections have them. Red-light cameras are used extensively in Canada and are becoming increasingly common in the United States.

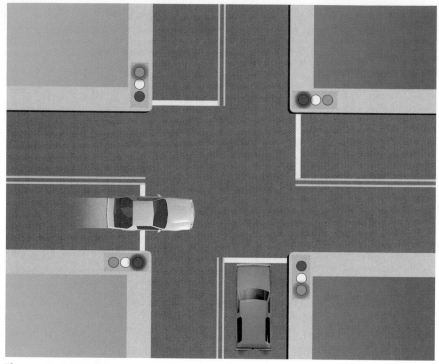

Figure 8–4 Just because your light is green does not mean it is safe to proceed.

changing to red. If you are turning left, make sure that you know whether you have to wait for a green arrow or can go as soon as there is a sufficient break in oncoming traffic.

Do not treat your initial forward movement like a drag race. Pedestrians or other hazards may come into view as you accelerate, and you will not have time to stop. At the same time, you risk

REALITY CHECK *The Right-Hand "Quick Starter"* _____

Rather than wait behind other cars at a red light, impatient drivers will sometimes leave the regular stream of traffic and pull over into the far-right lane to get a "line position" for the next green. The "lane" they use is often a bicycle lane or a lane filled with parked cars. These racers will then creep up to the crosswalk so that once the light turns green they can floor the accelerator of their cars and rapidly swerve back into the regular stream of traffic, missing parked cars or other obstacles ahead by a hair. If this happens to you, do not be tempted to race the offending driver because he or she has gotten in front of you. Reduce your speed and allow the other driver to get ahead of you. It is not worth a crash to prove a point.

Figure 8–5 Be careful not to get stuck in the middle of an intersection.

getting rear-ended if you move too slowly or stop once you begin your movement. Do not enter an intersection unless you are sure that you can get all the way across without getting in the way of cross traffic once the signal changes. In some jurisdictions, you can be ticketed for blocking an intersection. Even if the driver behind you is furiously honking at you to move, do not endanger your life or other lives by getting stuck in the middle of an intersection.

Automated Signals

Some signals at intersections are controlled with sensors in the

DRIVING TIPS *Intersections*

- Look carefully for pedestrians and other vehicles in an intersection before you proceed either on a green light or after you have stopped at a STOP sign or uncontrolled intersection.

- When entering a major roadway from a side roadway, always stop at the intersection, even when no STOP sign is posted.

- If you intend to park on the other side of an intersection, slow down, get into the far-right lane, and indicate your move toward a parking spot by signaling only *after* you have entered the intersection. If you put on your turn signal too early, drivers around you may assume that you are making a right turn at the intersection.

- When passing slow or stopped vehicles in or near intersections, use extreme caution—the other drivers may have spotted something, or someone, in the street that you cannot see. Pedestrians are often hidden from view by parked cars or other vehicles in an intersection. Be patient and avoid hitting the unseen pedestrian or vehicle.

Wild Wheels

Figure 8–6 How long is this extra-stretch limo, which can enter an intersection on a green light and complete its turn on a red light?

roadway that trigger a light change in response to traffic flow and congestion. Other signals are timed to go off at certain intervals that vary with the day and time. As a driver, you can adjust your speed to the timing of traffic lights to "make" all the greens and save both gas and wear and tear on your brakes. However, you should do this only if you can stay within the speed limit, maintain a safe space cushion around your vehicle, and not take your concentration off other vehicles on the roadway.

Approaching an Uncontrolled Intersection

Use extra caution when approaching an uncontrolled intersection. Because there are no signs or signals, drivers often do not pay attention to cross traffic, or they just assume that they are the only ones on the road and race right through. Scanning ahead is especially critical at uncontrolled intersections. Because

many are in residential areas, watch out for children, bicyclists, skateboarders and rollerbladers, balls flying into the road, dogs without leashes, and so on. Keep in mind that small children can easily be hidden by parked cars or bushes. Always reduce your speed when approaching an uncontrolled intersection and prepare to stop your vehicle.

Other Types of Intersections

When approaching an intersection that you have trouble identifying, slow down to give yourself extra time to recognize what you are facing and to react to any potential obstacles or problems.

Alley Intersections

Because drivers on a roadway have a hard time even seeing alleys, especially in urban environments, this type of intersection can be very dangerous. The driver in the alley who is watching for pedestrians on the sidewalk and vehicles in the roadway must be

Figure 8–7 Uncontrolled intersections are most common in residential areas.

AUTO ACCESSORIES *"Round-the-Corner" Mirrors* _____

The next time you drive out of an alley or parking garage where it is hard to see cross traffic, look for a small, round mirror mounted nearby on a wall, post, or overhang. These mirrors are designed to allow drivers and pedestrians to see one another at dangerous narrow intersections where the driver's line of sight is blocked, often by a building.

more patient than usual while waiting for a safe opportunity to join the through traffic. Make sure that it is the *best* opportunity, not just the first opportunity, and never assume that you have a clear path.

When driving in an alley you must be extra cautious. Alleys are not designed for high-speed travel. They are typically narrow and have limited views because of the existence of obstacles such as the walls of the buildings through which the alley runs, parked trucks, and trash dumpsters. Keep your speed low—if signs are not posted you should not exceed 10 to 15 miles per hour (15 to 25 km/h)—and watch out for vehicles exiting parking lots and garages.

Traffic Circles

Also called rotaries or roundabouts, **traffic circles** are circular roadways that allow traffic from many different directions to intersect without having to stop at traffic signals. Although you are not likely to encounter these at all in many parts of North America, in other parts they are common.

As you progress through a traffic circle, watch out for vehicles on both of your sides. Some traffic circles have more than one lane of travel. As a general rule, the inner lane(s) of the circle should be used for through traffic,

Figure 8–8 You may have to go around a traffic circle more than once to reach your exit safely.

USING SAFE *Large Parking Lots*

Parking lots may seem like one of the easiest places to drive, but they can actually be very dangerous. Pedestrians and vehicles mix directly on the roadway, cars continually pull in and out of spaces, and drivers often ignore signs and roadway markings. When navigating through a parking lot, you must *scan* aggressively from side to side for pedestrians, especially small children, who may dart from between cars into your path at any moment; drivers who back out of spaces without first looking behind them; and drivers ahead of you who slam on their brakes when they see an opening. *Assess* what may happen. Can that shopper loaded down with merchandise see you coming? Is the driver in front of you looking for a parking space or trying to get out of the lot? *Find* an escape route by maintaining a large following distance in front of you. *Execute* your decision to avoid a potential collision with a pedestrian or another car by tapping your horn or flashing your lights to communicate your presence.

and the outer lane should be used by vehicles preparing to exit the circle. Moving to the outer lane can be a tricky maneuver because you must simultaneously follow the turn and watch for other vehicles that are trying to do the same thing you are. Do not cross lanes too early to reach your exit. You can always continue to go around the circle, and next time you will be more prepared to exit at the appropriate off-ramp.

Large Parking Lots

Safety is often compromised in parking lots where large numbers of cars and pedestrians heading every which way are in close proximity. The excitement associated with shopping, concerts, and sporting events makes it more difficult for drivers to concentrate. Pedestrians are hard to spot among parked cars, and when traveling in groups, often assume that there is "safety in numbers."

Figure 8–9 Dangers lurk in every direction in crowded parking lots.

Drivers often go too fast within large parking lots, treating the lot as an extension of the surrounding street scene. In crowded lots, some drivers compete fiercely for scarce parking spots, ignoring intersections within the parking lot or between the lot and the roadway. Congestion naturally leads to frustration and impatience. In these situations you must slow down, stay calm, and remain at peak alertness. This is not a time to change radio stations or argue with passengers.

8–2 RIGHT-OF-WAY

Right-of-way is the right to use a certain part of a roadway when two or more users of the roadway want to use it at the same time. When you give the right-of-way, or "yield," to another driver or pedestrian, you are giving that person first use of the road. When someone gives the right-of-way, or "yields," to you, that person is giving you first use of that stretch of roadway.

Understanding and obeying right-of-way laws is one of the most important components of safe driving. Each jurisdiction has such laws to increase safety for motorists, bicyclists, and pedestrians alike. They are founded on common sense and rely on drivers' patience and courtesy to be effective. In a certain situation, you may want to give the right-of-way to someone else even if the law says you have the right-of-way! Why? To contribute to an orderly flow of traffic, to avoid collisions, or even just to be nice.

In fact, the law *requires* you to give up your right-of-way if you have the last clear chance of avoiding a crash.

Never assume that others will give the right-of-way to you, even if you legally have the right-of-way. Giving up your right-of-way is a small price to pay to avoid collisions. Equally important, *never demand or insist on taking the right-of-way.* If you are the type of person who gets mad at someone for cutting you off, ask yourself if proving a point to a total stranger is really worth a crash. The answer is no! Let the other driver go and forget the whole thing.

Right-of-Way at Intersections

Always give the right-of-way to pedestrians still in or near the crosswalk and vehicles still in an intersection. As a general rule, if the roadway you are on has traffic controls and the cross-street traffic does not, you must give the right-of-way to the cross traffic.

At uncontrolled intersections, intersections with STOP signs on all the corners, and intersections with flashing red or broken signal lights, the first vehicle approaching or entering the intersection has the right-of-way. If two vehicles reach the intersection at the same time, keep in mind the **right-hand rule:** Drivers on the left should always give the right-of-way to drivers on the right. If three or four vehicles reach the intersection from different directions at the same time, each driver should wait to take his or

Figure 8–10

Figure 8–11 Signal-controlled intersections

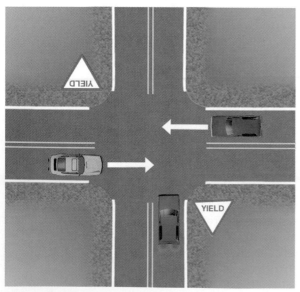

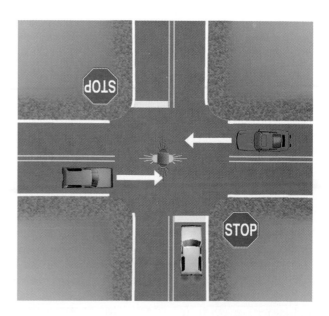

Figure 8–12 Semicontrolled intersections

Figure 8–13 Uncontrolled intersections or intersections with STOP signs on all the corners

her turn to cross the intersection. This situation calls for caution and clear communication among all drivers as to who will go first, second, and so on.

Always give the right-of-way to pedestrians before coming to a sidewalk and all vehicles in the roadway when approaching from an alley, private driveway, or private road. This means you will have to stop *twice:* once for pedestrian traffic on the side-

walk and once before entering the roadway.

In general, the driver of a vehicle entering a traffic circle must give the right-of-way to vehicles already in the circle. The driver of a vehicle within the circle must give the right-of-way to other vehicles that wish to exit the circle. However, because laws differ from jurisdiction to jurisdiction, you should check with your local law enforcement or

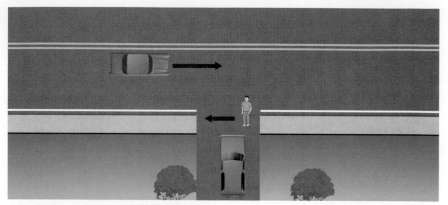

Figure 8–14 Alleys and private roads

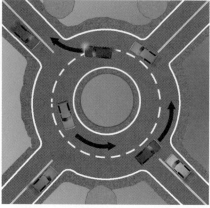

Figure 8–15 Traffic circles

motor-vehicle department to find out exactly what the rules are.

If you are making a left turn, all approaching vehicles have the right-of-way. Wait until the road is clear of oncoming traffic to make your turn. If you are in an intersection when your light turns yellow, wait until oncoming traffic has stopped, then proceed. If the light turns red while you are waiting to make your left turn, stay calm and proceed cautiously only when oncoming traffic has stopped. Cross

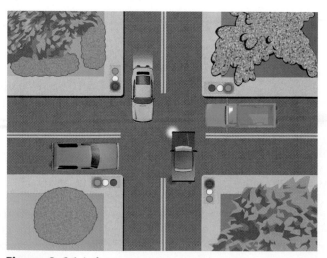

Figure 8–16 Left turns

DRIVING TIPS *Right-of-Way*

- Always give up the right-of-way, even if you think you have it, to avoid a collision.

- If you force another vehicle to slow down or stop, you have not given up the right-of-way.

- Although traffic signals and signs determine who has the right-of-way, other drivers will not necessarily observe them. Watch out for the driver who rolls through a STOP sign, ignores a YIELD sign, or runs a red light. Even if you have the clear right-of-way, always keep alert.

- In case of doubt, always yield the right-of-way. This will contribute to greater safety on the roadway, and other drivers will signal their appreciation of your courtesy.

traffic must give the right-of-way to you even though they now have a green light.

Other Right-of-Way Situations

Negotiating different types of intersections is not the only situation in which right-of-way comes into play.

Passing

On a multilane roadway, always give the right-of-way to any other vehicle passing you and to any

vehicle close enough to prevent you from passing safely.

Merging Lanes

If the lane in which you are traveling ends, either because the road narrows or because an obstacle is in your lane, you will be forced to merge into another lane. When this occurs, you must give the right-of-way to vehicles passing you in this other lane.

Roadway Parking

A car parked on the side of a road that is pulling into the roadway

Figure 8–17 Drivers in merging lanes must give the right-of-way to through traffic.

Figure 8–18 Watch out for pedestrians who illegally "take" the right-of-way.

must give the right-of-way to through traffic on the road.

Pedestrians

Pedestrians crossing in or near a crosswalk have the right-of-way. If a pedestrian has entered the roadway, but not at a crosswalk, be prepared for that pedestrian to illegally take the right-of-way from you. Take all measures to avoid hitting the pedestrian and to warn him or her of your presence, such as honking your horn or flashing your lights. All drivers have a duty to protect pedestrians even if the pedestrians are breaking the right-of-way laws.

If no painted crosswalk is at an intersection, a pedestrian still has a right to cross the street, although if it is a controlled intersection the pedestrian must cross the street only with a green light. Treat any intersection without painted crosswalks, which often occurs in residential and rural areas, as if there were imaginary crosswalk lines painted on the street.

Blind pedestrians with guide dogs or white canes have the right-of-way at all times no matter where they are in the street.

Emergency Vehicles

Emergency vehicles include police cars, ambulances, fire department vehicles, paramedic vans, and military vehicles. You must give the right-of-way to any approaching

DRIVING MYTHS   *Should I Stop or Should I Go?* _____

Do you have to stop on a divided roadway if an emergency vehicle with its siren on and flashing its lights is on the *other* side of the street? Many people think they have to stop, but in most jurisdictions you do not have to. Check with local authorities to find out what the law is where you live.

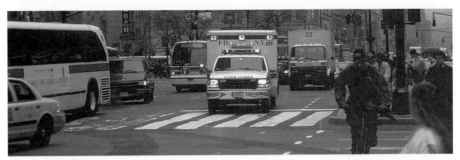

Figure 8–19 Emergency vehicles have the right-of-way in *every* situation.

emergency vehicle by moving to the far-right side of the road as near to the curb as possible and stopping when you hear sirens and/or see flashing lights. Never stop in an intersection unless specifically directed to by law enforcement or other emergency personnel. On multilane highways or freeways where it may be unsafe or impractical for you to stop, you must slow down and help clear a path for the emergency vehicle to get by you. Wait for emergency vehicles to fully pass you before you turn back into the normal stream of traffic.

Funeral Processions and Motorcades

A group of vehicles forming part of a funeral procession or motor-cade has the right-of-way over other vehicles. These vehicles are generally easy to identify because they travel at a slow speed; have funeral signs, flags, or other markings on their cars; are escorted by police; and/or each car in the motorcade has its headlights on. The driver of the lead vehicle in the procession must obey all traffic signs and signals, but other members of the procession may follow this lead vehicle without stopping, as if they were an extension of the lead vehicle.

8–3 RAILROAD CROSSINGS

Railroad crossings are the sites of hundreds of deaths and thousands of injuries across the United

In the United States, a train collides with a person or vehicle every 100 minutes.

Figure 8–20 More than half of all collisions between cars and trains occur at intersections just like this one.

States and Canada each year. Although the number of collisions and fatalities at highway–rail crossings has consistently decreased over the last decade, they are still one of the deadliest types of intersections. Most of these collisions are caused by human error: drivers who do not obey warning signals or devices, try to outrun a train, or ignore crossing barriers.

It takes approximately two-thirds of a mile (1 km) for an eight-car passenger train going 60 miles per hour (100 km/h) to stop. A 150-car freight train going 30 miles per hour (50 km/h), the speed under which most highway–rail crashes occur, needs a distance of 3,150 feet (950 m) to stop. Even if the engineer spots your car on the tracks ahead, it is next to impossible for him or her to stop the train in time to avoid hitting your vehicle. Train–car collisions are not a pretty sight. The weight difference between a train, which can weigh more than 10,000 tons, and a car is like that between a car and an aluminum soda pop can.

Think about that the next time you *flatten* a littered can on the road.

Railroad Crossing Controls

Controlled railroad crossings include signs, warning lights, signals, roadway markings, lowered crossing gates, or some combination of these. Warning signs are often posted well in advance of the tracks, anywhere from 200 to 800 feet (60 to 250 m), telling you to slow down and be prepared to stop.

Although many railroad crossings have at least a warning sign of one type or another, most railroad crossings in North America do not have the full set of controls such as signals, crossing gates, and signs. **Uncontrolled railroad crossings**, which are often found in rural areas, have neither warning signs nor signals. When you encounter an uncontrolled railroad crossing, treat it as if you were approaching a YIELD sign at a regular roadway intersection.

REALITY CHECK *Playing "Chicken" with a Train* _____

If you live in a rural area where weekend nights are slow and there is not much to do, you and your friends might be tempted to head for a remote stretch of railroad track to play an old and dangerous car game of "chicken." When a train approaches, you wait until the last minute before you hit the gas and try to cross the track only a few feet before the train hits your car. Sounds fun, right? The only problem is that in your desire to look cool in front of your friends you have forgotten that you are about to compete with a piece of metal weighing 6,000 times more than your car. Talk about the odds being against you! Playing chicken with another driver is stupid enough, but playing chicken with a train is certain suicide.

Approaching a Railroad Crossing

Follow these steps when approaching a railroad crossing:

1. Reduce your speed. Signal to any drivers behind you that you are slowing down by using several light taps on your brakes. Turn off the stereo, stop talking on the car phone or with passengers, turn off the air conditioning or heating, and lower the windows so that you can hear if any trains are coming. Do not assume that you

DRIVING TIPS *Railroad Crossings*

- Never rely on crossing signals or gates to warn you of an approaching train. Just like anything else, they can break. There is no substitute for slowing down, looking, and listening.

- Always wait for the vehicle in front of you to clear the tracks before you proceed. You do not want to be stuck behind a car or truck if it stalls in the middle of the crossing and exposes you to potential danger.

- Never pass another car, no matter how slow it is going, at a railroad crossing.

- Be extra careful when following motorcyclists or bicyclists across railroad tracks. They may lose traction on the slippery tracks or lose control if their tires get caught in the grooves of the rails. If the tracks cross the roadway at an angle, be prepared for the cyclist to swerve to cross the tracks at a right angle.

- When you are following buses, trucks, or vehicles carrying flammable or other hazardous cargo, always increase your following distance. Be prepared to stop behind them when they get to any railroad crossing, not just ones with warning signs and signals. Many jurisdictions have laws requiring that certain buses and trucks stop at all railroad crossings.

- Never stop your vehicle on railroad tracks. If your car stalls on the tracks and you cannot restart it immediately, get clear of your vehicle. Do not try to push it out of the way. Instead, seek immediate help from a towing service and/or local authorities.

- Trains travel at all hours of the day and night. It is never too late or too early for a train to be running, so always use the same care when checking for the presence of trains. Be especially careful at night at uncontrolled railroad crossings. If the train is moving slowly enough or if the weather limits your ability to see or hear, you may not realize that it is there.

- If you happen to cross railroad tracks frequently and are used to never seeing train traffic on them, do not assume that the tracks are never used just because they appear to be in bad condition and overgrown with weeds. Even if certain stretches of track are not often used, railroad companies may run maintenance trains down these tracks from time to time.

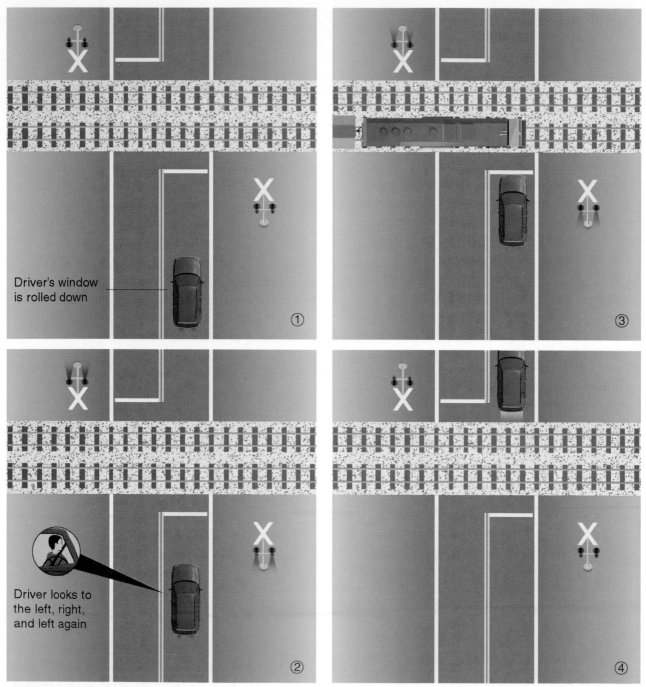

Figure 8–21 Approaching a railroad crossing

will be able to detect the distinctive *clackety-clack* sound of an approaching train, which is harder to hear on today's more smoothly welded rails. Never try to beat a train to a crossing, whether controlled or uncontrolled. Your ability to guess the speed of the train may not be as good as you think it is.

2. Determine whether any control is at the crossing and, if so, obey it. Never attempt to cross railroad tracks if warning lights are flashing or try to go around the ends of lowered crossing gates. If there is no control or the control is not operating, look and listen in both directions—left, right, and left again.

3. If you have determined that no train can be either seen or heard, move forward across the tracks. If a train is approaching, stop well away from the tracks. Laws vary by jurisdiction, but a minimum of 20 feet (6 m) is about right.

4. Once you have waited for a train to pass, never rush forward just as soon as it passes you. Take your time, not a foolish risk. Another train may be behind it or one may be coming from the opposite direction that you can neither see nor hear because of the presence of the first train. Once you are sure that no other trains are crossing at the same time, move across the tracks quickly and with enough momentum so that if your car stalls you will have enough motion to coast past the tracks and avoid a potentially dangerous situation.

factoid

More than half of all train–car collisions are caused by drivers trying to go around lowered gates or ignoring flashing lights.

WHO'S AT FAULT?

1. Taking a local shortcut to avoid traffic, Driver 2 had just made a quick right turn off 7th Avenue and was proceeding eastbound down the alley at approximately 30 miles per hour (50 km/h). Driver 1 had just finished a meal at the fast food establishment on the corner and was pulling into the alley. Driver 1's view was limited because of a high fence at the edge of the parking lot. Driver 2 ran into Driver 1's front end. **Who's at fault?**

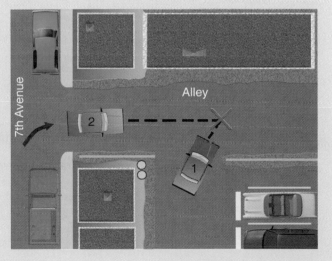

2. Driver 1 signaled in preparation for a left turn at the intersection. Upon seeing Driver 2 approaching the intersection, Driver 1 judged that he had just enough time to make it through the intersection and proceed rapidly with the turn. As Driver 1 was completing his turn, he sighted a bicyclist crossing his path from the left. Driver 1 was unable to stop in time and struck the bicyclist. **Who's at fault?**

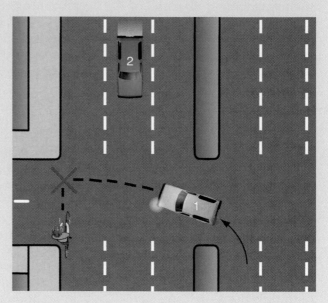

YOUR TURN

8–1 Intersections

1. What is the difference between a controlled and semicontrolled intersection?

2. What is the proper way to approach an uncontrolled intersection?

3. What are some of the hazards associated with alleys, traffic circles, and parking lots?

8–2 Right-of-Way

4. What is right-of-way?

5. What is the right-hand rule?

8–3 Railroad Crossings

6. What is the difference between a controlled and uncontrolled railroad crossing?

7. What is the proper procedure for crossing railroad tracks?

SELF-TEST

Multiple Choice

1. When approaching an intersection, always look:
   a. right, left, ahead, and right again.
   b. left, right, ahead, and left again.
   c. ahead, left, right, and left again.
   d. left, ahead, right, and left again.

2. A semicontrolled intersection is:
   a. an intersection with only STOP signs on all approaches.
   b. an intersection with both STOP and YIELD signs on all approaches.
   c. an intersection with traffic controls on one or more approaches, but not all approaches.
   d. an intersection with traffic controls on only two approaches.

3. When can you stop in an intersection?
   a. when directed to do so by a firefighter
   b. when you think it will help an emergency vehicle
   c. when all the signal lights are not working
   d. when you are waiting for a parking space on the other side

4. You should slow down when approaching a:
   a. "fresh" green light.
   b. green arrow.
   c. "stale" green light.
   d. flashing green light.

5. If you are in an intersection making a left turn when the light turns red, you should:
   a. back up.
   b. proceed cautiously when oncoming traffic has stopped.
   c. drive straight through the intersection.
   d. stay where you are and wait for the next green light.

Sentence Completion

1. You must give the right-of-way to any funeral procession or police-escorted _____ .
2. Never cross railroad tracks if warning lights are _____ .
3. A _____ sign means "give the right-of-way."
4. A _____ green light is one you have noticed has been green for a long time.
5. In some jurisdictions, you can be ticketed for _____ an intersection.

Matching

Match the concepts in Column A with examples of the concepts in Column B.

Column A	Column B
1. __ Clue to an approaching intersection	a. Two STOP signs
2. __ Controlled railroad crossing	b. Blind pedestrian
3. __ "Give the right-of-way"	c. YIELD sign
4. __ Uncontrolled intersection	d. Four STOP signs
5. __ Semicontrolled intersection	e. No signs or signals
6. __ Another way to say "traffic circle"	f. Crossbuck
7. __ Controlled intersection	g. Bus stop benches
8. __ Always has the right-of-way	h. Roundabout

Short Answer

1. What would you do if a pedestrian suddenly crossed in front of you outside of a crosswalk?

2. How many times do you have to stop as you move from an alley into a roadway?

3. When you give the right-of-way to another driver or to a pedestrian, what are you actually giving that person?

4. What does it mean to "roll" through a stop?

5. Who has the right-of-way in a traffic circle?

Critical Thinking

1. You approach an uncontrolled intersection at the same time as a vehicle to your right. You stop and let the vehicle to the right proceed. The other driver waves you to go first. Just then you hear a siren behind you. What should you do?

2. You are stopped at a red light at a fully controlled intersection and you are the first car behind the crosswalk line, in the right-hand lane. A teenage driver pulls up on your right in a souped-up hot rod, squeaking between your car and a row of parked cars along the curb. The teenager revs his engine as he pulls up even with you, shooting you a dirty look. He pulls up into the crosswalk, looking at the cross traffic's signal light. What should you do?

PROJECTS

1. Go out into your neighborhood and try to find an example of every type of intersection: a controlled intersection, a semicontrolled intersection, an uncontrolled intersection, a railroad crossing, an alley intersection, a traffic circle, and a parking lot intersection. Take a photograph or make a sketch of each one and show them to the rest of your class.

2. Find a stretch of railroad tracks in your community and see how many times roads and pedestrian paths intersect the tracks. Are all of these intersections controlled? Are some uncontrolled? Share the results of your investigation with your class.

Turning

Turning is more than simply changing direction. Whether you turn left, right, or completely around, you move in an instant from one flow of traffic to another. Maintaining peak alertness and scanning constantly are essential to safely executing a turn. You must visualize the turn you are about to make, plan your entry point, control the steering wheel and speed of your car, and maintain a comfortable cushion of space between yourself and other vehicles or pedestrians that can come at you from many different directions.

Upon completion of this chapter, you should be able to:

9-1 Turning Basics

1. Understand the difference between a protected and unprotected turn.
2. Understand the proper way to prepare for a left or right turn.

9-2 Left Turns

3. Understand the proper way to execute a left turn.
4. Describe some of the special dangers of left turns.

9-3 Right Turns

5. Understand the proper way to execute a right turn.
6. Describe some of the special dangers of right turns.

9-4 Reversing Your Direction

7. Understand the proper way to execute a two-point turn.
8. Understand the proper way to execute a U-turn.
9. Understand the proper way to execute a three-point turn.

KEY TERMS

protected turn	unprotected turn	U-turn
fully protected turn	two-point turn	three-point turn
semiprotected turn		

Figure 9–1 At some intersections, you may turn only when you have a green arrow.

9–1 TURNING BASICS

A **protected turn** is one made from a turn lane posted with signs, road marked with arrows, and accompanied by a traffic signal arrow. A green arrow or special green light for your lane allows you to turn while traffic from the oncoming lane(s) is halted with a red light. If the signal allows you to make a turn only when you have a green arrow (the green arrow turns to a red arrow or red light), it is a **fully protected turn**.

A **semiprotected turn** is one made from a turn lane but *not* accompanied by a special traffic signal light that directs your turn with a green arrow or a special green light. You are allowed to make such a turn either while you have a regular solid green light or when there is no light and a sufficient gap in traffic occurs.

Figure 9–2 When making a semiprotected turn, you may turn on a solid green light once a sufficient gap in traffic exists.

Figure 9–3 Be especially careful turning at intersections without arrows or turn lanes.

An **unprotected turn** is one not made from a turn lane at an intersection and where there are no arrows—whether designated by a signpost or road markings, or signaled by a traffic control—to guide your turn. It means that you have to make a turn either from the far-right lane (right turn) or from the far-left lane (left turn).

Preparing for a left or right turn and positioning your vehicle in the correct lane should begin approximately 300 feet (90 m) before you reach the intersection where you intend to make the turn. Scan the roadway in front of you, to your sides, and to your rear. Your eyes should be roving in all directions to make sure that no hazards or obstacles will interfere with

Figure 9–4 By properly scanning before making your turn, you can avoid this kind of situation.

DRIVING TIPS   *Avoid the "Pickle"* _____

Imagine a base runner in baseball who has been caught trying to steal a base halfway between two opposing players moving toward him to tag him out. If you do not scan the sidewalk far enough up and down the side of the street you are about to turn across, you may find yourself in the same jam. Right in the middle of your turn, a fast-moving pedestrian—often a skateboarder, rollerblader, or jogger—crosses the street right in front of you, leaving you nowhere to go! Avoid getting caught in this "pickle" by scanning the sidewalk to either side of the intersection for at least half a block before starting your turn.

your turn. In particular, be on the lookout for bicyclists, pedestrians, and other vehicles in your intended path. Make sure that you first look to see whether there are any signs that restrict or otherwise prohibit the making of your turn. If there is a light at the intersection, make sure that it allows you to make the turn you intend.

Once you have scanned the roadway, select the correct lane and move into it, at the same time reducing your speed. The sharper the turn, the slower you should be driving. Tap your brake pedal to warn vehicles behind you. If you are making a left turn, move just to the right of the center line or into another designated left-turning lane on the left side of the roadway. If you are on a one-way street, move just to the right of the left curbside of the far-left lane. If you are making a right turn, move to the right side of the far-right lane.

Most jurisdictions require you to signal at least 100 feet (30 m) before the turn. A good rule of thumb is to signal a turn 200 feet (60 m) before an intersection in urban areas and 300 feet (90 m) before an intersection in rural areas. Remember, however, not to signal your turning intentions too soon. If another turn is possible before you reach your intended turn, you will confuse the drivers behind you. Keep your signal on throughout the time that you are preparing for and making a turn.

Over time, you will learn to judge when to begin a turn. Your speed, the width of the traffic lanes, the turning radius of your car, and the presence of obstacles such as center dividers and parked cars are all factors to consider. If you start a turn too early or late, you may drift into an adjoining lane of traffic. As you proceed through a turn, keep your speed constant. Wait until you begin to enter the new lane before gradually accelerating to match the speed of traffic.

9–2   LEFT TURNS

Left turns can be one of the most hazardous maneuvers a driver can perform. For new drivers, judging

bumper sticker sightings

DON'T WORRY ABOUT WORLD PEACE. WORRY ABOUT YOUR TURN SIGNAL.

Figure 9–5 Wait until you have a clear view of oncoming traffic before turning left.

make the turn if you cannot see oncoming traffic clearly. Wait until the light switches to red and cars clear the intersection to give you a clear view before making your left turn.

Do not forget to watch out for drivers who may race through a yellow or red light at the last second, and do not be pressured into turning left if you are not ready. Remember that *you* must decide when it is safe to proceed. If drivers to your rear honk at you because they think you are taking too long or are waiting for too large a gap to turn, ignore them. Do not risk a collision because of someone else's impatience.

When you move into an intersection to begin a left turn, you may face a driver in an oncoming car whose real turning intentions are unclear. For example, the other driver may have activated the left-turn signal but now appears to be moving to the right to

when to cross in front of multiple lanes of oncoming traffic can be a nerve-rattling experience. Often your view of oncoming traffic is completely or partially blocked by a line of cars in opposing traffic waiting to make a left turn directly in front of you or by a large vehicle ahead of you. Do not

Figure 9–7 When turning left, make sure that you leave enough room for oncoming traffic to turn left as well.

proceed straight. Or the driver may not have activated a signal but has slowed and appears ready to make a rapid left. To avoid any possible confusion, leave enough space for both vehicles to turn in their respective directions.

Driver miscommunication is a major factor in many crashes. Motorists unfamiliar with an area or in a hurry can become indecisive and frustrated, changing their minds about a turn at the last second. They may be trapped in a lane that has changed unexpectedly from a regular traffic lane into a left-turn-only lane when they want to go straight. Whatever the reason, *never second-guess other drivers' intentions.* Wait until they make their move, and then proceed.

Types of Left Turns

The steps for making a left turn depend on what type of roadway you are turning from and what type of roadway you are turning onto. When turning left from a two-way street onto another two-way street, always turn from the lane proceeding in your direction that is closest to the middle of the street unless there is a road marking, sign, or signal that allows you to turn from one or more adjoining lanes. If there is only one lane from which to turn left, complete your turn in the left lane closest to the dividing line of the roadway you are turning onto. If no traffic signal arrow is controlling your turn, you should move slightly into the intersection to prepare for opposing traffic to

clear, allowing you to make your left.

On two-way streets, if there is only one lane from which to turn left follow these steps (see Figure 9–8):

1. Allow for a gap in oncoming traffic of at least 10 seconds on city streets and at least 15 seconds on higher-speed roadways.

2. Move into the intersection about 10 feet (3 m) from the center. Remember to first give the right-of-way to pedestrians or other vehicles in the intersection. Keep your wheels straight so that in case you get rear-ended you will not be pushed into oncoming traffic. Check oncoming traffic lanes to your left. Remember, a left-turning driver must give the right-of-way to any and all oncoming traffic and to pedestrians in the path of the turn.

3. Gaze down the path of your intended left turn as it curves into the lane just to the right of the center line of the cross-traffic roadway you are turning onto. Begin turning the steering wheel as you slowly accelerate. Follow the curvature of the imaginary turn you visualized seconds earlier, ending your turn in the far-left lane of the cross-traffic roadway.

4. Finish the turn by correcting your steering wheel to proceed straight in the far-left lane of the cross-traffic roadway. Make sure that your turn signal is shut off.

When turning left from a one-way street to another one-way

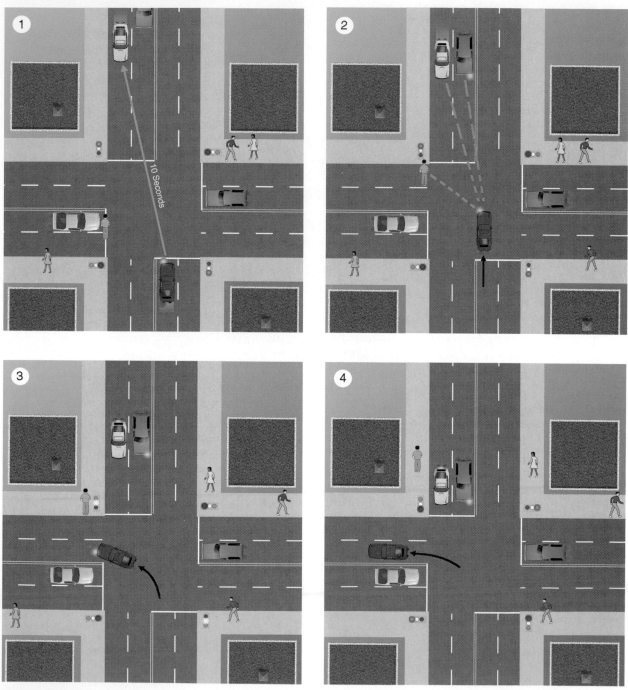

Figure 9–8 Making a left turn

street or two-way street, always begin your turn from the far-left lane and complete your turn in the far-left lane of the road you are entering. Most jurisdictions permit you to make a left turn from a one-way street to another one-way street on a red light. If you are turning onto another one-way street, check for bicyclists who may be riding on your *left* side because bicyclists are usually permitted to ride on either side of a one-way street.

Left-Turn Lanes

Often a left-turn lane is painted out of a center turn lane or a restricted central portion of the roadway, such as a median or a painted or "virtual" island. These left-turn lanes have specified entry points usually just before the space allowed for the actual turn. Solid double-yellow lines often immediately precede the designated entry point.

Some drivers illegally cross solid double-yellow lines—either into the opposite direction of traffic or outside of the designated roadway—to avoid having to wait to enter a turn lane. This can result in a collision if another driver who has waited correctly for the opportunity to move into the left lane merges without checking traffic on his or her left.

Always look in your rearview and sideview mirrors, and turn your head to make sure that you can enter the left-turn lane safely. Assume that the lane change you are making will involve traffic in

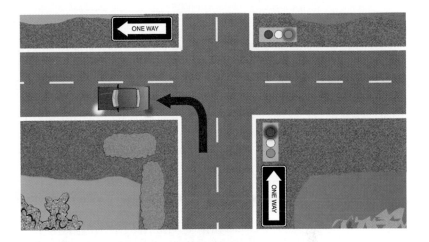

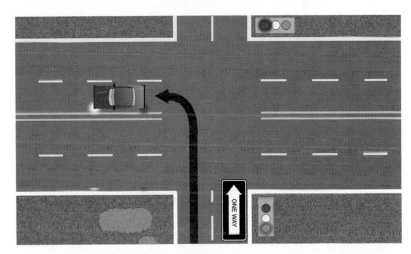

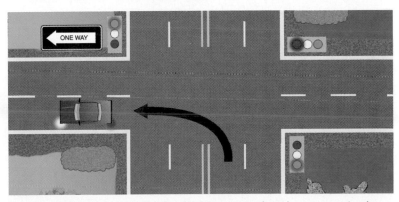

Figure 9–9 When turning left, always start and end your turn in the far-left lane.

Wild Wheels

Figure 9–10 What is the name of this 1961 vehicle, whose driver had to use a joystick rather than a steering wheel to make turns?

the lane next to you. Never enter a left-turn lane early by entering a restricted zone or a lane of opposing traffic. You risk a serious crash for which you will be completely at fault.

Just as dangerous as those drivers who enter a turn lane too early are those who enter it too late. This happens when a driver decides to make a left turn after already missing the opening to the turn lane and has to cross the solid white line separating the turn lane from the through-traffic lanes. This kind of last-second maneuver is both dangerous and illegal. Odds are, there will be a driver right behind you already in the turn lane preparing to turn, and you will drive right into him or her or cause a crash trying to avoid hitting that car. Instead of risking a collision, turn at the next intersection and retrace your steps.

Center Turn Lanes

If you wish to make a left turn on a street that has a center turn lane, you may only do so from this lane. Move completely within the lane so that through traffic is not blocked. Do not turn into the lane too early, or you may find yourself facing a left-turning vehicle moving in the opposite direction that is in the way of you making your left. If you get caught in this situation, it is always best to let the other driver go first.

Center turn lanes are also a convenient way to make a left turn from a driveway or side street onto a main road. For example, if

Figure 9–11 You can only make left turns from a center turn lane.

GENERAL GEORGE S. PATTON, JR.

United States General George S. Patton, Jr., performed military miracle after miracle in North Africa and Europe during World War II. "Old Blood and Guts," as the general was known by his soldiers, was famous for taking great chances with his personal safety in the front lines of battle. Ironically, rather than dying gloriously in combat, General Patton was killed several months after the war ended in Europe in a slow-speed automobile crash. The sedan in which he was traveling collided into a truck making a left turn into a driveway. The speed of the truck was estimated at approximately 10 miles per hour (15 km/h), and the speed of the car General Patton was riding in was estimated at less than 30 miles per hour (50 km/h). Patton's tragic death illustrates the fact that a poorly planned turn can kill even at slow speeds.

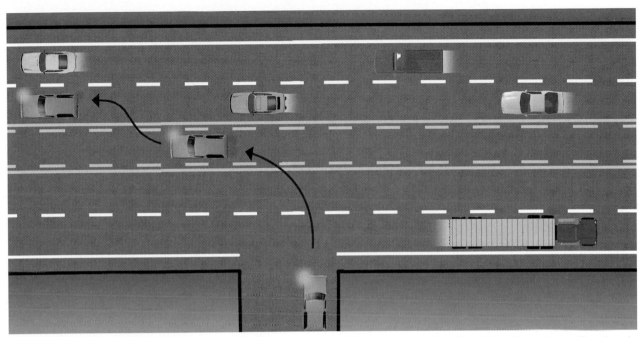

Figure 9–12 Vehicles turning onto a center turn lane from a side street must give the right-of-way to traffic already on the road.

there is a lot of traffic or it is hard to see, it may be difficult for you to make the complete left turn in one go. First, turn from the driveway or side street into the center turn lane. Second, let vehicles on the roadway going in your direction pass and then enter the far-left traffic lane. Remember that drivers already on the road have the right-of-way and will be traveling at relatively high speeds, so use extra caution before merging. If you are driving on a road with a center turn lane and *not* turning left, watch out for other vehicles making this maneuver that may cut in front of you.

"Stealing" Left Turns

Motorists making semiprotected or unprotected left turns some-times have to wait to complete their turn until the light turns yellow or even red and opposing traffic has stopped. In these situations, only the one or two drivers that have partly entered the intersection can legally turn left at each signal sequence. However, many drivers are too impatient to wait for a green light when they are second or third in line to turn. They try to "steal" left turns at intersections behind other cars *after* the light has turned red. By the time these drivers are completing their left turns, the light has been red for several seconds and cross traffic is already well within the intersection.

Stealing a left turn is both illegal and extremely dangerous. If you are stuck in heavy traffic, remember that *three rights make a*

USING SAFE   *"Stealing" Left Turns*

You are stopped at a red light at an intersection. Two left-turning drivers in oncoming traffic have just completed their turns, and your light changes to green. You accelerate into the intersection and nearly collide with a third driver trying to "steal" a left across your path. This is an all-too-common situation that you can avoid by using the SAFE process. While waiting at the light, use the opportunity to thoroughly *scan* the intersection. Note whether left turns are protected or semiprotected and if there are DO NOT BLOCK INTERSECTION signs. *Assess* whether there are any drivers who may try to sneak a left. Is traffic heavy, causing impatient drivers to take risks rather than wait for the next light? Are oncoming drivers queued up in the left-turn lane, displaying signs of nervousness, anxiety, or frustration? Are they creeping forward into the intersection? Are drivers in lanes adjoining yours showing signs of racing into the intersection, leading to a collision that could spill over into you lane? *Find* an "out" by checking the lanes on either side of you and the distance between your vehicle and oncoming left-turn drivers. *Execute* your decision to avoid a potential crash by starting your forward movement slowly and being prepared to tap your brakes to communicate the danger to drivers behind you.

left. You can get to the same point of your intended left turn by going up a block, making a right, turning right at the next intersection, and then making a right to get back to the original street where you intended to make your left. This may sound like a lot of trouble, but in the end, you will actually get where you want to go faster and more safely.

Heavy Traffic Situations

Turning left in the middle of a block to enter a driveway or alley in heavy traffic can be tricky. Because there are no intersection lines for the opposite traffic to stop behind, there is nothing to help create a gap in traffic to allow you to turn left. This situation calls for using the "Four C's": *crawling, communication, confidence,* and *caution.*

DRIVING TIPS   *Hesitant Left-Turners*

Everyone is familiar with the driver who is afraid to move toward the center of an intersection to prepare for a left turn. In heavy traffic, this failure to "move up" will probably mean that you will miss your chance to turn left, making you wait for the next green light. Be patient. Whatever you do, do not pressure the driver to move by honking your horn, flashing your lights, or gesturing in any way. It is not worth scaring the driver and causing a collision. Wait until you can safely advance into the intersection and then make your turn.

> ## AUTO ACCESSORIES *Steering Wheel Grip* _____
>
> You may have experienced problems turning your vehicle on a hot day because sweat on your hands causes your steering wheel to slip. To correct this problem, try putting on a vinyl or leather steering wheel grip. This accessory is inexpensive, easy to install, and makes turning safer. This type of grip is usually standard on expensive cars, so it will also give your vehicle a touch of class!

Before you turn your wheels to move across the stream of on-coming traffic, make sure that the traffic is coming to a gradual halt, or *crawling*, at less than 5 miles per hour (8 km/h), usually in response to a red light or STOP sign further down the road.

Once you have determined that the traffic is moving slowly enough for the other drivers to notice you, get the attention of the driver in the lane closest to you by means of hand signals. If you have to, roll down your window to make your arm motion more visible to other drivers. You may also use a light tap on your horn or a quick flash of your headlights to *communicate* your desire to cross in front of on-coming drivers.

If there is more than one lane of traffic to cross, the first driver who agrees to let you in may help you communicate with other drivers in lanes to his or her right. However, assume that drivers in lanes farther from you do not see you at all. Creep forward just enough so that your bumper is visible and double-check that drivers in these other lanes are stopping.

Unfortunately, some drivers will ignore you or intentionally close any gap in traffic and make it impossible for you to make a left. In these cases, do not attempt to force the gap. If you muscle your way in by sticking part of your car in front of an un-cooperative driver, you will either create gridlock when traffic starts to move again or confuse other drivers into dangerous evasive maneuvers that may cause a crash. It is better to take a deep breath and wait it out. Chances are, the next person will let you make your left and you will be safely on your way!

Once you have established eye contact with the driver in the lane closest to you and have gotten his or her agreement to go through, proceed with *confidence* across the lane. Proceed across while exercising constant *caution*. Because these lanes of traffic are typically slowing as well, it is usually not a problem to get other motorists to stop for you, especially because they realize you have already committed yourself to the turn.

9–3   RIGHT TURNS

Making a right turn is less complicated than making a left. Unless otherwise indicated with pavement markings or street signs at the intersection, a right turn always begins with your vehicle in the far-right lane, the one nearest the curb. As you slow down to prepare for your right turn, remember to tap your brakes to indicate to drivers behind you that you are preparing to turn. Keep in mind that through traffic may approach from the rear at high speeds, especially if the signal is turning yellow.

The steps for making a right turn are the same whether you are turning onto a one-way or a two-way street (see Figure 9–13).

1. After ensuring that the intersection is clear of pedestrians, find a gap in the cross traffic to your left. Allow for a gap in the traffic of 8 seconds on city streets and at least 10 seconds on higher-speed roadways.

2. Align your tires up to the point of the curb where it curves or comes to a right angle with the roadway of cross traffic. Just before turning, scan the intersection again for pedestrians that may have entered the crosswalk since the last time you looked.

3. Gaze around the curb along your path of turning and begin turning the steering wheel as you slowly accelerate. Keep in mind that your right rear wheel will have a smaller turning radius than your right front wheel. You will need to compensate for this as you turn your vehicle to avoid striking the curb. Follow the curvature of the curb as you visualized it seconds earlier, staying in the right lane of the cross-traffic roadway.

4. Finish the turn by correcting your steering wheel to proceed straight in the far-right lane of the cross-traffic roadway. Make sure that your turn signal is shut off.

Danger on Your Right Side

As you move into the right-hand side of the far-right lane before your upcoming turn, look for any bicyclists that might be riding either on the side of the road or in a designated bicycle lane that you will need to enter to make your right. Before moving into the bike lane, make sure that the area is clear of bicyclists. If any are nearby, take care that they know your intentions. Signal early and alert them of your presence, if necessary using a friendly tap of your horn.

Be aware that motorcyclists may be in your right-hand-side

REALITY CHECK   *Do Not Cut Corners* _____

Most jurisdictions prohibit persons from driving on or through any private property, road, or driveway to avoid obeying traffic rules or traffic control devices. Keep this in mind the next time you are tempted to cut through a gas station to avoid waiting in line to make your right turn.

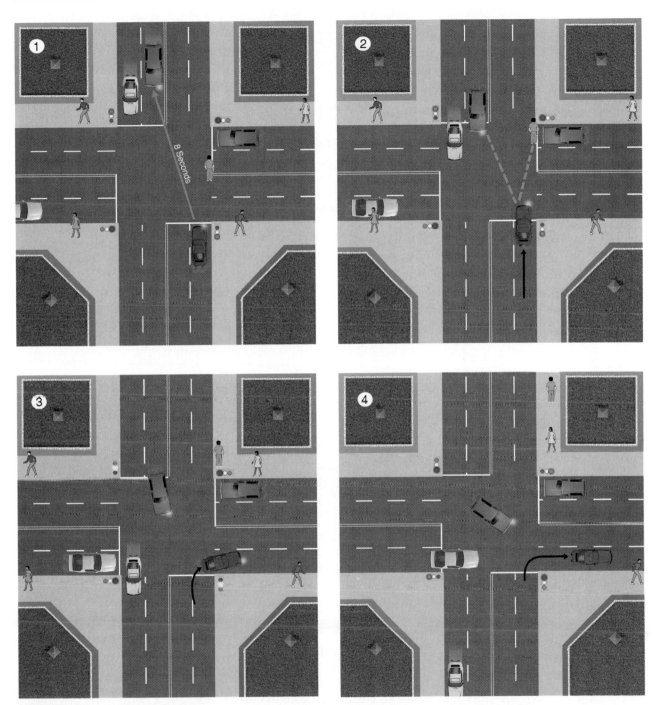

Figure 9–13 Making a right turn

Figure 9–14 Be careful making right turns on roads with bike lanes.

blind spot or accelerating to pass you on the right just when you are about to prepare for a right turn. Turn your head and look back to make sure that your blind spot is vacant. Do not rely on your rearview or sideview mirrors.

Danger on Your Left Side

Do not swing wide to your left to make a right turn. You will get in the way of traffic in the lane to your left, which can either be on-coming traffic or traffic going in your direction depending on the type of road you are on. If the type of vehicle you are driving forces you to swing wide left to clear the right-hand curb—for example, if you are towing a trailer or are in a recreational vehicle—signal your intentions to other drivers by using your hazard lights and hand signals.

Figure 9–15 Large vehicles must often swing left first to turn right.

DRIVING TIPS *Follow Your "Blocker"*

At times when you are preparing to make a right turn, your view of cross traffic from the left may be obstructed by a large parked vehicle. In this case, you can use a "blocker," just as a running back in football uses blockers to clear the way. Your "blocker" is a driver turning left from the cross street onto your street because that driver will have a better view of oncoming traffic than you do. When he or she executes the left turn, the path of cross traffic will be blocked, allowing you to execute your right turn at the same time.

Figure 9–16 When making a right turn at an intersection, always look for pedestrians on *both* streets.

Danger Ahead

Remember that you must first stop at the stop line or nearer crosswalk line before turning right. Look for pedestrians coming from both directions. As you turn, slow down for any pedestrian traffic on the crosswalk of the street you are turning onto that may dart onto the road from your right side. Also, look for pedestrians who are crossing the street opposite from you on your left.

Do not forget about oncoming traffic cars that will be turning left into either your lane or a nearby lane. Use courtesy and common sense to determine which car should end up in which lane. If both of you will be turning into only one open lane, always be ready to give the right-of-way to the left-turning driver. He or she is cutting across oncoming traffic and may need to accelerate into the lane to avoid getting broadsided by another vehicle.

Right Turns on a Red Light

Turning right on a red light is legal in every jurisdiction in North America except New York City and Quebec unless there is a sign specifically prohibiting it. Where it is allowed, always double-check for pedestrians, bicyclists, and any vehicles that might be either crossing the intersection on their green or making a left turn into your intended lane of travel. Remember that both pedestrians and vehicles approaching the intersection or in

Figure 9–17 When turning right, always give the right-of-way to left-turning drivers.

the intersection have the right-of-way over you. Even if a right turn on a red light is legal, you are not required to make the right if you feel safer waiting until the light is green. If you get behind someone who will not make the right on a red, be patient and wait for him or her to turn right when the light turns green.

9–4 REVERSING YOUR DIRECTION

Sometimes it is necessary to reverse the direction in which you are going. For example, if you missed a street that you needed to turn onto and there is no way to go around the block to get to it, you may have to turn around and go back in the opposite way. Because you will have to cross or back into one or more lanes of

traffic, this can be dangerous. In many places and situations, it is illegal. Depending on the circumstances and road conditions, there are several ways to turn around.

Two-Point Turns

Two-point turns require the use of a driveway either on your side of the roadway or on the opposite side. Each has important safety implications that you must keep in mind.

Reverse, Then Forward

It is safest to execute a two-point turn from a driveway on your side (the right side) of the street (see Figure 9–18).

1. Reduce your speed as you approach the driveway, tapping lightly on your brake pedal to warn drivers behind you that

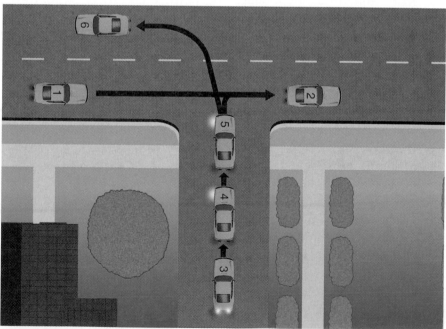

Figure 9–18 Making a two-point turn: "reverse, then forward"

you are slowing down. Make sure that the driveway is clear of vehicles, pedestrians, and other obstacles.

2. Go past the driveway, lining up your rear bumper with one end of the driveway and staying within a few feet (about 1 m) of the right-hand curb. Check again for any pedestrians or vehicles coming from behind you that may interrupt your maneuver.

3. Switch gears to REVERSE, turn your body to look out the rear and side windows, and slowly begin backing into the driveway, turning your steering wheel to the right. Be sure to straighten out the steering wheel as you complete your turn backwards into the driveway. Stop the car once you are fully in the driveway.

4. Switch gears to DRIVE or FIRST, and signal a left turn. Creep slowly up to the sidewalk and stop. Make sure that no pedestrians are in your path.

5. Creep up to where the driveway meets the street and stop.

6. Scan traffic in both directions, and when you have a large enough opening to allow you to smoothly accelerate into the lane, make your left turn and rejoin traffic in the direction opposite that which you were going moments earlier. Make sure that your turn signal is shut off.

Forward, Then Reverse

It is best to use a driveway on the opposite side of the street to reverse your direction if you want to go forward first, then reverse (see Figure 9–19).

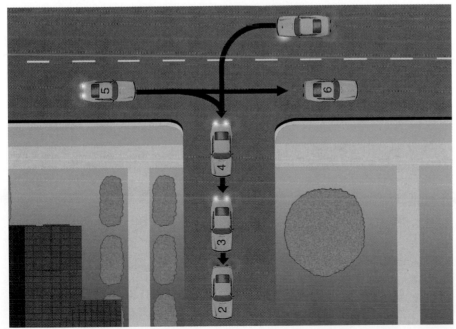

Figure 9–19 Making a two-point turn: "forward, then reverse"

1. Choose a driveway with a clear view of traffic in both directions. Make sure that no obstacles, such as parked cars, are on the road very close to the driveway that may block your view. Move into the far-left lane of traffic going in your direction. Reduce your speed, tapping lightly on your brake pedal to warn drivers behind you that you are slowing down. Signal a left turn after making sure that the driveway is clear of vehicles, pedestrians, and other obstacles.

2. Turn into the driveway, straightening the wheel out as you fully enter it. Come to a complete stop. Make sure that your turn signal is shut off.

3. Shift your transmission into REVERSE, and go *very slowly* out of the driveway. Look over your shoulder and use your rearview and sideview mirrors to make sure that no pedestrians are in the way or vehicles are approaching from your right. Stop first before reaching the sidewalk.

4. If clear of pedestrians, proceed across the sidewalk and stop a second time before reaching the roadway.

5. When you are sure that traffic is clear in the far-right lane of oncoming traffic going in the direction you want to go in, sharply turn the steering wheel while reversing slowly out into the roadway. Look over your shoulder *the whole time*. This will mean steering the wheel with one hand while your other is supported against the back of the passenger seat, a maneuver you should practice many times before actually using it on the streets. Do not try to back across one lane of traffic into another lane farther away from the curb.

6. As you enter into the far-right lane of travel, straighten out your steering wheel and come to a stop, switching gears to DRIVE or FIRST, and proceed forward.

It is possible to pull forward into a driveway on the right side and then back into the opposite lane to reverse your direction. However, this is extremely dangerous and should be avoided at all costs. You will be backing up across *two* lanes of traffic, a risky move even in the quietest residential areas.

U-Turns

When a vehicle makes a **U-turn**, it actually traces a path in the shape of a large "U." U-turns are another way to reverse your direction of travel. They are often dangerous, and in many situations and places, they are illegal, so a good rule of thumb is to avoid performing a U-turn if you are unsure whether it is allowed (see Figure 9–21).

1. The first step in making any U-turn is to check for any signs that tell you U-turns are not permitted. If you do not see any signs, then think about where you are. Unlike

Figure 9–20 Before making a U-turn, ask yourself if it is legal where you are.

other kinds of turns, whether a U-turn is legal or not can depend on your location. For example, U-turns are illegal in most business districts, in school zones, and in front of fire stations. Often no signs

will be present to indicate specifically whether a U-turn is legal or illegal. It is up to *you* to know the difference.

2. Allow at least 400 feet (120 m) visibility in both directions. Make sure that nothing is blocking your view, such as buildings, blind curves, and hills, and that you have enough time and space to complete the turn on the roadway. Consider the turning radius of your vehicle and get over as far to the right as necessary. Vehicles with long wheelbases, such as trucks and sedans, need more room to maneuver. Allow yourself a gap in traffic of at least 20 to 30 seconds if you are unsure whether your vehicle can fully make the U turn on a narrow road. Check traffic in

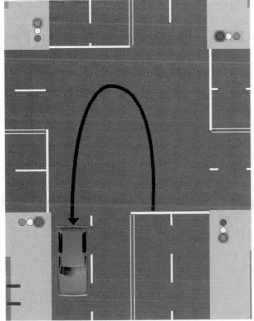

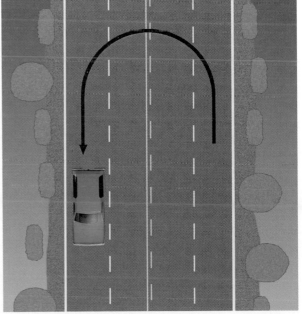

Figure 9–21 Make sure that you have plenty of room and time to make a U-turn.

ⓐuto slang

Smooth-talking drivers do not "make a U-turn," they "pull a U-ee."

both directions and signal a left turn.

3. Turn the wheel to the left completely, moving forward at a slow speed. If it looks like you can make the turn without hitting the other curb or a parked car, complete the turn until your vehicle is facing in the opposite direction. As you complete the turn, straighten out your wheels and proceed forward. Make sure that your turn signal is shut off.

Three-Point Turns

If no driveways are available for you to make a two-point turn and circumstances prevent you from making a U-turn, you can make a **three-point turn** to reverse your direction. This is a difficult maneuver and should not be tried on the streets until you have practiced it a lot in a safe area away from traffic, like an empty parking lot. You should limit your use of this maneuver to rural roads, residential areas with no driveways, dead-end streets, and emergencies (see Figure 9–22).

1. Make sure that no traffic is approaching you either from the rear or from the front for at least 500 feet (150 m). Stop your vehicle close to the right curb. Double-check that traffic is clear of other vehicles and pedestrians in both directions.

2. Activate your left-turn signal, and turn your car's steering wheel sharply to the left while you start going forward until you get into the opposite lane of traffic (at an angle). Ap-

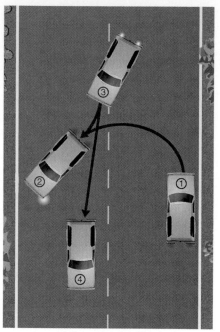

Figure 9–22 Making a three-point turn

proach the opposite curb within a few feet (about 1 m). Stop your car and turn the steering wheel to the right. Make sure that your turn signal is shut off.

3. Check for traffic again by looking over your shoulder. If it is still clear, put your transmission into REVERSE, and back up into the far-right lane of traffic going in your new direction of travel. Come to a complete stop.

4. Switch gears to DRIVE or FIRST and proceed forward.

Other Ways to Reverse Your Direction

The easiest and safest way to reverse your direction is to drive around the block. If all the roads are low-speed roads or roads with signal lights, make three rights and a left. If you are on a high-speed roadway intersected by smaller streets with no signal lights, make three lefts and a right. It is always easier to make your left off of a high-speed street onto a side street if there is no signal light than onto a high-speed road from a side street.

Another alternative is to turn around within the "alleys" of a large parking lot, making sure to slow your speed as you move across the lot. Watch out for people getting in and out of cars and drivers that may be busy trying to park. Exit the lot by making a turn in the reverse direction from which you were originally going.

WHO'S AT FAULT?

1. Driver 1 was proceeding northbound on Avenue A and turning right (eastbound) on a green signal at the intersection. Driver 2 was southbound on Avenue A and had pulled into the intersection on the green light to make a left when oncoming traffic was clear. Driver 2 made her left moving toward the lane closest to the curb. In doing so she struck Driver 1, who was making a right and attempting to move immediately into the same lane. *Who's at fault?*

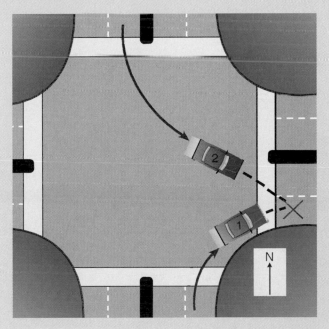

2. All vehicles were stopped at red lights waiting to make left turns or proceed straight once the lights turned green. Lane A is a left-turn-only lane. Lane B is a left-turn or straight lane. When the left-turn green arrow activated, Driver 4 followed Driver 5 in making a controlled left turn from eastbound Central Boulevard onto northbound Third Street. Driver 6 followed Driver 3 in making a controlled left turn from westbound Central onto southbound Third.

Driver 2 was in Lane B waiting for the green light to proceed straight through the intersection on Central. Driver 1, wishing to make a left turn as permitted in Lane B, honked his horn at Driver 2, who could not legally proceed straight. Driver 2, being unfamiliar with the intersection, became nervous and darted forward to clear the way for Driver 1, at which time he was struck on the right front by Driver 3. **Who's at fault?**

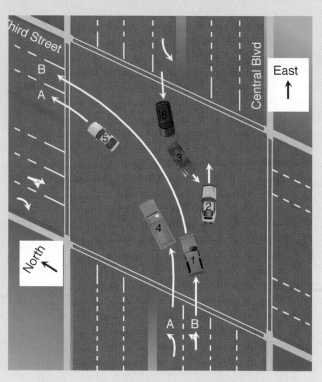

YOUR TURN

9–1 *Turning Basics*

1. What is the difference between a protected and unprotected turn?
2. What is the proper way to prepare for a left or right turn?

9–2 *Left Turns*

3. What is the proper way to execute a left turn?
4. What are some of the special dangers of left turns?

9–3 *Right Turns*

5. What is the proper way to execute a right turn?
6. What are some of the special dangers of right turns?

9–4 *Reversing Your Direction*

7. What is the proper way to execute a two-point turn?
8. What is the proper way to execute a U-turn?
9. What is the proper way to execute a three-point turn?

SELF-TEST

Multiple Choice

1. A semiprotected turn is made:
   a. from a turn lane but with no special traffic signal.
   b. from any lane but with a special traffic signal.
   c. with help from a traffic officer.
   d. from a turn lane with a special traffic signal.

2. You should signal a turn in a city at least _____ from the intersection.
   a. 100 feet (30 m)
   b. 200 feet (60 m)
   c. 300 feet (90 m)
   d. 500 feet (150 m)

3. You should signal a turn in a rural area at least _____ from the intersection.
   a. 100 feet (30 m)
   b. 200 feet (60 m)
   c. 300 feet (90 m)
   d. 500 feet (150 m)

4. Making a left turn in heavy traffic calls for:
   a. communication, consideration, caution, and coexistence.
   b. crawling, caution, charisma, and communication.
   c. consideration, coexistence, crawling, and cunning.
   d. confidence, caution, crawling, and communication.

5. "Forward, then reverse" is a technique used to make a:
   a. two-point turn on the right side of the street.   c. two-point turn on the left side of the street.
   b. U-turn.   d. three-point turn.

Sentence Completion

1. When turning left, move about 10 feet (3 m) from the _____ of the intersection.

2. Most jurisdictions permit turning left on a red light from a one-way street to a _____ .

3. If you enter a _____ too early, another left-turning driver may block your way.

4. Turning _____ on a red light is legal in every jurisdiction in North America except New York City and Quebec.

5. It is safest to execute a two-point turn from the _____ side of the street.

Matching

Match the concepts in Column A with examples of the concepts in Column B.

Column A	Column B
1. __ Danger ahead for a right turn	a. Reverse, then forward
2. __ Two-point turn	b. Illegal in most business districts
3. __ Left turn on a city street	c. Drive around the block
4. __ Entering a turn lane too soon	d. Narrow dead-end streets
5. __ Answer to a difficult left turn	e. Gap of 10 seconds
6. __ Three-point turn	f. Crossing solid double-yellow lines
7. __ U-turn	g. Three rights make a left
8. __ Safest way to reverse direction	h. Pedestrians

Short Answer

1. What is a fully protected turn?
2. What are the dangers of entering a turn lane too late?
3. Three-point turns should be limited to which situations?
4. Which lane do you turn into when turning left or right?
5. What does it mean to "steal" a left turn at a red light?

Critical Thinking

1. You are lost on a narrow street in an unfamiliar industrial zone with moderate traffic at night. The area is not well lit and it is hard to tell where the few side streets lead to, if they lead anywhere at all. You need to reverse your direction and head back the way you came. What should you do?

2. You are preparing to make a left turn in a high-traffic business area and have properly waited for a sufficient gap in oncoming traffic to start your left. You commit to the maneuver, beginning to cross before more oncoming traffic approaches, when at the last second a rollerblader comes out of nowhere, zipping across the crosswalk at a blinding speed directly in your path of travel. Oncoming traffic does not appear to be slowing down for you and may soon broadside your vehicle. What should you do?

PROJECTS

1. Knowing the turning radius of your vehicle is an important factor in making a U-turn. Go to an empty parking lot and empty a pail of water on the ground. Drive through the water and turn as sharply to the left as you can. When you have made a complete U-turn, stop and measure your vehicle's turning radius with measuring tape. Compare your results with those of others in your class. List the vehicles in order from shortest to longest turning radius to see how they vary by type of vehicle.

2. Take a clipboard, paper, and pen out to a busy intersection in your town and note how many drivers try to "steal" a left turn. Share your results in class. Appoint a representative to discuss your findings with the traffic section of your local police department and see if they are aware of the size of the problem.

The Driving Environment

City Driving

On city streets, you face a variety of complex traffic situations. Intersections occur frequently, pedestrians and bicyclists cross your path from every direction, and business advertisements compete with traffic controls for your attention. Parked cars, buses and delivery trucks, crowds of people, and buildings block your surrounding view. Maneuvering space and escape routes are limited. Urban parking spaces can be hard to find and are typically more dangerous to enter and exit. Stop-and-go traffic, detours for road repairs, and turning restrictions can make city driving frustrating.

Upon completion of this chapter, you should be able to:

10–1 *The City Driving Environment*

1. Understand the importance of scanning ahead and reducing speed in city driving.
2. Understand the difference between riding and covering the brake.

10–2 *Lane Positioning*

3. Understand why lane positioning is important in city driving.
4. Understand the proper way to change lanes.
5. Describe the advantages and risks of using one-way streets.

10–3 *Passing*

6. Understand the proper way to pass another vehicle.
7. Describe some of the dangers of passing on urban roadways.

KEY TERMS

covering the brake
riding the brake
gridlock

one-way street
pass

10–1 THE CITY DRIVING ENVIRONMENT

All of the driving you do in cities will be in either residential districts or business districts. Although the rules and regulations of city driving are the same for both types of districts, different risks are associated with each.

Typically, the streets in residential districts are not very congested, the pace of traffic is slow, and there are fewer controlled intersections. Although this might seem like a safe place to drive, many risks are hidden from view. Streets are not brightly lit, and because residents are familiar with the streets and flow of traffic, some may disregard STOP or YIELD signs or pay less attention than they should while driving.

Many residential streets are used by local children as their playground. Kids may chase a ball into the street from a park or driveway without looking. Children on minibikes, bicycles, skate-boards, go-carts, pedal-powered toys, and other recreational equipment can be right around the corner. As you drive through neighborhoods, be thinking of what defensive measures you can take with your vehicle to avoid a tragic collision.

Business districts have their own hazards. Although roadways are usually wider, have controlled intersections, and are more brightly lit, they are often packed with traffic. Vehicles often travel at much faster speeds in a business district than in a residential one, making the chances of a serious collision greater. Rows of parked cars, big delivery trucks, and blind alleys often conceal pedestrians or other vehicles that you may only see clearly when it is too late. Drivers competing for a lane opening or parking space can be rude and aggressive.

When driving on crowded urban roadways, every second counts. You cannot afford to look too long at business signs, street addresses, and other distractions.

Figure 10–1 Maintaining a space cushion is difficult on crowded urban streets.

If a driver ahead of you hits his or her brakes in heavy traffic and you are not paying attention, you could rear-end the other vehicle before you even know what happened. Because you have such a small margin for error, you must make an extra effort to stay focused and continually scan ahead in urban environments. To avoid the danger of "information overload" when traveling in an unfamiliar city, consult a local map to familiarize yourself with the layout of the city and the major through streets.

Expect pedestrians and bicyclists to be *everywhere*. People go to and from office buildings, stores, hotels, and restaurants; get in and out of parked cars, buses, and taxis; or just "cruise" the streets. Delivery drivers race to and from their trucks. Couriers weave in and out of traffic on bicycles. Pedestrians in crowds are more likely to cross streets ille-gally. Those who are drunk or mentally ill may not pay any attention at all to traffic.

Because of the number of potential hazards and limited space available on city streets, you must make a conscious effort to watch your speed. Cars can and do kill people even at relatively slow speeds. Slowing down will give you more time to assess a dangerous situation on the roadway and respond safely to it. For example, if a car suddenly darts out of an alley ahead of you into traffic, you will be able to apply your brakes early with less risk of causing a crash. If a bicyclist is about to jump the curb and move onto the street directly in front of you, you will have time to warn him or her of your presence with a polite toot of your horn.

Covering the Brake

In city driving, you must be prepared to stop or slow suddenly. It takes time to move your right foot from the accelerator to the brake, and it is not uncommon for people to panic in an emergency situation and completely miss the brake pedal. To avoid this problem, you can use a technique called **covering the brake**. This involves taking your right foot off of the accelerator and holding it over the brake pedal as you cruise forward on your car's momentum. If you have to stop quickly, your foot is already in position to immediately hit the brake.

When covering the brake, be careful not to rest your right foot

factoid

Crashes at speeds as low as 12 miles per hour (20 km/h) can result in fatal injury to occupants of vehicles.

Figure 10–2 For many pedestrians, the shortest distance between two places is a straight line.

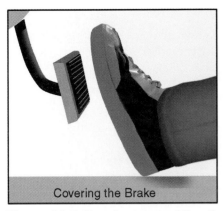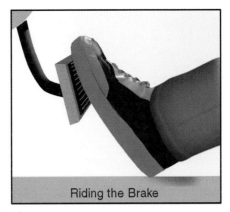

Covering the Brake

Riding the Brake

Figure 10–3 Covering versus riding the brake

on the pedal. This is known as **riding the brake**, and it will both add wear and tear to your brakes and confuse other drivers by constantly activating your brake lights. If people behind you think you are going to stop or slow down and then see you continue moving forward, they may not stop as quickly when you really do need to use your brakes.

Parked Cars

When driving in cities, you must constantly watch for cars entering and exiting parking spots. On busy streets, especially in downtown areas, parking spaces can be rare. Drivers may circle a block a couple of times looking for a vacant spot or one about to be vacated. This can lead to dangerous, erratic driving behavior, especially if these drivers see signs that someone is preparing to leave—for example, a person unlocking the door of a parked car or a vehicle's back-up lights. Sometimes these drivers swerve across several lanes or slam on their brakes, after passing what looks like a depart-

ing vehicle, in the hope that they might get that space.

If you are the one looking for a spot, resist the urge to drive dangerously when you see an opening. This is an invitation to get rear-ended. Instead, reduce your speed and scan far ahead so that you will have plenty of time to identify a possible parking space, indicate your intention to park with a turn signal, and come to a gradual stop near the space.

If you are *not* looking for a parking space, be aware that other drivers may be. Be on the lookout for cars entering and exiting parking spaces. Because vehicles must often back up into traffic to squeeze into a space when parallel parking, they can cause an entire lane to quickly stop. Look for wheels turned out, exhaust, brake lights, and other signs of cars leaving parking spaces.

When driving past a row of parked cars, keep your brake covered. Look through the rear windows of the parked cars to see if any drivers are inside. Be prepared for doors to open suddenly. If

MARGARET MITCHELL

In 1939, Margaret Mitchell gained world fame with her Civil War novel *Gone with the Wind*, which won a Pulitzer Prize and was made into an Academy Award–winning motion picture. On the evening of August 11, 1949, Mitchell and her husband John Marsh drove into downtown Atlanta, parked their car, and walked together across the street toward a theater where they planned to see a movie. When they were halfway across the street, a driver traveling at a very high speed came around a curve and braked violently when he saw the pedestrians. His car skidded nearly 70 feet (20 m), swerved toward Mitchell, and struck her near the curb. She never regained consciousness before dying at a local hospital almost five days later. When asked why he was exceeding the 25 miles per hour (40 km/h) speed limit, the driver said that "everybody does it." Because city streets are more congested with traffic and have limited visibility, it is essential that you drive at or below the posted speed limit to safely navigate around all potential hazards.

your lane is wide enough, stay at least a door's width away from parked cars. If necessary, tap your horn to warn a person getting out of a vehicle of your presence. Keep an eye on the lane next to yours. You should always be prepared to stop behind the door of a parked car, but if you cannot stop, you at least want to avoid swerving into the path of another vehicle to your right.

Gridlock

On city streets in and around urban areas, traffic can get so heavy that vehicles come to a virtual stop. This situation, called **gridlock**, is most common during rush-hour periods and special events such as concerts, athletic contests, and parades. Collisions, police officers issuing tickets, and other distractions can contribute to gridlock and make urban driving a nightmare.

When you know that you will encounter heavy traffic, plan alternative routes. Use side streets to get past logjams on through streets. If none are available, try to rearrange your schedule to travel at a different time. If you drive into the city to work, talk to your employer about working earlier or later. Familiarize yourself with the commuter lane rules

AUTO ACCESSORIES *Fuel Additive*

Because of constant stopping and starting, city driving can be brutal on your engine. A good way to lessen some of this harsh treatment is to use a fuel additive every time you fill up your tank. The additive assists in keeping your engine clean, avoiding rust, and preventing pinging and knocking. It is a small investment that can extend the life of your car.

during certain times of the day. Watch TV or listen to the radio for up-to-date information on roadway construction, closures, and other problems. By avoiding heavy traffic, you will save yourself unnecessary headaches.

10–2 LANE POSITIONING

Defensive driving requires you to position your vehicle within a stream of traffic so that you have the greatest possible space between your vehicle and any potential dangers. This is especially true in an urban environment where careful lane positioning is the key to avoiding many of the hazards associated with city driving.

Choosing a Lane

Most people either pick a lane to travel in out of habit or do not think about it all. However, certain lanes are more appropriate than others, depending on the circumstances. The amount of congestion, the direction of cross traffic, and the availability of turn lanes determine the best lane of travel, as will your immediate goal on the

road—for example, to continue straight ahead, park on the street, enter the driveway of a strip mall, or turn at the next intersection. By waiting until the last minute to get into the proper lane before turning or trying to park, drivers needlessly risk causing a crash.

As a general goal for city driving, you should choose a lane that is uncongested or less congested than the other lanes. That does not mean you should dart in and out of lanes to get into the one with the "shortest" line in heavy traffic situations. This only slows everyone else down and creates a dangerous situation for other drivers. When you pick a lane, stay there until you need to turn off the road, pass another vehicle, or avoid a traffic hazard. By selecting the less-traveled lane, you increase your distance from other cars and expand your safety cushion.

Two-Lane Roads

On two-lane, two-way roads, traffic often bunches up along the right-hand side of the road. Buses and taxis picking up or dropping off passengers, vehicles double parking or backing up into parallel

Wild Wheels

Figure 10–4 What are these accordion-like buses, which require special skill to navigate on crowded city streets, called?

REALITY CHECK *Squeaking Past the Bus*

In city traffic, it is common to get stuck behind a stopped bus, delivery truck, or double-parked car. Avoid the temptation to "squeak" past the vehicle by intruding into the occupied adjoining lane. You could get sideswiped by a vehicle in that lane or, worse, cause it to swerve into oncoming traffic, resulting in a serious collision. You might also get caught between that vehicle and the one you are trying to pass if it suddenly starts forward. Instead of rolling the dice, wait until the vehicle in front of you moves or another lane becomes free and you can pass safely.

Figure 10–5 "Squeaking" past a large bus or delivery truck will decrease your space cushion and create problems for everyone.

parking spaces, slowly creeping traffic-enforcement vehicles checking parking meters, and delivery trucks making their "stop and go" rounds can effectively block an entire lane.

Avoid the temptation to "creep" over the center dividing line of the road and quickly swerve by a problem. Not only will you be moving into the lane of opposing traffic, but you also will be increasing your speed at the same time. This maneuver is guaranteed to eventually cause a crash. The next time you encounter this situation as a driver, relax, slow down behind the obstacle, and wait patiently for it to move. If it has not moved within a reasonable amount of time, wait until the roadway is completely clear of opposing traffic before *slowly* moving out over the center line to bypass the obstacle.

Multilane Roads

On streets with more than one lane going in the same direction, the left lane is usually the fastest lane. That does not mean, however, that it is the smoothest lane of travel. Traffic can be held up in the left lane by drivers waiting to turn left. This is especially true on streets with intersections that have no left-turn lanes to keep the through lanes clear. Also, you must make room for vehicles that "spill over" into your lane when the right lane ends or when it is filled with parked cars, forcing right-lane traffic into your lane. On crowded multilane streets, the right lane may actually get you to your destination more quickly.

Traveling in the left lane is also more dangerous. Because city streets can be narrow and crowded, there is an increased risk that vehicles will cross over the center line into your direction of traffic. They might swerve into your lane to pass or avoid a pedestrian or obstacle. They might make left turns in front of you to enter a driveway or parking lot, or they might make a wide right turn that causes them to cross right into your path.

Figure 10–6 On city streets with lots of signals, the left lane can become very congested.

To avoid possible conflicts with oncoming traffic, it is safer to stay out of the left lane unless you are planning to turn left soon. If you have to travel in the left lane, stay to the right side of the lane. If possible, keep an escape route open on your right in case you have to swerve to avoid a car coming at you. If you do face an oncoming car in your lane, slow down, flash your headlights, sound your horn, and give the other driver as much room as possible to clear your vehicle. If the adjoining lane is free, move into the lane only after first checking that it is clear.

Although it is generally safer and quicker, the right lane has its own hazards. You are farther from oncoming traffic, but you are closer to any parked cars. Although right turns are typically easier and smoother than lefts, special right-turn lanes are not as common as left-turn lanes. Sometimes the right lane is wide enough at intersections to allow both through traffic and right-turning vehicles, but this is not always the case. Also, the extra area available to drivers to make right turns at intersections is typically shorter than a left-turn lane, so in some places congestion can actually be worse in the right lane.

On two-way streets with three or more lanes going in the same direction, choose the center lane(s) for the smoothest flow of traffic. This will allow you to avoid both left- and right-turning vehicles *and* parked cars.

Figure 10–7 Congestion can also build up in the right lane at urban intersections.

road weirdness

Once a year, when the circus comes to town, the Mid-Town Tunnel in New York City is shut down to allow all the circus animals to march through it and onto Manhattan streets.

Changing Lanes

Changing your lane of travel should never be done too often or without taking the proper precautions. Never try to change lanes in or near an intersection. Make sure that you have a clear view of the road ahead and no obstacles are in either lane. When changing lanes, follow these steps (see Figure 10–8):

1. Check your rearview and side-view mirrors for traffic behind

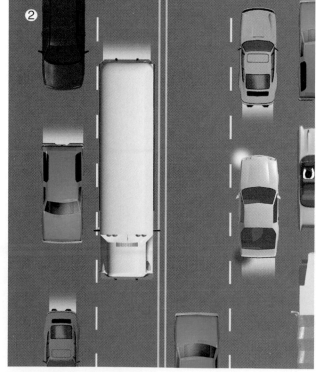

Figure 10–8 Changing lanes

you and in the lane you wish to move into. Turn your head to make sure that no vehicles are in your blind spots.

2. When traffic is clear, signal your intention to change lanes. Allow other drivers plenty of time to see your signal. Make sure that you have enough room to change lanes safely. For example, if traffic in the other lane will not create space to "let you in," avoid the lane change.

3. Move into the other lane while maintaining a constant rate of speed. Change lanes as smoothly as possible. If you turn the wheel too sharply, you will oversteer and risk losing control of your vehicle.

4. Cancel your turn signal, if necessary. Check the rearview and sideview mirrors again to get oriented to your new position in the flow of traffic.

One-Way Streets

One-way streets are common in urban environments because they can handle a heavier volume of traffic in one direction than two-way streets. Because you do not have to face oncoming traffic, they are also safer. However, when you are unfamiliar with an urban area, it is easy to get lost in a maze of one-way streets that all seem to lead you away from your destination. Always consult a detailed street map before trying to get through the maze.

When driving on one-way streets with two or more lanes, always choose the lane with the fewest hazards. If there is a middle lane, it usually has the smoothest traffic flow. On two-lane roadways, use the right-hand lane unless you have to make a left turn off the street soon. If parking is permitted on only one side of the roadway, choose a lane that is not next to parked cars.

Before turning onto a one-way street, make sure that you have correctly identified it as a one-way street, and that you are turning in the proper direction. Watch for posted ONE WAY, DO NOT ENTER, WRONG WAY, and NO LEFT TURN or NO RIGHT TURN signs. Even if there are no signs, other clues can help you identify a one-way street. If parking is allowed on both sides of a one-way street, all vehicles will be pointing in the direction of traffic. Also, one-way streets do not have yellow lines. Once you have correctly identified the one-way street, move into the appropriate lane at least a block ahead of time, and turn into the first available lane going in your direction.

When exiting a one-way street, be sure to correctly identify the street that you will be turning onto. Watch for signs and roadway markings that tell you whether you are turning onto another one-way street or a two-way street. In general, use the left lane for left turns and the right lane for right turns. If there are three lanes, the middle lane should be reserved for driving straight ahead. Some one-way streets have special lanes for turning left or right only. If you are turning onto a multilane street, you may be able to turn from more

guess the vanity plate

DELMAR

H8DCITY

Figure 10–9

than one lane. Also, do not be surprised if a one-way street turns into a two-way street, which is usually indicated by special signs or signals.

Figure 10–10 One-way streets are a common feature of the urban driving environment.

While driving on one-way streets, be prepared for a driver unfamiliar with the area to be driving the wrong way down a one-way street, heading directly for you in your lane of traffic. Do not panic! Slow down and try to get the driver's attention by flashing your headlights or honking your horn, loudly and continu-ously if necessary. If this does not work, pull over to the side of the road and avoid the driver, putting as much space as possible be-tween your two vehicles.

If you accidentally go the wrong direction on a one-way road, slow down to a near stop, turn on both your headlights and hazard lights, and honk your horn as necessary to get the attention of drivers who may be heading to-ward you. If you see a nearby driveway, pull into it as soon as you can safely do so. If no drive-way is available, slowly make your way to the first available street or alley. If no street or alley is nearby, try to make a U-turn. However, if there is not enough space avail-able to make a U-turn, carefully execute a three-point turn when traffic clears, and reverse your di-rection. Once you are going in the proper direction, do not forget to turn off your headlights and haz-ard lights.

Traffic Flow

When only one vehicle drives slower than the rest, it creates problems for all the drivers nearby, who must alter their speeds and

Figure 10–11 Changing lanes at the last second near a stop light is an easy way to get into a collision.

paths of travel to deal with the slow driver. Try to stay with the traffic flow and avoid driving too fast or too slowly. This reduces the chance of you causing a collision by crowding traffic ahead or causing vehicles behind you to pass. At the same time, "going with the flow" is *not* an excuse for speeding. Even if everyone else is exceeding the speed limit, you must obey the law. If you are in the far-right lane and still feel pressured to speed by drivers tailgating you, be patient and let them pass you.

Traffic flow is often irregular on city streets. When possible, avoid driving next to other cars in adjoining lanes. Side-by-side driving reduces your space cushion and blocks your view of the surrounding area, which increases the chance of a collision. In congested areas, you often have no choice, but as soon as traffic starts to clear up, make sure that you get plenty of separation from other vehicles on the road.

When traffic in your lane is moving but traffic in an adjoining lane is stopped, watch out for impatient drivers who will dart out to escape the holdup. Often these drivers do not adequately check for traffic in your lane before suddenly

REALITY CHECK   *The Constant Lane-Changer*

Beware of the driver who makes frequent, unnecessary lane changes. This type of driver impatiently changes lanes to get into the "faster" one, and then when other traffic catches up, changes into the new "faster" lane. Constant lane-changers often fail to signal, and they do not check long enough to make sure that the way is clear before making a lane change. If you are not careful, they may change lanes right into the side of your car! Stay clear of these drivers.

swerving over. If *you* get stopped in a long line of cars, think twice about pulling out to save a few seconds of waiting in traffic. Drivers in your lane probably are not just testing their brakes. It is likely that they have stopped to allow a bicyclist or pedestrian to cross. If you pull out of your lane and hit the gas without checking first, you stand a good chance of running someone down.

Keep in mind that vehicles in the "open" lane of traffic that you are trying to get into will be approaching from your rear at relatively high rates of speed. They may be unable to stop if you suddenly enter their lane. Also, chances are that you are not the only driver who is tempted to move into the open lane to pass. While you are watching for everyone else, make sure that you are not entering the path of a car pulling out behind you or driving forward into a vehicle pulling into the lane ahead of you.

10–3 PASSING

One skill you will need to develop as a driver is how to overtake or **pass** another vehicle on the road. Passing requires practice and maturity. You must learn how to judge the relative speeds and distances of vehicles, including vehicles going in opposite directions. Just as important, you must be able to identify whether passing is appropriate in different situations. Even if a passing maneuver is legal, it may not be safe.

General Passing Rules

Passing laws vary by jurisdiction, but there are some general guidelines you should follow wherever you travel. Never try to pass more than one vehicle at a time. It is extremely difficult to look over, through, or around more than one car at a time ahead of you. This is especially true in city driv-

Figure 10–12 When driving in cities, allow extra time for unexpected detours.

REALITY CHECK *Detours*

Detours are common on city streets, usually as a result of street construction, maintenance, or some special event or emergency. When confronted with a detour, always follow the detour signs set up by law enforcement or work crews to keep traffic flowing. Do not stop your vehicle to ask a worker or traffic control officer what the reason for the detour is or how long it will last. You will hold up traffic and contribute to making the detour situation worse than it already is.

ing, where your view of oncoming traffic is severely limited. You simply cannot see far enough ahead of you to determine whether you have enough room to pass.

In most situations, you should attempt to pass on the *left,* and only when it is safe to do so. Laws vary by jurisdiction, but passing on the right is generally allowed only under the following circumstances:

- If the vehicle you are passing is making or about to make a left turn
- If you are on a roadway not occupied by parked vehicles and clearly marked for two or more lanes of moving vehicles in the same direction as you are going
- If you are on a one-way street, or on any roadway on which traffic is restricted to one direction of movement, that is free from obstructions and wide enough for two or more lanes of traffic

When Not to Pass

There are many situations when passing is either forbidden by law

or clearly unsafe and should not be attempted. Most jurisdictions prohibit passing another vehicle within 100 feet (30 m) of an intersection, railroad crossing, or any bridge, tunnel, abutment, or underpass where your view is blocked. Similarly, you should not pass another vehicle if you are coming to the crest of a hill or a curve where you cannot see enough of the road ahead to be certain of completing your pass safely.

Do not try to pass a vehicle going at or near the legal speed limit. Not only will you have to travel at an illegal speed limit to pass it, but your higher speed will make it easier to misjudge the gap in oncoming traffic. Passing is also forbidden if it would require driving off the paved or main portion of the roadway or crossing a solid-white-line lane divider. Even if you are in a legal passing section of a two-lane roadway, it is against the law to pass if the visibility of oncoming traffic is limited or not distant enough to allow you to complete your pass safely.

Avoid trying to pass near stopped or slow-moving roadway

REALITY CHECK *Know Who Not to Pass* _____

Almost everyone has had the experience of trying to pass a driver who refuses to let you by. This driver speeds up, slows down, swerves, or otherwise obstructs the completion of your pass. Whether this driver feels that he or she was "cut off" by you a few miles/kilometers back, does not like the way you look, or is simply looking for someone to pick a fight with does not matter. What does matter is how you choose to deal with the situation. With road rage a reality of driving today, the best thing you can do is back off and let the other driver feel that he or she has won the "battle." If necessary, slow down and pull over to let the problem driver get far away from you. Take a few moments to relax and then re-enter the roadway and continue driving.

USING SAFE *Passing*

To pass safely, first ask yourself whether the pass is necessary and legal. Use the *SAFE* process. *Scan* for oncoming vehicles, vehicles approaching from the rear, merging vehicles, and any activity on the side of the road. Taking into account the limits of your vision and depth perception, determine how long it will take to make the pass and whether you are able to correctly judge the distance necessary to do it safely. The faster that your vehicle and the vehicle you are trying to pass are traveling, the more time and room you will need to safely complete the pass. *Assess* the driving environment and road conditions, including traction, weather, visibility, width of the road, obstacles, and amount of traffic. Make sure that pedestrians, bicyclists, or anybody else will not be placed in jeopardy by your pass. *Find* safe points ahead to begin and complete your pass. Allow yourself a reasonable margin of safety. Once you have determined that it is safe, you are ready to *execute* the pass.

users, such as bicyclists, pedestrians, and certain vehicles. If the unexpected happens—a driver opens a door of a parked car or a slow-moving car makes a quick U-turn right in front of you—you will have almost no time to avoid a serious collision. On narrow city streets, buses, recreational vehicles, trucks, and vehicles pulling trailers preparing to turn sometimes cross two or even three lanes of traffic to make it around obstacles and corners and may run right into you. It is also a good idea to avoid passing other vehicles moving downhill, especially trucks, because they tend to pick up speed. Never try to pass if obstacles that would interfere with your maneuver are on the road.

Finally, never pass if you have any doubts about your ability to legally do so or if there is any

Figure 10–13 Would you attempt to pass in this situation?

doubt as to the intentions of the driver ahead of you. A slowing car could be stopping or preparing to turn. If you are about to pass on the left, do not rely on a right-turn signal to tell you it is safe to do so. The driver may have left the signal on from a previous turn, moved the turn-signal lever in the wrong direction, or changed his or her mind.

Making the Pass

Follow these steps to properly pass another vehicle on the road (see Figure 10–14):

1. Make sure that you are at least at a safe 3-second following distance behind the vehicle you wish to pass. Check your rearview and sideview mirrors for traffic behind you and to your sides. Turn your head to make sure that no vehicles are in your blind spots. Signal your intention to pass to other drivers. If necessary, flash your headlights or tap your horn to get their attention.

2. Move into passing position and obtain a speed advantage over the other vehicle. Do not linger in the other vehicle's blind spots. Overtake the vehicle, passing with a sufficient clearance of both the passed vehicle and of any oncoming traffic ahead of you.

3. Recheck conditions ahead of you and to the sides. Create a return space by making sure that you can see the front of the vehicle you have just passed in your rearview mirror.

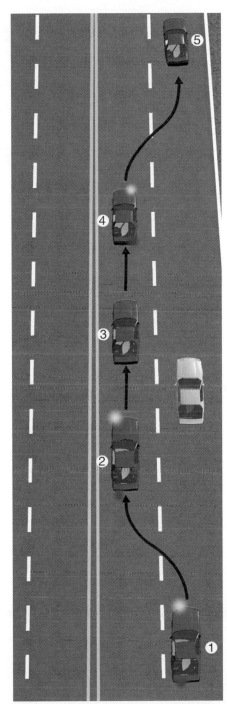

Figure 10–14 Passing another vehicle

Figure 10–15 If you are tailgating a driver who stops abruptly, you will be unable to avoid a crash.

Do not count on other cars making room for your return. If you have to, tap your horn to communicate to other drivers that you need to move back into the line of traffic.

4. Signal your return into the lane and check your blind spots.

5. Move into your return space, creating following-distance space for the vehicle you just passed. Resume normal driving speed.

Being Passed

As soon as you are aware that another driver is attempting to pass you, maintain or reduce your speed to make it easier for that driver to execute the pass. Never speed up or otherwise block the passing vehicle. This is both illegal and dangerous. If you see a hazard ahead that would make another driver's pass of your vehicle dangerous, tap your brakes as a warning not to pass. If he or she does not see your warning or ignores it, reduce your speed as the other driver passes you to increase the space available for that car to re-enter the lane and slow or stop before reaching the obstacle. Have an escape route ready just in case.

REALITY CHECK   *Let the Fast Pass* _____

Clear out of the faster, left-hand lanes when other, faster drivers appear behind you. Even if they act rudely and flash their lights, honk, or tailgate, do not "up the ante" by staying in your lane. Even worse, do not slow down or hit your brakes to warn these drivers to "back off." Maintain your speed and move to the right as soon as it is safe to do so. If they are speeding, you may later have the satisfaction of seeing them pulled over and cited by a police officer down the road.

WHO'S AT FAULT?

1. Driver 1 was proceeding eastbound on a residential street at approximately 20 miles per hour (30 km/h). Driver 3 had just completed parallel parking on the eastbound side of the street ahead of Driver 1. Driver 2 was traveling westbound and had slowed to approximately 15 miles per hour (25 km/h). She had moved well toward the center of the street to avoid the parked cars on the north side of the street. Driver 1, estimating that he had adequate space to maneuver between Driver 2 and Driver 3, continued eastbound in the only lane available and was unable to stop when Driver 3 opened the door to exit his vehicle. Driver 1 applied his brakes but still knocked Driver 3's left front door completely off. **Who's at fault?**

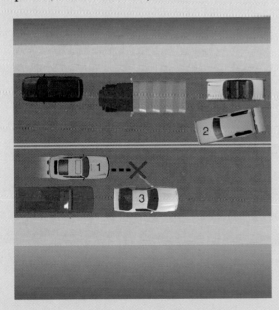

2. Driver 1 was proceeding northbound on Central Avenue approaching a signal-controlled intersection at approximately 35 miles per hour (55 km/h) in the number 2 lane. Drivers 3 and 4 were stopped at the red light ahead. Driver 2, who was northbound in the number 1 lane immediately next to Driver 1, was slowing in preparation to stop. Driver 1 had just purchased a hamburger at a fast food restaurant and was eating as he drove. While approaching the intersection he took a bite out of his burger, being careful not to spill it on his clothes. As he looked up, Driver 1 realized he was about to rear-end Driver 3. He simultaneously swerved to his left and stomped on the brake. Driver 1 managed to avoid hitting either Driver 3 or 4, but he slammed into Driver 2, who collided with the center median. **Who's at fault?**

YOUR TURN

10–1 *The City Driving Environment*

1. Why is scanning ahead and reducing speed important in city driving?

2. What is the difference between riding and covering the brake?

10–2 *Lane Positioning*

3. Why is lane positioning important in city driving?

4. What is the proper way to change lanes?

5. What are the advantages and risks of using one-way streets?

10–3 *Passing*

6. What is the proper way to pass another vehicle?

7. What are some of the dangers of passing on urban roadways?

SELF-TEST

Multiple Choice

1. Holding your right foot over the brake pedal as you cruise forward on your car's momentum is called:
   a. riding the brake.
   b. readying the brake.
   c. covering the brake.
   d. holding the brake.

2. When driving past parked cars, stay at least _____ away.
   a. 10 feet (3 m)
   b. a door's width
   c. a car's width
   d. 3 feet (1 m)

3. When traffic gets so heavy that vehicles come to a virtual stop, the result is:
   a. chaos.
   b. signal failure.
   c. road closure.
   d. gridlock.

4. Which determines the best travel lane?
   a. the amount of congestion
   b. the direction of cross traffic
   c. the availability of turn lanes
   d. all of the above

5. On two-way streets with three or more lanes going in the same direction, you should drive in the _____ lane.
   a. left
   b. center
   c. right
   d. turn

Sentence Completion

1. _____ streets are common in cities because they can handle a heavier volume of traffic.

2. Never try to _____ more than one vehicle at a time.

3. You should maintain a _____ following distance behind a vehicle you wish to pass.

4. When possible, it is best to pass on the _____ side of the vehicle ahead of you.

5. When driving in the left lane, avoid the temptation to "creep" over the _____ to swerve by an obstacle.

Matching

Match the concepts in Column A with examples of the concepts in Column B.

Column A

1. __ Illegal pass
2. __ One-way street
3. __ Hazard in the left lane
4. __ "Going with the flow"
5. __ Road closed
6. __ Gridlock
7. __ Hazard in the right lane
8. __ Best travel lane

Column B

a. Parked cars

b. Bumper-to-bumper traffic

c. Traveling at the same pace as other traffic

d. Within 100 feet (30 m) of an intersection

e. WRONG WAY

f. Oncoming traffic

g. DETOUR

h. Least congestion

Short Answer

1. Why should you avoid side-by-side driving?

2. Why is riding the brake dangerous?

3. How can you identify a one-way street?

4. What dangers might you face on residential streets?

5. What should you do if traffic in your lane is stopped but is moving in an adjoining lane?

Critical Thinking

1. As you are turning left onto a two-lane street, you notice that the lines dividing the street lanes are all white across the entire street and that cars parked on both sides of the road are pointing in the direction opposite yours. A car is traveling toward you in the right-hand lane. What should you do?

2. You are traveling uphill behind a slow-moving truck in the right lane of a busy four-lane street. You drop back to see if the left lane is clear for passing and then move into the left lane. As you are passing the truck at the legal speed limit, a pickup speeds up close behind you honking and flashing its lights. What should you do?

PROJECTS

1. Interview a professional bus, limousine, or taxi driver about the particular hazards he or she faces every day while driving in the city. Share the results with your class.

2. Look at a city map with your classmates and discuss which areas may be more congested at rush-hour times. Find some alternative routes that you could use to bypass the areas that have heavy traffic or gridlock problems.

Highway and Rural Driving

In some ways, rural roadways are safer than city streets. They are less congested, they have fewer distractions, and there is more room to make evasive maneuvers in an emergency. Because they are less crowded, however, rural roads have higher speed limits than city streets. You face *fewer* hazards on a highway than you do on an urban road, but you reach them more *quickly*. Rural roads generally are not cleaned or repaired as often as city streets, and they have fewer warning signs, sharper curves, steeper hills, and fewer controlled intersections. It also usually takes longer for medical help to arrive after a collision.

Upon completion of this chapter, you should be able to:

11–1 *The Rural Driving Environment*

1. Understand what makes rural roads and intersections dangerous.
2. Understand the proper way to enter, cross, and exit a divided highway.

11–2 *Defensive Driving on Highways*

3. Understand the importance of scanning ahead and reducing speed in rural driving.
4. Describe some of the dangers of passing on highways.

11–3 *Other Dangers of Highway and Rural Driving*

5. Understand what velocitation and highway hypnosis are.
6. Understand what you should do if you encounter a slow-moving vehicle or wild animal on the road.

KEY TERMS

highway	Y-intersection	slow-moving vehicles (SMVs)
divided highway	crossover	off-road vehicle
median strip	velocitation	
T-intersection	highway hypnosis	

11–1 THE RURAL DRIVING ENVIRONMENT

Most rural roadways serve small communities or link local roads with major roadways like interstates. The most heavily traveled roads in rural areas are highways. A **highway** is a main public roadway designed to carry traffic for long, uninterrupted periods at medium-to-high speeds. Unlike freeways, where access is limited to on-ramps and off-ramps, highways can have intersections with cross traffic, side roads, driveways, and other means of direct access.

Divided Highways

The typical highway is a two-way, two-lane road separated by double-yellow lines. Major rural highways, including interstates, often have four or more lanes. Many multilane highways are **divided highways** in which opposing directions of travel are separated by a fixed barrier or area of space called a **median strip.** These open areas may be paved, dirt, or land-

scaped. The widths of median strips vary depending on the location of the highway and the surrounding environment. The more open the area is, the wider median strips tend to be. Median strips may be even with the road, but they are usually angled downward to help channel off water during rainstorms.

Rural Roads

Most rural roads lack the engineering advances featured on modern freeways and interstates. Many are old, narrow, and originally designed for slower speeds. Rural roads may be paved with many different materials, including concrete, asphalt, macadam (crushed stones), and even cobblestone or brick. The traction of each of these surfaces varies with weather conditions and has a different "feel" when you drive on it. Some lightly traveled rural roads are not paved at all.

Roads with "washboard" surfaces are built in uneven sections, leaving ridges that can cause your

Figure 11–1 Opposing directions of travel are separated on a divided highway.

Figure 11–2 Narrow roadways are a common feature of the rural driving environment.

tires to lose their grip as you move from one section to another. Certain roads or lanes may be grooved or rutted. Potholes and other damaged sections of the roadway may be left unrepaired for long periods or covered over with uneven patches of asphalt as quick fixes. Many rural roads are not cleaned regularly, and dirt, sand, gravel, and leaves can accumulate to create slippery patches. Collision debris, pieces of truck tires, and dead animals are also familiar obstacles.

Do not rely on warning signs to indicate rough conditions on rural roads. Pay attention to the sounds your tires make as you drive over different surfaces. Reduce your speed when you suspect any difficulties with traction. Although you cannot expect to detect every potential problem, you will be better prepared for a loss of traction by maintaining a safe speed. Be especially careful when moving from a well-paved highway onto a dirt or gravel road, in which case the sudden reduction in traction could cause you to lose control of your vehicle.

Rural Intersections

Many rural intersections have only signs or no traffic controls at all. **T-intersections,** in which side roads join a main road with through traffic at a right angle, are especially common and can be dangerous. Drivers on the through road may have difficulty seeing vehicles entering from the side road. There may not be warning signs for through traffic, and STOP or YIELD signs on the side road could be blocked from the view of drivers on the main road by trees or bushes. If the intersection is on a curve or hillside and visibility is limited, drivers on the side road may misjudge the time it takes to accelerate to keep ahead of approaching traffic. If they are turning from a gravel or dirt road, they may temporarily lose traction in an attempt to jump quickly onto the main road, causing a collision with an approaching vehicle.

Figure 11–3 You are likely to encounter unusual intersections on old rural roadways.

In rural areas, roads sometimes meet at unusual angles called **Y-intersections.** These intersections, which commonly form a "Y" shape, are often the site of junctions of minor and major roads. Y-intersections can be confusing, especially to beginning drivers. Drivers may either fail to stop or stop when they are not supposed to. Watch for posted warning signs when approaching Y-intersections and be ready to swerve or stop to avoid hitting confused drivers.

Entering or Crossing a Divided Highway

Roads that intersect divided highways often continue across a median strip. Those vehicles turning left onto the highway from the road, turning left onto the road from the highway, or driving straight across the highway must use a special paved area of the me-

dian. Because these types of intersections are usually controlled by signs, not signals, traffic can build up on the median strip. If the median is "full," cars turning left off the highway may have no place to go. There is also the risk that too many cars might try to squeeze onto the median, and the last car might be caught sticking partially onto the highway. Given the high speed limits on most highways, this is extremely dangerous.

To turn left onto a divided highway or proceed straight across it, follow these steps (see Figure 11–4):

1. Come to a complete stop at the intersection. Stay well clear of the right lane of the highway. Remember that cars on the highway will be driving *extremely* fast.

2. Look ahead at the median strip to determine how wide it is and how many vehicles can safely occupy it with at least a car length of space to spare. If the median is full, patiently wait until one of the cars on it has turned onto the highway or proceeded across it.

3. Look left at oncoming traffic on the highway. Watch for any vehicles turning left off the highway onto the median strip that might fill the gap you are waiting for. Also, watch for any oncoming vehicles on the median that are turning left across your path onto the side of the highway that you want to cross. Although you have the right-of-way, do not assume that

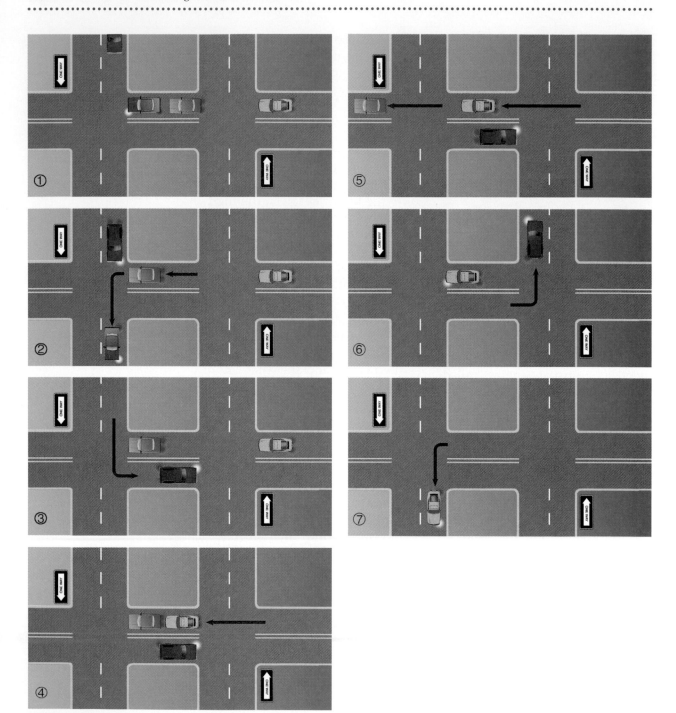

Figure 11–4 Crossing a divided highway

drivers turning onto the highway will wait for you.

4. Once the way is completely clear of any approaching vehicles and there is enough room for you to safely occupy a place on the median, look left again and then proceed cautiously across the highway.

5. Wait for any vehicles in front of you to turn left or proceed straight across the other side of the highway. When you are "next," move to a safe spot on the median to wait for a gap in traffic. If there is no STOP sign or limit line to help you position your vehicle, move to within about half a car length of the edge of the median. Come to a complete stop.

6. If you are turning left, activate your left-turn signal. Look across the highway for oncoming vehicles that will go straight onto the median to drive across or turn onto the other side of the highway. Look to your right for a gap in traffic on the highway.

7. If you are driving across the highway, proceed across when the way is clear. Watch for vehicles exiting the highway onto the road you are taking. If you are turning left onto the highway, watch for oncoming vehicles turning right onto the same side of the highway. Turn left into the left lane of the highway just as you would on a two-lane, one-way street. Make sure that your turn signal is off. Because you will be entering the passing lane,

change into the right lane as soon as it is safe to do so.

Turning Left off a Divided Highway

When turning left off a divided highway to turn onto an intersecting road or make a U-turn, you must first turn onto the median strip to wait for a gap in oncoming traffic. Keep in mind that you will be slowing down in what is normally the passing lane. To avoid holding up traffic, get into the left lane and signal your intention to turn well in advance of the intersection. As you approach the intersection to prepare to turn, frequently check your rearview mirror for fast-moving cars behind you and look for an escape path on the median in case you risk being rear-ended.

Some intersections of divided highways have turn lanes. If the median is already occupied by cross traffic or other cars turning left, turn lanes provide a safe place for you to wait for an opening on the median. If there is no turn lane, you may have to stop in the left lane. Keep your wheels straight while waiting to turn. If you get hit from the rear, it is better to be pushed straight ahead than into other vehicles on the median or oncoming traffic on the other side of the highway. Keeping your wheels straight also gives you the opportunity to rapidly accelerate. You may not be able to avoid a rear-end collision, but the faster you are traveling when struck from behind the better chance you have of avoiding a serious injury.

Figure 11–5 Driveways and side streets may be hard to spot on rural highways.

Intersections at divided highways that do not have room for left-turn lanes may have special roads called "jughandles" that exit the highway to the right and loop back so that drivers can cross the highway. These types of intersections are usually controlled by signals, and special signs are posted on the highway indicating that drivers who want to turn left off the highway or make a U-turn must first exit to the right.

Unmarked Driveways

Driveways to farms and ranches appear frequently on rural stretches of highways. Some of these unmarked roads are hidden by bushes, crops, or trees. Watch for mail and newspaper boxes, gates, openings in fences or shrubbery, tire tracks turning off and onto the highway, and other signs of a property entrance. Reduce your speed as you approach these areas and be prepared for a vehicle to dart out into your path.

Entry/Exit Problems

Many highways either do not have acceleration lanes or have very short acceleration lanes, so pay close attention to YIELD or MERGE signs before entering a highway. Wait for a long gap in

REALITY CHECK   *Mailbox Bashing* _____

A favorite pastime of some teens is to drive around and smash mailboxes along rural roads and highways. One person drives, while the passengers take turns hanging out of the windows to take swings at mailboxes. This "prank" is illegal and extremely dangerous. Not only does the driver risk losing control of the car and having a collision, but also the "basher" may lose his or her balance and fall out. If you are caught mailbox bashing, you can be arrested for vandalism and cited for reckless driving.

traffic before you accelerate and merge with through traffic. If you are on the highway, keep an eye out for other vehicles that may quickly enter the roadway. You may have to reduce your speed or, if you are on a multilane highway, change lanes to allow the other driver to merge smoothly. When you see signs warning you of merging traffic ahead, check your rearview and sideview mirrors for vehicles behind you and try to spot any drivers on a side road or at an intersection ahead that might be preparing to merge.

There are often no exit ramps on highways either, so remember to slow down more quickly than you would on a freeway as you approach highway exits. Pay attention to speed reduction signs and signal well before you turn off. If you are on a multilane highway, make sure that you get in the far-right lane long before you reach the exit.

Crossovers

Many divided highways have **crossovers**, special areas where vehicles can turn around to go in the opposite direction. Unpaved crossovers are usually restricted to law-enforcement and emergency vehicles. Warning signs may be placed near the crossovers indicating that they are reserved for official use, but do not assume that you can use a crossover if you do *not* see a warning sign.

Rural Railroad Crossings

Railroad crossings in rural environments are less likely to include the full range of roadway markings and control devices like signs, signals, lights, gates, and warning bells that exist at most urban railroad crossings. This is especially true of electronic controls because of the high cost of supplying electricity to distant, widely scattered crossings. In open areas with little human activity, these crossings may not be controlled at all. Rural railroad crossings are also more dangerous than urban ones because trains tend to move faster in the countryside than they do in or around cities.

Be extremely careful when approaching railroad crossings in rural areas. Railways are often slightly elevated above the ground, so watch for the road to dip up near tracks. Make sure that you can see clearly in both directions and that your view down the tracks is not blocked by trees, rocks, or other obstacles. Be especially careful at night. In dark, rural areas, sometimes the only way you can see a train is by its lights.

Roadside Stands and Service Stations

Roadside stands and service stations are sometimes located very close to rural roadways. Because many highways were built during a time of slower-speed driving, today's greater speeds pose a great degree of danger. When you pass one of these places, reduce your speed, increase your following distance, and watch for pedestrians or cars pulled over to the side of the road.

factoid

Nearly 65% of all motor vehicle fatalities at railroad crossings occur in rural areas.

DRIVING TIPS *Meeting a Line of Cars*

On open highways with only one lane of traffic going in each direction, any collision, animal crossing, or other obstacle can tie up traffic for hours. As you approach a long line of cars, immediately reduce your speed and tap on your brakes to warn others behind you that they must stop ahead. If necessary, switch on your emergency flashers to get their attention.

11–2 DEFENSIVE DRIVING ON HIGHWAYS

Depending on the jurisdiction, speed limits on rural highways can be as high as 75 miles per hour in parts of the United States and 110 kilometers per hour in parts of Canada. Sharp curves, detours, lane endings, areas with gusting winds, and other hazards on major rural roads are usually accompanied by speed reduction signs, but do not rely on these warning signs to always be there. Remember the basic speed law: *Do not drive faster than conditions allow.* The faster you drive, the harder it is to control your vehicle, the less time you have to swerve, the more room you need to stop, and the higher the risk of a serious injury or damage to your car in a collision. Almost two of every three traffic fatalities occur in rural areas, and excessive speed is usually the reason.

Reduced Visibility

Your line of sight on rural roads is often more limited than it is on city streets or freeways. Trees, bushes, crops, billboards, fences, and other obstructions close to the road can reduce your ability to see oncoming vehicles, cross traffic, signs, or signals. The higher speeds of highways make it even more difficult to recognize details. Your side vision can be reduced to a virtual blur.

Figure 11–6 Visibility on rural roads is often limited.

Figure 11–7 It can be difficult observing details at highway speeds.

Traffic safety engineers try to compensate for the reduced visibility of high-speed travel when they design signals, post signs, and paint roadway markings on rural highways. Signs are generally placed farther ahead of hazards, signals may be larger than those in cities, and roadway markings are painted well in advance of intersections and crossings. Rural intersections may have unusual signals or signs to get your attention early. For example, you might see a yellow signal ahead of an intersection concealed by a hill, sharp curve, or trees that flashes only when the light at that intersection is red.

Make sure that you remember to look off-road, as well as directly ahead of you. A dust cloud off to the side could mean that a vehicle is just about to enter the highway, a herd of livestock is approaching a crossing, or a tractor is cruising along the edge of the road on the dirt shoulder. Fenced-in property is bound to have occasional outlets or driveways. Water towers, power lines, telephone poles, or other structures may indicate a nearby road or railway that will cross your path.

Look for patterns in traffic controls and roadway surfaces to better anticipate dangers or changing conditions ahead. While scanning, gather information about your environment. Keep a mental note of roads or service stations you pass, safety features like wide shoulders and medians, how often and where you see patrol cars, the distance to rest stops (which often have telephones and water), whether call boxes are on the road, and other information that could be of use to you in the event of an emergency.

Increasing Following Distance

On city streets, a following distance of 3 seconds is safe under normal driving conditions. At highway speeds greater than 50 miles per

DRIVING TIPS **Solo Signaling** _____

Even if you are the only one on the highway, do not fall out of the habit of signaling before turning, pulling over, or any other maneuver requiring you to signal. The next time you are turning or passing another vehicle you might cause a collision by forgetting to signal properly.

hour (80 km/h), however, you need at least 6 seconds to stop or avoid an obstacle. Maintaining a long following distance will also help you save fuel and wear on your brakes. Drivers ahead of you may momentarily use their brakes to slow down—for example, because they see a warning sign, an upcoming curve, or a law-enforcement officer—and then speed up again when the danger or threat is past. When you see brake lights ahead, take your foot off of the accelerator to let your car's speed decrease naturally and to avoid having to use your brakes. Then if you *do* have to use your brakes, you will not have to push them as hard.

Highway Passing

The higher speeds of highway travel and the dangers associated with rural environments like low traction and inadequate lighting at night mean that you must take extra precautions when passing on highways. On multilane highways, you should stay in the right lane unless you are passing another vehicle or preparing to turn. In some jurisdictions, it is actually illegal to travel in the left lane unless you are passing.

When passing on a two-lane highway, never move to the left of the center line unless you can see far enough ahead to know whether you can pass safely. Make sure that you have enough room to return to the right side of the roadway without affecting the safe movement of oncoming traffic or the vehicle that you are passing. Consider the width and condition of the shoulder before passing. The wider your escape route, the better. Check for warning signs of upcoming intersections, merging traffic, railroad crossings, bridges, underpasses, no-passing zones, and other places where passing is prohibited or dangerous.

Pass only on long, straight sections of the road where you can see

MICHAEL HEDGES

Born on December 31, 1953, acoustic guitarist Michael Hedges helped establish the "New Age" Windham Hill record label in the early 1980s. Hedges was known for his unusual tunings and his two-handed picking style. He described his own music as "heavy metal" and "acoustic thrash." Others compared his skill and intensity with that of rock guitarist Eddie Van Halen. On December 2, 1997, a work crew discovered Hedges's body in his crashed BMW at the bottom of an embankment on California Route 128, in rural Mendocino County near San Francisco. The California Highway Patrol determined that Hedges had died several days earlier when his car skidded off the road as he was going around a curve. Rural roads can be deadly if you do not remain vigilant about the hazards they present. When dealing with the sharp curves and steep hills that you will encounter on rural roads, the best way to keep control of your car in a dangerous situation is to slow down.

Figure 11–8 Make sure that you finish your pass *before* you reach a no-passing zone.

clearly ahead of you. Avoid passing on or near curves or hills. Especially avoid passing on roads going uphill within 1,000 feet (300 m) of the crest. Use your low-beam headlights to improve your visibility as you pass another vehicle. Never try to pass if your sight distance is limited by rain, snow, fog, blowing dust, or other severe weather.

Keep in mind that until an approaching vehicle is close to you, it is almost impossible to estimate its rate of speed. Just because you are going the speed limit does not mean that the oncoming driver is. Do not take chances. To be on the safe side, make sure that oncoming vehicles are at least a half a mile ahead (1 km) of you before you attempt a pass.

If you are passing another vehicle on a multilane highway, first check *all* lanes of traffic going in your direction. If you are in the center lane, make sure that no vehicles are in either the left or right lanes that might interfere with your pass. Watch for any vehicles that might enter your passing lane. Do not rely only on your mirrors, even if you have been "tracking" other cars for a while. Signal early, and look over your shoulder to check that your blind spots are clear before making your pass.

USING SAFE   *Rural Roads*

Use the SAFE method to reduce the dangers of driving on rural roads. *Scan* ahead for traffic controls, debris on the roadway, dust clouds, animals, brake lights, vehicles jutting into the road from hidden driveways, slow-moving vehicles, and pedestrians and parked cars by roadside stands. In conditions of low light or bad weather, watch for headlights of oncoming cars, taillights of cars ahead of you, and pedestrians or animals that reflect the light from your headlights. *Assess* the width and condition of the roadway and shoulder, the visibility of oncoming drivers, the following distance of traffic behind you, and the off-road environment. *Find* an escape route in case an oncoming car veers into your lane, an animal or pedestrian darts across your path, or you suddenly come across debris blocking the road. Watch your speed, especially on curves, and be prepared to *execute* your decision to avoid a collision by moving off the road, by changing lanes, or by emergency braking.

Always avoid passing in the presence of oncoming traffic. Good defensive driving calls for allowing yourself the widest possible margin for error in case of an emergency.

Always pass on the left when possible. Sometimes, however, you have to pass on the right on a multilane highway—for example, if a driver is preparing for a left turn or is not keeping up with the flow of traffic. Wait until the lane is clear, activate your right-turn signal, double-check for vehicles in your blind spots by looking over your shoulder, and enter the lane smoothly. Watch for other vehicles ahead of you that might be preparing to turn right.

Remember that you can enter the lane of oncoming traffic to pass another vehicle only if the yellow line on your side of the road is broken. On some highways, especially where curves and hills prevent normal passing, extra lanes are added at intervals to each side of the roadway to make passing safer and easier.

11–3 OTHER DANGERS OF HIGHWAY AND RURAL DRIVING

When driving on highways and rural roadways, be aware of some of the unique hazards and challenges that you will face.

Velocitation and Highway Hypnosis

Driving on a roadway that is extremely familiar or that is long,

straight, or boring can cause you to take your mind off what you are doing. Two common psychological effects of open highway driving are velocitation and highway hypnosis. **Velocitation** occurs when you find yourself unconsciously driving much faster than you intended. (The root word of velocitation is "velocity," which means "speed.") **Highway hypnosis** results when you literally become hypnotized by the road. After a few seconds in this hypnotic state, you will feel as if you just awakened from a dream, leaving you with no recollection of the last few seconds you spent driving down the road.

To prevent either problem from occurring, drive only when you are rested and mentally fresh. Break up long journeys into short segments, and avoid trying to make the trip in one long haul. Stop frequently for food and rest. Break up the monotony of open highway driving by talking to passengers and changing drivers. When practical, take "the road less traveled." By taking time to explore and enjoy your route, you may enjoy the trip more than the destination.

Slow-Moving Vehicles

Various types of **slow-moving vehicles (SMVs)** are common on highways. "Wide-load" vehicles carrying homes, trailers, and heavy equipment are usually accompanied by lead and trailing vehicles with warning lights or signals. Construction zones may have pavers, bulldozers, and a va-

Figure 11–9 Approach slow-moving vehicles with caution.

riety of other heavy equipment going to and from the job site. Near farms, you are likely to encounter combines, tractors, harvesters, and cultivators, especially in late summer or fall. During or after a snowstorm you may encounter snowplows and sanding trucks.

SMVs present two major dangers to motorists. First, because they are not designed for high-speed travel—many cannot go more than about 20 miles per hour (30 km/h)—they can cause rear-end collisions or traffic backups on highways. Second, because they are wider than most vehicles or have equipment that projects into the roadway in a dangerous manner, they are difficult to pass. In some cases you may not be able to see cables, booms, cranes, or other pieces of equipment that stick out. Some SMVs can take up the entire road. If the vehicle is on an unpaved road or riding par-

tially on the shoulder, it can send rocks careening into your vehicle or kick up clouds of dust that reduce visibility.

When you approach an SMV, reduce your speed and take a moment to identify the vehicle and its potential dangers to you. Look for warning signs, reflectors, signals, or orange-and-red, triangular-shaped SMV emblems mounted on the rear end. Approach with caution. Because your lane may be sharply narrowed, do not attempt to pass unless you have a clear view of the road ahead. Do not speed past an SMV. From a distance you might not have accurately judged the "reach" of the equipment attached to the vehicle. Instead, pass slowly and carefully.

Watch for oncoming cars that might try to pass SMVs on the *other* side of the road. Drivers might not see you and may swerve into your lane as they

Figure 11–10 The SMV emblem

Figure 11–11

Figure 11–12 Drivers of off-road vehicles may not always observe posted regulations.

pass. Even if they avoid colliding with you, they might hit the SMV and cause equipment on the vehicle to fall into your path. Move into the right side of the lane when passing oncoming SMVs to give yourself as large a space cushion as possible.

Off-Road Vehicles

Some public lands, including fire trails, logging roads, service roads, and sand dunes, are open to use by specially equipped **off-road vehicles.** These include "dirt bike" motorcycles, ATCs (three-wheeled cycles), quadrunners (four-wheeled cycles), dune buggies, and snow-

mobiles. Off-road vehicles are generally less stable than passenger cars or light trucks, and most provide little protection to operators in a collision with a motor vehicle. When driving in rural parks and recreation areas, watch for signs warning of off-road activity. Many of these vehicles are noisy, so use your ears as well as your eyes to detect them.

There are restrictions on where and how off-road vehicles are permitted to use or cross highways. For example, operators are usually required to cross a two-way highway at a 90-degree angle. If off-road vehicles are permitted on roadways, any extra lights they

DRIVING TIPS *Government Land to Avoid* _____

If you are driving in an off-road area, especially in the western United States, that you suspect may be restricted government land (such as a military base or test site), seek the advice of a sheriff's office or highway patrol station before proceeding.

have must be covered or disconnected. Be alert to off-roaders who ignore or do not know the rules. Some can get so caught up in the excitement of what they are doing that they drop their guard or behave irresponsibly when driving on or near public roadways.

Livestock Crossing Areas

Although it may seem dangerous, many farmers and ranchers must cross their livestock across open highways. Sometimes these crossing points are marked, sometimes they are not. Always be on your guard when traveling through pasture land. If you suddenly encounter a herd of animals crossing the roadway, slow your speed to a crawl and stop far from the herd to avoid frightening them. Always obey the instructions of livestock handlers. Once the farmer or rancher has moved the herd across the highway and well beyond the shoulder, proceed forward with caution. If necessary, wait for any dust stirred up by the animals to settle to make sure that you can see ahead clearly.

Horse-Drawn Vehicles and Riders

In areas where you are likely to encounter horses (such as farms, ranches, horse-friendly suburbs, and parks with specially marked trails), exercise extreme caution and watch for warning signs. If you do come across a person riding a horse or a horse-drawn

vehicle, avoid using your horn. This may "spook" the animal and endanger the life of the rider or those in the vehicle. Reduce your speed or stop, if necessary, to let the animal cross the road.

If you approach people on horseback on the side of a road, wait until the road is clear of oncoming traffic and drive around them slowly and cautiously. In some jurisdictions, you must reduce your speed in the presence of a frightened horse or stop if directed to do so by the rider.

Wild Animals

A deer is a large animal, and it can do substantial damage to your vehicle if you hit one. Collisions with wild animals, primarily deer, account for hundreds of thousands of crashes and more than 100 fatalities each year in North America. The deer population has swelled in the last decade, making crashes with deer a growing risk on rural roadways.

Smaller animals such as raccoons, skunks, opossums, foxes, coyotes, and rabbits can also cause

Figure 11–14 Most serious collisions with wild animals involve deer.

Wild Wheels

Figure 11–13 What is the name of this early steam-powered version of an off-road vehicle that carried passengers up a steep, winding mountain road to a remote hotel in Colorado?

factoid

There are more than half a million collisions with deer in the United States each year.

DRIVING MYTHS   *Do Not "Look for the Whites of Their Eyes"*

The saying "look for the whites of their eyes" may have worked in the early days of motor vehicles when a deer or moose would be easily surprised by an approaching vehicle and look in that direction. Today, however, many animals are so used to vehicles that they may not even turn around to look at you. When traveling at night, your best precaution when you are in an area populated by deer is to slow down and keep scanning for signs of their presence.

auto slang

"Road kill" is the term commonly used to describe the remains of an animal that has had an ill-fated encounter with a motor vehicle.

deadly crashes by causing drivers to swerve or brake sharply to avoid a collision. It is instinctive not to want to hit an animal, but driving into another vehicle or tree or causing a car to rear-end you by slamming on your brakes is a far worse scenario.

The first thing you can do to avoid a crash with an animal is to watch for warning signs indicating that wildlife inhabits the area. These signs are usually posted at places where collisions have occurred in the past. When driving near wooded country or farmland, control your speed and stay alert. Be especially careful at dawn, in the evening, and in November and December, when deer are most active. If you see one animal, you should assume that others are nearby.

If you see an animal by the side of the road, reduce your speed and drive very slowly past it. Remember that frightened animals can bolt in any direction, so keep your brake covered, watch for oncoming traffic, and have an escape route planned. If an animal is on the road directly in front of you, slow down and honk your horn. Do *not* flash your lights. This can cause the animal to "freeze" in its tracks.

If you think you are going to collide with an animal, even a large one, it is better to brake than to swerve out of the way. Swerving might confuse the animal as to which way you are going and cause it to run right into you. You might also get into a worse collision. Some insurance companies will hold *you* liable if you have a crash trying to avoid an animal, but not for damage resulting from hitting it. If it is a large animal like a deer or moose, take your foot off the brake the moment before you actually make impact. This will cause the front of your car to rise and reduce the chance of the animal hitting your windshield.

WHO'S AT FAULT?

1. Driver 2 was proceeding southbound on State Highway 1 through Nobles National Forest at night. His speed was about 40 miles per hour (65 km/h), just at the posted limit. Driver 1 was traveling northbound on the same highway at approximately 45 miles per hour (70 km/h) when a coyote appeared in his headlights on the road ahead. Surprised, Driver 1 swerved into the oncoming lane to his left. Driver 1 impacted Driver 2 head on. *Who's at fault?*

2. Driver 1 and Driver 2 were proceeding along a two-lane country road at about 50 miles per hour (80 km/h). Driver 1 suddenly realized that she was coming up behind a slow-moving tractor. She attempted to pass but discovered that she was in a no-passing zone. When she applied her brakes to retreat back to her position in her lane, she was hit from behind by Driver 2. *Who's at fault?*

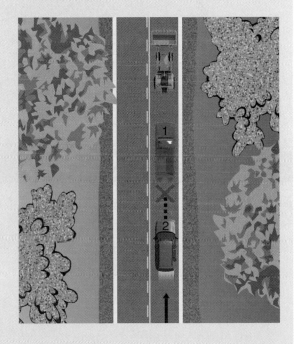

YOUR TURN

11–1 The Rural Driving Environment

1. What makes rural roads and intersections dangerous?

2. What is the proper way to enter, cross, and exit a divided highway with a median strip?

11–2 Defensive Driving on Highways

3. What is the importance of scanning ahead and reducing speed in rural driving?

4. What are some of the dangers of passing on highways?

11–3 Other Dangers of Highway and Rural Driving

5. What are velocitation and highway hypnosis?

6. What should you do if you encounter a slow-moving vehicle or wild animal on the road?

SELF-TEST

Multiple Choice

1. Divided highways are highways that:
   a. are built on two levels.
   b. have a fixed barrier or space between opposite directions of travel.
   c. do not have a median strip.
   d. are maintained by both state/provincial and federal agencies.

2. Which of the following is *not* a common feature of a rural highway?
   a. unmarked driveways
   b. uncontrolled railroad crossing
   c. acceleration lanes
   d. passing lanes

3. The SMV emblem is:
   a. orange and red, and triangular.
   b. orange and red, and round.
   c. blue and red, and triangular.
   d. red and triangular.

4. On highways, how far ahead should oncoming vehicles be for you to safely attempt to pass?
   a. ⅓ mile (500 m)
   b. ½ length of a football field (45 m)
   c. ¾ length of a football field (70 m)
   d. ½ mile (1 km)

5. A crossover is:
   a. a rural railroad crossing.
   b. a place to turn around on a divided highway.
   c. a type of rural intersection.
   d. a pedestrian walkway over a highway.

Sentence Completion

1. A _____ is a main public roadway designed to carry traffic for long, uninterrupted distances at medium to high speeds.

2. The area of ground that separates some divided highways is called a _____ .

3. In rural areas, _____ are often the site of junctions of major and minor roads.

4. _____ occurs when you find yourself driving much faster than you intended.

5. _____ are usually required to cross a two-way highway at a 90-degree angle.

Matching

Match the concepts in Column A with examples of the concepts in Column B.

Column A

1. __ Off-road vehicle
2. __ Unmarked property entrance
3. __ Uneven road
4. __ Use to cross some divided highways
5. __ Crossover
6. __ Highway hypnosis
7. __ Slow-moving vehicle
8. __ Livestock crossing area

Column B

a. "Washboard"
b. Mailbox
c. "Jughandle"
d. For official use only
e. Feeling like you just woke from a dream
f. Wide load
g. ATC
h. Large cloud of dust by roadway

Short Answer

1. How do you turn left off a divided highway?
2. What are the dangers of T-intersections?
3. Why can it be hazardous to enter or exit a highway?
4. How do traffic safety engineers compensate for reduced visibility on rural roadways?
5. What dangers do slow-moving vehicles pose to motorists?

Critical Thinking

1. You are driving on a level two-lane highway with heavy shrubbery on both sides. A pickup carrying a large load of hay is moving slowly in front of you in a passing zone. Scanning ahead, you see no oncoming vehicles for more than half a mile (1 km). You signal and pull into the oncoming traffic lane to make your pass. Just as you pass the pickup and are signaling your intent to return to the right-hand lane, you see a car preparing to pull out from a hidden property entrance 100 yards (90 m) ahead to your right, and headed in your direction. What should you do?

2. It is early evening in December, and you are driving to your grandmother's house out in the country. The road to her house is a narrow and winding two-lane highway with a steep embankment to your left and a shallow wide ditch running alongside to your right. As you go around a curve at 35 miles per hour (55 km/h), a skunk appears in your headlights directly in front of your car. What should you do?

PROJECTS

1. *Find a quiet and level rural road with a speed limit of 50 miles per hour (80 km/h) or more. While you are driving, select two landmarks ahead of you that you estimate to be half a mile (1 km) away from each other. When you reach the first landmark, check your odometer. Make sure that you are maintaining a constant speed at or just below the road's speed limit. When you reach the second landmark, check your odometer again. Note how accurate your estimate of the distance between the landmarks was. Repeat the procedure several times to see if you get more accurate with practice.*

2. *Take a drive on a local rural road or highway. Have a friend write down every potential hazard you encounter—for example, sharp curves, debris on the road, unmarked driveways, animal crossing areas, short acceleration lanes, and uncontrolled railroad crossings. Share your observations with your class.*

Freeway Driving

Unlike city streets and rural highways, access to freeways is controlled and limited. Because there are no intersections, traffic flows smoothly with a minimum of interruptions and a lower risk of collisions. Freeways are also better maintained and equipped with more safety features than highways. Slow-moving vehicles, bicyclists, and pedestrians are normally not permitted. The high rates of speed, however, coupled with congestion, can still make freeways dangerous. Even though there are fewer crashes on freeways than on highways and fatality rates are far lower, freeway driving still demands special skills.

Upon completion of this chapter, you should be able to:

12–1 The Freeway Driving Environment

1. Describe some of the hazards and safety features of freeways.
2. Describe the four basic types of interchanges and where they are used.
3. Understand the importance of scanning, space cushioning, and lane positioning in freeway driving.

12–2 Entering Freeways

4. Describe what you should do when driving on an on-ramp.
5. Understand the purpose of acceleration lanes.
6. Describe the proper way to merge into freeway traffic.

12–3 Exiting Freeways

7. Describe the proper way to exit a freeway.
8. Describe some of the dangers of off-ramps.

12–4 Other Dangers of Freeway Driving

9. Identify the dangers of "weave" lanes and double-merge lanes.
10. Describe the proper way to approach a tollbooth.

KEY TERMS

freeway	merging area	double-merge lane
interchange	deceleration lane	express lane
on-ramp	off-ramp	tollway
acceleration lane	"weave" lane	tollbooth

Figure 12–1 Despite high speeds, freeways are among the safest roads.

12–1 THE FREEWAY DRIVING ENVIRONMENT

Freeways are divided roadways with at least two lanes going in each direction that are designed to carry heavy traffic efficiently and rapidly. Depending on their location and function, freeways may go by other names. In many parts of North America, for example, freeways are called expressways or autoroutes. Freeways that go around urban areas are sometimes called beltways, and those within a park or parklike area and often restricted to noncommercial vehicles may be called parkways.

Freeways are built to maximize safety at high speeds. Lanes and shoulders are wider than average, and fixed objects such as signs and bridge supports are kept well clear of the roadway. Grades are even and curves banked to improve visibility and vehicle control. However, you have less time to react to an emergency situation on a crowded freeway than on an open highway. Escape routes are limited. There are also more vehicles to worry about because freeways can have five, six, or even more travel lanes in addition to special lanes for cars entering and exiting the freeway.

Interchanges

To reduce confusion, congestion, and the dangers of high-speed collisions, **interchanges** are used instead of intersections to allow drivers to enter, exit, or cross a freeway without interrupting the normal flow of traffic. There are four basic types of interchange:

- A *cloverleaf interchange* is where two freeways intersect. Ramps allow drivers to move from one freeway to the other without having to turn left, turn right, or stop for cross traffic.

- A *diamond interchange* is where a freeway intersects a highway with relatively less

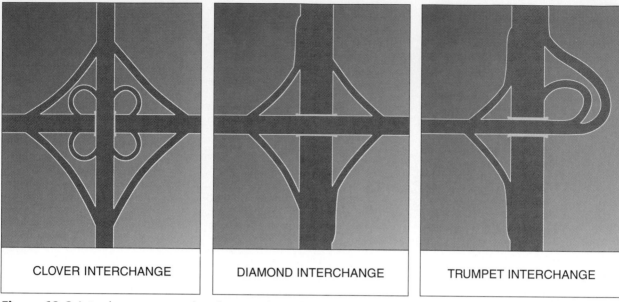

| CLOVER INTERCHANGE | DIAMOND INTERCHANGE | TRUMPET INTERCHANGE |

Figure 12–2 Interchanges are used on freeways instead of intersections.

traffic. Drivers exiting the freeway must stop or yield before turning left or merging right into cross traffic. Drivers entering the freeway use entrance ramps.

• A *trumpet interchange* is where a freeway and highway form a "T." Drivers exiting the freeway merge on

the highway after one direction of traffic crosses over or under the freeway. Drivers entering the freeway from the highway use entrance ramps.

• A *directional interchange* is where several freeways and/or highways meet. Traffic is channeled in various

Figure 12–3 What type of interchange is this?

directions through a complicated series of elevated ramps so that drivers do not have to stop for cross traffic.

Scanning for Danger

When driving on the freeway, you should *repeatedly* scan ahead, behind, and to your sides. Note where other vehicles are at all times and which lanes have a heavy volume of traffic. Pay close attention to signs, signals, and roadway markings on freeways to identify upcoming areas of merging traffic, exits, and lanes or shoulders closed for construction work. Increase your following distance behind large vehicles that can block your view of the surrounding area.

Try to identify possible hazards long before you reach them. Watch especially for traffic backups—caused by collisions, obstacles in the road, severe weather, and vehicles entering the freeway—to give you time to change lanes or slow down gradually. Long-distance sight on freeways is normally very good, so you can usually spot a mass of cars—or brake lights when it is dark or hard to see—long before you get there.

Be on the lookout for speeders, constant lane changers, tailgaters, cars suddenly stopping or even backing up, and drivers having difficulty staying in their lanes.

Increasing Your Space Cushion

Another key to defensive driving on freeways is to leave as large a gap as possible between yourself and other drivers. Remember that higher driving speeds require larger space cushions. The faster you travel, the more room you need to stop or swerve to avoid a collision. Because freeways are more crowded than highways and escape routes are limited, you must work harder to increase the space cushion around your vehicle. This requires *constantly* responding to the actions of drivers around you both in your lane and in adjoining lanes.

Choosing a Lane

To achieve a smooth flow of traffic, all freeway drivers have a responsibility to use the appropriate lane based on the volume and speed of traffic and the exit they plan to use. The far-left lane

DRIVING TIPS *Facing Your Fear of the Freeway* _____

Facing a high volume of fast-moving traffic on multiple lanes of traffic for the first time can be scary. If you are uncomfortable driving on the freeway, stick to "surface streets"—city streets that you can use as an alternative to the freeway—until you gain more confidence behind the wheel. Practice driving on the freeway at quiet times, such as early weekend mornings, in the company of an experienced driver.

DRIVING TIPS *Trapped in the Carpool Lane*

Even if you are qualified to use the HOV lane, do not get in the lane if you are not prepared to drive the prevailing speed up to the posted maximum. If you are maintaining
the speed limit in the carpool lane but traffic is still bunching up behind you, wait for an
appropriate time to legally merge into a through lane and let the other drivers by. Do
not be pressured by tailgaters into crossing solid yellow or white lines into another freeway lane. If you find that vehicles in the carpool lane are consistently speeding, it is
probably in your best interest to simply stay out of the lane.

should be used by faster-than-
normal traffic and for vehicles
passing slower traffic. At rush-
hour times, the far-left lane is often the smoothest lane because
on most freeways it is farthest
from merging traffic. On the
other hand, travel in the far-left
lane can sometimes be inter-
rupted by merging traffic if it ad-
joins a carpool lane, a left freeway
on-ramp, or another freeway
transition lane.

The far-right lane should be
used for traffic that is proceeding
more slowly than normal traffic

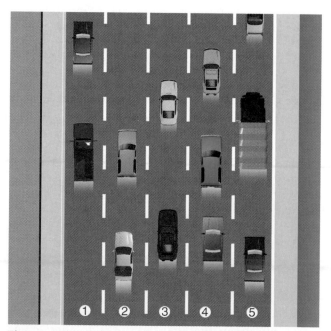

Figure 12–4 The speed and volume of traffic, the type
of vehicle you are driving, and the distance from your intended exit all determine which lane you should use on
the freeway.

DRIVING TIPS · *Lane Numbering*

Freeway lanes are numbered, starting with the left lane closest to the center of the roadway and moving across the freeway to the lane on the extreme right. On a three-lane freeway, for example, the left lane is Lane 1, the center lane is Lane 2, and the right lane is Lane 3. The next time that you hear a radio traffic report about a crash in the "number two lane" or that "the number one lane" is closed for construction, you will know which lanes to avoid.

or is either entering or exiting the roadway. Avoid driving in the far-right lane when possible. Not only will you have merging conflicts, but you will also have to drive behind trucks, buses, recreational vehicles, and other large vehicles that can block your surrounding view of the roadway.

The center lanes should be used for through traffic. Because you do not have to deal with vehicles merging into or out of your lane on a regular basis and a "passing lane" is available to your left, center lanes are the ones that normally have the smoothest flow of traffic. The closer you get to the far-left lane, the faster the through traffic generally is. On a five-lane freeway, for example, vehicles in Lane 2 generally drive faster than vehicles in Lane 3, which go faster than vehicles in Lane 4. In reality, however, it does not always work out that way. It is up to you to assess traffic conditions and pick a through lane appropriate for your relative speed.

Changing Lanes

Changing lanes at high speeds in a crowded, multilane environment requires extreme caution and patience. When several lanes are moving in the same direction, drivers often compete for the same space. It

LATRELL SPREWELL

On March 2, 1997, Latrell Sprewell, a three-time All-Star guard with the Golden State Warriors basketball team, was changing lanes and cutting through traffic at high speeds on Interstate 680 near the town of Pleasant Hill in Northern California. After first moving into an EXIT ONLY lane, he lost control of his car while attempting to re-enter the freeway. He struck several sand barrels, hit a wall, and collided with another vehicle, flipping it over and injuring both the driver and the passenger. Sprewell pleaded no contest to a charge of reckless driving and was sentenced to three months of home detention, placed on two years probation, and fined $1,000. Weaving in and out of traffic to avoid slowing down or to pass other vehicles is both dangerous and illegal.

is often difficult to guess other drivers' intentions, and sometimes you cannot see their signal—if they do signal. Openings in traffic can appear and disappear in seconds, and many motorists change lanes without thoroughly checking their blind spots because they do not want to "waste" an opportunity.

When changing lanes on a freeway, remember to *change only one lane at a time.* Even if two or three adjoining lanes appear to be clear, resist the urge to change more than one lane at a time. Most people simply cannot process the amount of visual information required to execute a multilane maneuver safely. Therefore, it is illegal to change more than one lane at a time in many jurisdictions.

To safely change lanes on a freeway, follow these steps (see Figure 12–5):

1. Make sure that there is enough space between your vehicle and the car in front of you. If not, reduce your speed to increase your following distance. Watch for signs that the other driver intends to change into the same lane. Is the turn signal on? Is the driver looking over his or her shoulder? Is the car veering toward the other lane?

2. Assess possible merging conflicts in the lane you wish to enter. Look for vehicles ahead of you in the other lane, behind you in your lane, behind you in the other lane, and in the lane *next* to the lane you wish to enter. Use both your rearview and sideview mirrors, and look over your shoulder

to check your blind spots in the direction you want to move.

3. If the way is clear, signal your intention to change lanes by activating your turn signal. Thoroughly check traffic around you *again*. Make sure that the situation has not changed since you turned on your signal. Is a car ahead of you in the other lane suddenly slowing down? Is a motorcycle accelerating behind you in the other lane? Give other drivers around you plenty of time to see your signal. Delay your lane change if necessary until it is safe to move over.

4. If the way is clear, move into the other lane *with your head turned in the direction you are moving.* Check for any late-developing potential conflicts with quick, darting glances around you.

5. As soon as you have entered the lane, face forward again and establish your position in the new lane. Cancel your signal.

When you encounter other drivers about to enter the freeway near you, avoid potential conflicts by changing lanes to allow them to safely enter the freeway. Even if you are not in the far-right lane (or far-left lane if the entrance ramp is on the left), you may need to allow other vehicles in that lane to move over to make room for cars entering the freeway. You may also have to move over for merging traffic from a carpool lane.

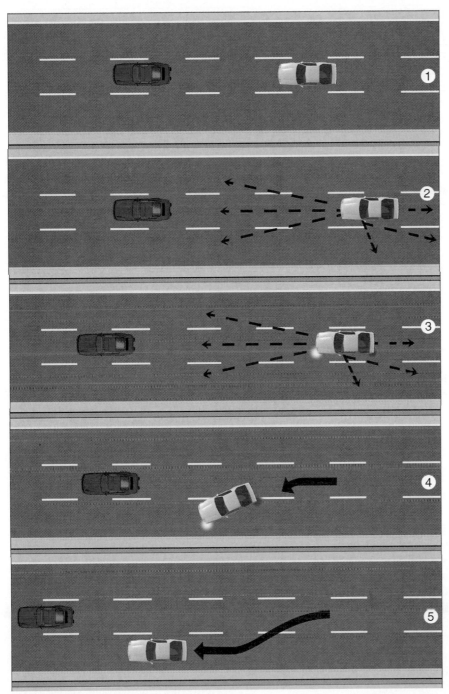

Figure 12–5 Changing lanes on a freeway

Passing on Freeways

Just as in all other driving environments, the general rule is to pass on the left. However, freeway traffic conditions sometimes prevent you from doing so. Many drivers drive too slowly or too fast for the lane they are in, causing traffic to back up where it should be flowing smoothly. For example, if you are behind a dangerously slow car in the middle lane of a normally flowing five-lane freeway, and there are no opportunities to use the two left lanes to pass but the right lanes are clear, you may have no choice but to pass on the right.

If you are constantly being passed on the right, you are probably driving too slowly for your lane. This is dangerous because it leaves you no escape path in case of an emergency. Work your way over to the right—one lane at a time—until other vehicles are passing you only on your left.

When passing other vehicles on a freeway, continually scan around you for potential conflicts. Use both your rearview and sideview mirrors and check your blind spots by looking over your shoulder. Watch for brake lights, turn signals, and people turning their heads in preparation for a lane change. As you change lanes, flash your lights or tap your horn if necessary to get the attention of other drivers who may be merging into the space you are about to occupy.

Always try to maintain as large a space cushion as possible around your vehicle when passing or being passed. If a car passing you is too close, move away from the other vehicle within your lane until the other driver has passed. When passing other cars, make sure that you have adequate room on both sides of your vehicle. If possible, avoid passing vehicles on both sides of you at the same time. If you have *any* doubts about the safety of your pass, wait for a better opportunity. Remember that conditions change quickly on a freeway, so even if you "lose" a chance to pass, another is likely to come along shortly.

12–2 ENTERING FREEWAYS

Entering freeways can be challenging, especially for inexperienced drivers. If you are entering a freeway from a surface street, you must quickly adjust both to a rapid increase in speed and a high volume of traffic. The first step in learning how to safely and comfortably enter freeways is to familiarize yourself with the three major parts of a freeway entrance: the on-ramp, the acceleration lane, and the merging area.

On-Ramps

Access to freeways from surface streets is limited to one-way entrance ramps or **on-ramps.** Entrance ramps may go up or down to the freeway, depending on whether the surface street passes above or below it. Watch for green directional signs at the top or base of on-ramps directing you to the

Wild Wheels

Figure 12–6 What is the name of this car, capable of violating the freeway speed limit even in FIRST gear?

Figure 12–7 Access to freeways is limited to on-ramps.

freeway. Most on-ramp signs provide the freeway name, route number, direction, and destination (usually the name of a city).

On-ramps for a particular direction on the freeway may be located on either side of the surface street, so pay close attention to signs indicating which lane you should get into on the surface street as you approach the underpass or overpass. If the surface street has numerous lanes and traffic is heavy, it might be difficult changing from the far-left lane to the far-right lane or vice versa to reach the appropriate entrance ramp. If you miss the on-ramp you want, continue on the surface street until you can safely turn around and try again from the opposite direction. Do not try to move across two or

Figure 12–8 It is sometimes easy to confuse entrance ramps with exit ramps, so pay careful attention to all signs.

Figure 12–9 Scan for a gap in freeway traffic from the on-ramp to give you more time to prepare to merge.

more lanes of traffic at the last second to reach the ramp.

Once you have entered an on-ramp, make sure that you maintain a safe following distance behind any vehicle in front of you. Depending on freeway traffic conditions, the driver ahead of you may suddenly brake to look for a gap. Because you will be scanning freeway traffic as you move along the entrance ramp, your full attention will not be on the vehicle directly in front of you. A long following distance will give you extra time to react if the other driver suddenly slows or stops. Remember to also keep an eye on drivers behind you on the ramp. Tailgaters on freeway on-ramps may rear-end you if *you* have to suddenly hit your brakes. Their aggressive behavior is also a sign that they may try to cut you off as you prepare to merge, accelerating past you onto the freeway before you can enter it.

Adjust your speed on freeway on-ramps to traffic conditions.

Watch for backups caused by freeway traffic or ramp signals, and tap your brakes if necessary to warn drivers behind you to slow down and prepare to stop. If you mistakenly take the wrong on-ramp, continue onto the freeway and get off at the next available exit to turn around on the freeway or retrace your steps on surface streets to reach the correct on-ramp. *Never* back up on a freeway on-ramp under any circumstances.

On-ramps may be short, steep, sharply curved, or separated from freeway lanes by walls, landscaping, or other obstacles that block your view. It is important that you be ready to scan for a gap in traffic as soon as you have a clear line of sight. Observe traffic on all lanes of the freeway as well as ahead of you and behind you on the ramp. Look over your shoulder and use sideview and rearview mirrors to find a gap that you can safely enter. Activate your turn signal well before you reach the freeway.

Figure 12–10 Use extra caution when using an on-ramp with double-merge lanes.

If you are on a metered on-ramp and have to stop, keep in mind that you will have less roadway to use for accelerating into traffic.

Acceleration Lanes

Unlike most rural highways, freeways usually provide an **acceleration lane.** This is a temporary lane on the freeway that is an extension of the on-ramp and that allows entering vehicles to match freeway driving speeds before merging into traffic.

Do not ever be tempted to "dive into" a stream of traffic, counting on freeway drivers to get out of your way, without properly searching for an opening. If you have not found an opening in traffic by the time the acceleration lane ends,

USING SAFE   *Entering Freeways*

When entering a freeway from surface streets, you must adjust to a rapid change in speed. Use the SAFE process to reduce the risk of a collision. As you make your way up or down the on-ramp, *scan* toward the freeway lane you will be entering. Look over your shoulder and check your mirrors for vehicles that may be approaching from the rear. Watch for the brake lights of the car directly ahead of you in case the driver is forced to stop or abruptly slow down to merge. *Assess* the relative speed of traffic in the lane of the freeway into which you will be merging. Most often, this will be the far-right lane. Consider the types of vehicles to determine where you are likely to end up when you reach the merging area. The far-right lane is often used by "big rigs" and other slow-moving vehicles, but you also have to be careful of fast-moving drivers who are preparing to exit the freeway or those who have just entered the freeway. This problem often occurs in metropolitan areas, where access points are spaced close together and cars are constantly entering and exiting the freeway. *Find* a gap in traffic and adjust your speed as necessary to *execute* your merge safely.

Figure 12–11 Acceleration lanes give you time to match the speed of freeway traffic before merging.

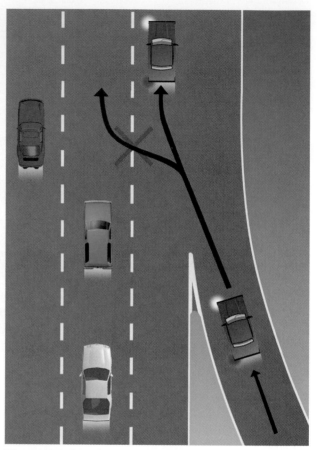

Figure 12–12 Always merge into the first through lane of freeway traffic.

continue driving onto the shoulder if necessary to wait for a safe gap. Even in heavy, bumper-to-bumper traffic, you should never completely stop in the acceleration lane to merge into traffic. A driver behind you looking for a gap might not realize that you have stopped and rear-end you.

If vehicles in front of you stop in the acceleration lane, be patient and reduce your speed. Tap your brakes to warn drivers behind you on the on-ramp to slow down. Allow stopped or slow-

ing drivers directly in front of you to find a gap first before merging onto the freeway yourself. Never try to rush past another vehicle in the acceleration lane. The driver of the other vehicle may not see you and could attempt to merge onto the freeway just as you are trying to pass, resulting in a crash.

Merging Area

The **merging area** is the space where the acceleration lane merges with the freeway. Before reaching the merging area, you should be traveling at about the same speed as other vehicles already in the traffic flow. You should also target which vehicle you are going to get behind after you merge.

As you enter the merging area, steer gradually into the through lane. Make periodic speed adjustments to blend into traffic smoothly. Continue to check traffic in all lanes, and watch for drivers that unexpectedly slow down, accelerate, or change lanes. Do not rely on your mirrors. Turn your head in the direction that you are merging to make sure that your blind spot is clear.

Position your car at a safe distance behind the vehicle you decide to follow. Once you are safely in the through lane, cancel your turn signal. Check for vehicles around you once again. Be especially careful of drivers still in the acceleration lane who may cut in front of you or directly behind you. If traffic is stop and go, common courtesy often comes into play, and merging cars and through-traffic cars take turns.

Most drivers will cooperate with you, but be prepared for the occasional drivers who will not let anyone in ahead of them. Let these drivers pass and take the next spot.

Always merge into the first through lane of the freeway. Never try to cross one or more freeway lanes while merging. In those rare instances when you enter a freeway on the left side, keep in mind that you will be merging into the fastest lane of traffic and must accelerate more quickly than you would if entering the freeway on the right.

12–3 EXITING FREEWAYS

Exiting a freeway is normally smoother than entering one. Exits are easier to identify on a freeway than on ramps are from a city street or highway. You also have more time to prepare to exit than you do to merge onto the freeway. Also, exit ramps have no meters or carpool lanes to worry about. However, exiting freeways

Figure 12–13 Get into the proper exit lane well ahead of the exit to avoid last-second merging conflicts.

REALITY CHECK *A Missed Exit Is Not the End of the World*

If you have missed your exit, do not panic and stop, back up, or swerve across several lanes in a last-minute desperate attempt to make it. Instead, continue to the next exit and use surface streets to drive back to your intended point of exit. If you have missed an exit for another freeway, take the next exit and follow signs to get back on the freeway going the opposite direction.

can still be dangerous. Ramp overflows, short or sharply curved exit ramps, and crossing acceleration and deceleration paths all can cause problems.

Most freeways give you plenty of time to prepare for an exit. For example, distance signs for an exit may appear 5 miles, 2½ miles, and ¼ mile before the exit in addition to the EXIT sign at the exit itself. Do not wait until the exit is a few hundred feet (100 m) away to begin making your move toward the proper exit lane. Sudden, surprise exit moves could cause other drivers around you to make evasive maneuvers that may result in a crash. If possible, signal and move into the proper lane at least 1 mile (1½ km) before your exit. This is especially critical in heavy traffic, when it may be difficult to find an opening for last-minute lane changes. If you see an EXIT ONLY sign for your exit, move into the lane indicated by the arrow as soon as it is safe to do so.

Deceleration Lanes

Just as acceleration lanes allow drivers entering a freeway to adjust to high-speed conditions without disrupting the flow of traffic, **deceleration lanes** allow driv-

ers exiting a freeway to adjust to slower-speed conditions without blocking traffic on the through lanes. Just as with acceleration

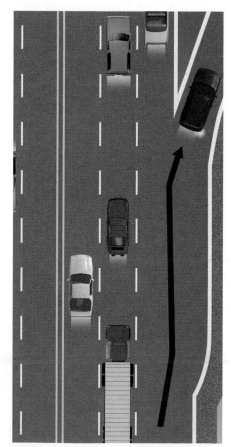

Figure 12–14 Deceleration lanes give you time to reduce your speed before getting on surface streets.

lanes, you will normally be able to recognize a deceleration lane by its distinctive lane-line markings. Make sure that you signal and enter a deceleration lane well in advance. Check your rearview and sideview mirrors for other vehicles, and look over your shoulder to be certain that your blind spots are clear. Watch for vehicles to your rear that may try to sneak past you to exit ahead of you.

Avoid slowing down to enter the deceleration lane. Instead, wait to reduce your speed until you are completely out of the freeway traffic flow. Once you have entered the deceleration lane, cancel your signal and make sure that you have a comfortable space cushion with vehicles ahead of you and behind you. If a driver behind you is too close, tap your brakes to warn him or her that you are slowing down. If you are too close to a vehicle in front of you, first take your foot off the accelerator and then use your brakes if necessary to increase your following distance. This is especially important if you are behind a large vehicle that can block your view of the off-ramp ahead.

Gradually reduce your speed as you drive along the deceleration lane. Watch for posted speed reduction signs or warning signs about sharply banked off-ramps. Keep in mind that some deceleration lanes are very short, requiring you to reduce your speed more quickly than normal.

Off-Ramps

Deceleration lanes lead directly to one-way exit ramps called off-ramps. Exit ramps direct vehicles exiting the freeway up or down to another roadway. Because off-ramps can be very short or have sharp curves, you must adjust to the off-ramp speed limit before actually getting onto the ramp. In some cases, this requires a rapid decrease in speed. If you enter an exit ramp too quickly, you may lose control of your vehicle. Warning signs are usually posted on dangerous off-ramps, but there is no substitute for properly scanning ahead to assess potentially hazardous conditions.

When exit ramps merge directly into street or highway traffic, watch for YIELD or MERGE signs and use caution. Exit ramps may also end in an intersection with a STOP sign or signals. After you exit the freeway, anticipate the dangers associated with city and highway driving intersections, two-way traffic, and pedestrians. It is often difficult to adjust to slower speeds after driving on the freeway, so keep an eye on your speedometer to make sure that you are driving at the proper speed.

12–4 OTHER DANGERS OF FREEWAY DRIVING

Although freeways are among the safest roadways, a number of hazards are associated with freeway driving that can challenge even the most experienced drivers.

"Weave" Lanes

One of the most dangerous situations facing freeway drivers is that

Figure 12–15 Drivers entering and exiting the freeway must sometimes share the same lane.

of shared acceleration and deceleration lanes, often called **"weave" lanes** because vehicles exiting and entering the freeway have to weave in and out of the same lane. This situation occurs when an off-ramp is placed immediately after an on-ramp and both share at least one access lane. Vehicles entering and exiting the freeway at the same place *share* the right-of-way. The result is a nerve-racking jockeying for position between drivers who are trying to do opposite things.

When driving in one of these lanes, actively scan so that you know where vehicles around you are at all times. Increase your space cushion as much as possible, and communicate your intentions to other drivers using turn indicators, hand signals, a flash of your headlights, or a tap of your horn. Watch for brake lights. Find an escape route in case another driver makes an unexpected move.

Double-Merge Lanes

Some on-ramps have two lanes that merge together at the end of the ramp so that a single **double-merge lane** enters the freeway. On other double-merge on-ramps, the two lanes stay separate throughout the entire merge onto the freeway! These situations call for drivers to merge twice—once with other vehicles into the acceleration lane or from one merge lane to another, and then again into freeway traffic. On freeways with carpool lanes, one of the double-merge lanes may be designated for carpoolers. In these situations, the carpool lane is usually uncontrolled while the other lane is metered, making the merging situation even more complicated.

If you are entering the freeway in the entry lane closest to through traffic, you must find an appropriate merging space with the through traffic *and* watch for vehicles in the outer entry lane. Outer entry-lane vehicles often dart ahead of cars in the inner entry lane. Vehicles in the inner lane behind you may move over quickly and occupy the gap in through traffic which you had intended to use. Continue to scan on all sides of your vehicle when executing this tricky maneuver.

Double-merge exit ramp lanes are less problematic, but you must always be ready for other drivers to make erratic lane changes on the exit ramp. Other drivers may find themselves stuck in the "inner" exit-ramp lane without wishing to leave the freeway at that location. These drivers will sometimes attempt to cross over two lanes to get back into the flow of through traffic, a dangerous maneuver that can easily lead to a crash.

Express Lanes

Express lanes are special reversible freeway lanes that go into and out of cities. During morning rush-hour times they are opened to traffic entering the city, and in evening rush-hour times they are opened to traffic leaving the city. To maintain a smooth flow of traffic and minimize merging conflicts, express lanes normally have only one entrance and few exits. Make sure that you read signs carefully before entering an express lane, especially if there is no traffic around to indicate the current direction of travel.

Rush-Hour Traffic

Freeways are designed for high-speed driving, but at rush-hour times, traffic can be extremely congested. As city populations increase, freeways are becoming increasingly crowded places. Local jurisdictions have attempted to tackle this problem with more road construction, tollways, commuter lanes, carpool lanes, metered on-ramps, and various forms of public transportation. Space and funding for road improvements are limited, and many drivers simply refuse to give up the convenience of using their own vehicle to get to and from work or school.

Rush-hour traffic can be frustrating. Many drivers wait an hour or more to cover a distance that might take half as long at nonpeak hours. The problem becomes worse when there is a crash, breakdown, or lane closing. Rush-hour traffic can also be hazardous. The most dangerous situation occurs when traffic backs up periodically and unpredictably, so drivers continually alternate between high and low speeds on different sections of the freeway. Traffic flow can vary greatly by lane as well. Vehicles can be completely stopped in one lane

Figure 12–16

AUTO ACCESSORIES *Freeway Maps*

In large cities such as Toronto, Chicago, and Los Angeles, you can purchase special maps to help you navigate the complex networks of modern urban freeways. Without having to wade through several giant fold-out maps of neighboring counties, you can get a bird's eye view of the principal interchanges, connecting freeways, and exits of a large metropolitan area in a handy-sized map that can be safely read in stopped traffic.

and traveling 55 miles per hour (90 km/h) in the next!

Under these kinds of conditions, many impatient drivers try to jump from one lane to the next to get into a "faster" lane. This is almost guaranteed to cause a crash. Vehicles in fast-moving lanes may be forced to suddenly stop, causing one or more rear-end collisions. On congested freeways, sometimes *no* escape paths are available in emergencies. One crash can easily lead to a chain of other collisions. If you get stuck in rush-hour traffic on the freeway, stay calm. Keep your radio tuned to traffic reports and look for variable message signs for updates on conditions ahead. If necessary, carefully consult a map for an alternative route when you are completely stopped. If you lose all patience, get off at the next exit and wait it out before putting yourself or others at risk.

Never attempt to use the freeway shoulder or median to get past a traffic backup on the freeway. This is both hazardous and strictly illegal. These spaces are often the only available routes for emergency vehicles to get past traffic. If you get in the way of a fire truck, ambulance, or police car, you could be putting other people's lives at risk.

Tollways

Some freeways require drivers to pay a fee, or toll, to use it. **Tollways** are also called turnpikes, toll expressways, or toll roads, depending on where in North America you are. Some tollways are connected to freeways and provide an alternative to the most heavily traveled sections of freeways. In these situations, signs are posted on the freeway indicating which lanes and exits lead to tollways ahead. You are usually given plenty of time to get into the proper lane, although the costs of using the tollway may not be posted. Sometimes a freeway turns into a tollway, in which case you are normally warned to get off the roadway by a certain exit to avoid paying a fee.

At some point on a tollway, you must stop at a **tollbooth** to pay the fare. Tollbooths are usually located at entrances and exits to tollways in a toll plaza that includes extra lanes to minimize congestion. Approaches to tollbooths include a combination of rumble strips, flashing yellow lights, signs,

Figure 12–17 Before entering a tollbooth lane, make sure that you know whether you have to provide exact change.

and roadway markings warning of the toll plaza area ahead. Each booth in a toll plaza has its own lane, with some lanes reserved for certain types of vehicles such as trucks, buses, and vehicles towing trailers. A green signal above a tollbooth indicates that it is open to traffic, while a red signal indicates that it is closed.

There are three basic types of tollbooths. One type scans your vehicle for an electronic transponder usually mounted on the inside of your front windshield. This type of tollbooth requires you to slow down, not stop, as you pass through it. Another type is machine-operated and requires you to briefly stop to toss exact change or a previously purchased "token" coin into a bucket or net. The third type of tollbooth is operated by an attendant, who can give you change.

As you approach a toll plaza, prepare to slow down. Choose an appropriate tollbooth as early as possible, and make sure that it has a green light above it. Once you enter a tollbooth lane, remain in it. Many crashes at tollbooths are caused by drivers changing lanes at the last second looking for a booth with the shortest line. Allow yourself plenty of time to stop at the booth or, if you have a transponder, proceed slowly through it. Observe the traffic controls on the other side of the booth—usually red and green signals—and continue once the payment of the fee is registered. As you leave the tollbooth, watch for other vehicles leaving on both sides of you. Gradually accelerate and watch for drivers who may merge into your lane as you enter the freeway, highway, or city traffic.

bumper sticker sightings

> TRAFFIC TAKES ITS TOLL . . .
> PLEASE HAVE EXACT
> CHANGE READY

WHO'S AT FAULT?

1. Driver 1 was in a tractor-trailer truck proceeding westbound on the interstate at about 5 miles per hour (8 km/h) in Lane 3 in heavy traffic. He spotted his off-ramp ahead and began moving right to prepare to exit. Driver 2 had just come from the transition road from southbound Highway 15 and was attempting to merge left into Lane 3 of the interstate. Her speed was about 30 miles per hour (50 km/h). While merging right, Driver 1 collided with Driver 2. *Who's at fault?*

2. Drivers 1 and 2 were both stopped side-by-side at a red light on a metered on-ramp to the freeway shortly after dark. Just as the light turned green, both drivers "floored" their accelerators and raced toward the freeway. Driver 1's left front tire struck the barrier, causing his vehicle to spin sideways. Attempting to avoid Driver 1's tail, Driver 2 veered right and suffered a head-on collision with the cement barrier on the right. *Who's at fault?*

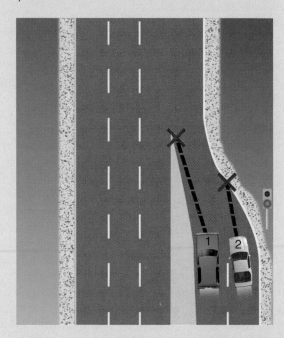

YOUR TURN

12–1 The Freeway Driving Environment

1. What are some of the hazards and safety features of freeways?

2. What are the four basic types of interchanges and where are they used?

3. How are scanning, space cushioning, and lane positioning important in freeway driving?

12–2 Entering Freeways

4. What should you do when driving on an on-ramp?

5. What is the purpose of acceleration lanes?

6. What is the proper way to merge into freeway traffic?

12–3 Exiting Freeways

7. What is the proper way to exit a freeway?

8. What are some of the dangers of off-ramps?

12–4 Other Dangers of Freeway Driving

9. What are the dangers of "weave" lanes and double-merge lanes?

10. What is the proper way to approach a tollbooth?

SELF-TEST

Multiple Choice

1. Lane 1 on a five-lane freeway is:
   a. the far-left lane.
   b. the far-right lane.
   c. the center lane.
   d. the carpool lane.

2. When driving on a freeway, signal and move into the proper exit lane at least _____ before your exit appears.
   a. 2 miles (3 km)
   b. ½ mile (1 km)
   c. 5 miles (5 km)
   d. 1 mile (1½ km)

3. A freeway that goes completely around an urban area is called a:
   a. parkway.
   b. beltway.
   c. turnpike.
   d. directional interchange.

4. A temporary lane on the freeway that allows entering vehicles to meet freeway driving speeds before merging into traffic is called a(n):

   a. acceleration lane.   **c.** deceleration lane.

   b. express lane.   **d.** on-ramp.

5. If you are consistently being passed on the right side on a freeway, you should:

   a. move to the left.   **c.** move to the right.

   b. speed up.   **d.** stay where you are.

Sentence Completion

1. _____ are special reversible freeway lanes that go into and out of cities.

2. It is illegal to change more than _____ lane(s) at a time in many jurisdictions.

3. A _____ is where a freeway and highway form a "T."

4. The _____ is the space where the acceleration lane merges with the freeway.

5. You must pay a fee to use a _____.

Matching

Match the concepts in Column A with examples of the concepts in Column B.

Column A	Column B
1. __ Shared right-of-way	**a.** Carpool lane next to a regular lane
2. __ Payment at a tollbooth	**b.** Far-right lane
3. __ Used by trucks and buses	**c.** Token
4. __ Express lane	**d.** "Weave" lane
5. __ Danger on on-ramp	**e.** Short acceleration lane
6. __ Sign of lane change	**f.** Driver turning head
7. __ No crossing solid yellow/white lines	**g.** Short deceleration lane
8. __ Danger on off-ramp	**h.** Open to traffic leaving city at end of day

Short Answer

1. What should you do if you mistakenly take the wrong on-ramp?

2. What should you do if you have not found an opening in traffic and the acceleration lane ends?

3. How fast should you be driving in the merging area?

4. Who has the right-of-way in a "weave" lane?

5. What is the most dangerous situation you face in rush-hour traffic?

Critical Thinking

1. You are in the far-right lane on a freeway preparing to get off at the next exit. Merging traffic is causing a backup in your lane. Just as you commit yourself to enter the "weave" lane, you notice that a car entering the freeway is moving up fast behind you on your right. What should you do?

2. You are traveling in the center lane of a three-lane freeway behind a slow-moving tractor-trailer truck. The lanes to the left and to the right are clear, so you decide to pass the truck on the left. As you pull alongside, you observe that several other "big rigs" are in a line ahead of the truck you are passing. Although you are traveling at 65 miles per hour (100 km/h), the posted maximum limit, another driver in a sports car moves up close behind you in your lane and flashes his lights at you to speed up. What should you do?

PROJECTS

1. Look at a detailed road map of a large urban area. Find the freeway interchanges and classify each one as a cloverleaf, diamond, trumpet, or directional interchange. How do the actual interchanges differ from the models shown on page 274?

2. Select a point at the edge of the same map and plot out the most direct route to get to downtown. Next, plot out one or two alternative routes that you think would bypass the heaviest traffic during rush-hour times. Drive each of your routes during both rush hour and at a time with light traffic. Were you able to follow your planned routes? Did you get lost, or did the trip go smoothly? Did the alternative routes save you time and hassle?

13

Sharing the Road

As a driver, you have a responsibility to share the road with many types of roadway users. Most people that you will encounter on streets and highways will be driving cars or light trucks. However, bicycles, motorcycles, large trucks, and buses are also permitted on public roadways, and pedestrians use or cross streets to get to their destinations. Understanding the dangers you face from other roadway users and the dangers they face from you is an important part of defensive driving.

CHAPTER OBJECTIVES

Upon completion of this chapter, you should be able to:

13–1 Pedestrians

1. Understand what responsibilities motorists have to pedestrians.
2. Understand what responsibilities pedestrians have to motorists.

13–2 Bicycles

3. Understand what responsibilities motorists have to bicyclists.
4. Understand what responsibilities bicyclists have to motorists.

13–3 Motorcycles

5. Understand what responsibilities motorists have to motorcyclists.
6. Understand what responsibilities motorcyclists have to motorists.

13–4 Trucks and Buses

7. Describe the "no zones" of a large truck.
8. Describe some of the dangers of passing trucks.
9. Understand what precautions you should take when driving near stopped buses.

KEY TERMS

pedestrian	motorcycle	"no zones"
jaywalking	moped	off-tracking

Figure 13–1 City streets are often crowded with pedestrians.

13–1   PEDESTRIANS

The term **pedestrian** broadly refers to any person who uses or crosses a roadway on foot or by means of a self-propelled device other than a bicycle. People who walk, run, jog, skateboard, or rollerblade are pedestrians, as are disabled persons who use wheelchairs, walkers, or crutches. You can expect frequent encounters with pedestrians on city streets, especially near commercial districts, parks, shopping areas, and schools. On weekends and after school and work hours, residential areas can also be crowded with pedestrians.

Driver Responsibilities to Pedestrians

In most jurisdictions, drivers must give the right-of-way to any pedestrian crossing a street at an intersection, using a crosswalk, or using the sidewalk when crossing an entrance to a driveway or alley.

They must also give the right-of-way to any blind pedestrian wherever he or she is. In general, however, you should always give the right-of-way to *any* pedestrian you meet for the simple reason that while you are safely enclosed in a metallic shell, pedestrians

Figure 13–2 You have a responsibility to look after the safety of pedestrians.

REALITY CHECK *Help the Unseen Pedestrian*

We have all seen it happen. A pedestrian is trying to cross a busy street and the vehicle in the lane nearest the pedestrian stops to allow him or her to cross. Unfortunately, approaching drivers in adjoining lanes do not see the pedestrian or understand why the vehicle ahead has stopped. They continue at full speed and reach the pedestrian's path just as the pedestrian is coming into view from behind the stopped vehicle. If you are the driver of that stopped vehicle, you should do everything you can to help protect the pedestrian. Warn the motorists behind you to stop by using hand signals or tapping your brakes. If necessary, honk your horn or flash your lights to alert the pedestrian that danger is approaching.

only have as much protection as their clothes provide.

Most collisions between vehicles and pedestrians occur in or near intersections. Some of these crashes are the result of pedestrians who cross illegally against a red light or pedestrian signal. Others are caused by drivers who run a red light or fail to give the right-of-way. Still others are caused by carelessness on the part of both drivers and pedestrians. Drivers may hit a pedestrian hidden from view by a high-profile vehicle in another lane as they

pass or move to the corner to turn. Similarly, pedestrians may step off the curb right into the path of a car without looking because they think they have the right-of-way or they are looking only at the signal.

As you approach an intersection, watch for trucks and buses in front of you or in adjoining lanes that may block your view of the crosswalk area. To avoid hitting any pedestrians who may be crossing near the vehicle blocking your view, make sure you stop at the stop line or nearer crosswalk

bumper sticker sightings

IF YOU DON'T LIKE THE WAY I DRIVE, GET OFF THE SIDEWALK!

Figure 13–3 Many pedestrians are dangerously exposed to traffic while working.

Figure 13–4 If another vehicle is blocking your view of pedestrian traffic, make sure that the front of your car remains behind the front of the other vehicle when you stop.

line. If there is no crosswalk or limit line, act as if there were and stop before where the first crosswalk line would be. If you are preparing to make a right turn, carefully creep forward to the corner and check for pedestrians who may be hidden from view.

Pedestrian Responsibilities to Drivers

Just as drivers have a responsibility to watch out for the safety of pedestrians, pedestrians have a responsibility to avoid creating dangerous situations. Pedestrians have a much better view of the road than do drivers, have fewer distractions to worry about, and can stop or change directions much more quickly than a person in a vehicle. Although they have the right-of-way in many situations, pedestrians bear much of the burden for their own safety on the road.

Use common sense and remember how vulnerable you are. If you are crossing a street at a crosswalk where there may be a pedestrian crossing sign but no other traffic controls, wait for a gap in traffic to cross. This is especially true on roads with high-speed traffic. Even if vehicles are always required to stop for you, it is safer to attempt to cross when no vehicles are nearby. The more time a driver has to see you cross, the better prepared he or she will

Figure 13–5 Pedestrians have a responsibility not to create dangerous situations.

be to slow down. You will also have less distance to cover to reach the other side of the street in case the driver does not see you. Drivers appreciate the courtesy—and good sense—of pedestrians who avoid interrupting the flow of traffic.

REALITY CHECK *Pedestrian Guidelines*

- Do not cross a street outside of an intersection except in rural areas where it would be impractical to walk for long distances to find one.
- Do not cross or enter a street from between parked cars.
- Do not chase or follow balls, toys, or pets into the street without first checking for traffic.
- Do not walk in the street if you do not have to. If there are sidewalks, use them. If there are no sidewalks, walk on the left side of the street facing traffic and try to stay as far away from oncoming vehicles as possible.
- Do not step into the street from the curb before you can do so legally and safely.
- Do not assume that you are safe in a crosswalk. Always watch for cars and other vehicles approaching you.
- Do not assume that just because you see a driver that he or she sees you. Always try to establish eye contact with drivers as you cross in front of them.
- Do not assume that just because you are wearing light-colored or reflective clothing at night that you are visible to all drivers.
- Do not use sidewalks or cross streets when your hearing is limited by a radio or a portable CD or cassette player. Turn your music down or take off your headphones.
- Do not hitchhike. It is dangerous and often illegal.
- Do not walk on freeways. It is usually illegal and extremely dangerous.

Figure 13–6 Jaywalkers are common at urban intersections.

Jaywalking

Jaywalking is crossing the street without regard for traffic rules or signals. The most dangerous form of jaywalking is crossing a street at a place other than an intersection or crosswalk. Many jurisdictions and localities have laws regulating or prohibiting jaywalking. Because of different urban environments and customs, some jurisdictions rigorously enforce such laws, whereas others are very lax about it. Regardless of whether it is legal or not enforced, jaywalking is dangerous. Most fatalities in traffic collisions involving pedestrians are jaywalkers. As a pedestrian, you should cross streets only at intersections and crosswalks when it is legal and safe to do so.

Although it is difficult to predict when people will jaywalk, drivers who pay careful attention to their surroundings can anticipate jaywalking situations. For example, people are more inclined to take shortcuts across the street on long blocks or in bad weather. Jaywalkers might also dash across a street to reach a crowded restaurant or to get to a movie theater if they are worried about being late. Unsupervised children in residential areas may jaywalk to and from school and playgrounds. The more people present, the

DRIVING TIPS *Roads That Are Not "Pedestrian Friendly"* _____

Always watch for pedestrians on the road in areas without sidewalks. If you approach a pedestrian whose back is to you, especially on a narrow road, reduce your speed and flash your lights or "toot" your horn as you pass to let him or her know of your presence.

higher the risk that you will encounter a jaywalker; so if the sidewalks are crowded, be on your guard!

13–2 BICYCLES

Bicyclists ride on all types of roadways except freeways. They are commonly found in residential areas, in certain business districts, near schools, on scenic roads, and by parks, lakes, rivers, and other recreational areas.

Because bicycles are used for both transportation and recreation by people of all ages and sizes, you should expect to find

Figure 13–7 Bicycling is a popular form of transportation and recreation throughout North America.

them almost anywhere. In addition, because bicyclists ride close to traffic and are vulnerable to injury in a collision, drivers have a special duty to pay attention to them and provide for their safety.

Driver Responsibilities to Bicyclists

When sharing the road with bicyclists, expect sudden moves on their part at all times. Debris, minor oil slicks, a pothole, an opening door of a parked car, and other hazards can force a bicyclist to swerve suddenly into the lanes of traffic. Especially in residential areas, bicyclists will often ride in the middle of the street and disregard STOP signs and other traffic controls. Be alert for children on bikes and tricycles who are riding on the sidewalks, weaving between cars and pedestrians, driving the wrong way on one-way streets, and darting out from behind parked cars and other obstructions.

Never pass a bicycle if the street is too narrow for you to pass safely. Slow down and create a wide space when passing a bicyclist, especially on high-speed roadways where your pass may create a wind burst that

---

DRIVING MYTHS *Do They Think They Are Cars?* _____

Many people think that bicycles are not allowed to move over into the left-hand lane or left-turn lane of a roadway to make a left turn. In fact, they are, even though in dense or high-speed traffic it is wiser for bicyclists to get off their bike at an intersection and walk the bike across.

Right-Turning Bicyclists _____

Bicyclists often fail to stop or even slow down when making right turns. If you see a bicyclist approaching from the right at an upcoming cross street and he or she shows no sign of stopping or yielding, expect the rider to go through the intersection or fail to turn sharply enough to safely execute the turn. Reduce your speed and prepare to stop until the danger is past.

could interfere with the safe handling of the bike. If you think a bicyclist is endangering himself or herself by riding too far out in the street, "toot" your horn as a warning. Check your blind spots for bicyclists when you execute a turn or open your door to exit your vehicle after parking. On rainy days, remember that bicyclists may be unable to stop as quickly because many brakes on bicycles operate less effectively when wet.

Bicyclist Responsibilities to Motorists

Bicyclists often forget or are unaware that they have an obligation to obey the rules of the road just like any motorcyclist or motorist. This means signaling all turns with proper hand signals, stopping at all

Bicyclist Guidelines _____

- Do not turn quickly or erratically on a bike. This can surprise motorists and cause them to instinctively swerve out of their lane.
- Do not carry more persons on a bicycle than it was designed for. If it is not a tandem bike (a bicycle built for two riders), then this means only *you* should be riding!
- Do not hitch a ride by holding on to or attaching your bicycle to a moving motor vehicle.
- Do not install any type of siren or whistle on your bike.
- Do not perform any "trick" riding maneuvers such as weaving or riding with no hands on roadways.
- Do not ride your bike if you have a leak in a tire, which can lead to a blowout and loss of control of the bike.
- Do not use your bike on slippery roadways or in the rain or snow.
- Do not use portable music devices with headphones when riding a bike.
- Do not stop between a car and a curb at the corner of an intersection. If the car makes a right turn, you may be in its path.

intersections that require a stop for motor vehicles, and riding on the right-hand side of the street or in a designated lane instead of on the sidewalk.

While riding your bicycle, always wear a safety helmet. Make certain that your bicycle is in proper working condition and includes extra safety devices as needed for the type of riding you are doing. Use both hands to control the bike, except when making turn signals with your left or right arm, and follow well behind moving cars in case they stop quickly. If you are with a group of riders, ride single file on public roadways. Watch your speed as you ride down hills.

As a bicyclist, you have a responsibility to avoid dangerous actions that put you and other users of the roadway at risk of a collision. Riding against the flow of traffic, going too fast down hills, ignoring signals and STOP signs, riding in the middle of the street, and disregarding right-of-way laws are guaranteed to cost you a ticket, time in the hospital, or even your life.

13–3 MOTORCYCLES

A **motorcycle** is any two- or three-wheeled motor vehicle having a seat or saddle for riders and weighing less than 1,500 pounds (3,300 kg) with at least 15 horsepower. More powerful than many automobiles, motorcycles are capable of incredible speed and acceleration. They are also more maneuverable and easier to stop than cars. On the other hand, cars provide protection from weather and collisions, are more stable, and are easier to see because of their size and wide array of lights.

Motorcyclists are directly exposed to rain, snow, gusting wind,

factoid

The motorcycle fatality rate is sixteen times that of passenger vehicles.

Figure 13–8 A motorcycle collision is almost guaranteed to result in injury or death for the rider.

and other types of bad weather. Noise from their own engine and wind reduces their hearing ability. Rocks and dirt kicked up from vehicles ahead can cause them to lose control of their vehicle, and slippery patches or obstacles on the road can instantly result in a crash. Like bicyclists, motorcycle riders have virtually no protection in a collision with another motor vehicle or fixed object. It is no surprise that motorcycles are one of the most dangerous forms of transportation on the road.

Driver Responsibilities to Motorcyclists

Failure of drivers to spot motorcyclists in traffic is the primary cause of crashes involving motorcycles. Because motorcycles are smaller than motor vehicles, drivers who are not consciously scanning for motorcycles can miss seeing them in other lanes or at intersections. Train yourself to check for motorcycles at all times while you drive, especially before passing, changing lanes, turning, or backing out of driveways.

Before executing any maneuvers, double-check your estimates of a motorcyclist's speed and distance, which are easy to misjudge because of the bike's small size. Also, keep in mind that the relatively small sideview mirrors on motorcycles offer a limited field of vision and are often vibrating, so if you are behind a motorcyclist, you should assume that he or she cannot see you.

Motorcyclists need all the space they have within a lane to make

Figure 13–9 Always check for motorcycles in your blind spots before changing lanes.

evasive maneuvers. If you hit a pothole in your car, you feel a bump. If a motorcyclist hits one the wrong way, he or she can be thrown over the handlebars. Be prepared for riders to make sudden moves, including lane changes, to avoid a roadway hazard. Increase your following distance behind motorcycles to at least 5 or 6 seconds on city roads and 8 or 9 seconds on highways. You should always increase the space cushion between you and a motorcyclist in severe weather, on slippery roads, in gusting wind, on grooved highways, and while crossing metal-grated bridges.

When being passed by a motorcyclist, maintain your lane position and speed and let the motorcyclist pass. Be aware that motorcycle turn signals usually are not self-canceling and that a motorcyclist's signal may be "left over" from an earlier maneuver. Do not assume that a signaling motorcyclist is preparing to turn so that you can suddenly pass on the rider's left or right. Also, be very cautious when passing a motorcycle with a passenger. Any wrong movement of the passenger can throw off the motorcycle and result in either erratic recovering movements or a crash.

Motorcyclist Responsibilities to Drivers

As a motorcyclist, you can do a lot to reduce the risk of being involved in a collision or to minimize the severity of a crash should one occur. The most important precaution you can take is to understand your motorcycle well before taking to the roadways. Most jurisdictions require you to get a special motorcycle license and pass a written exam and riding test before you can legally use a motorcycle.

Keep your motorcycle in proper working condition. Do not add dangerous accessories to your bike, overload it, or modify it so that it becomes a menace to other drivers—for example, by extending the front forks or by putting on "sissy bars."

In the event of a crash, proper safety equipment often means the difference between a motorcyclist's life and death. Most jurisdictions require some or all motorcycle operators and passengers to wear a helmet. Other important safety gear for motorcycle riding includes face shields or

Figure 13–10 To legally ride a motorcycle on most roadways, you must get a special license and pass a riding test.

GARY BUSEY

Gary Busey is a popular TV and movie star with more than fifty film credits. After his breakout performance in *The Buddy Holly Story*, a role that earned him an Academy Award nomination for Best Actor in 1978, Busey went on to appear in a number of movies, including *Big Wednesday, Lethal Weapon,* and *Under Siege.* As a member of a group of celebrity motorcycle enthusiasts, Busey campaigned against mandatory helmet laws in California. On December 4, 1988, he lost control of his Harley-Davidson, flew off the cycle, and hit the curb of the roadway head first. Busey was not wearing a helmet and suffered extensive head trauma requiring brain surgery. He eventually recovered, but after this near-death experience, he became an outspoken advocate of helmet use. If you ride a motorcycle, remember that head injuries are the leading cause of death in motorcycle crashes. Protect yourself by always wearing a helmet that fully complies with safety standards.

goggles, leather boots for protection from exhaust-pipe burns, and abrasion-resistant clothing that covers both arms and legs in case of a collision. A rainsuit will make riding in severe weather less uncomfortable. Finally, because remaining visible helps avoid collisions with motorists, wear bright colors with reflective stickers to make yourself seen in all weather conditions.

Ride to the *side* of a lane, not in the middle of a lane, to get a better picture of what the driver in front of you sees. The left side of a lane is safest to use because it gives you the best view of traffic ahead and makes you more visible to other drivers. Do not ride too closely to the rear of motor vehicles. The closer you get, the less time you have to react to quick stops by those vehicles. Avoid riding in drivers' blind spots, weaving in traffic, or "splitting" lanes—riding between lanes of slow-moving or stopped traffic—even though it is legal in some jurisdictions. An unsuspecting motorist who cannot see you could easily hit you changing lanes or passing another vehicle.

Figure 13–11 If this rider gets involved in a collision, he has a good chance of being killed or suffering irreversible brain damage.

factoid

Motorcycle riders who do not wear helmets are 40% more likely to sustain a fatal head injury in a motorcycle crash than riders who do wear helmets.

Figure 13–12 You should ride a motorcycle on the side, rather than in the center, of a lane for better visibility.

At intersections, driveways, parking spaces, and other dangerous spots for motorcycles, slow down and anticipate trouble. Reduce your speed when approaching areas of the road you suspect are slick, oily, or wet. Exercise caution when crossing railroad tracks, bridge gratings, and potholes. In wet weather, ride in the wheel tracks of vehicles ahead of you for maximum traction and remember to use both front brakes in braking situations. Always communicate your position and intentions to other drivers. Assume that you are invisible to other motorists. Use hand signals when possible, as well as your turn signals, which are hard to spot from a distance.

Always reduce speed before entering turns. Although this is one of the first things new motorcycle riders are taught, they seem to forget it or ignore it after riding for some time. Once you bank for a turn, it is difficult, if not impossible, to apply brakes firmly without losing control of your motorcycle. Also, avoid the temptation to "pop wheelies," stand on your seat, "do donuts," or otherwise show off on a motorcycle, especially on a public roadway. This is sure to cause a crash.

Do not try to take advantage of your motorcycle's speed and maneuverability when passing other motorists. Before passing another vehicle, position yourself on the left side of the lane behind it. Always use an entire lane to pass instead of riding between lanes of normal-speed traffic, and avoid crowding the car or truck as you pass. Never rely on your sideview mirrors when passing or making a lane change. Most bike mirrors are convex, which means that vehicles appear farther behind you than they actually are. Always look over your shoulder and use your mirrors.

When riding in groups, break up the group into four or fewer motorcycles. Large groups of motorcycles can become confusing for riders in the group and other drivers on the roadway. When passing others, do so individually, not in pairs or groups. Use single-file formation on all curves, turns, and highway entrances and exits. At all other times, use either single-file or staggered formation such that one rider is to the left, the next is to the right and behind, the third rider is to the left and behind the second rider, and so on.

factoid

About 70% of collisions involving motorcycles occur in or near intersections.

guess the vanity plate

Figure 13–13

Ride with passengers only once you are a good enough rider to be able to do so safely. Passengers should get on a motorcycle only after it has been started. Have them sit as far forward as possible with both feet on footrests at all times, keeping their legs and feet away from the muffler. Instruct them to hold on firmly to your waist, hips, or belt; keep their movement and talking to a minimum; and lean into turns when you lean. Remember that this extra weight affects the handling of your motorcycle, especially during turns and at slow speeds. Your braking distance is also increased.

Mopeds and Motorized Cycles

A **moped** is any two- or three-wheeled device with pedals that has an automatic transmission and a motor that produces less than 2 horsepower and that is not capable of exceeding 30 miles per hour (50 km/h) on level ground. Mopeds can be propelled by either pedals or the motor. A cross between a bicycle and a motorcycle, a moped is usually subject to the same rules of the road as cars and motorcycles. Most jurisdictions require riders of mopeds to have driver's licenses.

Mopeds are underpowered and should be ridden on the right side of the roadway, like a bicycle, and not in the regular stream of traffic. You should never ride a moped on a freeway. Because many jurisdictions have restrictions on where you can ride mopeds, check your local laws before using one. This also applies to motorized bicycles, minibikes, motor scooters, "tote-goats," trail bikes, and other motorized cycles.

13–4 TRUCKS AND BUSES

Commercial tractor-trailer trucks, often called "semis" or "big rigs,"

Figure 13–14 Even though they have motors, mopeds should be ridden on the right side of the roadway like bicycles instead of in the lanes of traffic.

are easy to see, but their enormous size makes them a far greater hazard to motorists than pedestrians, bicycles, or motorcycles. In general, the bigger a vehicle, the slower its acceleration, the larger its blind spots, the more room it needs to maneuver, and the longer it takes to stop or be passed. Commercial trucks in North America can be up to 120 feet (35 m) long and weigh more than 80,000 pounds (175,000 kg). Because trucks are so much larger and heavier than cars, the driver of the car is almost always the one killed in a fatal crash involving both types of vehicles.

"No Zones"

Many people think that because truck drivers ride much higher than other drivers that they can see better. Because of their large size, however, truck drivers have larger blind spots, called "no zones," than do passenger-car drivers. In addition to blind spots on either side of the cab, there is a deep blind spot up to 200 feet (60 m) long directly behind large trucks in which the driver cannot see you and in which your own view of traffic is severely limited. Drivers in truck cabs with long hoods cannot see up to 20 feet (6 m) in front of their bumper. This is enough room for a car to slip into a position of danger and be completely unnoticed by the driver. Even truck cabs with no hood, called cab-overs, can have a front blind spot up to 10 feet (3 m) long.

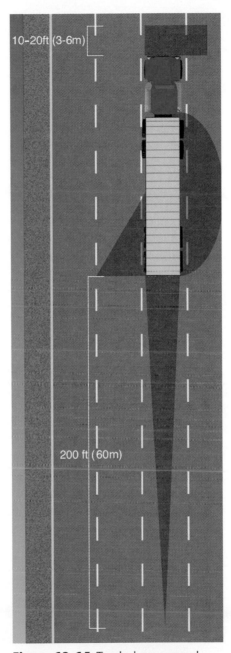

10–20ft (3-6m)

200 ft (60m)

Figure 13–15 Trucks have several "no zones" that cars do not have.

factoid

One of every eight traffic deaths results from a collision involving a large truck.

Driving Behind Trucks

Always increase your following distance when driving behind trucks. This is the only way that you will be able to see down the roadway beyond the truck. On inclines, compensate for the truck's loss of speed by slowing down yourself. When you are behind a truck at a stop, especially on an incline, allow extra room for the truck to maneuver. Because of gravity, gearing, and the type of load it is carrying, the truck may first rock backwards toward you before going forward. If you are too close and you are unable to back up, you may get into an easily avoidable crash. When following or being passed by trucks in rain or on wet or muddy roads, watch out for "splash and spray" from rear wheels that can temporarily block your view.

Passing Trucks

Before you attempt to pass a truck, make sure that you first know its size. Some trucks have two or even three trailers. It is easy to misjudge the length of these "longer combination vehicles," especially at night or in severe weather. If you commit to a pass without correctly assessing how long it will take you to get by the truck, you may find yourself stuck facing oncoming traffic with no escape route.

You should also take into account the type of terrain you are on when passing a truck. On an upgrade, trucks often lose speed, making them easier to pass than on a level roadway. On a downgrade, a truck's momentum will cause it to go faster. Truck drivers also use downgrades to get up enough speed to make it over the next hill. In general, never try to pass a truck going downhill.

Do not cut right back in front of a truck after passing it. You may end up directly ahead of the truck and force the driver, who may be unable to see you, to abruptly slow down, causing a crash. Instead, wait until you can see the cab of the truck in your rearview mirror before pulling back into the lane.

Remember to compensate for the "wind effect" that occurs when you pass a truck or are being passed by one. The truck itself can generate air currents that may rock your car, or it can temporarily block crosswinds. The return of strong gusts once your vehicles have separated may surprise you

USING SAFE *Passing Big Rigs*

Passing large tractor-trailer trucks requires respect for the limitations and special performance characteristics of these vehicles. Use the SAFE method to reduce the risk of a collision when passing a big rig on a two-lane highway. Before you make the decision to pass, maintain a long following distance for as long as it takes to properly *scan* far ahead. If you are too close to the rear of the truck, you will not be able to see potential hazards down the road that could force the truck driver to take evasive action and collide with your vehicle or cause an oncoming car to crash into you. You must also be able to see whether there is enough space ahead of the truck for you to easily fit after passing. *Assess* the road and weather conditions to determine whether it is safe to pass. Do you and the truck driver have good visibility? Is it raining, dark, or foggy? Is the sun in your eyes? Is the road icy or curving? Is the road uneven or full of potholes or debris? Is it narrow? Are you in a no-passing zone? Are there soft shoulders or drop-offs? Are you moving uphill or downhill? Is there a lot of oncoming traffic? Note the length of the truck, the nature of its cargo, and the condition of its tires. After observing the truck driver's behavior, is he or she likely to help you pass by slowing down? If it is safe to pass, *find* the proper place to *execute* your pass with a minimum of interference to the truck driver. Make sure that throughout the pass, you have an escape route in case of an unexpected danger.

and cause you to lose control of your vehicle.

Trucks sometimes drive in clusters so that they can "draft," or ride behind the wind break of vehicles directly ahead, to reduce gas consumption. Never try to pass more than one truck at a time. If

Figure 13–16 Adjust for the "wind effect" when passing or being passed by a truck.

you find yourself stuck behind a slow truck or a line of drafting trucks, be patient and wait for a safe opportunity to pass. Do not assume that you will be able to squeeze in between two trucks. Most jurisdictions require a truck driver to turn off the roadway in a safe area or turnout if that driver is impeding the progress of more than a certain number of other vehicles (usually five); so if you are on a crowded two-lane highway you should not have to wait long.

Do not attempt to pass closely behind or in front of a truck backing into a loading dock or other parking area. The driver might be fully concentrating on maneuvering into a tight space and may not see you as you try to sneak past.

Merging Trucks

When entering highways and freeways, truck drivers often need extra time to adjust to high-speed traffic. Considering the reduced visibility a truck driver has, as well as the limitations of having to shift up to ten gears, it is both courteous and good defensive driving to slow down and move to another lane to allow the truck to enter the roadway smoothly and safely.

Oncoming Trucks

Many motorists make the mistake of judging an oncoming truck to be traveling slower than it really is. This optical illusion is caused by the truck's large size, which allows it to be seen from far away. One of the main causes of collisions between cars and trucks at intersections is the inability of motorists to accurately determine the speed of an approaching truck before making a left turn. When in doubt about the speed of an oncoming truck, do not turn left in its path or drive toward it in an attempt to pass another vehicle. The truck may be going faster than you think.

Figure 13–17 Be careful not to underestimate the speed of oncoming trucks before turning or passing.

Large trucks use air brakes rather than the hydraulic brakes found in cars and light trucks. These brakes take longer to engage, adding many feet/meters to a big rig's stopping distance. It takes more than 100 yards (90 m)—the length of a football field—for an average fully loaded tractor-trailer truck traveling at 55 miles per hour (90 km/h) to stop. It takes even longer if the truck's brakes are hot. If you guess wrong when passing another vehicle or turning in front of an oncoming truck, the driver will not be able to stop to avoid a collision.

Off-Tracking

Off-tracking occurs when a truck driver swings wide on a turn to minimize interference with through traffic on the cross street. Because right turns are sharper than left ones, off-tracking is greater on right turns. Off-tracking is dangerous but often unavoidable because of the large size and limited turning radius of trucks. Left-turning drivers will first swing wide to the right, and right-turning drivers will first swing wide to the left, to enter a cross street. The sharper the turn, the narrower the intersection, and the longer the truck—the wider the driver must go. Off-tracking can force a truck's trailer to cut off or "squeeze" roadway users to the sides.

If a truck is stopped at or approaching an intersection, never attempt to "cut in" along the right side of the roadway as the driver first maneuvers left, or you will find yourself sandwiched between the turning truck and the curb. Trying to pass a right-turning truck driver on the left can also present dangers. If the truck swings wide enough, it can force you to stray into oncoming traffic or the median of the cross street. Always give a truck driver sufficient clearance and time to complete a turn safely.

Commercial Buses

Buses present many of the same problems as large commercial trucks for the motorist. They are long, heavy, difficult to maneuver and stop, and have large blind spots. Like big rigs, they can be deceptively fast when approaching from a distance, take a long time to pass, tend to go slower uphill and faster downhill, swing

Figure 13–18 What is the name of this 200-ton mining truck, which can share the road with a car by driving *above* it?

Figure 13–19 Off-tracking presents a danger to vehicles on both sides of a right-turning truck driver.

Figure 13–20 Watch for pedestrians around stopped buses.

wide on turns, and produce a wind effect at high speeds.

The unique danger presented by buses, especially those used for public transportation, is that they make frequent stops to drop off and pick up passengers. Buses pull into and out of traffic at designated curbside stops, and on major urban streets, they can tie up traffic in the right lanes. Therefore, some cities have special bus lanes to separate buses from the through-traffic lanes.

When driving behind a bus, increase your following distance to improve your visibility and avoid a rear-end collision. Expect the bus to suddenly stop or change lanes. When approaching a stopped bus, exercise extreme caution. Buses often stop at corners, blocking your view of cross traffic. Pedestrians may suddenly rush across the street to catch a bus. Never try to pass a bus on the right unless it is in the left lane of a multilane roadway. You may pass a bus on the left only if you use a separate lane going in the same direction or if the bus pulls out of through traffic into a special bus-stop lane.

School Buses

School buses are yellow and normally found in residential areas early in the morning and in mid- to late afternoon. Because children are often unaware of traffic rules and safety and less predictable than adults, you must be especially careful when driving near school buses. When a school bus is stopped and has its red lights flashing and/or its mechanical STOP sign arm extended, you must come to a complete stop *unless* you are on the opposite side of a divided roadway.

Watch for children getting on or off the bus, especially small children, whom the bus driver

Figure 13–21 Exercise extra caution around school buses.

may not see or who dart across the street at the last second without checking for cross traffic. Glance periodically in your rearview and sideview mirrors. If you see a vehicle approaching from behind in another lane that shows no indication of stopping, tap your brakes and/or use hand signals to get the driver's attention. If necessary, honk your horn to alert the bus driver and children.

Resume driving only once the school bus is in motion, the lights have stopped flashing and the STOP sign arm has been retracted, or if the bus driver has indicated that you should proceed. Always give a moving school bus extra space cushioning, especially while passing. Bus drivers may become distracted by rowdy children and be unable to give their full attention to the road.

WHO'S AT FAULT?

1. Driver 1 was stopped behind a bus in the right lane of a four-lane roadway when a passenger exited the bus and crossed the road between the car and the back of the bus. When the pedestrian walked into the left lane, she was hit by Driver 2. ***Who's at fault?***

2. A motorcyclist traveling 25 miles per hour (40 km/h) was splitting lanes on a freeway with bumper-to-bumper traffic. Driver 1 was traveling in front of the motorcyclist and changed lanes without looking over his shoulder, striking the motorcyclist. ***Who's at fault?***

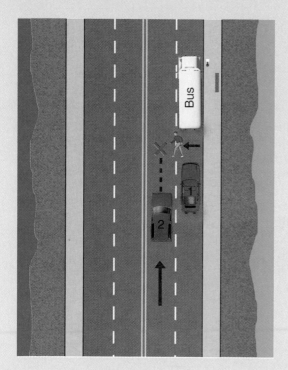

YOUR TURN

13–1 Pedestrians

1. What responsibilities do motorists have to pedestrians?

2. What responsibilities do pedestrians have to motorists?

13–2 Bicycles

3. What responsibilities do motorists have to bicyclists?

4. What responsibilities do bicyclists have to motorists?

13–3 Motorcycles

5. What responsibilities do motorists have to motorcyclists?

6. What responsibilities do motorcyclists have to motorists?

13–4 Trucks and Buses

7. What are the "no zones" of a large truck?

8. What are some of the dangers of passing trucks?

9. What precautions should you take when driving near stopped buses?

SELF-TEST

Multiple Choice

1. Most collisions between vehicles and pedestrians occur in or near:
   a. driveways.
   b. intersections.
   c. parking lots.
   d. bus stops.

2. A motorcycle is any two- or three-wheeled motor vehicle having a seat or saddle for riders and weighing less than 1,500 pounds (2,400 kg) with at least _____ horsepower.
   a. 15
   b. 25
   c. 30
   d. 50

3. Bicyclists ride on all types of roads except:
   a. freeways.
   b. scenic roads.
   c. service roads.
   d. divided highways.

4. The bigger the vehicle, the _____ its blind spots.
   a. smaller
   b. larger
   c. higher
   d. lower

5. The blind spot directly behind a commercial truck can be up to:
   a. 50 feet (15 m).   **c.** 150 feet (45 m).
   b. 100 feet (30 m).   **d.** 200 feet (60 m).

Sentence Completion

1. Your following distance behind a motorcycle on city roads should be at least _____ seconds.
2. When you are passing a large truck, wait until you see the _____ of the truck in your rearview mirror before pulling back into the lane.
3. _____ can be propelled by either pedals or the motor.
4. The _____ occurs when you pass or are being passed by a large vehicle such as a truck or bus.
5. Many motorists make the mistake of judging an oncoming truck to be traveling _____ than it really is.

Matching

Match the concepts in Column A with examples of the concepts in Column B.

Column A	Column B
1. __ Off-tracking	**a.** "Tote-goat"
2. __ Lane-splitting	**b.** Retractable STOP sign arm
3. __ "No zone"	**c.** Trucker maneuver to save fuel
4. __ Dangerous pedestrian practice	**d.** Jaywalking
5. __ Draft	**e.** Motorcyclist maneuver to avoid traffic
6. __ School bus	**f.** 20 feet (6 m) in front of bumper
7. __ Big rig	**g.** Swinging wide to make turn
8. __ Cross between bicycle and motorcycle	**h.** Up to 120 feet (35 m) long

Short Answer

1. What is the major cause of collisions between cars and motorcycles?
2. What should you do if you approach a pedestrian from behind on a road with no sidewalks?
3. If you are stopped behind a school bus with its lights flashing, when can you resume driving?
4. What precautions should you take when carrying a passenger on a motorcycle?
5. When is it legal for a pedestrian to cross a roadway outside of a crosswalk?

Critical Thinking

1. You are traveling uphill on a two-lane highway behind a slow-moving big rig. As you round a curve, you notice that there is another large truck in front of it. After the road straightens out, you enter a passing zone about 3 miles (5 km) from the crest of the hill. What should you do?
2. You are traveling in the center lane of a three-lane freeway. A fast-moving motorcyclist in the left lane pulls up and changes lanes in front of you. You notice that a short distance ahead traffic is backed up in the center and right lanes. The motorcyclist still has his right-turn signal on, and the left lane is clear for you to pass if you act quickly. What should you do?

PROJECTS

1. *To get a feeling for what it is like to share the road from a few different perspectives, take a walk that extends around at least two square blocks near your home. Note which way you look when you cross the street, whether there is a sidewalk for you to walk on, whether drivers respect your right-of-way, and how much of the roadway and oncoming traffic you can see from the side of the road. Take the same route on a bicycle (if you have one) and in your car. Describe how your perspective and concerns are different in each of your roles as pedestrian, bicyclist, and motorist.*

2. *Observe the activity of pedestrians and motor vehicles at a busy intersection. Are drivers being considerate of pedestrians and bicyclists? Do pedestrians take unsafe actions such as step off the curb when the WALK sign goes on without looking each way first or jaywalk across the street? Do bicyclists making right turns stop at red lights or ride right through them? Do they turn left from the left lane or walk their bike across? How would you drive defensively through this intersection?*

Challenging Driving

USE LOWER
GEARS

6%

Challenging Driving Conditions

Before going out on the road, it is important to realistically evaluate the driving conditions that you will encounter. Your driving environment will rarely be perfect. An important part of defensive driving is learning how to respond to challenging driving conditions. If your visibility is reduced or if you are negotiating bad roads or challenging terrain, you must take extra precautions.

Upon completion of this chapter, you should be able to:

14–1 Reduced Visibility

1. Describe some of the dangers of driving with reduced visibility.
2. Understand what it means to "overdrive" your headlights.
3. Understand how you can prevent being blinded by the headlights of other vehicles.
4. Describe ways to minimize the risks of sunshine glare.

14–2 Challenging Road Conditions

5. Understand what precautions you should take when driving on poor road surfaces.
6. Understand how to "rock out" your vehicle if you get stuck.
7. Describe how to safely approach narrow roads, bridges, and tunnels.

14–3 Challenging Terrain

8. Describe how to drive uphill and downhill using either an automatic or a manual transmission.
9. Describe some of the special dangers of mountain driving.

KEY TERMS

overdriving your
   headlights

"rock out"

shoulder

soft shoulders

drop-offs

switchbacks

runaway vehicle ramps

Figure 14–1 Darkness severely limits your ability to scan the roadway and identify possible dangers.

14–1 REDUCED VISIBILITY

Traffic death rates are three times greater at night than during the day. The most obvious reason why night driving is so dangerous is darkness. Ninety percent of a driver's ability to react depends on vision, and vision is severely limited at night. Darkness makes it harder for you to see and for others to see you. It is harder to determine the size, speed, color, and distance of objects ahead of you. This is especially true for older drivers, who may need twice as much light to see as well as younger drivers.

Looking Beyond Your Headlights

Headlights can give you a false sense of security on the road. At night, a person's 20/20 daylight

SAM KINISON

Stand-up comedian Sam Kinison made his reputation as a loudmouthed wild man. His brand of humor was not for everyone, but he had a loyal following of fans. On the evening of April 10, 1992, Kinison was driving from California to Laughlin, Nevada, on U.S. Highway 95 to perform at a sold-out show. At about 7:30 PM, as he neared the California–Nevada border, an oncoming pickup swerved into Kinison's lane as the driver attempted to pass traffic. The truck hit Kinison's Pontiac Trans Am head-on. Kinison was able to pull himself from his wrecked car but died within minutes of internal injuries at the scene of the collision. His wife, with whom he had just returned from a honeymoon in Hawaii, was severely injured. When driving at night, you need to be extremely cautious when executing a difficult maneuver such as passing. If you cannot see well enough to know it is safe, be patient and stay where you are. Taking driving risks in challenging driving conditions is far more likely to cause collisions and cost lives.

factoid

Headlights give off only $\frac{1}{2,250}$ as much light as the sun on a clear day.

vision can be reduced to 20/50, so do not assume that just because you have "perfect" eyesight you do not need to pay more attention to the road. In addition, the narrow width of headlight beams can limit your view of the surrounding area to merely outlines and forms, and off-road areas may not be visible at all.

Always try to look beyond your headlights to get a better picture of possible dangers ahead. Scan beyond the center of the lane in which you are driving, not just to the edge of the area illuminated by your headlights. Reduce your speed and give yourself an extra space cushion to react to unexpected hazards. Look for flashes of light in the distance that may signal the presence of another vehicle or traffic signals. Watch for reflections off of signs, roadway markings, and pedestrian clothing.

Avoid using a light *inside* your car while driving at night. This will greatly reduce your night vision. It is also not a time to take your concentration off the road. If you need to check your map or read the song titles on a new CD, pull over to a safe area and do it there, not while you are driving.

Overdriving Your Headlights

Large objects can only be seen about 500 feet (150 m) away with high beams and 150 feet (45 m) away with low beams. People, animals, and small objects may be visible only at much shorter distances. If pedestrians are wearing dark clothes, you may not see them until they are right in front of you.

Do not "overdrive" your headlights. That is, do not travel at speeds that prevent you from stopping within the distance lighted by your headlights. To prevent **overdriving your headlights,** follow these steps (see Figure 14–3).

1. Select a fixed object ahead of your vehicle, such as a sign or

Figure 14–2 Headlights allow others to see you at night long before you meet them on the road.

DRIVING TIPS *Dirty Windows and Lights*

Over time your vehicle will build up a film of dirt, especially if you have been driving on wet or dusty streets. Make sure that you keep your windows clean. Dirt on the glass will reflect rays of light, either from the sun or from headlights, and add to glare. Do not forget your headlights. Dirt on headlights can reduce their effectiveness by as much as 75%. When you stop to get gas, it is a good idea to clean your windshield *and* wipe your headlights.

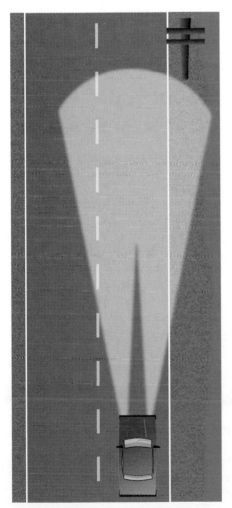

Figure 14–3 Avoid overdriving your headlights.

telephone pole, the moment your high-beam headlights pick it up.

2. Count off 6 seconds.

3. Is the object still ahead of you or is it behind you? If it is ahead of or even with you, you are driving at a safe speed. If you have passed it, you are driving too fast! Slow down and repeat the process again until the next object you choose is within the 6-second range.

Remember that most posted speed limits on roadways are generally considered reasonable for daylight but too fast for nighttime. On some freeways and interstates, you may see a special nighttime speed limit, which is usually 5 to 10 miles per hour (8 to 15 km/h) below the normal limit. Do not wait for a sign, however, to tell you when to slow to a safe speed.

Make sure that your headlights are aimed properly. Misaimed headlights make it harder for you to see and can blind other drivers. Also, if one of your headlights burns out, replace it immediately. Not only is it both dangerous and

illegal to drive with only one headlight, but if your second light goes out, you will be in serious trouble.

Figure 14–4 If you replace your headlights when they burn out, do not forget to realign them.

High and Low Beams

When traveling on dark or poorly lit roads with little oncoming traffic, use your high beams to get a bigger picture of the road. Switch to low beams as soon as you see the headlights of an oncoming car to avoid temporarily blinding the other driver. You should also switch to low beams when you see the taillights of a vehicle in front of you. High beams will reflect off the rearview and sideview mirrors and into the eyes of the other driver. Laws vary by jurisdiction, but generally, you should dim your headlights at least 500 feet (150 m) ahead of approaching vehicles and when you are within 200 feet (60 m) of a vehicle ahead of you.

Blinded by the Light

Staring into the headlights of oncoming cars can blind you, especially if they are high beams. Reduce your speed and look off to the right-hand side of the road as other cars with their high beam lights on approach you. Make brief, frequent glances ahead of you to keep your bearings, always keeping oncoming cars in the corner of your vision. If you do get blinded by oncoming traffic, slow down or pull off the road until your eyes recover.

REALITY CHECK *The Blind Leading the Blind* _____

If an approaching driver in the oncoming lanes of traffic forgets to turn off his or her high beams and they are interfering with your vision, briefly flick on your high beams as a reminder to turn them off. If the other driver does not switch to low beams after you signal, do not play tit-for-tat by keeping your high beams on or by wildly flashing your lights. Driving is not child's play, and you may cause a collision by trying to "teach the person a lesson." The offending driver may have an emergency situation or some other valid reason for using high beams that you do not know about.

Adjust your rearview mirror to the "night" setting for night driving. This will reduce the glare caused by the headlights of cars behind you, especially if they have their high beams on. Never wear sunglasses at night to reduce the glare caused by oncoming cars. Unlike a shaded rearview mirror, sunglasses darken your *entire* view of the road, not just part of it. For the same reason, you should avoid using tinted windows in your car.

Dawn and Dusk

Pay very close attention to your driving during the periods of dawn and dusk. Your eyes must constantly adapt to changing light conditions. Many drivers do not have their headlights on, yet the low level of available light can still make it hard to see other vehicles. Morning and evening commuter traffic is often heavy during these times, and many drivers are tired and not at peak alertness. Unlighted traffic signs, roadway markings, bicyclists, and pedestrians are often difficult to spot.

Jurisdictions have different laws that specify when you must drive with your headlights on. Some, for example, require that you do so from ½ hour after sunset until ½ hour before sunrise, or at anytime you cannot see 1,000 feet (300 m) ahead of you. If you are not sure what the law is, the safest thing to do is to use your headlights as soon as the sun sets and until sunrise.

When driving, use your low-beam headlights, *not* your parking lights. Parking lights are designed to let other drivers see you when you are temporarily parked. Driving only with your parking lights on is dangerous and in many jurisdictions is illegal. When turning at dawn or dusk hours, use your turn signals earlier than normal to give other drivers more time to see them.

Sunshine Glare

Sometimes sunshine can be dangerous, especially at daybreak or in late afternoon when the sun's rays shine directly into your windshield or rearview mirror. Glare can make it hard to see and can contribute to driver fatigue. If you are driving into the sun, you may not see the brake lights or turn signals of cars in front of you. If the sun is behind you, you may be unable to see in that direction at all.

When sunshine glare is a problem, assume that other drivers

AUTO ACCESSORIES *Sun Visor Extensions* _____

Most sun visors in cars do not cover the middle area at the top of the windshield between the driver's-side and passenger-side sun visors, allowing blinding sunlight to enter and catch you off guard. Purchase a special sun visor extension to cover up this gap.

Figure 14–6 Sunshine glare can limit your vision just as much as darkness.

cannot see you or your turn signals before executing a maneuver. Maintain an extra space cushion around your car. Take more time to prepare for lane changes. If you are at an intersection, look in each direction one extra time before proceeding. Activate your turn signal earlier, and if necessary, use hand signals. Tap your brake pedal lightly several times as you slow or come to a stop. Because glare can prevent other drivers in front of you from seeing your own vehicle, turn on your low-beam headlights to make yourself more visible.

14–2 CHALLENGING ROAD CONDITIONS

Many roadways have dangerous stretches that can limit your view ahead, force you to take extra precautions to avoid a collision, or even cause you to lose control of your vehicle.

Unpaved and Gravel Roads

Dirt and loose gravel can reduce your traction, causing you to slide or skid. At higher speeds, your car can swing from side to side, or

REALITY CHECK   *The Blinding Commute*

Many of us have to face driving with the sun shining at a low angle directly into our eyes on a near-daily basis in the morning or late afternoon when we commute to and from work or school. To reduce glare, keep a pair of sunglasses handy in the car. Attempt to rearrange your work schedule so that you will not have to commute when the sun is blinding you. Revise your journey to go north–south during the time when the sun is at its most intense. Save the east–west leg of your journey for when the sun has risen or set enough to avoid the problem.

"fishtail." Stopping distance is also increased. When driving on dirt or gravel roads, always increase your following distance behind other vehicles. Reduce your speed, especially on curves, and use lower gears to avoid wheel spin. Firmly grip the steering wheel to maintain control. Use the tire tracks left by other vehicles to keep your tires closer to the road surface. On dirt roads, keep your headlights on so that oncoming drivers can better see you through the clouds of dust kicked up by your vehicle.

Deep Sand and Mud

Unpaved roads often contain stretches of deep sand that are nearly impassable. Rain can also turn unpaved roads into virtually undrivable muddy messes. Even a small amount of mud can make an unpaved road slippery, and if the mud is thick, tires of other vehicles can form deep ruts that fill up with water. Always approach muddy roads with caution. Avoid sudden stops or sharp turns, and maintain a fast enough speed to let the vehicle keep its momentum without driving so fast as to lose your traction.

If you get stuck in mud or deep sand, first try to back out using the tracks you just made to help you steer. If this does not work, you can **"rock out"** as follows:

1. Start the car slowly in a low gear and keep the front wheels straight. *Gently* step on the gas pedal. Do not spin the wheels.

2. Go forward as far as you can. Firmly press the brake pedal to hold the car in place, and shift rapidly into REVERSE.

3. Back up slowly as far as you can. Again, do not let your wheels start to spin. Step on the brake and hold it. Shift back to a low gear and go forward again.

4. Repeat steps 1 to 3 in rapid succession, rocking the vehicle backward and forward until it springs free. To avoid doing damage to your transmission, always use the brake while switching gears. If someone is helping you rock out, make sure that they are clear of the tires before you press the gas pedal.

If the tire is still stuck, put small tree branches, cardboard, flat rocks, or some rough material such as stiff canvas or burlap under the stuck tire. You can also use special traction pads sold at auto supply stores.

Wild Wheels

Figure 14–7 What is the commercial name of this ultimate high-traction machine, known to the United States armed forces as the "High Mobility Multipurpose Wheeled Vehicle"?

DRIVING TIPS *Check Your Clearance*

If you are traveling on rough terrain and notice an object on the road, remember that you cannot always clear it even though it may look as though you can. The chassis, differential, tailpipe, and muffler all may have a lower clearance point than you think. Damaging these parts can lead to serious and expensive repairs.

Potholes

A pothole is a hole in the roadway surface caused by weather, overuse, or a combination of both. Cracks in the roadway can often develop into dangerous potholes. If you hit a pothole at a high speed, you can lose control of your car or do serious damage to the tires, wheels, or underside of your vehicle. Try to avoid potholes by carefully driving around them if you can, but do not swerve into another lane of traffic to do so. If you must drive over a pothole, slow your vehicle down to maintain better control of your car and to minimize any damage. If you hit a deep pothole, pull over into a safe spot and examine your vehicle. If you notice any damage or loss of tire pressure, drive to a gas station or mechanic and have it checked.

Figure 14–8 Large potholes can cause you to lose control of your vehicle and damage it as well.

Dips

Watch for areas of the road that sharply dip down. These areas are usually marked with warning signs and speed reduction signs. Some dips are a natural part of the roadway; others are intentionally created to channel water runoff. Always reduce your speed when approaching a dip. If you drive through a dip too fast you can seriously damage the front and rear ends of your vehicle, especially if it is long or loaded down with cargo or passengers.

Shoulders and Drop-offs

Normally a roadway has a **shoulder**, a continuation of pavement or other stable surface that extends beyond the road boundary lane. Shoulders have a number of purposes. They are designed to provide space for disabled vehicles, work crews, and evasive maneuvers in emergencies. They reduce hydroplaning by helping channel water away from the travel lanes. They also increase the distance between motorists and bicyclists or pedestrians who might also be using the roadway.

Soft shoulders are shoulders that either slope downward or do not provide effective traction. These are typically found on old rural roads that have not been or cannot be upgraded. You should avoid driving on soft shoulders unless absolutely necessary or in an emergency situation. **Drop-offs** are areas where the terrain literally drops off from the edge of the roadway without any shoul-

Figure 14–9 Soft shoulders are most common on rural roads and highways.

der. These are most common on mountain roads and on elevated roadways. Drop-offs are extremely dangerous, especially at night on unlit rural roads when it is almost impossible to see beyond the road boundary lane. If you have to pull over on the roadway, make sure that you have a shoulder to drive onto!

Narrow Roads

Narrow roads can be very dangerous because there is little room for driver error. Be prepared to slow down when reaching a narrow stretch of roadway to better gauge whether there is enough clearance for two cars to pass each other. If there is, proceed with caution, hugging as close as you can to the right-hand edge of the roadway. If there is not enough room, wait on the side of the road and signal the other driver through first with a hand gesture or some other form of communication. After the other driver has gone by, proceed through the narrow stretch safely.

Figure 14–10 Crossing the double-yellow lines to pass on a narrow road is illegal and *extremely* dangerous.

Sometimes you will encounter "temporary" narrow roads in construction zones. It is common for two-way traffic to be reduced to one lane, with workers posted at opposite ends of a section of roadway letting traffic go in one direction while vehicles going in the other direction wait their turn. Obey construction workers or trucking personnel just as you would police or emergency personnel when they are directing traffic.

Figure 14-11 Always use caution when approaching a bridge or tunnel.

Bridges and Tunnels

Bridges and tunnels can alter your perception of the driving environment. They both can be noisy, making it difficult for you to hear other vehicles that may be trying to pass you. Bridges can also distract you by tempting you to look over the edge. Do not let yourself gaze at a spectacular view while driving over a bridge. Keep your eyes on the road. If you must see

USING SAFE *Construction and Work Zones*

Using the SAFE method will help you negotiate construction and work zones. *Scan* ahead for orange construction signs, cones, barricades (sometimes mounted with flashing yellow lights), safety barrels, truck- or trailer-mounted arrow boards, and other traffic controls. Watch for flaggers in fluorescent vests and hard hats directing traffic. Keep an eye out for slow-moving vehicles, heavy equipment, road hazards such as cargo in the street, sand, mud, tar, oil, and work-related debris. After identifying a construction zone, *assess* potential dangers. Keep your speed low and your attention level high. Is construction going on now? Are any lanes closed ahead? Is traffic being rerouted? Are vehicles moving in your direction being stopped at intervals to let oncoming cars go by or to let a large truck in or out of the work site? Could delays cause frustrated or confused drivers around you to make sudden or unexpected movements? *Find* the best lane to get in as early as possible to avoid last-second lane changes and *execute* your decision safely. Increase your following distance, and look for escape routes on the shoulder or on the other side of cones or barriers. At night, especially in rural areas, it is hard to see what dangers are concealed in construction or work zones. Make sure that you can see what is behind any barrier set up in adjoining lanes before you have to take evasive action, if necessary, to avoid a collision.

Figure 14–12 Be alert to slow-moving vehicles in construction zones.

the view, cross the bridge again later as a passenger!

Tunnels can also play games with your senses. Sounds can be distorted, and lights can reflect off the walls. Many tunnels are not lit or are poorly lit. If you have claustrophobia, it can be difficult driving through tunnels, especially long ones.

Another challenge of bridges and tunnels is that they often have narrow lanes. On older roads, bridges may even be reduced to one lane. Guardrails and abutments reduce your options in the event of an emergency. If you are stranded on a bridge or in a tunnel, just getting out of your vehicle can be dangerous.

When you cross a bridge or enter a tunnel, reduce your speed. Carefully check any signs, signals, or roadway markings for information about the bridge or tunnel. Turn on your low-beam headlights to make yourself more visible to other vehicles. Watch for narrowing lanes, pedestrians and bicycles, and disappearing shoulders. Expect other cars to crowd the center lane.

14–3 CHALLENGING TERRAIN

Most roads are not completely flat. Even if you live in a relatively flat area of the country, you are likely to encounter hills

ROAD WEIRDNESS *Not for the Faint of Heart* _____

If you want a true driving challenge, visit historic San Francisco in Northern California. Two of the steepest vertical descents in the world, Filbert Street and 22nd Street, each have a 31.5% grade, and Lombard Street is billed as "The World's Crookedest Street."

at some point in your travels. Many national parks have mountains, so if you plan on going to Yosemite or Jasper you must be prepared to handle the special challenges of mountain driving.

Hills

When driving on hills, you must consider the force of gravity on your vehicle. The steepness of the grade, the speed you are traveling, and the weight of your vehicle can all impact how you drive. Whether you go uphill or downhill, you must consider how much power you need to use and how to apply your brakes. Whether you use a vehicle with a manual or automatic transmission, you need to exercise more caution when driving on hills and mountains.

When you drive uphill, you are driving *against* the force of gravity. This means that you need more power to keep moving at the same speed. If you have an automatic transmission, you must apply more pressure on the gas pedal to avoid losing speed. When you get to a comfortable speed, keep your foot at that point until the road starts to level off. On very steep hills, switch to a lower gear to help the engine work more efficiently. If you have a manual transmission, downshift to a lower gear to avoid losing power and speed. The grade of the hill will determine which gear to use. The steeper the grade, the lower the gear.

When you drive downhill, you are driving *with* the force of gravity. This means that you need less power to keep moving at the same speed. If you have an automatic transmission, ease off the gas pedal as you drive downhill. If you start going too fast, gradually apply the brakes to slow down until you reach a comfortable speed. On long or steep hills,

Figure 14–13 Turnouts allow faster-moving vehicles to pass slower-moving traffic on narrow roads.

switch to a lower gear to maintain better control of your vehicle and reduce wear on your brakes. Avoid riding your brake.

If you have a manual transmission, switch to a lower gear to maintain better control of your vehicle and reduce the drag on your engine *before* you start driving downhill. If you switch gears after you begin to move downhill, you may be forced to apply your brakes while shifting. This is especially true on steep hills, where if you wait too long to downshift you may not have enough braking power to switch to a lower gear without braking continuously for a long time.

Mountain Driving

Mountain roads are typically narrower than average roads. They also have sharp curves and steep grades that make it difficult to see the road ahead and put more stress on your vehicle's engine, transmission, and brakes. Some turns, called **switchbacks**, are so sharp that they reverse direction. If you find yourself behind a truck, bus, or any other large vehicle, your view of the road is even more limited. The absence of walls, barricades, or guardrails on many stretches of mountain roads leave little margin for error. If you stray into oncoming traffic on a mountain road, you risk not only colliding with another vehicle but of driving off the edge of a cliff.

Always pay careful attention to signs and roadway markings on mountain roads. Keep your speed low, especially on curves. Expect problems and delays caused by fog, snow, and ice. Watch for washed-out areas and road damage or debris from landslides. Give yourself an extra space cushion when driving behind other vehicles. Use your low-beam headlights to make yourself more visible. When you approach any area in which it is difficult to see ahead of you such as a blind curve,

Figure 14–14 Switchbacks are a common hazard of mountain driving.

lightly tap on your horn or flash your lights to warn any drivers that might be coming your way.

Driving down a mountain is riskier than going up. As you move downhill, you can accelerate quickly unless you resist the force of gravity. *Never* coast down a mountain road in NEUTRAL or with the clutch disengaged. This is both dangerous and, in some jurisdictions, illegal. Some mountain roads include **runaway vehicle ramps** for those vehicles that experience braking problems on long, steep grades. These "ramps" are usually short, steep uphill roads that help the driver stop by quickly reversing the effects of gravity. Sometimes they are long pits filled with sand or gravel that help stop a vehicle. Runaway vehicle ramps may also have sand, plastic barrels, or some other energy-absorbing material at the end to stop the vehicle if it cannot do so on its own.

Passing on Mountain Roads

What do you do if you meet a car going in the opposite direction on a one-lane or very narrow mountain road? The general rule is to give the right-of-way to uphill traffic. The car that faces downhill has the obligation to back up until the driver has room to pass. Each situation, however, may call for a different solution. If you get in this kind of jam, be courteous. For example, if you are going uphill and the mountain is on your right, it may be safer for *you* to back up because you are on the right side of the road. Also, even if you have the right-of-way it may be easier for you to back up if you are closer to a side road, turnout, or driveway.

Be extra cautious when passing vehicles going in your direction. It is common to get stuck behind large trucks, recreational vehicles, and cars with trailers when driving uphill in the mountains. As more and more cars back up behind you, you may feel more pressure to pass so you do not "hold them up." Be patient! Wait for an appropriate place to pass with a clear view of the road ahead. Many mountain roads have special passing lanes at periodic intervals for this very reason. There are also pull-out areas for slow vehicles to pull over and get out of the way of faster traffic.

Figure 14–15 Runaway vehicle ramps provide an escape route on steep downhill grades.

Figure 14–16 Mountain roads require patience and extra caution.

Effects of High Altitude

The lower oxygen available at high altitudes can make you sleepy, especially if you are not used to it. High altitudes can also increase your heart rate and cause shortness of breath and headaches. The effects are worse if you are already tired or ill. If you have any of these symptoms while driving on a mountain road, pull off at a turnout, scenic overlook, or some other safe place clear of traffic to rest. If you are traveling with others, try changing drivers to give yourself a break. Also, consider selecting an alternative route at a lower altitude.

Because the air is thinner, cars tuned up at lower altitudes do not run as efficiently at higher altitudes. Engines heat faster, and the risk of stalling is greater. Keep in mind that you will have less power going uphill, a time when you need it the most. While driving on mountain roads, periodically check your temperature gauge. If the car is close to overheating, pull over and allow your engine to cool down. If you cannot pull over right away, turn on your heater to draw off some of the heat built up in the engine coolant. Always carry a bottle of water in the car for your radiator when you are driving in the mountains, especially if it is hot outside.

WHO'S AT FAULT?

1. Driver 1 was traveling uphill on a two-lane road behind several slow-moving cars. Losing patience, she attempted to pass three cars at once. Just as she reached the top of the hill, she saw Driver 3 moving down the hill in the oncoming lane at a high rate of speed. Driver 1 tried to get over into the right-hand lane, but Driver 2 refused to let her in. To avoid a head-on collision, Driver 1 moved over to the right and hit Driver 2, forcing him off the road. ***Who's at fault?***

2. Driver 1 was traveling on the single downhill lane of a three-lane mountain road and approached a line of cars stopped by a flagger at a construction site. Despite several orange construction signs, he failed to realize that the cars were stopped until the last second and slammed on his brakes, skidding into the left oncoming lane of traffic. Driver 1 hit Driver 2, who was driving at the posted speed limit in the left lane and did not have time to get into the free right lane. ***Who's at fault?***

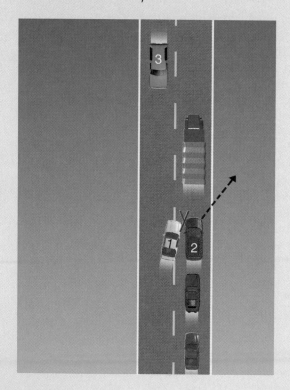

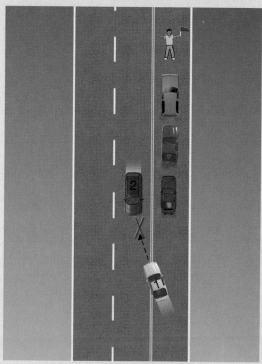

YOUR TURN

14–1 Reduced Visibility

1. What are some of the dangers of driving with reduced visibility?

2. What does it mean to "overdrive" your headlights?

3. How can you prevent being blinded by the headlights of other vehicles?

4. What can you do to minimize the risks of sunshine glare?

14–2 Challenging Road Conditions

5. What precautions should you take when driving on poor road surfaces?

6. How do you "rock out" your vehicle if you get stuck?

7. How do you safely approach narrow roads, bridges, and tunnels?

14–3 Challenging Terrain

8. How do you drive uphill and downhill using an automatic transmission? a manual transmission?

9. What are some of the special dangers of mountain driving?

SELF-TEST

Multiple Choice

1. Large objects can be seen at about _____ away with low beams.
   a. 50 feet (15 m)
   b. 100 (30 m)
   c. 150 (45 m)
   d. 200 (60 m)

2. You should dim your headlights within at least _____ of approaching vehicles.
   a. 200 feet (60 m)
   b. 300 feet (90 m)
   c. 400 feet (120 m)
   d. 500 feet (150 m)

3. When entering a tunnel, you should turn on your:
   a. low beams.
   b. high beams.
   c. parking lights.
   d. emergency flashers.

4. On some freeways and interstates, a special nighttime driving speed of _____ below the normal limit is posted.
   a. 5 to 10 miles per hour (8 to 16 km/h)
   b. 10 to 15 miles per hour (16 to 24 km/h)
   c. 15 to 20 miles per hour (24 to 32 km/h)
   d. 20 to 25 miles per hour (32 to 40 km/h)

5. Unless otherwise specified by local laws, you should put your headlights on at dawn, dusk, or any-time you cannot see _____ ahead of you.

   a. 700 feet (215 m)   **c.** 500 feet (150 m)
   b. 2,000 feet (610 m)   **d.** 1,000 feet (300 m)

Sentence Completion

1. Dirt and gravel roads can reduce your _____, causing you to slide or skid.

2. To avoid damaging your transmission while "rocking out," always use the _____ while switching gears.

3. _____ either slope downward or do not provide effective traction.

4. The _____ on your rearview mirror reduces the glare from headlights behind you.

5. Some mountain roads have _____ in case vehicles experience brake failure on long, steep grades.

Matching

Match the concepts in Column A with examples of the concepts in Column B.

Column A

1. __ Bridge and tunnel hazard
2. __ Construction zone hazard
3. __ Mountain road hazard
4. __ Shoulder
5. __ Effect of high altitude
6. __ Commuting hazard
7. __ Dip
8. __ Pothole

Column B

a. Used to channel water runoff
b. Sleepiness
c. Two-way traffic reduced to one lane
d. Drop-offs
e. Sunshine glare
f. Noise
g. Space for broken down vehicles
h. Can damage wheels

Short Answer

1. What is dangerous about switchbacks?
2. How can you test whether you are overdriving your headlights?
3. How do you communicate to an oncoming driver that his or her high beams are blinding you?
4. When driving downhill, what can you do to maintain better control of your vehicle?
5. Who generally has the right-of-way if two drivers going in opposite directions meet on a narrow mountain road?

Critical Thinking

1. You are driving up a two-lane mountain road approaching a sharp curve with a steep drop-off. Suddenly you notice that a small pile of rocks is in your lane ahead. You cannot see oncoming traffic from where you are, and no shoulder is on either side of the road. What should you do?

2. You are on a two-way, four-lane road approaching an intersection with a green traffic signal. An oncoming driver in the left lane has his left-turn signal on, preparing to turn onto the cross street when the way is clear. A car is to your rear, but because the sun is directly behind you, it is difficult to determine how far back it is. The left-turning driver is not slowing down, and you suspect that the oncoming driver cannot see you because of sunshine glare. What should you do?

PROJECTS

1. *Use a newspaper or the Internet to determine what time sunset is on a given day. On that day, select a safe location where you and a friend can view traffic on a major roadway. Every 5 minutes, note on a piece of paper whether some, most, or all vehicles have their headlights on from sunset until it is completely dark outside. Describe the weather conditions. Is it cloudy? raining? clear? Check with the local law-enforcement agency or transportation department to determine when drivers in your jurisdiction must turn on their headlights in the evening. What percentage of drivers comply with the law? Share the results with your class.*

2. *As a passenger, go for a drive and find five different challenging road conditions where you live, including gravel roads, unpaved roads, roads with dips or potholes, roads with soft shoulders or drop-offs, narrow roads, bridges, tunnels, and construction zones. Identify their location and what makes them dangerous. Share the results with your class.*

Driving in Bad Weather

It is always best to avoid driving in bad weather. Sometimes, however, you cannot delay a trip because of rain, snow, ice, fog, gusting wind, extreme cold or heat, or other hazardous conditions that may test the limits of both you and your vehicle. When driving in severe weather, you must exercise common sense and good judgment. Because you face both reduced visibility *and* challenging road conditions, you must be extra cautious when executing all driving maneuvers.

CHAPTER OBJECTIVES

Upon completion of this chapter, you should be able to:

15–1 Rain

1. Describe some of the dangers of driving in rain.
2. Understand what hydroplaning is and how you can prevent it.
3. Understand what you should do if you encounter deep water on the road.

15–2 Snow and Ice

4. Understand how to prepare for driving in winter conditions.
5. Describe some of the dangers of snow-covered and icy roads.

15–3 Other Severe Weather Conditions

6. Understand what precautions you should take when driving in fog.
7. Understand what to do if you are caught in a severe storm.

15–4 Cold and Hot Weather

8. Describe some of the problems caused by extremely cold temperatures.
9. Understand what to do if your engine overheats.
10. Understand what precautions you should take when driving in the desert.

KEY TERMS

hydroplaning
vapor lock

15–1 RAIN

Rain makes road surfaces slippery. It also makes it harder for you to see others and for others to see you. Water pounding on your windshield, the motion of wiper blades, and darker skies significantly reduce your visibility. "Splash and spray" from oncoming or passing traffic can temporarily blind you. Painted roadway markings can virtually disappear, making it difficult to stay within your lane. In heavy rainfall, both hearing and seeing in the driving environment can be difficult.

Driving in Rain

When driving in the rain, always use your low-beam headlights to increase visibility. Watch for other vehicles that may not have their lights on. Activate your windshield defroster and rear window defogger to keep your windows clear of condensation. Remember that other roadway users may have trouble controlling their vehicles in the rain, especially bicyclists and motorcyclists. Also, pedestrians may unexpectedly dart across the street to get out of the bad weather.

When driving in the rain, increase your space cushion in case you or other drivers begin to skid. Increase your normal dry weather following distance by at least 5 seconds. Signal your turns, stops, and lane changes earlier than usual. To increase contact with the road and improve traction on wet road surfaces, drive in the "tracks" left by the vehicle in front of you.

Never drive at normal, fair-weather speeds when it is raining. A good rule of thumb is to reduce your speed by 25% below the posted limit on straight roads and 50% on curves. If you have a manual transmission, avoid quick downshifts because this can cause a skid. Do not make sudden

factoid

The first windshield wipers were offered by Trico in 1916.

Figure 15–1 Visibility is severely limited in heavy rain.

DRIVING TIPS *A Slick Combination*

The first 10 to 15 minutes of any rainfall can be the most dangerous. Oil and grease that have built up on the road combine with the water to create a very slippery surface. If possible, wait until the road oils have been washed off the roadway by more rain before driving.

movements of the steering wheel or turn too sharply. Use lower gears on hills for added control.

Avoid applying your brakes too suddenly or too hard on wet road surfaces. Because wet brakes may "pull" or stop more slowly than dry brakes, plan ahead and brake earlier than normal. Let the car coast to reduce speed when possible.

If the rainfall becomes so heavy that you cannot see with the wiper blades at maximum speed, pull over to a safe area and wait it out. Make sure that you park far away from traffic. Vehicles parked on the side of the road are often struck by drivers who cannot see well in bad weather. Do *not* set the parking brake. In the event of a rear-end collision, the less resistance your car offers to the impacting vehicle the better.

Hydroplaning

Hydroplaning occurs when a thin sheet of water gets between the road surface and a vehicle's tires, causing them to lose contact with the road. The vehicle then begins a skatinglike movement across the road. Hydroplaning can start at speeds as low as 30 miles per hour (50 km/h) and in water little more than ⅛ inch (3 mm) deep.

When your speed increases, so do the chances of hydroplaning. Your ability to slow, stop, or even

factoid

The collision rate is up to 50% higher on days with heavy rainfall than on dry days.

JEROME BROWN

After an All-American football career at the University of Miami, Jerome Brown was selected in the first round of the 1987 NFL draft by the Philadelphia Eagles. As a defensive lineman with the "Birds," he appeared in seventy-six games and in 1991 played a pivotal role in the success of the league's best defense, tying for most tackles by a defensive lineman in the National Football Conference. Off the field, "Number 99" gave his time and energy to helping others in Philadelphia and in his hometown of Brooksville, Florida. On June 25, 1992, twenty-seven-year-old Brown was killed along with a twelve-year-old relative when his Corvette skidded out of control and flipped on a rain-slick U.S. Highway 41 in Brooksville. The next time you drive on a wet road, remember that you have less ability to slow, stop, or steer than you do on a dry road.

Figure 15–2 Driving through standing water increases the risk of hydroplaning.

steer your vehicle is greatly reduced. Once you begin to hydroplane, any sudden jerking of the wheel or even a strong gust of wind can send you into an uncontrollable skid that can result in a crash. If you do begin to hydroplane, take your foot off the gas pedal. *Resist your instinct to use the brakes.* Keep your steering wheel straight and let the car's momentum ease down until the tires grip the road again and you regain control.

Before going out in rainy weather, check your tires. Tires with deep, open treads allow water to escape and help prevent hy-

droplaning at moderate speeds. Tires with worn tread and those that are underinflated have less grip on the road surface, increasing your chance of hydroplaning. To properly handle skids, it is better to have tire pressure on the high side, rather than the low side, of the manufacturer's specifications.

Be alert to warning signs of standing water on the roadway, which can lead to hydroplaning. These include visible reflections on the surface of the water, "dimples" created by rain drops as they hit the water, a "slushing" sound made by your tires, and a "loose"

REALITY CHECK   *Wet Leaves*

Especially in the fall, roads may be covered with leaves that become very slippery when they get wet from rain or fog. Even if the leaves are dry on top, they may still be wet underneath. Wet leaves can reduce the braking distance of your vehicle and even cause you to skid. When you approach a road surface covered with leaves, slow down and try to stay on clear pavement.

feeling in your steering wheel. If you are driving after a rainstorm has just ended, continue to be cautious. Rain leaves puddles in the road for several hours, sometimes even days, after the showers stop that can cause your car to hydroplane.

Deep-Water Driving

If you come to a point on the road with deep water, it is best to use an alternative route, even if it is far out of your way. If water on the road ahead is running, which is typical of areas prone to "flash floods," the worst possible thing you can do is try to cross. Moving water as shallow as 18 inches (45 cm) can carry away an average car. If there are no alternative routes, find a warm, dry place to wait it out, and try again later when the water level drops.

If you have to go through a stretch of standing deep water, make sure that the water level does not reach the bottom of your car. Consider the difference in ground clearance between other vehicles trying to cross the water and your own vehicle. Use signs, fire hydrants, and other fixed objects to help gauge how deep the water is. If the water is too deep, you risk getting water into your engine through the carburetor, air filter, or exhaust pipe that can cause it to stall. Water can also short out your electrical system. Do not assume that just because you are in a jeep, truck, or sport utility vehicle you can make it safely across deep water. There may be underwater dips or trenches that you cannot see at all.

To cross safely, wait until other cars ahead of you go through the water and clear it. If they stall, you do not want to be behind them with nowhere to go. Shift to a lower gear to keep the engine turning faster, which reduces your chance of stalling. Proceed slowly. Crossing quickly will splash water and drown your engine. Stay close to the higher

Figure 15–3 Think twice about driving through deep water.

center of the road and away from the soft shoulder, where you may have reduced traction. Gently ride your brakes as you go through the water to keep your brake linings in contact with the brake drums. The heat from the brake pressure will prevent your linings from getting soaked and keep them operating more efficiently. After passing through the water, continue to ride your brakes to dry off any water that may have accumulated on your brake pads.

15–2 SNOW AND ICE

Snow, especially in combination with gusting winds, can greatly limit your vision. Road markings are often covered up with accumulations of snow, and traffic signs and signals may also be hard to see. A blanket of snow can hide familiar landmarks, making it easier to become lost. If the sun is shining, sunlight can reflect off snow and ice on the ground and add to glare.

"Winterizing" Your Vehicle

Make sure that your vehicle is properly prepared for winter driving by checking all of the car's systems. Add a deicing solvent to your windshield washer solution—*not* antifreeze—to prevent icing. Carry tire chains properly fitted to your tires and chain repair links, especially if you will be driving in the mountains. Also carry along a tarp to lay on to install the chains, if you want to keep your clothes dry. Check your

Figure 15–4 Make sure that your windows, mirrors, and lights are completely free of snow and ice before going out in winter conditions.

DRIVING TIPS *Winter Driving*

- Check the current road conditions and weather forecast before starting your trip. Stay off the road when traveler's advisories are issued. Once you are on the road, periodically check the radio for updated changes in the weather.

- Before going on a long trip, let a family member, friend, or co-worker know where you are going, when you plan to get there, and which routes you plan to take. When you arrive at your destination, let that person know you have made it safely.

- Leave early. Expect your trip to take up to twice as long as normal because of delays and roadway closures.

- Keep your gas tank at least half full at all times. Bad storms can cause traffic to be delayed or rerouted away from roadside services that are usually available.

- Use low-beam headlights to increase visibility in winter driving conditions.

- On a long drive through snow, maximize visibility by making sure that you periodically check for and remove ice and snow from your windows, mirrors, roof, and hood, and from under the fenders.

- Keep your window cracked open while driving to prevent any carbon monoxide from seeping into the passenger compartment of your car from a leak in your exhaust system.

- Put an extra car key in your pocket. If you accidentally lock yourself out of your vehicle, you do not want to wait outside in the cold weather for help to arrive.

- If you get trapped in a blizzard, stay in your car unless help is visible within 100 yards (90 m). Hang a distress flag from your radio antenna or, if stranded in a remote area, spread a large, brightly colored cloth over the snow to attract the attention of rescue personnel. Run the engine and heater about 10 minutes each hour to keep warm.

- If you ever get stuck in snow, make sure that your exhaust pipe is not blocked. This can cause your engine to stall and carbon monoxide to build up inside your vehicle.

spare and make sure that you have a flashlight, ice scraper, snow brush, ice pick (for hardened ice under the fender), snow shovel, gloves, road flares, and jumper cables. If you will be driving in remote areas, make sure that you have the ability to call for help, either with a car phone or CB radio. Take along extra clothes and warm blankets in case you get stuck.

Starting on Snow

When starting your car on a snow-covered road, first clear a path in front of the wheels by gently driving back and forth. Use a shovel if the snow is deep. With your wheels pointed straight, shift to DRIVE if you have an automatic transmission or SECOND gear if you have a manual transmission. Gently press on the accelerator. Ease out without spinning

DRIVING TIPS   *While You Were Sleeping*

During winter, take extra precautions in the morning when you first drive your vehicle. You may not know what the weather conditions were like overnight. Even though the roads may appear to be dry, moisture from light rainfall or even fog could have frozen in certain areas.

It can take three to ten times farther to stop on winter-slick pavement than on a dry road.

the wheels of your car, which will only get you deeper in the snow.

Driving on Snow and Ice

In extremely cold temperatures, such as around 0°F (−32°C) or lower, fresh, powdery snow offers decent traction. At warmer temperatures, however, snow becomes a watery slush as it melts, creating a very slippery surface. The greatest danger occurs when temperatures approach the freezing point (32°F or 0°C) and slush turns into a slick sheet of ice. If it is raining at the freezing point, or sleeting, ice can form instantly on

the road. Ice is one of the most hazardous conditions you can face as a driver. Not only does ice reduce your traction to almost nothing, it is virtually impossible to see. Roads that look wet may in fact be glazed with what is called "black ice."

Because cold air circulates below bridges and overpasses, they tend to freeze before other roadway surfaces. Even if the roads are completely dry, bridges and overpasses may still have ice on them. If it is cold enough, water from melting snow can even freeze in the shaded areas of an otherwise dry, sunlit roadway, creating dangerous patches. Intersections and

Figure 15–5 After a snowfall be especially careful at intersections, where packed snow and slush can freeze and form an invisible layer of ice.

other areas of the roadway with heavy traffic also tend to be icy because the weight of vehicles continually packs down the snow and slush into ice.

During snowstorms, maintenance crews often lay down sand and/or salt to melt ice on the roadway, especially on bridges, intersections, and other dangerous areas. Although sanding/salting is effective at improving traction on the roadway, do not assume that a treated area is free of ice. Remember that a road with *any* ice is extremely dangerous.

To improve your traction in snow, try to stay within the tire tracks created by other vehicles and off the snow and ice between the tracks, on the road shoulders, and in the central part of the road as much as possible. Reduce your speed to no more than half the posted maximum on snow-covered or icy roads, and execute all maneuvers slowly and smoothly to avoid losing traction. If you ever feel your drive wheels start to slip, immediately ease off the gas pedal.

Increase your following distance by at least 10 seconds on winter-slick roads. Stay far enough behind other vehicles that you only have to stop when absolutely necessary because it may be difficult for you to get enough traction to start again. Always give yourself

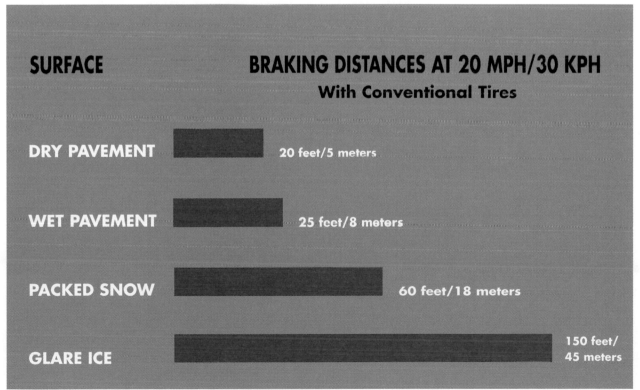

SURFACE

BRAKING DISTANCES AT 20 MPH/30 KPH

With Conventional Tires

DRY PAVEMENT — 20 feet/5 meters

WET PAVEMENT — 25 feet/8 meters

PACKED SNOW — 60 feet/18 meters

GLARE ICE — 150 feet/45 meters

Figure 15–6 Braking distance varies dramatically in different weather conditions.

extra room to stop when approaching signs and signals. You could easily get into a crash if you slide into oncoming traffic at an intersection. Use lower gears on hills for added control. Be careful not to downshift or brake abruptly as you are going downhill or the car may skid.

On a snow-covered or icy road, brake as you approach a curve but coast around it smoothly without touching either the brake pedal or accelerator. Accelerate only *after* straightening your wheels. Braking or accelerating during a turn on snow may cause you to oversteer or understeer, resulting in a skid and possible loss of control of your vehicle.

Snow Tires and Tire Chains

Road and weather conditions can change rapidly during winter. It is therefore important that your car be equipped with proper snow tires or chains. Snow tires have a large, open tread that allows the snow to escape from under the tire to better grip the roadway. Tire chains provide even better traction on snow-covered roads and, with practice, take only about 5 minutes to install per wheel. Before using

Figure 15–7 Make sure that you have the proper chains installed before entering a chain zone.

chains, practice installing them in your driveway first.

On some roads and highways, especially in the mountains, it is required by law that you use or carry tire chains during certain times in winter. Posted CHAINS REQUIRED signs usually appear about a mile (1½ km) before a checkpoint. You will not be allowed to proceed past the checkpoint without chains or, depending on what kind of vehicle you have, proper snow tires. Areas where chains are required often have special posted speed limits, usually a maximum of 25 miles per hour (40 km/h).

Pull well off the roadway before installing chains. Chains must be placed on all four tires. If you use the services of a private chain installer, make sure that you bring your own tire chains because such businesses are usually prohibited from selling or renting their own. After you have reached the end of a chain control area, wait until you can get off the road safely before removing the tire chains.

Parking on Snow or Ice

Avoid parking on snow-covered or icy roads. It may be extremely difficult to later get out of the space. If you have to park downhill, always make sure that there is enough room to pull out of the parking space without backing up, which can be very tough with reduced traction. Never set your parking brake after driving in snow. It can freeze and leave you unable to move your vehicle. Instead, leave your car in PARK or, if you have a manual transmission, REVERSE.

Snowplows

Snowplowing by road maintenance crews often opens up only one central lane in each direction of a multilane roadway. Because it is often difficult to see exactly where the road markings are, watch for oncoming traffic that may be traveling closer to the road's center line than normal. Before passing a snowplow, make sure that you can see clearly

Figure 15–8 Watch for oncoming traffic crowding the center line on roads cleared by snowplows.

DRIVING TIPS **When "Hazard Lights" Are Hazardous** _____

If you have to pull over on the side of a roadway in heavy rain, thick fog, or a severe storm, do not put on your emergency flashers. This can mislead other motorists into running off the highway and into your vehicle. As vehicles approach you from the rear, drivers might mistake your emergency lights for fleeting glimpses of your regular brake lights. In conditions of low visibility, drivers often follow the rear taillights of vehicles ahead of them to gauge their own lane position. If you are stopped on the side of the road, these approaching drivers could easily drift off the roadway and rear-end your vehicle.

ahead. Blowing snow can reduce visibility and hide the width of the blade. If a snowplow is approaching you in the oncoming lane of a two-lane road, move as far to the right as possible. Never drive next to a snowplow because they often move sideways to avoid hitting drifts or to cut through a snow pack.

15–3 OTHER SEVERE WEATHER CONDITIONS

In addition to rain, snow, and ice, you may encounter other severe weather conditions on the roadway.

Fog

Fog is most common early in the morning, late at night, at high altitudes, and near bodies of water. You may not think of fog as severe weather, but fog can be one of the most dangerous driving environments you will encounter. Some of the worst crashes in history have occurred in fog. Fog can reduce your visibility drastically, sometimes to within only a few feet (1 m) of your car. If you cannot see other vehicles or pedestrians, remember that they cannot see you either.

Greatly reduce your speed when approaching a patch of fog. Maintain an extra space cushion

guess the vanity plate

DELMAR

GSTBSTR

Figure 15–10

Figure 15–9 Some of the worst traffic collisions in history occurred in fog.

USING SAFE *Driving in the Wind*

Severe wind can come from any direction, making steering difficult. If you are not alert, crosswinds can literally force you into an adjoining lane, off the road, or into the path of oncoming traffic. Use the SAFE process. *Scan* ahead for warning signs in areas prone to strong, gusting winds. Observe how the wind is affecting other vehicles. Look at trees and foliage to try to gauge the direction and intensity of the wind. *Assess* how the wind may affect your own vehicle. Will tailwinds cause your vehicle to build up speed, increasing your stopping distance? Are you facing a head wind, making it necessary to accelerate harder to maintain a steady speed or pass? Are you in a high-profile vehicle such as a van, recreational vehicle, or pickup with a camper shell, making handling more difficult? Are the roads slippery, making gusting winds even more dangerous? Are you passing over or under a bridge, emerging from a tunnel, or driving between hills or tall buildings that can create a funneling effect? *Find* an "out" in case buffeting winds push you out of your lane and *execute* the appropriate defensive driving techniques to maximize control of your vehicle. Increase your space cushion, especially around vehicles that may have trouble handling the wind, such as motorcycles and cars pulling trailers. Slow down if you feel the wind "pulling" your vehicle, and firmly grip the wheel. If you are on a multilane road, stay in the right lane. If you are on a two-lane highway, move to the right side of your lane when facing oncoming traffic or when being passed by trucks, buses, or other large vehicles that can magnify the effects of wind.

around your vehicle. Fog can alter your depth perception, and vehicles may be closer to you than you realize. Use your low-beam headlights to increase visibility. Fog reflects light, so using your high-beam headlights can actually *reduce* your view of the surrounding area. If the fog becomes so thick that you cannot see at all, pull over as far away from the roadway as you can and wait for it to clear.

Dust and Sand Storms

Dust and sand storms are common in deserts, agricultural areas, and sandy beach areas. Do not attempt to drive through such a storm, even at a reduced speed.

Other drivers behind you may be driving much faster than you and could rear-end you. Also, your visibility can be reduced to zero. While the storm may not be so bad where you are, dust and sand storms often change very quickly

Figure 15–11 Posted signs warn you of areas known to have gusting winds.

in intensity over an area and you could get in real trouble down the road. If you see a thick cloud of dust or sand ahead, pull off the road as far as you can and stop the car. Roll up the windows and stay where you are until the storm passes.

Hail

Hail usually accompanies spring and summer rains. Heavy downpours of pea-sized hail can dramatically reduce visibility and layer the road with slippery balls of ice. Larger baseball-sized hail can crack windshields and dent car bodies beyond repair. If the weather forecast calls for hail, and you value your safety and the appearance of your vehicle, find a covered place to park your car and stay there until the storm passes.

Lightning Storms

During a lightning storm, get indoors or stay in your car. Stay away from open areas and high objects such as tall poles or trees that can attract lightning. Avoid any contact with water, metal, or electrical devices such as a radio or cellular phone. If you happen to be in the open far away from your vehicle and cannot get to shelter, head for the lowest area possible and get on the ground.

Tornadoes and Hurricanes

Although tornadoes are most common in the American Midwest, they have been reported from time to time throughout most of North America. What makes a tornado so deadly is the speed, unexpectedness, and deadly force with which it strikes. Should you ever be driving and see a tornado, pull over immediately and find shelter in a basement or low-lying area such as a bridge underpass. Never try to "chase" a tornado to take photographs or to videotape it. Tornadoes can quickly change directions, and before you know it, you are trapped.

Hurricanes form in tropical waters and are common along the southern United States coastline, especially in the fall. They are characterized by driving rain, surging water, and extremely strong winds. If you get caught in your vehicle during a hurricane, try to park under a covered area. Do not park near trees, telephone poles, or similar objects that can topple and crush you and your vehicle.

15–4 COLD AND HOT WEATHER

Vehicles are designed to operate in both cold and hot weather, but extreme temperatures create special problems.

Cold Weather

Air is denser in cold weather, resulting in a leaner mixture of fuel and air in your engine. This means that in colder temperatures your engine has to work harder to vaporize fuel. If your car has any vacuum leaks, such as loose or cracked vacuum hoses or a loose carburetor, sticky valves, faulty seals around an injector, or a faulty thermostat, the air–fuel mixture can become even leaner. If your engine is performing poorly in cold weather but normally in warm weather, have a mechanic check your engine.

If your engine does not have enough antifreeze or has the wrong kind of antifreeze, the radiator can freeze in cold weather. This will block the coolant from getting to your engine, causing it to overheat. Make sure that you follow the directions in your owner's manual regarding the proper maintenance of your cooling system.

Starting in Cold Weather

Cold weather puts added strain on your engine, especially when you first start it. The battery has less power, and oil, transmission fluid, and other lubricants tend to thicken. In winter, keep your battery charged on a regular ba-sis. You do not want your battery to fail when you are out in severe weather and far from a service station.

Depending on what type of battery you have and how old it is, your car can only sit in cold weather for a limited time. If possible, keep your vehicle parked in a closed garage. If you are not going to use your car for a long time, have someone else periodically start it and run the engine for about 10 minutes. If the car is going to be parked in extremely cold weather, attach an electric engine-block heater to the engine to keep it warm.

Frosted-up Windows

Cold temperatures can cause your windows to ice up, reducing your visibility. Scrape the outside of the windows thoroughly before driving. Once the engine is warmed up, use the defroster to completely clear the frost from

Figure 15–12 Wait until your window is completely defrosted before you start driving.

DRIVING TIPS   *"Locked" Out by the Cold* _____

Water that splashes onto your door or trunk locks can freeze over and prevent you from getting into your vehicle. If the ice is not too thick, pouring hot water on the lock may do the trick. If you have a pair of fire-retardant gloves to protect your hands, you can also try heating your car key over a flame and then inserting it into the lock. You can also spray or squirt a chemical deicer or isopropyl alcohol into the lock. To prevent locks from freezing during winter, treat them in the fall with liquid graphite.

the inside of the windows. Trying to drive with limited visibility because you are too impatient to wait for the windows to defrost is just asking for a collision. Keep an eye out for other drivers who may have a hard time seeing you through *their* iced-up windows.

During winter, moisture from your breath, perspiration, snow on your shoes, or even a leak in your heater core can cause your windows to continue fogging up even with the defroster on. The more people there are in the vehicle, the worse the problem can get. Keep a window open and the ventilation system set on "fresh air" to help eject moist air from your car. You can also use a quick blast from your air conditioner, which will actually clear your view faster than air from your defroster. Although defroster air is warm, air from your air conditioner is very dry and evaporates the condensation much more effectively.

Hot Weather

Just as the cold temperatures of winter put added stress on your vehicle, so do the hot tempera-

tures of summer. In general, heat causes liquids to evaporate. Motor oil, automatic transmission fluid, and power-steering fluid are all crucial to the safe operation of your vehicle and should be checked regularly during hot weather conditions. Heat can also shorten the life of a car's battery and cause belts and hoses to crack and tear. Before summer driving season, make sure that you take proper preventive maintenance measures as described in your vehicle owner's manual.

Vapor Lock

In very hot weather, gasoline can boil and turn to vapor. This may cause some engines to "lock," or stop running. If this happens to you, turn off your engine and let it cool down. Once the vaporized fuel in your fuel line returns to its liquid form, you should be able to restart your engine.

Vapor lock is almost a thing of the past. Today's cars have fuel pumps in the fuel tank rather than on the engine, which "pushes" rather than "sucks" gasoline into the engine. This results in a more efficient flow of pressurized, cool

factoid

Driving with the air conditioner on reduces gas mileage by approximately 2.5 miles per gallon (6 km/L).

fuel in the fuel lines, making vapor lock almost impossible. Find out what kind of fuel system your vehicle has. If you have an older car, be aware of the risk of vapor lock in hot weather.

Overheating

Driving for long periods in hot weather, especially in heavy traffic, going up steep inclines, or using your air conditioner at full blast on a very hot day can all cause your engine to overheat. The risk of damage to your engine from overheating is even greater if you have not maintained the proper coolant level or used the wrong type of coolant.

If your engine starts to overheat, move to a safe place off the roadway and stop your vehicle. Turn off your air conditioner if it is on. Open your windows. Put

Figure 15–13 Wait for your radiator to cool down before adding water.

your heater on the maximum setting to draw heat away from the engine. Shift the transmission into NEUTRAL, and give the engine a little gas by pressing on the accelerator. If this fails to work, turn off the engine and get out of your vehicle. Stand away from the hot engine until steam has stopped escaping. Cover your hand with a thick towel or a heat-resistant glove and open the hood to allow more heat to escape.

In an emergency situation, you can add water to the radiator to serve as a temporary coolant. With a thick towel or heat-resistant glove, give the radiator cap a one-quarter turn. Keep your face turned away to prevent accidental scalding. Retreat several steps from the vehicle while the pressure under the cap escapes. Once the pressure is released, turn the radiator cap and remove it. Add a measure of water into the radiator after it is *completely* cooled down. This can take as long as an hour, so be patient. Putting cold water in your radiator right after the engine has overheated can cause the radiator to crack.

Start the engine again and return to the radiator. As water circulates through the engine, the fluid level in the radiator will drop. Add water as necessary. If it appears that the engine is running again without overheating, replace the radiator cap tightly in place and resume your travel. If your engine starts to overheat again after you add water, do not drive the vehicle. Call a tow truck or your automobile club for roadside assistance.

Crazy **auto laws**

You had better not get caught with anything but your arm out the window in Ohio, where it is against the law to stick your feet out the window to cool off.

Figure 15–14 Which auto manufacturer made this "dune buggy" for the moon, used for the first time in 1971?

Get your car checked out at as soon as possible in case you have a leak in your coolant system or another engine problem. Have the radiator pressure-tested and flushed, if necessary. Replenish the coolant in the container if the level is low.

Driving in the Desert

The combination of heat and isolation make the desert a dangerous place to drive, especially during summer months. Your car requires more maintenance in desert driving than in any other environment, so you should be extra careful that you properly service your vehicle, especially on long trips. If your car breaks down in the desert, it could be several hours or, if you are off a major highway, even days before you can get help or auto service.

DRIVING TIPS   *Desert Driving*

- Before going into the desert, let someone know where you are going and when you plan to return.

- Stay on the main roads. If you go "off-road," you could get stuck in sand, more easily get a flat tire, or get lost.

- Check the radiator fluid level each time you stop for gas. Unless you are using a sealed battery, check the battery fluid at least once a day.

- Check tire pressure daily. Do not bleed air from hot tires. Instead, prevent an excess buildup of pressure in your tires by driving your vehicle only for moderate time periods. If you think the car is riding hard on the tires, pull over and let the tires cool off.

- Do not make your engine work too hard by driving fast.

- In the summer, avoid driving during the hottest period of the day, which is between 11 AM and 4 PM.

- Carry at least two extra bottles of water in the car—one for you, to avoid dehydration, and one for your radiator—as well as an extra can of gas, spare hoses and fan belts, and maps of the area.

- Keep good quality sunglasses in the car to help reduce sun glare. It is also a good idea to keep a hat in your car. If you have to walk a long distance to get help, you will need protection from the sun.

- If you get stuck in the desert, stay with your vehicle. Your car is easier to spot than you are. Use your horn and, at night, your lights to get the attention of aircraft or other searchers.

WHO'S *AT FAULT?*

1. Driver 1 was proceeding eastbound in Lane 1 of the interstate about 65 miles per hour (100 km/h) in heavy rain. Driver 2, worried about driving on a wet surface, was traveling about 15 miles per hour (25 km/h). The posted speed limit was 55 miles per hour (90 km/h). Because of the great difference in their speeds, Driver 1 came upon Driver 2 very rapidly and attempted a last-second pass that caused his car to begin hydroplaning. A few seconds later, Driver 1 spun 180 degrees around and struck a barrier on the center divider. Driver 2 was not involved in the crash. **Who's at fault?**

2. Driver 1 was proceeding eastbound about 30 miles per hour (50 km/h) as she rounded the curve. In the middle of the curve she came upon Driver 2, who was proceeding about 20 miles per hour (30 km/h). The posted maximum speed limit for the turn was 35 miles per hour (55 km/h). As Driver 1 attempted to apply her brakes to avoid hitting Driver 2, she encountered a patch of ice on the road. The brakes locked and Driver 1 slid toward the edge of the eastbound lane until her vehicle left the road and impacted the mountainside. Driver 2 was not involved in the crash. **Who's at fault?**

YOUR TURN

15–1 Rain

1. What are some of the dangers of driving in rain?

2. What is hydroplaning and how can you prevent it?

3. What should you do if you encounter deep water on the road?

15–2 Snow and Ice

4. How should you prepare for driving in winter conditions?

5. What are some of the dangers of snow-covered and icy roads?

15–3 Other Severe Weather Conditions

6. What precautions should you take when driving in fog?

7. What should you do if you are caught in a severe storm?

15–4 Cold and Hot Weather

8. What are some of the problems caused by extremely cold temperatures?

9. What should you do if your engine overheats?

10. What precautions should you take when driving in the desert?

SELF-TEST

Multiple Choice

1. Hydroplaning can occur at speeds as low as:
   a. 45 mph (70 km/h).
   b. 30 mph (50 km/h).
   c. 15 mph (25 km/h).
   d. 35 mph (55 km/h).

2. The fastest way to clear moisture from your windshield is by using:
   a. the air conditioner.
   b. the defroster.
   c. the heater.
   d. washer fluid.

3. On a winter-slick road, increase your following distance by at least _____ seconds.
   a. 3
   b. 4
   c. 5
   d. 10

4. If your car engine starts to overheat, the first thing you should do is:
   a. drive to the nearest mechanic.
   b. turn off the air conditioner and turn on the heater.
   c. pop open the hood slightly to let some heat escape.
   d. pour cold water into the radiator.

5. A car traveling at 20 miles per hour (30 km/h) will take _____ to stop on ice with conventional tires.
   a. 75 feet (25 m)
   b. 120 feet (35 m)
   c. 150 feet (45 m)
   d. 175 feet (55 m)

Sentence Completion

1. Using your high beams can actually reduce your view of the surrounding area when driving in _____.

2. Use lower gears on _____ to maintain better control on wet or icy roads.

3. Do not set your _____ after driving in snow because it can freeze and leave you unable to move your vehicle.

4. The greatest danger of reduced traction on winter-slick roads occurs when temperatures approach the _____.

5. _____ occurs when a thin layer of water gets between the road surface and your vehicle's tires, causing them to lose contact with the road.

Matching

Match the concepts in Column A with examples of the concepts in Column B.

Column A	Column B
1. __ Way to improve traction on wet roads	a. Ride your brakes
2. __ Safe speed for driving in rain	b. 25% below posted limit
3. __ Indication of hydroplaning	c. Slow down and keep firm grip on wheel
4. __ Crossing deep water	d. Carry extra water for radiator
5. __ Response to gusting winds	e. Drive in tracks of vehicle ahead of you
6. __ Winter driving tip	f. 25 miles per hour (40 km/h)
7. __ Tire chain area speed	g. Allow extra traveling time
8. __ Desert driving tip	h. "Loose" feeling in the steering wheel

Short Answer

1. How would you approach a curve on a snow-covered or icy roadway?
2. Why is it dangerous to use hazard lights if you are parked by the roadway in bad weather?
3. What are the advantages of increasing your space cushion on slick roads?
4. Why should you avoid parking on snow-covered or icy roads on hills?
5. Why is vapor lock rare in modern cars?

Critical Thinking

1. You are in the right lane of a four-lane highway behind a large tractor-trailer truck driving at the speed limit. Although it is no longer raining, there are large puddles all over the roadway. "Splash and spray" from the truck is reducing your visibility. What should you do?

2. You parked on an uphill stretch of road, only to discover in the morning that it snowed overnight. What should you do?

PROJECTS

1. Go to a local auto supply store and see what products they offer for driving in bad weather. Write down a list of items you would include in an emergency preparedness kit for winter driving and desert driving.

2. Visit a public library and locate a copy of the local newspaper for your town or city for the past year. Find out which section of the paper contains stories about bad traffic crashes. Count the number of crash stories in January, April, July, and October. Which month had the most crashes? the fewest?

Collisions

Most collisions are easily preventable. If drivers paid more attention to the road and made better choices before an impending crash, tens of thousands of lives and billions of dollars would be saved each year. By understanding what causes collisions and how to avoid them, you will be a safer driver. If you are ever involved in a crash, it is important for you to know what to do and what your responsibilities are at the scene. Your own life, and the lives of others, may depend on it.

Upon completion of this chapter, you should be able to:

16–1 Collisions

1. Understand why a vehicle crash is a "collision" rather than an "accident."
2. Describe the different types of collisions.

16–2 What to Do at the Scene of a Crash

3. Understand what responsibilities you have at the scene of a collision in which you are involved.
4. List the steps you should take when giving aid at a crash scene.

16–3 Preventing Collisions

5. Describe the four choices you have to avoid an impending crash.
6. Understand what you should do if a collision is unavoidable.

16–4 Vehicle Restraint Systems

7. Describe the purpose of safety belts and air bags.
8. Understand the proper way to wear safety belts.

KEY TERMS

solo collision	rollover	safety belts
head-on collision	"hit and run"	passive restraint
side-impact collision	Good Samaritan law	air bags
rear-end collision	"brake and hold"	child safety seat
chain reaction		

16–1 COLLISIONS

When a collision occurs, *everyone* pays. Besides the direct costs to those involved in a crash of medical care, legal fees, funeral costs, and property damage, there are indirect costs to society in the form of higher auto and medical insurance premiums, traffic delays, crowded court dockets, and loss of wages and worker productivity. Being involved in a crash or having a friend or loved one hurt or killed in a collision has emotional costs that are impossible to calculate.

Causes of Collisions

Collision is a more accurate description of a vehicle crash than *accident*. The word *accident* im-

plies that nothing could be done to prevent the crash. In fact, almost all collisions are caused by driver error. The most common causes of crashes are speeding, failure to give the right-of-way, driving under the influence of alcohol or other drugs, failure to obey traffic controls, improper turning, and following another vehicle too closely. If you stay alert to traffic conditions, manage your speed, and remain aware of vehicles around you at all times, you should be able to avoid getting into a crash in almost all circumstances.

Types of Collisions

All crashes are really *two* separate collisions. The first is the collision of the vehicle with some obstacle.

Traffic-related injuries are the leading cause of injury deaths in North America.

Figure 16–1 What are the direct and indirect costs of this collision?

The second collision is that of the human occupants with the interior of the vehicle. It is the second collision that often causes injury and death. Injuries may be sustained because of the jarring effect of a collision—for example, whiplash in a rear-end crash—or the collapse of a vehicle's protective shell, especially in high-speed collisions or crashes involving a physical mismatch between the vehicle and the obstacle. However, most people are hurt when *they* impact the wheel, dashboard, or windshield of their own vehicle after it has been stopped by the force of the impact.

There are many types of collisions. A **solo collision** involves only one vehicle, such as when a driver drives into a ditch because he or she fell asleep at the wheel or failed to take a curve properly. These collisions can be deadly if the crash involves a hard obstacle such as a wall, bridge support, or large animal or if the vehicle falls off a cliff or into a deep ditch.

A **head-on collision** occurs when two vehicles collide front to front. This type of collision results in the most serious injuries and the highest rate of death because the force of impact combines the kinetic energy of both vehicles. A **side-impact collision** occurs when two vehicles collide side to side, side to front, or side to rear. The worst injuries in this type of collision result when one vehicle directly impacts the passenger compartment of another. A **rear-end collision** occurs when one vehicle hits another from behind. This type of crash results in the most damage when the vehicle impacted is not moving.

A **chain reaction** is a series of collisions involving vehicles that impact one after another. In most cases, chain reactions involve

auto slang

A "fender bender" is a minor collision that usually involves minor property damage and minimal injuries.

EDWARD GIVENS

Edward Givens' lifelong dream was to be an astronaut. As an Air Force pilot and instructor, he had logged more than 3,500 hours of flight time. After completing the USAF Aerospace Research Pilot Program, the thirty-six-year-old Texas native was selected by NASA in 1966 to be one of nineteen American astronauts to train for manned space flight. Unfortunately, Givens never got his chance to walk on the moon. On June 6, 1967, a fatigued Givens was returning from a training mission at the Manned Spacecraft Center near Houston, Texas, shortly after midnight. He fell asleep at the wheel, plunging off the road into a ditch, killing himself and injuring two passengers. As fellow Apollo crewmen carried his flag-draped casket to its final resting place, Givens was mourned by his wife, three children, his parents, and several hundred people whose lives he had touched. Givens' untimely death was all the more tragic because his "accident" was entirely preventable.

Figure 16–2 Rear-end collisions often lead to chain reactions on crowded roadways.

rear-end collisions. These are most common on highways and freeways where cars are driving close together at high speeds or in conditions of low visibility.

Some collisions can result in a **rollover**, in which a vehicle is flipped upside down or literally rolls over one or more times. Roll

overs can be very serious because the occupants may impact with all sides of the vehicle's interior, often resulting in head and neck injuries. If you are thinking about buying a sport utility vehicle or other vehicle with a high center of gravity, make sure that it has some form of rollover protection.

Figure 16–3 Rollovers are rare, but when they do occur, there is a risk of the roof collapsing or being crushed on impact with the ground.

REALITY CHECK   *"Set-up" Collisions* _____

Some collisions are staged by criminals who seek to defraud insurance companies for fake or exaggerated injuries and property damage. In the "swoop and squat" scheme, for example, the driver of a car you are following (the "squat" car) suddenly slams on the brakes when another vehicle (the "swoop" car) makes a sudden lane change directly ahead, giving the driver of the "swoop" car no time to stop before rear-ending the "squat" car. Pay close attention to drivers who drive slowly for no apparent reason, act rashly by trying to cut in quickly ahead of you, or otherwise behave out of the ordinary. The best defense against these criminals is to maintain a large space cushion around your vehicle at all times. Do not fall into the trap of tailgating someone who *wants* to be tailgated!

16–2 WHAT TO DO AT THE SCENE OF A CRASH

Although state and provincial laws differ slightly, all jurisdictions require you to stop at the scene of a crash to give aid and exchange information, notify others in the event of property damage, and report the incident to the proper authorities.

Stopping at the Scene

The first duty you have if you are involved in a collision is to im-mediately stop. You need not have suffered injury or damage to your own vehicle to be "in-volved" in a crash. You must stop if you directly *or* indirectly cause a collision to occur. *Never, under any circumstances, leave the scene of a crash unless directed to do so by law-enforcement or emergency personnel.* If you do leave the scene, or fail to stop following a crash in which you were involved, you could be prosecuted for the felony crime of **"hit and run."** This is an ex-tremely serious offense that can result in severe penalties if you are convicted.

Figure 16–4 Failure to stop at the scene of a collision in which you are involved could result in your arrest.

In most jurisdictions, stopping immediately does not mean that you must stop at the exact spot where the collision occurred. If your vehicle is still maneuverable and you are not injured, you are usually required to stop as close to the crash site as you can while making sure to move your vehicle out of harm's way. This means getting your vehicle out of the traffic lanes and away from any debris or wreckage on the road left by the collision.

As soon as you have pulled off the road to a safe spot and come to a stop, turn on your car's hazard lights and extinguish any lighted cigarettes. Watch for traffic from both directions before you exit your vehicle. Locate any crash victims by looking under and through all wreckage. Account for any who may have been thrown from their vehicle by talking to those who are uninjured or only slightly injured. If victims cannot turn off their ignition, do it yourself. Be alert to fire, downed power or telephone lines, flammable materials that may be leaking, and other hazards. Use extreme caution if you choose to approach a burning vehicle to rescue occupants. If you choose to do so, put out the fire using a fire extinguisher, dirt, or heavy fire-retardant blanket.

If you are not involved in a crash, you are usually not legally required to stop at a crash scene. Never stop, however, just to look, because by doing so you may block the route of law enforcement, fire and paramedic personnel, or tow trucks. You will also contribute to traffic congestion.

Giving Aid

Many people who die from injuries sustained in a collision might otherwise live if they were to get immediate care from others. It may take anywhere from 10 minutes to an hour or longer for emergency medical help to arrive, depending on the site of the crash. If you are one of the first to arrive at the scene of a crash or are yourself involved in a crash and are uninjured, you can do a lot to prevent further injuries and save lives. However, provide care to the injured only if you feel confident that you know what you are doing. If you are nervous, uncertain, or scared, do not attempt to render first aid. Ask others at the scene as to their knowledge of first aid. If someone else is more qualified or capable, let him or her take charge.

On the other hand, do not hesitate to help someone in need if you are the only person available or no one else steps forward. If you are concerned about liability, keep in mind that most jurisdictions have a **Good Samaritan law**. This law protects those who try to give first aid in emergency situations from being liable for injuries or fatalities that they may cause or assist in causing because of the quality of first aid they administered. In some jurisdictions, failure to provide "reasonable" assistance to any person injured in a crash, including making arrangements for the person to be taken to a

Protect Yourself While Helping Others _____

Because of the potential of transmitting disease via the mouth, especially when other injuries may increase the chances of blood being in the mouth, it is prudent to wear some form of mouth-to-mouth resuscitation barrier that prevents you from making actual contact with the mouth of the injured. Have several of these barriers in your car at all times. To reduce the risk of exposure to acquired immunodeficiency syndrome (AIDS), hepatitis, or other blood-borne diseases, use latex gloves, waterproof material such as plastic sheeting, or clean clothing to stop bleeding in other areas of the body. You can also try applying pressure with the victim's own hand.

physician or hospital for medical treatment, is a punishable offense.

Do not move crash victims or allow them to move unless their location puts them in immediate life or death danger. Hazards that would justify moving an injured person include being in the path of oncoming traffic, being submerged in water, being nearby downed power lines, or being near fire. Moving an injured person could make the injury much worse, especially in the case of head or spinal trauma. These types of injuries are often difficult to diagnose because there may be no blood or other evidence of a wound. If you have to move an injured person, make sure that his or her head and neck are in alignment, then delicately drag the person backwards by holding on to the person's clothes or armpits. Do not drag the person sideways.

Assess who needs help the most. Check for any crash victims who may be unconscious. If a victim is neither moving nor talking, ask the person if he or she is okay. If the victim does not answer, his or her airway may be blocked.

Open the injured person's airway by slightly lifting the chin. Do *not* tilt the head backwards. Place your ear next to the person's mouth and nose to feel and listen for any sign of breath. Look at the person's chest to see if it rises and falls, indicating breathing. If an injured person is not breathing, begin rescue breathing as soon as possible. Only a few minutes of nonbreathing can result in permanent damage to the brain or death.

Once you have made sure that the injured are conscious and breathing, check for bleeding. Apply a sterile bandage, if available, using additional dressings over the existing bandage as needed. If blood is moving rapidly from a specific wound, apply pressure with your fingertips over the bleeding area. Carefully elevate the wound as necessary to reduce bleeding, moving the injured person's body as little as possible.

Make the victim as comfortable as you can. Cover the injured with blankets or clothing to minimize shock, and loosen tight clothing. Do not give any food or liquid to the injured. Once you

Figure 16–5 Stay with victims of a collision until professional help arrives.

have begun to administer first aid, do not abandon a victim unless it is to attend another injured person in more need of assistance. Never take any injured to the hospital by yourself or in your own vehicle. Wait for professionals who know how best to transport people with different types of injuries.

Warning Others

After attending to the injured, mark the crash scene with flares, reflective emergency triangles, or other warning devices. Depending on the speed of traffic, they should be placed immediately behind and from 100 to 500 feet (30 to 150 m) behind the vehicles involved in the collision. Generally, the higher the speed of traffic, the farther back the warning devices should go. If the crash occurred near the crest of a hill or in a sharp curve, place warning devices where approaching drivers who do not have a good view of the crash site will be able to see them well in advance.

Figure 16–6 Place flares behind disabled vehicles to warn other drivers.

Never light a flare anywhere near gasoline, diesel fuel, motor oil, or other flammable materials that might have been discharged on the road following a crash. If you have no flares or marking devices, raise the hood of your vehicle to draw more attention to the scene. Tie a piece of cloth or an article of clothing to the radio antenna, a door handle on the side of the vehicle facing traffic, or the corners of the trunk or hood. If you have help to spare, have a person warn drivers approaching from the rear with brightly colored clothing during the day or a flashlight at night.

Calling for Help

If you have a cellular phone or CB radio, dial 911 or the local emergency telephone number to obtain help for any injured parties, even if the injury appears to be slight. If you do not have your own phone or radio, try to find a public pay phone or ask to use the phone of a nearby business or residence. Some freeways have emergency roadside phones that you can use.

Be prepared to tell the dispatcher your name and telephone number, what happened, the number of victims, and the exact location of the crash. If you are on a stretch of roadway with no specific address, be able to provide the names of nearby landmarks, mileposts/distance mark-

ers, cross streets, off-ramps, or any distinguishing geographic features. Ask the dispatcher for advice on how to care for the victims until help arrives. Make sure that you stay on the line until he or she hangs up.

If your vehicle is undrivable after a collision, contact your automobile club or a private towing service to have it towed to a garage or your residence.

Exchanging Information

Once first aid has been rendered to any victims, you have a responsibility to gather and exchange information with both the other parties to the crash and law-enforcement officers. The information you are required to provide varies by jurisdiction, but you should be prepared to exchange the names and addresses of all drivers and passengers, vehicle registration numbers, li-

Figure 16–7 When calling for help, stay on the line until the dispatcher hangs up.

Figure 16–8 Gather and exchange as much information as you can after a collision.

cense plate numbers, and driver's license numbers.

Insurance company names, policy numbers, policy expiration dates, and contact information should also be exchanged. If other parties have no insurance information available, ask them if they are insured. If they are not, ask them if they have filed any substitute for insurance such as a bond or deposit of funds, which are accepted in some jurisdictions. If they still reply in the negative or cannot produce evidence

of any such substitute, make sure that you get as much information as you can, including the make, model, and year of the vehicle.

Keep calm and do not argue at the crash site with other drivers and passengers about who was "at fault." Instead, gather any evidence you can that will support what you believe to be the true version of events. Get the seat locations of different passengers, and note the extent and nature of everyone's injuries. If you have a camera, take photos of the crash

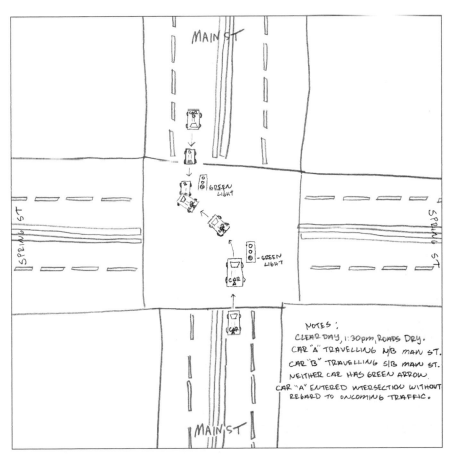

Figure 16–9 Make a sketch of the collision to help protect yourself in the event of a dispute with other parties involved in the crash.

More than half of all insurance claims for collision-related injuries are for neck sprains.

scene. It is especially important that you talk to any witnesses of the collision and jot down their names, addresses, telephone numbers, and what they saw. Make a sketch of the collision indicating each vehicle's speed, lane, and direction of travel, and record any relevant circumstances such as the weather, time of day, and location of the crash. Do not sign any papers given to you. Wait for law enforcement to arrive and cooperate in their reporting of the incident.

Property Damage

If you hit a parked vehicle or cause property damage, you have the responsibility to attempt to locate and notify the operator or owner of the property. If you are unable to locate the property owner, leave a note in a conspicuous place on the vehicle or damaged property with your name, contact address, the name of the owner of the vehicle you are driving (if you are not the owner), and a statement of what happened. Check with your insurance company and local law enforcement for any other requirements. In the case of an unattended vehicle, it is best to place the note underneath a windshield wiper blade. If you damage someone's property—for example, if you knock over someone's fence—you might leave the note in a mailbox or with a neighbor.

Reporting the Crash

The final responsibility you have after a collision is to report it to the proper authorities. Notify local police if they did not appear at the scene and give them details of any injuries or property damage. File a report with local law-enforcement officials and the Department of Motor Vehicles or equivalent authority in your jurisdiction. Even if police appeared at the crash scene, *you should always file your own report*. Most jurisdictions require a report if there was a fatality, an injury, or property damage exceeding a certain amount. Some jurisdictions require a report no matter how small the property damage is.

Telephone your car insurance company *immediately* after the collision and provide them with all the details you can. Send them copies of any reports, photos, and any other information that they require. Contact a physician if you suspect that you may have been hurt. It can take hours or even days for symptoms of a neck sprain or other injuries to appear.

16–3 PREVENTING COLLISIONS

In most cases, you can avoid an imminent collision by executing an evasive maneuver. By properly scanning and remaining aware of your driving environment at all times, you will give yourself more time and space when the unexpected occurs.

"Brake and Hold"

Most drivers have a reflex action to **"brake and hold"** when faced with an impending collision, no matter where it is coming from or what type it is. Although it may not be the best thing to do in a

USING SAFE **Preventing Collisions** _____

The SAFE process is the key to responding to specific circumstances that may lead to a collision. Always *scan* the road well ahead of you, *assess* potential hazards and other drivers' actions, *find* an escape route to avoid a collision, and *execute* the best alternative smoothly and safely. Many crashes occur because drivers fail to respond, or respond improperly, to an emergency situation. Whenever and wherever you drive, constantly be thinking of an escape route if a collision were to be imminent.

given situation, sometimes it is the only option you have. If you find yourself in congested traffic and there is no escape route to avoid the collision, you may have no other choice but to stop as quickly as possible. In lower-speed situations, such as driving less than 30 miles per hour (50 km/h), it may be more effective for you to brake and hold than to swerve.

When braking, hold the upper portion of the steering wheel with both of your hands. If you do not have an air bag, keep your arms between your body and the steering wheel, not to the sides, to help cushion your head and upper body in the event of a crash. Press your body up against the back of your seat and place your head directly against the headrest. Follow procedures for emergency braking according to whether you have an antilock braking system or non-ABS system.

Speeding up

You can often avoid an impending crash by speeding up. This is especially true when you are about to be hit from the side or rear. Situations in which speeding up can help you avoid a crash include when you are in an intersection, when a driver traveling next to you in the same direction moves toward you without seeing you, or when you are about to be rear-ended and you have clear space ahead to accelerate and escape danger. Even if you cannot avoid a crash by speeding up, you may be able to shift the impact toward the rear of your vehicle, thus minimizing injuries to yourself and passengers.

DRIVING MYTHS **When It Is Legal to Speed** _____

Many drivers incorrectly believe that they should never accelerate beyond the speed limit under any circumstances. You may legally exceed the speed limit in an emergency situation if your speeding is for a good reason such as avoiding a crash. Once the danger is passed, however, you must resume a normal driving speed.

Steering Left or Right

When there is not enough time to brake and you have some room to maneuver on one or both sides of an impending obstacle, you may be able to avoid a crash by steering to the left or to the right. If you are traveling more than 30 miles per hour (50 km/h), you can generally react more quickly by turning the steering wheel than by applying your foot to the brake pedal and trying to stop the car in time.

Remember that to your left you can usually expect either oncoming traffic or traffic traveling in your own direction but at higher speeds. To your right you will most often find slower lanes of traffic, the shoulder of the road, the curb, or parked cars. Avoid making too sharp a turn at higher speeds to maintain control, especially if you are driving a vehicle with a high center of gravity.

Driving off the Roadway

Driving off the roadway can be a good solution to avoiding crashes. Many drivers do not think of this option or do not dare do it because they believe it is against the law or unsafe. In fact, it is legal to drive off the roadway if you do so prudently to avoid a collision.

First, however, consider your environment. Certain terrain off the roadway can lead to more problems than a collision. It is better to sideswipe a car than it is to drive off a cliff or run into a concrete barricade. On the other hand, driving off the road onto farmland, front lawns, level highway medians, or shallow ditches may be a safe option. You must also consider your vehicle. A high-clearance 4×4, for example, can manage harsher terrain than a low-to-the-ground sports car.

When driving off the roadway, you may have to deal with several types of surfaces, making traction unpredictable. Slamming on your brakes can cause a skid, an uncontrolled re-entry across other lanes of traffic, or a rollover. Instead, ease your foot off the accelerator to slow your vehicle down naturally.

Avoiding Head-on Collisions

The possibility of serious injury and death is more likely with a front-impact crash than any other type. Be aware of situations in which a head-on collision is more likely, such as on two-lane highways, on narrow lanes around roadway construction, and near obstacles on the road.

If a car is coming at you head-on and is likely to collide with you, flash your headlights and/or honk your horn—loudly and continuously if necessary—to get the other driver's attention so that he or she will slow down or veer away. Move your vehicle to the right. A head-on driver will be more likely to move back onto his or her side of the roadway to your left than toward your right. By turning to your right, you have a better chance of being sideswiped by the driver than being struck head-on.

Figure 16–10 What was the name of this three-wheeled "little death trap" manufactured by BMW in the 1950s?

Avoiding Side-Impact Collisions

Despite recent safety advances in side protection such as reinforced steel beams in doors and side-mounted air bags, most vehicles are less well-equipped to withstand a side impact than they are a head-on impact. If you are at risk of colliding with the side of another vehicle, honk your horn and flash your lights to warn the other driver. Swerve right rather than left when there is no time to look first.

If you are the one about to be impacted, your best option is to accelerate rather than brake if the way is clear. Accelerating will get you past the danger more quickly. Braking may actually contribute to a side-impact collision, especially if the other driver has judged that your speed is sufficient to avoid a crash. If the way ahead is not clear, another alternative is to turn in the direction that the other vehicle is moving to force the impact behind you to the rear of your vehicle. If you turn in the direction of the approaching car, you risk colliding head-on with it.

Avoiding Rear-End Collisions

One of the most common types of multiple-vehicle collisions, rear-end crashes are most often caused when a driver follows another vehicle too closely. If you practice defensive driving and maintain a large space cushion and following distance, you should be able to avoid rear-ending a vehicle in front of you in *all* situations.

Drivers who risk hitting you from behind are another matter. To prevent an imminent rear-end crash with a vehicle behind you, tap your brakes rapidly and continuously to flash a warning to the approaching driver. Release the parking brake if it is on. Position your steering wheel straight, especially if you are stopped waiting to make a left turn. If your wheels are already pointed in the direction you want to turn, the impact may send you into lanes of oncoming traffic. This might result in a more serious head-on or side-impact collision, as well as the initial rear-end crash.

If the way ahead is clear, move forward as rapidly as possible to approach the speed of the oncoming car. This will reduce the force of the impact and give the approaching driver more time and space to stop if he or she recognizes the imminent crash. If moving forward means crossing an intersection, do so only if it is clear of traffic. If it is not clear, you risk a side-impact collision that may be more dangerous than being rear-ended. If you cannot move forward, look for another avenue of escape to the right or left if those areas are clear.

When a Crash Is Unavoidable

Recognizing that a crash is imminent does not mean that the world is coming to an end and that you have absolutely no control over the situation. You may

auto slang

When one vehicle hits the side of another at a right angle, the impacted vehicle is said to have been "T-boned" by the other vehicle.

driving tips

If your vehicle is rear-ended, prepare to begin braking immediately after you have recovered from the force of the impact to minimize the chances of your vehicle moving into any other cars or obstacles in front of you.

actoid

Although the use of safety belts by the driver and front-seat passengers is required in almost every jurisdiction in North America, more than 30% of Americans and more than 10% of Canadians do not buckle up.

have only seconds to do something about it, but if you do the right thing, you can greatly reduce the severity of the impact.

The first thing to remember is to *hit something soft if you can,* such as shrubbery, crash barriers, or a field of crops. The second is to *choose where your vehicle will be hit.* All vehicles are designed with crash-resistant features that work to protect the passengers by spreading out the force of the impact throughout the car. Familiarize yourself with these safety design features in your vehicle. Knowing your car's strengths and weaknesses may save your own life and others in a crash situation.

16–4 VEHICLE RESTRAINT SYSTEMS

Every vehicle is equipped with devices to protect the driver and passengers in the event of a collision or an evasive driving maneuver. These restraints significantly help to reduce injuries and deaths.

Safety Belts

Safety belts are among the most important safety features in your vehicle. They provide protection against most kinds of collisions, they keep you behind the wheel so you can steer to avoid a crash, and they prevent you from being thrown from your car. Most vehicles have a lap belt and a shoulder belt, although much older vehicles only have lap belts. On most vehicles, when you turn on the ignition a light appears on the instrument panel and a buzzer or

chime sounds to remind the occupants to attach their safety belts.

The lap belt is designed to restrain your pelvic area, and should

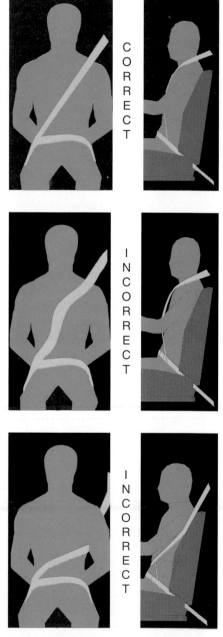

Figure 16–11 Safety belts include lap and shoulder belts.

actoid

In 1984, New York became the first jurisdiction in the United States to pass a mandatory safety belt law.

be adjusted to fit snugly across your hips and below your stomach. If the lap belt is too loose, it may slide up over your pelvis and injure your abdomen in a crash. The shoulder belt goes over the shoulder and across the sternum at the center of the rib cage. It should be loose enough to allow you to fit your fist between the belt and your chest, but not so loose that the belt hangs over your arm. If the shoulder belt is too loose, there is a greater chance that your upper body will strike the vehicle interior. Never leave the shoulder belt *under* your arm. This will not only result in unrestricted forward motion of your upper body, but also can cause severe internal injuries in a crash.

Most shoulder belts will adjust automatically as you pull them across your body. Other belts have a tension device that works like a window blind. If it is too short, you pull it out farther. If it is too long, you pull it tight gently and let it roll back into its housing un-til it reaches the length you want. Always take the time to untwist safety belts before buckling them.

In some cars, lap belts and shoulder belts are combined, allowing you to buckle both across your lap and chest in one motion. In other cars, the shoulder belt is a **passive restraint**, meaning that it operates without action by the occupants. When you sit in the car and shut the door, the belt automatically moves into place across your shoulder. *If you have separate lap and shoulder belts, remember to buckle your lap belt across your hips,* because otherwise you can slide out of the shoulder belt and be injured in a collision. Safety belts differ from vehicle to vehicle, so read your owner's manual for instructions on proper belt use.

As a driver, it is your responsibility to make sure that you and all passengers are wearing their safety belts properly. In some jurisdictions, a driver can be ticketed if any of the passengers are

guess the **v**anity plate

Figure 16–12

DRIVING MYTHS   *Safety Belts*

Some people argue against wearing safety belts. One common myth about safety belts is that in a crash they can trap you inside your vehicle. In fact, it takes less than a second to undo a safety belt, and if you are wearing one, you will be in a much better condition to undo it and get out of the car than if you did not wear it. Another myth is that safety belts are unnecessary on short trips or when driving on local streets. The reality is that more than half of traffic-related deaths occur within 25 miles (40 km) of home and on roads with speed limits under 45 miles per hour (70 km/h). A third myth is that if you are not wearing safety belts you may be thrown clear of the vehicle in a crash and walk away without a scratch. It is much more likely that a person ejected from a car will suffer extreme injuries or death. Your chances of survival are much better if you stay inside your vehicle.

not wearing safety belts, even if the driver is buckled up. Some insurance companies will even refuse to cover you if you or your passengers were not wearing safety belts when a collision occurred.

Air Bags

A major cause of serious chest and facial injuries in head-on collisions is driver contact with the steering wheel rim or hub. **Air bags** are a type of passive restraint system that cushion the force of impact and distribute it over a wider surface of the torso. Air bags are concealed in the steering wheel and dashboard and are designed to instantly inflate on impact in front-end collisions over a certain speed. Some air bags also deploy in side-impact collisions. When used with safety belts, air bags provide greater protection against contact between a vehicle's occupants and the interior.

It is important to remember that air bags are supplemental restraint systems. *Even if your car has air bags, you must still wear your safety belts!* Although air bags will protect you from hitting the steering wheel, the dashboard, or the windshield, they will not secure you behind the wheel of your vehicle. Only a safety belt can do this.

Child Safety Seats

The factory-installed restraint systems in cars are designed for adults. To protect infants and young children, you must install a separate **child safety seat**. These seats are placed directly on top of the car seat and are held in place by the vehicle's safety belts. The child seat itself has its own restraints, and these must be correctly fitted to the child to be safe and effective. Parents using child safety seats should always carefully follow the instructions that come with the seat.

DRIVING MYTHS *Air Bags*

Many people believe that air bags can seriously injure occupants if they deploy at the wrong time or too forcefully. In fact, the chance of an air bag deploying when it is not needed is almost zero. To protect passengers, air bags must deploy at an explosive $1/20$ of a second. They deflate almost as quickly, so there is no possibility of suffocation. In rare instances, air bags can cause serious injuries for drivers who are so short that they sit closer than 10 inches (25 cm) to the steering wheel. Small children or infants in rear-facing carriers who are seated in a front-passenger seat with an air bag may also be at risk for serious injury. If you cannot adjust your seating and pedals to allow a safe distance between your body and the air bag, or if young children have to ride in the front seat, contact your dealer or mechanic regarding federal procedures that may permit you to have an air bag turn-off switch installed on your vehicle.

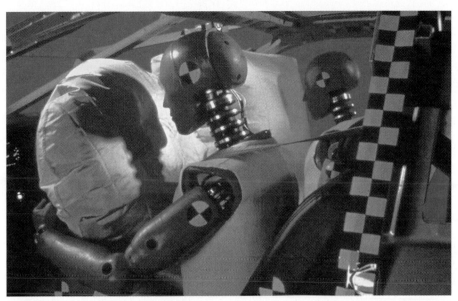

Figure 16–13 Air bags prevent contact with the interior of the car in a collision.

factoid

"Vince" and "Larry" are the famous crash-test dummies used by the United States Department of Transportation.

There are three basic types of child safety seats. Rear-facing seats are designed for infants from the time they are born until they weigh 20 pounds (9 kg) or are one year old. They have a detachable base so that the seat can double as a carrier. Convertible seats are for toddlers weighing between 20 and 40 pounds (9 to 18 kg) or who are one to four years old. These seats convert from rear-facing to forward-facing as the child gets older. Booster seats are used for older children not quite ready for regular safety belts. Children should be placed in properly installed safety seats until they weigh about 80 pounds (35 kg) or are eight years old, and most jurisdictions require that children ride in them until they weigh at least 40 pounds (18 kg) or are four years old.

Child safety seats should always be placed in the back seat to separate children as far as possible from the force of a head-on collision. This is especially true of rear-facing seats. Newborns and infants in a rear-facing safety seat placed on the passenger seat are at risk of being injured by an air bag if it inflates in a frontal collision.

WHO'S AT FAULT?

1. Driver 1 was going north and stopped at the intersection. Driver 2 was stopped directly behind Driver 1. Driver 3 was speeding and failed to stop in time to avoid colliding with Driver 2. Seeing that she was about to be rear-ended, Driver 2 hit her brakes and gripped the steering wheel with both hands. The force of impact pushed Driver 2 forward into the rear of Driver 1. ***Who's at fault?***

2. Drivers 1 and 2 were stopped in the right-hand lane of a four-lane highway after a fender bender. As they stood outside their vehicles arguing about who was responsible, Drivers 3 and 4 approached the site while driving side by side in adjoining lanes. Blocked from entering the left-hand lane by Driver 3 and going too fast to stop, Driver 4 went off the road into a bush to avoid hitting either Driver 1 or 2, damaging the front of her car. ***Who's at fault?***

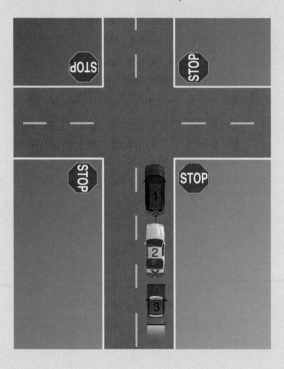

YOUR TURN

16–1 Collisions

1. Why is a vehicle crash a "collision" rather than an "accident"?

2. What are the different types of collisions?

16–2 What to Do at the Scene of a Crash

3. What responsibilities do you have at the scene of a collision in which you are involved?

4. What steps should you take when giving aid at a crash scene?

16–3 Preventing Collisions

5. What are the four choices you have to avoid an impending crash?

6. What should you do if a collision is unavoidable?

16–4 Vehicle Restraint Systems

7. What is the purpose of safety belts and air bags?

8. What is the proper way to wear safety belts?

SELF-TEST

Multiple Choice

1. Almost all collisions are caused by:
   a. accidents.
   b. miscommunication.
   c. driver error.
   d. defective vehicles.

2. You can legally exceed the speed limit if you are:
   a. driving off the road.
   b. avoiding a collision.
   c. traveling on rural roads.
   d. going with the flow of traffic.

3. Serious injury and death are more likely in which type of collision?
   a. rear-end
   b. head-on
   c. side-impact
   d. chain reaction

4. If you are facing an impending head-on collision, the first thing you should do is:
   a. swerve to the left.
   b. swerve to the right.
   c. flash your lights and/or honk your horn.
   d. "brake and hold."

5. Good Samaritan laws protect people who:
   a. leave the scene of a collision.
   b. give first aid in emergencies.
   c. are liable for a collision.
   d. stage a crash.

Sentence Completion

1. Most drivers have a reflex action to _____ when faced with an impending collision.
2. A _____ is a series of collisions involving vehicles that impact one after another.
3. If you fail to stop at the scene of a crash in which you are involved, you could be prosecuted for _____.
4. A shoulder belt that operates without involvement by the occupants of a vehicle is an example of a _____.
5. In a _____ collision, the occupants may impact with all sides of the vehicle's interior.

Matching

Match the concepts in Column A with examples of the concepts in Column B.

Column A	Column B
1. __ "Set-up" collision	a. Common on crowded roads
2. __ Crash scene responsibility	b. Choose where you will be hit
3. __ Option when crash is unavoidable	c. "Swoop and squat"
4. __ Evasive maneuver	d. Discuss who is "at fault"
5. __ Solo collision	e. Colliding with a tree
6. __ What not to do at a crash scene	f. Putting out flares
7. __ Rear-end collision	g. "T-boned"
8. __ Side-impact collision	h. Driving off the roadway

Short Answer

1. In which situations might speeding up prevent a collision from occurring?
2. If you are involved in a crash, what information should you be prepared to exchange?
3. Why can all crashes be considered two separate collisions?
4. Why is it important to file your own report of a collision?
5. What are the dangers of a vehicle with passive restraints?

Critical Thinking

1. You are stopped at a red light at the intersection of two four-lane roads in the right lane. Looking in your rearview mirror, you see a car approaching from behind traveling too fast to avoid rear-ending you. At that moment, you notice another car approaching the intersection from your left in the left lane of the cross street. What should you do?

2. As you are traveling on a lonely rural road, you come across a collision between two vehicles in the middle of an intersection. The driver of one vehicle is slumped forward over the wheel, and the driver of the other vehicle is lying on the ground bleeding. What should you do?

PROJECTS

1. Clip articles from your local newspaper describing automobile collisions. Select three crashes, and for each one, write down the most likely cause and what could have been done to avoid it. Share the results with your class.

2. Because people have been reportedly killed by air bags, they remain a controversial passenger restraint system. Call your or your parent's insurance company to find out what their policy on air bags is. Do they offer a reduction in your premium if you have them installed on your vehicle? Call a local automobile dealer to find out how much it costs to have air bags installed, or if they are already installed, how much it costs to replace them once they deploy. Contact the National Highway Traffic Safety Administration or Transport Canada to find out what the current federal guidelines are for the safe use of air bags. How do you apply to get a turn-off switch installed? Are all new vehicles required to have air bags? What about side-impact air bags?

17

Emergencies

Mechanical failures can lead to emergencies if your vehicle is in motion when the malfunction occurs. Blowouts can cause you to lose control of your car. If your brakes or steering fail, you may be at great risk for a collision. Loss of traction caused by weather or road conditions can cause you to skid. Dead batteries and other system failures can leave you stranded. No matter how alert you are or how well you take care of your vehicle, you must be prepared to deal with unexpected and unusual emergencies. Knowing what to do in these situations can mean the difference between life and death.

Upon completion of this chapter, you should be able to:

17–1 Blowouts and Flat Tires

1. Understand what to do if your vehicle has a blowout.
2. Understand how to replace a flat tire.

17–2 Mechanical Failures

3. Understand what to do if your vehicle breaks down on a freeway.
4. Understand what to do if your brakes fail.
5. Understand the proper way to jump-start a dead battery.

17–3 Skids

6. Describe the four types of skids.
7. Understand the proper way to respond to a skid.

17–4 Other Emergencies

8. Understand what to do if you get trapped in deep water.
9. Understand what to do if your car is on fire.
10. Understand what precautions you can take to avoid being the victim of a car jacking.

KEY TERMS

blowout	skid	cornering skid
brake fade	power skid	downshifting skid
jump-start	braking skid	car jacking

17–1 BLOWOUTS AND FLAT TIRES

A **blowout** is a sudden loss of air pressure in a tire. Hitting a deep pothole or a sharp object on the road (such as a nail or screw) can sometimes cause a blowout, even of a brand-new tire. However, properly maintained steel-belted tires can withstand most damage from road debris. In most cases, if you get a nail stuck in your tire, it will not cause a blowout and you can have it removed and the tire repaired for a small cost at a service station.

Most blowouts are caused by excessive tire wear. The average automobile tire has a tread life of about 60,000 miles (96,000 km), but you can shorten a tire's life by hard cornering and braking, driving in hot temperatures, driving at

Figure 17–1 Not all blowouts involve old or worn-out tires.

high speeds, "burning rubber" on quick starts, driving on rough road surfaces, and overinflating or underinflating your tires. Do not wait until your tire is "bald," the rubber is cracked, or there are bulges on the sidewalls to replace them. By practicing simple preventive maintenance—regularly checking your tire pressure and tire tread depth, rotating and balancing your tires, and having your wheels aligned—you can prevent a blowout from ever occurring.

Responding to a Blowout

Blowouts can be scary. If you experience a blowout while driving, your natural instinct will be to slam on the brakes. However, this can cause you to completely lose control of your vehicle. Instead, hold on tightly to the steering wheel, which may be vibrating badly. Gradually remove pressure on the accelerator, and allow the car to slow down by itself. Concentrate on staying inside your lane. If a front tire blows, the vehicle will pull hard in the direction of the blowout and the steering will vibrate. Steer away from the direction of the blowout to regain control of your vehicle. If the rear tire blows, the back of the car will weave from side to side just like a skid. To regain control, steer in the direction of the skid.

After checking that the way is clear, slowly and gradually pull completely off the road and out of the path of other vehicles, even if this means driving for a while

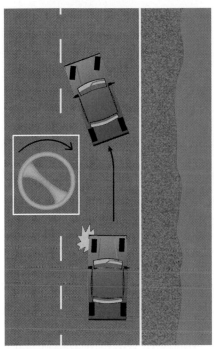

Figure 17–2 If you have a blowout, concentrate on staying within your lane.

on your wheel rim. After all, having to buy a new wheel rim is preferable to causing a collision.

Flat Tires

If you have had a blowout or if a tire has gone flat during the course of your drive, you must either call for roadside assistance or replace the flat tire yourself. You must first determine whether it is safe to change the tire in the location where your car is stopped. If you are too close to passing traffic and there is no way to move your vehicle to another location, do not attempt to change the tire yourself. Instead, seek professional roadside assistance.

Fixing a flat tire is fairly easy given plenty of room to operate and the proper equipment, but many people either are not prepared or do not know how to do it. Newer vehicles usually include a repair kit with instructions and a spare tire in the trunk, but before you get on the road, you should check to make sure that your vehicle has a spare in good condition and the necessary equipment to replace a tire, including a jack, wheel blocks, and lug wrench. Because many lug wrenches provided by car manufacturers are very short and can be difficult to use, you may want to consider purchasing a "cross" lug wrench. This type of lug wrench allows you more leverage to unfasten really tight lugs.

To replace a flat tire, follow this procedure:

1. Park on level ground. If your vehicle has an automatic transmission, switch gears to PARK. If you have a manual transmission, put the stick in REVERSE. Turn on your emergency flashers and apply the parking brake. Make sure that everyone is out of the vehicle. If you have reflective warning triangles or flares, set them out immediately behind and 100 to 500 feet (30 to 150 m) to the rear of your vehicle.

2. To make sure that the vehicle does not move while you are changing the tire, put two blocks—for example, bricks, pieces of wood, stones, or heavy metal bars—in front

Wild Wheels

Figure 17–3 What is the name of this 1911 vehicle, which could potentially experience *eight* flat tires?

Figure 17–4 Make sure that your vehicle is equipped with a complete tire repair kit.

of and behind the tire *diagonally opposite* the flat tire.

3. Put the jack under the vehicle as indicated in your owner's manual. Slowly crank the jack to raise the car. Make sure that the jack is securely in place when you first make contact with the vehicle's undercarriage. Continue cranking until the flat tire is partially up but still making contact with the ground and is incapable of being turned. Be careful not to expose any part of your body underneath the car in case the jack fails and the vehicle falls down.

4. If there is a wheel cover, remove it to get access to the lug nuts, the bolts that hold the wheel in place on the car. Loosen, but do not remove, each of the lug nuts using a lug wrench. If your wheel has not been removed for a long time, the lug nuts may be difficult to take off. Try placing the lug wrench on one of the lower lugs (toward the ground) so that it stays on by itself, with the handle facing parallel to the ground. Position your body sideways to the car and apply strong pressure with your foot downward onto the handle part of the wrench to loosen the lug. Work your way around the wheel, loosening the lug nuts diagonally in succession.

5. Finish jacking up the car until the flat tire is just off the ground. Remove the lug nuts with the lug wrench. Take off the entire wheel with the flat tire and set it down. Place the spare tire on the wheel mount, making sure to line up the holes of the wheel onto the holes of the wheel mount. Place the lug nuts back into the holes and tighten them. Replace the wheel cover onto the spare.

Figure 17–5 Emergency spares are not meant to be used for normal everyday driving.

6. Lower the car down by cranking the jack in the opposite direction from which you cranked it up. Stay clear of the vehicle until the car is all the way down. Remember to recover the blocks you used to keep the car in place.

On many cars, the spare is not a full-sized tire. Emergency spares are not designed to be used for normal driving but to get you home or to an auto repair shop. Full-sized spares that come with cars are often of inferior quality to your regular tires. Whatever type of spare you have, check your owner's manual or with the manufacturer to see how long you can safely drive on it and what its limitations are. As a rule of thumb, you should replace your spare with your second set of tires. Dry rotting and heat can cause a spare to deteriorate over time. If you have an older car with a spare that has been sitting in the trunk for years, odds are the spare tire is not safe to use.

17–2 MECHANICAL FAILURES

Tire failures are one of the most common causes of vehicle breakdowns, but other systems in your car can malfunction and cause an emergency while you are driving.

Brake Failure

One cause of vehicle breakdown is brake failure. In most cases, brakes do not literally "fail." Most cars on the road today have some type of power-assisted braking system. Engine failure or interruption of the flow of brake fluid can cause the power-assist or full-power feature of the brakes to fail. The brakes still work, but you have to apply much more pressure on the pedal.

Brakes can also "go out" if your brake pads become totally worn out. However, it takes time for pads to wear out, and you will notice a gradual reduction in the effectiveness of your brakes before they reach this point. If one day

Most emergency spares are designed not to exceed 50 miles per hour (80 km/h).

you cannot stop your vehicle because you ignored grinding noises coming from your brakes, *you failed, not your brakes!*

In most vehicle braking systems, the front and rear wheels are controlled by a separate mechanism. If one part of the system ever fails, you can still use the foot brake to stop the car. In the unlikely event that both parts of your regular braking system fail, you must respond quickly. *Unless you have an ABS braking system,* pump your brakes rapidly to engage any remaining brake fluid pressure to the brakes. If this does not work, use the power of the engine to reduce your speed by downshifting. If you are driving a vehicle with an automatic transmission, do not be afraid to downshift to SECOND gear and then to FIRST gear in quick succession to slow the car down.

Gradually apply the parking brake. Because this brake controls the rear two wheels of the vehicle, you must use the brake in a controlled way to prevent a skid. If you have a hand-cranked parking brake, slowly apply pressure on the release button of the parking brake as you pull the lever up. If you have a foot-pedal parking brake, hold the parking brake release handle while you are applying pressure on the brake with your foot.

As you are carrying out this procedure, find an escape route. Head for a safe place to stop the vehicle on the side of the road and steer safely out of traffic. If there is no safe place to go or if your speed is still too high, use whatever means are available to produce enough friction to stop, such as brush vegetation on the side of the road, an uphill slope, or a runaway vehicle ramp.

Overheated Brakes

When you use your brakes continuously over time—for example, when descending a long, steep mountain road—your brakes may overheat. To prevent this overheating, called **brake fade**, try to let your engine do most of your braking for you by changing the transmission to a lower gear. However, if the road is extremely steep or a lot of traffic is going downhill, staying in a low gear may not slow you down enough. In this case, pull off to the side of the road and give your brakes a rest. If this does not resolve the problem, wait for roadside assistance. Do *not* continue to drive the vehicle.

Steering Failure

Most cars today have some type of power-assisted steering. A power-steering failure is most common when the engine stalls. Without the power provided by the engine, your steering wheel moves, but it is much more difficult to turn. In the event of a power-steering failure, grip the steering wheel firmly and exert as much force as you can to get it to turn in the direction you need to go to get off the roadway and out of traffic.

If the wheel will not turn at all or the vehicle does not respond as the wheel turns, your steering system has failed completely. Any at-

DRIVING TIPS ***Freeway Breakdowns*** _____

A freeway is the most dangerous place that you can have a breakdown. There is not much room to pull over, and other vehicles *constantly* pass you at high speeds. If you have to stop on the freeway, signal and drive completely off the freeway onto the shoulder. Activate your emergency flashers. Set out warning devices, raise the hood of your car, or attach a white cloth or handkerchief to your antenna or roadway-facing door handle to get the attention of police officers or tow-truck operators that regularly patrol the area. Use a call box if one is available nearby to get professional help. Stay in your vehicle if it is completely off the freeway, and lock your doors until help arrives. If other drivers stop to offer their assistance, roll your window down slightly and ask them to call the police. Avoid walking on a freeway after a breakdown, especially at night or in bad weather. If no one is stopping and you are close to an exit with a source of help, such as a service station or place with a telephone, walking may be the best option if you can do so without risking your safety. Always walk on the right side of the roadway facing traffic. Never attempt to cross a high-speed, multilane freeway on foot.

tempt to steer the vehicle could be very dangerous, so shift the transmission into NEUTRAL and apply the brakes immediately until you stop. Turn on your emergency flashers.

Stalled Engine

Engine failure usually happens as a result of a mechanical failure, but it can also occur as a result of a common driver error—forgetting to put gas in the car! An engine can also stall if it gets wet or is exposed to excessively cold weather.

If the engine dies or stalls while you are driving, first try to re-engage the engine. Shift the transmission to NEUTRAL and try turning the ignition several times. If the engine comes back to life, shift out of NEUTRAL and back into a driving gear to proceed on your way. If shifting to NEUTRAL does not work, take a strong grip of the steering wheel, pull off the roadway to a safe place, and stop your vehicle. Keep in mind that it may be extremely difficult to turn the wheel and apply the brakes with a loss of engine power.

Stuck Accelerator

A stuck accelerator is rare and is often caused by an obstruction on

Figure 17–6 If your power steering fails, the wheel will be very difficult to turn.

REALITY CHECK   *"Stuck in the Middle with You"* _____

If your vehicle becomes disabled in the middle of traffic and you cannot pull over, which sometimes happens in stop-and-go traffic, keep your wheels pointed straight and turn on your emergency flashers. When it is safe to do so, get everyone out of the vehicle and onto the shoulder or median. If possible, use the shoulder rather than the median. The shoulder is generally wider than the median, traffic is slower in the right lanes, emergency vehicles can reach you more easily, and if call boxes are available they are located on the shoulder. If the shoulder is dangerously narrow, carefully walk to a wider point and face traffic so that you can see oncoming vehicles.

the floor in front of the driver's seat, such as hardened mud or ice, or an object wedged against the accelerator pedal. However, it may also be caused by a mechanical problem with the vehicle.

To try to free or "unstick" your accelerator, first try lifting the accelerator pad up with the tip of your shoe. If this does not work and you have a passenger in the front seat, tell him or her to reach down underneath the dashboard and pull up the accelerator. If you do not have a passenger or this still does not solve the problem, shift into NEUTRAL immediately. Pull off the roadway, using your brakes to slow the vehicle down. Do not turn off the engine until you have come to a complete stop.

Headlight Failure

If your headlights go out, try flipping the "on" and "off" switch several times. If this does not work, try your high beams. These usually use different bulbs and may still work even if the low-beam bulbs will not go on. If nei-

ther your high beams nor low beams work, activate your emergency flashers. These lights will help you see the road ahead, and more important, they will make you visible to other drivers. Pull your vehicle off the roadway as soon as it is safe to do so.

Dead Battery

If you attempt to start your vehicle and you do not hear the ignition turn, your battery is probably dead. It may have been old, weak, or drained by a defective alternator or extremely cold weather. Perhaps you left the lights on by mistake after parking your car.

You can **jump-start** your car to recharge your battery. This involves using a set of jumper cables to start your vehicle by drawing on the charge from another vehicle's battery. If you do not carry your own set of cables, ask other drivers or check with a nearby parking garage or service station to see if they will loan you a set.

To jump-start your vehicle's battery, first make sure that the other vehicle's battery is in good working order and that it is the same voltage as your battery. The front ends of both vehicles should be face to face, or at such an angle that the cables can easily reach both batteries. *Do not let the vehicles touch each other.* The other vehicle's engine, lights, and accessories should all be off.

Figure 17–7 Keep a pair of jumper cables in your vehicle in case you need to jump-start your battery.

Now you are ready to attach the jumper cables and jump-start your vehicle. Note that there are two separate cables with hand-operated clamps at each end. The "positive" jumper cable is usually marked with a "+" sign and is red. The "negative" jumper cable is usually marked with a "−" sign and is black. To avoid accidental shock, *make sure that your hand remains on the plastic grip of the clips at all times.*

1. Attach one of the clips of the positive cable to the positive terminal of the working battery.
2. Attach the clip at the other end of the positive cable to the positive terminal of the dead battery.
3. Attach one of the clips of the negative cable to the negative terminal of the working battery.
4. "Ground" the other end of the negative cable by attaching the clip at the other end to your vehicle's frame, to the metal engine block, or to an engine bolt. Attach it as far away as possible from the battery and any moving engine parts. *Never attach the other end of the negative cable to the negative terminal of the dead battery.* This can cause damage to the other vehicle's battery or electrical system. Make sure that none of the cables are near fans or belts.

Try starting the vehicle with the dead battery. It should start on the first try. If not, try it again. Once your vehicle has started, let it run for a few minutes, then remove the cables while the engines on both vehicles are still running. Remove the negative cables first, then the positive cables. Be aware that the first cable you disconnect may cause a small spark. *Do not allow the clamps at the ends of the cables to touch each other or to touch car parts.* Close the hoods of both vehicles.

To recharge your battery, you must leave your engine running

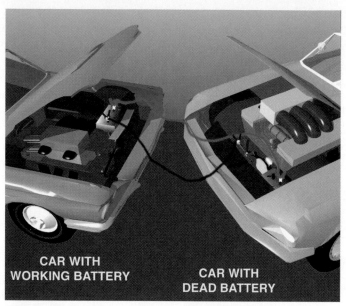

Figure 17–8 Make sure that you know the proper connections before trying to jump-start a dead battery.

for a while. If you can, drive around for at least half an hour. If you turn your engine off too soon, you will have to repeat the jump-start process. If your battery dies again, even when you have allowed plenty of time to recharge it, have a mechanic check the condition of the battery and look for problems in your vehicle's electrical system.

Windshield Wiper Failure

Like every other system on your vehicle, windshield wipers must be well maintained to work. Over time, excessive heat and cold causes wipers to rot or crack, reducing their effectiveness. If the rubber on the blades is very worn or has fallen off, the metal bracket that holds them will have direct contact with your windshield and will scratch the glass when the wipers are turned on. If you do not replace your blades regularly, you will have an unpleasant surprise when you find out that they are useless when you need them most.

Windshield wiper failure can be dangerous if it occurs while you are driving in the rain. Without your wipers to clear away the water beating on your front windshield, your visibility may instantly be reduced to zero. If your windshield wipers fail, first flip the wiper switch several times. If this does not work, maneuver your way to a safe place off the roadway as soon as possible. Call

Figure 17–9 If they are not regularly replaced, your windshield wiper blades will wear out and fail when you most need them.

a tow truck or wait out the rain before starting back on the road again.

Hood Latch Failure

If your hood latch fails, your hood can pop open all the way and completely block your view of the road. Although it may be your first instinct, the worst reaction you can have in this situation is to slam on your brakes. Stay calm. Switch on your emergency flashers and look for an opening between the hood and the dashboard. On many cars, this space is large enough for you to see traffic and get your vehicle safely off the roadway. If you cannot peek through the bottom of the hood, lean out of the side window to see. Ask any passengers to help by directing you and checking whether you have clear passage to the side of the road.

Once you are off the roadway and stopped, check to see whether the latch was not closed properly or if the latch mechanism is actually broken. If the latch seems to be functioning, shut the hood properly. When you begin to drive again, do so slowly and remain in the far-right lane so that you can be ready to move off the roadway quickly if the hood opens up again. If the mechanism is broken, you may be able to secure the hood shut with some wire, cable, or rope. Drive the vehicle to your mechanic as soon as possible to have the latch mechanism replaced or fixed. If you cannot secure the hood, call a tow truck.

17–3 SKIDS

When a vehicle experiences a loss of traction, the result may be a skid. When a skid occurs, all or

Figure 17–10 A skid can cause you to lose directional control of your vehicle.

some of the tires slide over the roadway, causing the driver to lose control over the vehicle's direction. Skids are most likely to happen when you are driving at high speeds in bad weather, on dirt or gravel roads, and on wet or icy pavement. However, they can also occur on dry surfaces and even at low speeds, given certain conditions.

Types of Skids

Although roadway conditions contribute to skids, in most cases they are caused by drivers going too fast for the current road or weather conditions, steering the car incorrectly, changing the car's direction too quickly, braking improperly, or applying too much pressure on the gas pedal at the wrong time.

A **power skid** is caused by accelerating too quickly, especially on a slick road surface. If you have rear-wheel drive, suddenly pressing on the gas pedal too hard can cause the back end of your car to skid to the side. The best way to avoid a power skid is too ease off the accelerator when you feel the tires start to spin. On slick roads or roads with poor traction, remember to always accelerate and decelerate very gradually.

If you apply the brakes while the vehicle is going too fast, one or more of the wheels may lock up and result in a **braking skid.** This type of skid occurs only in vehicles without an antilock-braking system and is more common on slippery or uneven roads. If the front wheels lock, the vehi-

cle will plow straight ahead, but if the rear wheels lock, your car may start to spin sideways. If you sense a braking skid, you should immediately take your foot off the brake pedal until the wheels start turning again.

A **cornering skid** occurs when your tires lose traction on a curve. This type of skid is usually caused by driving too fast. If the road is slippery or you have worn tires, the chances of a cornering skid are higher. If you feel your rear wheels start to skid away from the turn, take your foot off the gas and make steering adjustments to straighten out.

If you downshift from a high gear to a low gear too quickly, you may cause a **downshifting skid.** If you are driving a vehicle with a manual transmission, make a habit of engaging NEUTRAL each time that you downshift instead of moving from one driving gear directly to the next.

Responding to a Skid

If you experience a skid, your natural instinct will be to hit the brakes. However, slamming on your brakes will only cause you to skid more. The appropriate response to a skid depends on the road conditions. If you are skidding on a dry surface at a high speed, you must turn the steering wheel sharply in the appropriate direction to correct the skid. On a slippery road, however, you should only turn the steering wheel slightly to bring your vehicle back under control.

In general, follow these steps to get out of a skid (see Figure 17–12):

guess the vanity plate

DELMAR

SKDROW

Figure 17–11

1. Immediately take your foot off the gas to decrease your speed. *Do not use the brakes.*

2. Steer the car gently in the same direction as the skid. This will get the front end of the car to head in the direction that you are skidding. At higher speeds on a dry surface, you should turn the wheel more sharply. If you overcompensate by steering too sharply or quickly, you may start to skid in the other direction and "fishtail" from side to side.

3. When the vehicle begins to straighten out, turn the steering wheel back the other way, correcting the car's path of travel. You may need to correct your steering several times, turning slightly left and right until you get out of the skid. Once the vehicle is back under your control, gently apply your brakes to reduce speed.

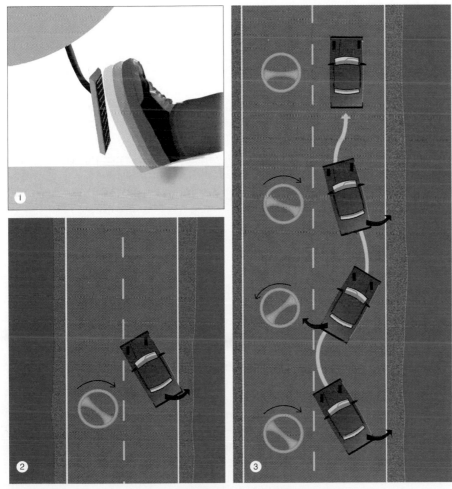

Figure 17–12 Always steer in the direction of a skid.

"Spinning Out"

If your vehicle starts to spin in circles during a skid, corrective steering will not help bring the vehicle back under control. In this situation, you have no choice but to hit the brakes as hard as you can, holding them down until the vehicle ultimately stops. If you have standard brakes, this will cause the brakes to lock up. Although your vehicle will continue to spin, it will travel along a straight line in its original general direction of travel. If you have ABS brakes, holding down the brake pedal will engage the brakes of all four wheels.

17–4 OTHER EMERGENCIES

Many emergencies are not caused by a vehicle malfunction or driver error. Debris on the roadway, deep water, and downed power lines are all potentially hazardous obstacles. Car fires are rare but require an immediate response. Car jacking is increasingly common in today's world. A defensive driver should be prepared to deal with each of these situations.

Roadway Debris

Occasionally you will encounter auto parts, pieces of tire, boxes, rocks, tree branches, furniture, and other unusual objects on the roadway. Avoid these when possible, but do not swerve into another lane unless you are first sure that the path is clear. It is better to hit an object and suffer some damage to your car than to uncontrollably swerve into another lane of traffic and cause a collision. If you do not know whether any vehicles are occupying the lanes to your sides, apply your brakes and slow down for the obstacle, stopping in front of it if necessary. Use your mirrors and look over your shoulder to make sure that the way is clear, and then drive around the obstacle at a slow speed.

Although extremely rare, your windshield may be blocked by a sheet of cardboard, plastic, canvas, or other similar material blowing around the road or that has come off a vehicle ahead of you. Loose materials such as hay, grass, or leaves may also get trapped on your windshield and block your view. If this happens, follow the same steps you would in the case

DRIVING TIPS   *When an Emergency Becomes Another Emergency*

When your vehicle breaks down or you are experiencing another kind of emergency, do not let your emergency get worse by stopping your vehicle where visibility is limited, such as around a curve or just over the crest of a hill. If you are unable to avoid stopping in one of these vulnerable positions, place flares and emergency warning triangles well behind your vehicle to give other drivers sufficient warning. This means that you need to place your first warning device *before* the curve begins or on the *other side* of the crest of the hill. Do not forget to use flares with extreme caution, keeping them away from flammable liquids such as leaking gasoline and oil.

of hood latch failure and steer your vehicle carefully off the roadway to remove the debris.

Deep Water Escape

Cars do not float very well or for a long time in water. If your vehicle gets trapped in deep water, you need to get out fast. Make sure that all other occupants' safety belts are undone. Do not, however, remove your safety belt *before* entering deep water. If you fall from a bridge or other elevated point into deep water, safety belts will help protect you from the impact. Go to the window that is highest out of the water, which may depend on where the heaviest load of your vehicle is. Try to open the window *immediately*.

If the window will not open, try the door. At first, the outside pressure on your door from the water will initially hold it closed. As the water level in your vehicle rises, however, the pressure will equalize and you will find the door easier to open. While you are waiting, breathe normally and make sure that the door is unlocked. If the doors or windows still will not open, attempt to kick out a window to escape.

Downed Power Lines

If you come across downed power lines on the road, avoid driving over them. Wait for a safe opportunity and maneuver around them slowly. If the power lines completely cover the road, especially if it is wet or standing water is nearby, turn around and choose an alternative route.

If power lines or other electrical wires fall onto your vehicle while you are inside, do not panic. Remember that your tires, which are your only points of contact with the ground, are made of rubber and will insulate you from any electrical shock. Stay in your vehicle until emergency personnel arrive. Do not try to exit the vehicle and hopscotch your way around very dangerous electrical wires. Switch on your emergency flashers so that other drivers will see you and know that you are in trouble. If necessary, use body movements to warn others to stay away from the scene and call for help.

Car Fires

The smell or sight of smoke, either coming from under the hood of the engine or in the passenger compartment, is a sign of a vehicle fire. If your vehicle is moving and you suspect that a fire is under the hood or inside the car, immediately pull off the roadway into a safe, open area without people. Turn off the ignition and make sure that all the occupants, especially infants, small children, and those with limited mobility, are out of the vehicle. Move as far away as possible in case of a fuel-tank explosion, and call the fire department.

If the fire is far from the fuel tank and is not widespread or if a passenger is trapped inside the vehicle, you may choose to try to control the fire. Aim to put out the fire at its source or base. *Never use water to fight a car fire.* If the fire is being fed by gasoline or oil,

Figure 17–13 Unless passengers are trapped inside, it is best not to try to put out a car fire by yourself.

the fire will literally float on the water or oil and may spread to other areas. If you do not have a dry-chemical fire extinguisher in your car, try to smother the fire by throwing dirt, sand, large blankets, or clothing onto it.

Never attempt to fight an uncontrollable fire that should be handled by professionals, especially if no one is trapped inside. It is not worth risking serious burns, or worse, when you can just walk away. A car can always be replaced, but you cannot.

Car Jacking

In recent years, there has been an alarming increase in assaults on drivers either to steal their cars or rob them of money or personal belongings. One of the most effective ways to prevent being a victim of a **car jacking** is to plan a route that does not go through dangerous areas. Try not to drive alone if possible, especially if you must go through dangerous or unfamiliar areas. Make sure that your doors are always locked and your windows are shut.

Constantly scan while you are driving, and remain aware of what is happening around you. Because car jackers can most easily approach if you are moving slowly or stopped, always leave enough room in front of you and to the sides to give yourself an escape route whenever you are

AUTO ACCESSORIES *Fire Extinguishers* _____

In case of a fire in your engine or passenger compartment, carry a small, portable A-B-C fire extinguisher in your vehicle. Make sure to secure it tightly to the vehicle with clasps or bolts so that it will stay in one place.

stopped at an intersection or in heavy traffic. At gas stations, turn off your engine and lock your doors when going to pay the attendant. If you have a vehicle breakdown, stay in your car and keep all your windows and doors locked tight. If anyone approaches to help you, write a note, motion with your hands, or "mouth" to them to call the police or a tow truck.

When parking your vehicle, make sure that you park in well-lit areas with other people around. If you are parked in a lot, avoid returning to your vehicle late when the lot is vacant, especially if you are alone. Have your door key ready in your hand when returning to your vehicle. Inspect your car from the outside first to see if anyone is on the other side, underneath, or hiding inside. If you do spot someone in or near your vehicle, move away from the area as fast as you can and call the police.

Some car jackers stage collisions by intentionally rear-ending your vehicle or causing a similar type of "set-up" crash. When you get out of the car to inspect the damage, they use the opportunity to take off with your vehicle. If you feel suspicious about the circumstances of a collision in which you are involved, and you are alone or feel scared, communicate to the other driver (without rolling down your windows) to follow you to the nearest police station. If you do not know where a nearby police station is, drive to a place close by where there are a lot of people. Leaving a crash scene may cause you trouble with law enforcement if your fears prove unjustified, but you have no other choice if you truly believe that your life is at stake.

The most important thing to remember if you are the victim of a car jacking, especially if you are threatened with a weapon, is to not resist. Hand over your keys, money, or whatever the car jacker wants. A car or wallet is not worth your life!

Police Chases

It is possible that at some time you may find yourself in the path of a criminal who is being chased by the police. During

---

REALITY CHECK **Fake Cops** _____

Car jackers have been known to dress up as uniformed police officers or to drive what appear to be regulation patrol cars. Because private security services are now common, it can be difficult to distinguish real patrol cars from those operated by security firms. To be safe, always ask a uniformed officer, or someone who claims to be a plainclothes officer, to show you his or her identification. Because realistic-looking imitation badges, as well as uniforms, can be easily purchased by anyone, a badge or uniform is not sufficient proof of identity.

these high-speed pursuits, the suspect often drives erratically and recklessly. Guidelines vary by jurisdiction, but the police officers may take great driving risks as well. If you find yourself in the path of a police chase, do not do anything sudden or rash. Keep your lane position and speed constant when the suspect vehicle passes you. Cooperate with the pursuing officers by following their instructions.

WHO'S AT FAULT?

1. Driver 1 was traveling north in the right-hand lane of a four-lane highway. Driver 2 was traveling in the same direction in the left lane behind Driver 1. Driver 3 was pulled over on the shoulder and changing her left-front tire. When Driver 1 saw the disabled car, he veered into the left lane to give it more room. Driver 2 reacted by swerving left, hitting the concrete barrier and ricocheting into Driver 1. Driver 1 slammed on the brakes, spun across the road, and flipped over. ***Who's at fault?***

2. Driver 1 was rounding a curve on a four-lane icy road at the speed limit. Just as the tires lost traction, she hit the brakes and skidded from the right lane all the way into oncoming traffic. Driver 2 was traveling in the opposite direction in the left lane, also at the speed limit, and had just gone around the curve when he saw Driver 1 spinning into his path. Both cars collided in the middle of the highway. ***Who's at fault?***

YOUR TURN

17–1 Blowouts and Flat Tires

1. What should you do if your vehicle has a blowout?

2. How do you replace a flat tire?

17–2 Mechanical Failures

3. What should you do if your vehicle breaks down on a freeway?

4. What should you do if your brakes fail?

5. What is the proper way to jump-start a dead battery?

17–3 Skids

6. What are the four types of skids?

7. What is the proper way to respond to a skid?

17–4 Other Emergencies

8. What should you do if you get trapped in deep water?

9. What should you do if your car is on fire?

10. What precautions can you take to avoid being the victim of a car jacking?

SELF-TEST

Multiple Choice

1. Braking skids only occur in vehicles that:
   a. have antilock brakes.
   b. are traveling too slowly.
   c. are traveling on dry pavement.
   d. do not have antilock brakes.

2. Most tire blowouts are caused by:
   a. driving too fast.
   b. excessive tire wear.
   c. too much air pressure.
   d. too little air pressure.

3. Power-steering failures are more likely to occur when the:
   a. engine stalls.
   b. coolant is low.
   c. brakes overheat.
   d. car skids.

4. If you are changing a left front tire, put two blocks in front of and behind the:
   a. left front tire.
   b. right front tire.
   c. left rear tire.
   d. right rear tire.

5. Brake fade occurs when:

    a. brakes overheat.   **c.** the brakes lock up.

    b. the parking brake fails.   **d.** you fail to "pump" the brakes.

Sentence Completion

1. The best way to avoid a power skid is to take your foot off the _____ when you feel the tires lose traction.

2. The "positive" jumper cable is _____ in color.

3. _____ hold the wheels in place on a car.

4. On many vehicles, the emergency _____ is not full sized.

5. Your _____ will insulate you from electrical shock if power lines fall onto your vehicle.

Matching

Match the concepts in Column A with examples of the concepts in Column B.

Column A	Column B
1. __ Skid in circles	**a.** Downshift
2. __ Cause of power skid	**b.** "Spin out"
3. __ Response to brake failure	**c.** Activate emergency flashers
4. __ Cause of cornering skid	**d.** Loss of traction
5. __ Response to headlight failure	**e.** Wheels lock up
6. __ Cause of braking skid	**f.** Accelerate too quickly
7. __ Response to engine stall	**g.** "Fishtail"
8. __ Skid from side to side	**h.** Shift to NEUTRAL

Short Answer

1. Why should you never use water to put out a vehicle fire?

2. What other emergencies might a stalled engine cause?

3. What direction do you steer in a skid?

4. What should you do if you are trapped in deep water and the windows will not open?

5. How do you "ground" jumper cables?

Critical Thinking

1. You are driving in the center lane of a rural interstate highway at night when your front left tire goes flat. You have an emergency spare and flashlight in the trunk. There is a narrow shoulder and no median. You remember seeing a sign for an exit about 10 miles (15 km) ahead. What should you do?

2. You are waiting at a traffic light in an unfamiliar area when a car behind you rear-ends your vehicle. Two young men get out of the car and approach you, one on either side. They seem less interested in the damage than in confronting you. There are no other pedestrians or vehicles nearby. What should you do?

PROJECTS

1. Practice jacking up your car and changing a front and rear tire so that you will be prepared in case you have a flat. Make sure that you have all the necessary equipment handy in your trunk.

2. If you do not already have a set, purchase a pair of jumper cables. Read the instructions carefully. Determine which end of the cables is positive and negative. Look at your battery to see where the voltage is indicated and where the terminals are located. Go to a service station or garage and practice attaching the cables to another vehicle under the supervision of a certified auto mechanic.

Driving Responsibly at Home and Away from Home

Driving Under the Influence

Driving under the influence means driving under the influence of any substance that affects your ability to drive safely, whether that substance is alcohol, an over-the-counter (OTC) medication, a prescription drug, or an illegal drug. Driving under the influence is one of the dumbest things you can do. Even if you avoid a collision driving home from a party or bar, you stand a good chance of ending up in jail if you are pulled over by the police. Being arrested for drunk driving is just the start of a long, costly, and humiliating process that could result in the loss of your driver's license, the confiscation of your vehicle, and time in prison. You will be punished, and rightly so, if you choose to endanger lives by drinking and driving.

Upon completion of this chapter, you should be able to:

18–1 *Alcohol and Other Drugs*

1. Understand what determines a person's BAC.
2. Describe the physiological effects of alcohol.
3. Understand how alcohol affects judgment.
4. Understand what happens when drugs are combined.

18–2 *Preventing Drunk Driving*

5. Describe the role of peer pressure in driving under the influence.
6. Understand how to avoid drunk drivers on the road.

18–3 *DUI and the Law*

7. Understand what it means to be charged with DUI or DWI.
8. Understand what the implied consent law is.
9. Understand what administrative per se laws are.
10. Describe the possible penalties for a DUI conviction.

KEY TERMS

blood alcohol
   concentration (BAC)
intoxication
oxidation
double vision
tunnel vision
inhibitions
synergistic effect
peer pressure

designated driver
driving under the influence
   (DUI)
driving while intoxicated
   (DWI)
implied consent law
breath alcohol test
field sobriety test

divided attention
   impairment
sobriety checkpoints
open container laws
administrative per se laws
ignition interlock device
sentence enhancement
zero tolerance laws

18–1 ALCOHOL AND OTHER DRUGS

Alcohol is the most widely abused drug and the one most often linked to motor-vehicle collisions in North America. About two of every five drivers in the United States and Canada will be involved in an alcohol-related collision at some point in their lives. Traffic crashes are the leading cause of death of people under twenty-five years of age, and more than half of them are alcohol-related. Many of the victims of drunk driving are not under the influence of alcohol themselves. It is estimated that each year 4 million innocent people are injured or have their vehicles damaged in drunk-driving crashes. If drivers followed a simple rule—*do not drink and drive*—the roads would be a safer place for everyone.

Types of Alcohol

Alcohol comes in a variety of forms, including beer, wine, and spirits. The alcoholic content of beers ranges from about 3% for a "light" beer to 12% for some "mi-

Figure 18–1 Alcohol abuse by teenagers is a major contributor to collisions.

crobrews." Wines have between 12% and 14% alcohol content. The strength of "hard liquor," or spirits, which include whiskey, gin, vodka, rum, brandy, and tequila, ranges from 20% to over 60% alcohol.

Blood Alcohol Concentration

The amount of alcohol in your body at a given time can be measured by determining your **blood alcohol concentration (BAC).** BAC is a percentage measurement of the level of alcohol

Type of Alcoholic Beverage	Percentage of Alcohol
Beer	
Domestic	3–5%
Imports	3–11%
Microbrews	4–12%
Wine	12–14%
Wine coolers	3–5%
Hard liquor	
Whiskey, vodka, rum, tequila	40%
Single malt scotch and some bourbon	40–63%
Fruit liqueur, blended liqueur,	
fortified wine (brandy, port)	20%

Figure 18–2 Alcohol content depends on the type of liquor that you are drinking.

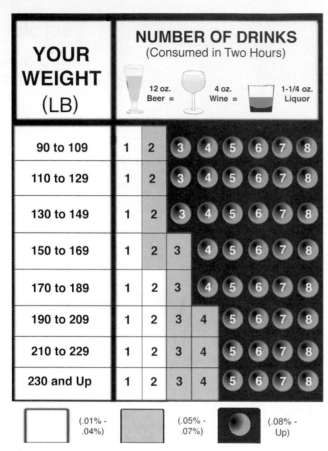

YOUR WEIGHT (LB)	NUMBER OF DRINKS (Consumed in Two Hours)							
90 to 109	1	2	3	4	5	6	7	8
110 to 129	1	2	3	4	5	6	7	8
130 to 149	1	2	3	4	5	6	7	8
150 to 169	1	2	3	4	5	6	7	8
170 to 189	1	2	3	4	5	6	7	8
190 to 209	1	2	3	4	5	6	7	8
210 to 229	1	2	3	4	5	6	7	8
230 and Up	1	2	3	4	5	6	7	8

(.01% - .04%)   (.05% - .07%)   (.08% - Up)

Figure 18–3 Your BAC determines your level of intoxication.

Every 0.02% rise in BAC doubles the risk of highway death.

in your bloodstream. For example, if you have a BAC of 0.10%, it means that your bloodstream contains one-tenth of 1% of alcohol. BAC can be measured using chemical tests that analyze your breath, blood, or urine. Your level of **intoxication** is determined by your BAC reading.

Alcohol can affect driving at a BAC as low as 0.02%, when reactions begin to slow and the first signs of poor judgment appear. At a BAC of 0.05%, driving skills begin to noticeably deteriorate. Rea-

soning is less reliable, muscles are too relaxed, and coordination is decreased. After reaching a BAC of 0.08%, your probability of a crash climbs rapidly. Judgment and inhibition are affected, as well as coordination, balance, vision, hearing, and speech.

If you have a BAC of 0.10% or higher, the chances that you will be involved in a collision dramatically increase. All mental and physical skills are extremely affected. Performing any task with your hands or feet, including walking without stumbling, is difficult. BAC levels above 0.30% can cause a driver to pass out and even go into a coma or die.

What Determines a Person's BAC

Two individuals having the same number of drinks may be affected quite differently by alcohol. A person's BAC depends on a number of variables:

- *The amount of alcohol consumed.* Alcohol is alcohol. Whether you drink a "shot" of scotch whiskey, a glass of wine, or a bottle of beer, your BAC will rise. Switching from beer to wine, or from hard liquor to beer, will not by itself affect your level of intoxication.
- *The amount of time over which the alcohol was consumed.* The faster you drink, the faster your BAC will rise. For example, your BAC rises faster if you have three drinks in 1 hour than if you have three drinks in 3 hours.

- *The amount of food in your stomach.* Some people falsely claim that "you cannot get drunk on a full stomach." In fact, food in your stomach will only slightly slow the absorption of alcohol into your bloodstream.

- *Your body weight.* A small person will be more affected by the same amount of alcohol than a larger person, who has more fluids in his or her body to dilute the alcohol.

- *Whether the alcohol is mixed with a carbonated beverage.* If alcohol is mixed with a carbonated beverage, it will enter your bloodstream faster and your BAC will therefore rise faster.

- *Whether you are a man or a woman.* Men have a higher tolerance to alcohol than women because their body contains a higher percentage of water, which helps dilute the alcohol.

How the Body Gets Rid of Alcohol

The body rids itself of alcohol by means of the liver, which turns alcohol into oxygen and carbon dioxide through a process called **oxidation**. Any alcohol that the liver cannot break down remains in the body. Your BAC increases when your alcohol intake and absorption rates are higher than the rate of the body's ability to oxidize the alcohol. You should never drive until you are ab-

solutely sure that enough time has passed for your liver to oxidize the alcohol. This means considering how many drinks you have had in a given amount of time. For example, after three 1-ounce (30-g) drinks in the space of an hour, a person would need to allow over 4 hours to pass before being rid of the alcohol in his or her system.

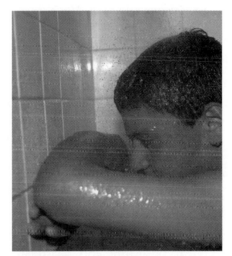

Figure 18–4 Only time, not cold showers or coffee, can sober you up.

Some people may tell you that you can "sober up" by taking a cold shower, drinking coffee, exercising, or other tricks. Even if they make you feel more alert temporarily, they will *not* decrease the amount of alcohol in your blood. Nothing can sober you up but time. It is also a myth that you can "build up a tolerance" to alcohol or that by driving slowly you can reduce the effects of alcohol impairment.

Once you let some time pass after having a few drinks, it is easy to convince yourself that you no longer feel the effects of the alcohol and are sober. This state of mind is a delusion because you are comparing your peak feeling of impairment with the return of only some of your physical and mental abilities as the body eliminates alcohol from the blood. Do not assume that sleep can magically remove all the alcohol from your system. If you have been drinking heavily late at night, the next day you may still have a dangerously high BAC which is in excess of the legal limits for driving.

The Physiological Effects of Alcohol

You must exercise mental and physical skills in tandem to safely control your vehicle. Alcohol slows the nervous system and dulls these skills to a great extent. Your vision, reflexes, and coordination, as well as your breathing and heartbeat, are all affected by alcohol. This makes performing multiple tasks at once, such as braking and steering, extremely difficult.

Vision

Good visual skills are crucial to carrying out the SAFE process. Alcohol relaxes the fine, delicate muscles that move the eyes and allow them to focus. This reduces your ability to scan effectively and blurs your vision. In some people, alcohol causes **double vision**, an uncontrollable rapid vibration of the eye that makes it virtually impossible to see at all.

Alcohol further impairs your awareness of the driving environment by distorting your depth perception, narrowing the scope of your peripheral vision, and impairing your night vision. Colors and shapes can be distorted, and you will be less able to interpret what you see. Your vision need only be mildly impaired by alcohol to have trouble identifying hazards.

You need your depth perception to judge the speed of oncoming vehicles, your stopping distance, and your distance from other vehicles, objects, and people around you. If you have been drinking, you may perceive a red light to be farther away than it actually is and have to slam on your brakes at the last second to avoid entering the intersection. You will not have a sense of where other vehicles are in relation to your own to make decisions about how to position yourself safely on the road. Drivers under the influence of alcohol also tend to stare at one spot and forget to scan constantly with their eyes. The combination of blurred peripheral vision and fixation on a narrow field ahead can result in **tunnel vision**, a 70% reduction in your field of vision.

You need more light to see dimly lit objects. Alcohol impairs your night vision as much as 25% by reducing the time it takes for the pupils of your eyes to respond to changes in light levels. Because your eyes take longer to adjust, you may be blinded more easily by oncoming headlights and continue to have blurred vision long after the oncoming car has passed.

Physical Reflexes and Coordination

The more alcohol that enters the bloodstream, the more the portions of the brain that control physical reflexes and coordination become depressed. This obviously has severe effects on your ability to execute driving maneuvers, which depends on both skills.

Your reaction time gets longer the more you drink. The brain works less efficiently, and instructions to the muscles are delayed. After two or more drinks, a typical driver becomes physically slower and less alert. The effect of alcohol on your muscles is to decrease coordination. Your muscles react more slowly to commands from your brain and function with less control. This can make your driving sloppy. You will tend to oversteer, understeer, brake late, overbrake, or not brake at all. At worst, you could lose control of the car. This impairment of coordination affects beginning drivers most because they have fewer reliable automatic reactions and ingrained skills.

Drinking can have many other unpleasant side effects. Consuming large quantities of alcohol can cause a driver to pass out behind the wheel. It can also produce "hangovers" hours later, after the immediate effects have worn off, that consist of feeling headachy, nauseous, dizzy, and tired.

How Alcohol Affects Judgment

When driving, your mental condition is just as important as your physical condition. The greatest number of alcohol-related collisions actually result from faulty thinking on the drinking driver's part, not the poor execution of physical skills such as steering. When you drink, your ability to reason and make sound judgments is decreased. Your ability to concentrate and to remember things is drastically reduced, and it takes longer to process information. Alcohol-impaired drivers may be more inclined to run a yellow light or attempt to pass without sufficient room. Even worse, they lose the ability to know that they are making poor decisions. This loss of self-judgment leads people who should not be behind the wheel into thinking that they are quite capable of driving.

Often a person drinking alcohol will get a sense of well-being and will experience an increase in confidence. In this state, sometimes described as euphoria, a person may believe he or she can do anything, or is more skilled and entertaining than he or she actually is. **Inhibitions** are the elements of your personality that stop you from behaving without regard to possible consequences. The loss of inhibitions is one of the reasons people drink, but it can also lead an individual to take chances that he or she normally would not take if sober. In addition, alcohol can magnify the feelings of an emotionally upset person.

Other Drugs

Alcohol is a drug, but what people normally think of as "drugs" can affect the mind and body very differently than alcohol. For example, drugs can remain in the body much longer than alcohol. The effects of some drugs can continue well after the drug itself can no longer be detected in the bloodstream. Other drugs can be detected long after the effects wear off. Most of the perceptual and motor abilities that are necessary for driving are affected when the driver is under the influence of either legal or illegal drugs.

OTC drugs such as aspirin and other pain relievers, cold and allergy remedies, and medicines for back pain and arthritis can cause dizziness, drowsiness, slower reaction times, reduced coordination, and other side effects that reduce your ability to drive safely. Prescription drugs, which usually contain either higher dosages of the same active ingredients found in OTC drugs or other, more potent drugs, can have even more powerful effects on your body and ability to drive. When you

auto slang

A "caffeine crash" is a collision caused by falling asleep at the wheel after the stimulant effect of coffee or other caffeinated products has worn off.

Figure 18–5 Legal drugs can impair driving skills just like illegal drugs.

take any OTC or prescription drug, check the label for warnings and ask your doctor or pharmacist if you will be able to drive safely.

Illegal drugs can put you and others at great risk for serious injury or death in a collision if you drive under their influence.

- Depressants produce side effects similar to alcohol, including irritability, confusion, drowsiness, dizziness, and poor eye–hand coordination, that are disruptive to basic driving skills.

- Narcotics can slow a driver's reaction time, impair motor skills, and cause dimness of vision. Stimulants adversely affect people's ability to drive by making the users aggressive and overconfident. Two common stimulants that people use every day are caffeine, which is found in coffee, tea, and cola soft drinks, and nicotine, which is found in cigarettes.

- A person under the influence of hallucinogens can become confused, unable to think clearly or concentrate, and have an altered sense of direction, space, and time.

- It takes only a small amount of the main active chemical in marijuana or hashish to impair your ability to see, steer, brake, and make correct driving decisions. Using these drugs results in drowsiness, fragmented thought patterns, and problems evaluating spatial relationships and the passage of time.

The effects of mixing any one drug with another drug or with alcohol are complex and can lead to serious impairment of driving skills. Alcohol in the bloodstream can trigger what is called a **synergistic effect** that enhances the side effects of certain drugs, including some legal drugs. When this happens, your body focuses on the elimination of alcohol as the primary drug in the body and ignores the other drug that you have taken. Because a "normal" dosage assumes that your body will eliminate part of the drug, the effects of the drug are multiplied.

18–2 PREVENTING DRUNK DRIVING

The best way to combat the problem of driving under the influence is to prevent people impaired by alcohol or other drugs from getting onto the road in the first place. *Everyone* at a place or event where alcohol is consumed is obligated to take an active role in keeping drinkers from driving.

Resisting Peer Pressure

The desire to "fit in with the crowd" can lead people to engage in dangerous and illegal behavior such as drinking and driving. The influence that others of your own age have on you is called **peer pressure.** People do things they would never do on their own to impress friends, classmates, co-workers, or members of the opposite sex. If others decide to act irresponsibly, do not participate. Honestly explain your choice and ask them to respect it.

Setting Limits on Yourself

Ideally, you should not have *any* alcohol in your system when you get behind the wheel. If you do drink, consider your weight and other factors that influence BAC. Most of us have some idea when we have had too much to drink. Our speech slurs, we become overly friendly, our voices get louder, and we get a little dizzy. Recognize the signs that your body is giving you and stop drinking. Trust your friends when they express concern that you have had too much to drink or if they ask for your car keys. If your behavior tells others that you have been drinking, you definitely do not belong on the road.

Do not try to match the drinking of other friends or party-goers.

Figure 18–6 If you decide to drink, set a drinking limit for yourself and stick to it.

Figure 18–7

Figure 18–8 If you are not sober enough to drive, arrange for alternative transportation to get home.

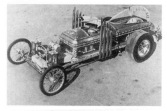

Wild Wheels

Figure 18–9 Who was the "designated driver" of this famous TV car?

"Nurse" a drink with small, occasional sips, skip a round, or have a nonalcoholic beverage. If you are afraid to admit that you do not want to drink, invent a creative excuse for not participating. Anything is better than drinking too much and later causing an injury or death on the road. Keep active and circulate among the crowd. If you are busy talking, dancing, or walking around, you will not be inclined to drink as much.

Alternatives to Drinking and Driving

If you know that you will be drinking, the best safeguard against getting behind the wheel is to have a nondrinking friend be your **designated driver.** In this way, you will not have to make a decision about whether to drive yourself home or not. Before going to a bar or party, choose someone who will volunteer not to drink during the event and who is willing to drive others

DRIVING TIPS *Get a "Safe Ride" Home* _____

Many communities sponsor Safe Ride programs to prevent people impaired by alcohol from trying to drive home on their own. Cab, shuttle, and vanpool companies team up with local bars and restaurants to provide free or inexpensive transportation on weekend nights and holidays. Some programs allow you to call a driver from wherever you are for a ride home during certain hours; others have designated pick-up and drop-off areas. If you drink, consider exploring what Safe Ride programs are available where you live.

REALITY CHECK *Celebrate Your "Independence" at Home*

The risk of facing drunk drivers is considerably higher on national holidays and during vacation periods. Statistically, the worst day of the year to drive in the United States is Independence Day. Other problem days in the United States for which the percentage of traffic fatalities that are alcohol-related is more than 50% are New Year's Day, Super Bowl Sunday, Memorial Day, and Thanksgiving. Canadian holidays such as Victoria Day, Canada Day, and St. Jean Baptiste Day are also characterized by increased alcohol consumption. Nearly 70% of roadway deaths on St. Patrick's Day are due to drunk drivers. Spring Break and the weeks surrounding the high school senior prom and high school graduation are also dangerous times to drive. Do not be a statistic. If you can, stay off the road during these risky periods, especially between 6 PM and 6 AM.

who are drinking. You and your friends can take turns being the designated driver on different occasions. Some establishments will provide free nonalcoholic beverages to designated drivers to encourage responsible drinking.

If you have not appointed a designated driver, call a friend or relative for a ride. Do not worry about your car until the next day, even if you parked in a bad area or if you risk a ticket. If you are concerned about your vehicle being towed, vandalized, or stolen, ask the person who comes to get you to bring a friend who can drive your car home. If you cannot get a friend or relative to help you, call a taxi or local "Safe Ride" program, or use some form of public transportation to get home. If none of these options is available at a party, ask the person giving the party if you can stay for the night.

Refuse to be a passenger in a car if you know or suspect that the driver has been drinking. You have the right to expect a driver to get you to your destination as

safely as possible. If you are sober, offer to drive. If the driver refuses, find another way to get home.

Avoiding Drunk Drivers on the Road

The danger of encountering drunk drivers on the roadway varies depending on when you drive. The alcohol involvement rate in crashes is five times higher at night than during the day. The risk of colliding with a drunk driver is also higher on weekends, holidays, and vacation periods. Always remember, however, that drunk drivers are on the road at all times.

No matter when you drive, be on the alert for the following signs of drivers who may be under the influence:

- Driving at inconsistent speeds, too fast, or too slow
- "Riding" the lane markers on the road or straddling the center line
- Weaving back and forth across the roadway

More than 60% of traffic-related fatalities occur at night.

- Drifting into other lanes or opposing traffic
- Driving at the edge of the roadway
- Driving on or next to the shoulder
- Traveling in a turn lane
- Braking erratically or stopping without cause
- Stopping and starting suddenly
- Responding slowly to traffic signals
- Tailgating
- Driving at night without headlights
- Passing other vehicles recklessly
- Almost hitting another vehicle or object in the road
- Leaving turn signals blinking or signaling turns inconsistently
- Making wide or abrupt turns

Drivers may also exhibit indications of being drunk, including tightly gripping the steering wheel, slouching in the seat, making strange or obscene gestures, driving with windows open in cold weather, sticking their heads outside the vehicle, driving with their face too close to the windshield, and not turning their head to scan ahead.

Once you have identified a driver you suspect to be under the influence of alcohol or other drugs, keep your distance as much as possible. If the other driver is ahead of you, do not pass him or her from behind. If the other driver is be-

hind you, pull off the road or onto a side street when it is safe to do so. If you believe that the driver is jeopardizing the safety of the roadway and is likely to get involved in a collision, note the color, make, and model of the vehicle and its direction of travel, as well as the license number if you can see it without endangering yourself. As soon as possible, report the driver to the police. As in any driving situation, remember that the best way to protect yourself from injury or death in a collision with a drunk driver is to wear your safety belt.

18–3 DUI AND THE LAW

Because of the high numbers of fatalities resulting from drunk driving, many jurisdictions have enacted extremely strict laws against driving under the influence. Drunk driving is considered a serious *criminal* offense, and the public supports the need for harsh penalties. However, most people are not aware of just how much power the law has to stop drunk driving. Consider the following:

- You can be "legally impaired" without ever having a drink if you have taken other substances—including OTC and prescribed drugs—that affect your ability to drive safely.
- Thanks to the sophisticated tools of modern technology, you can be proven legally drunk even if all your physical and mental faculties appear in perfect working order.

• Police can and do arrest people whom they believe are under the influence of alcohol or other drugs before they start their cars, while they are sitting still in a parked or wrecked vehicle with the motor off, and even when they have pulled off the road to "sleep it off."

DUI and DWI

When you are arrested by the police for drunk driving, they will charge you with either **driving under the influence (DUI)** or **driving while intoxicated (DWI)**, depending on how that jurisdiction chooses to call it. In many jurisdictions, you will automatically be charged with DUI or DWI if you are found to have a BAC level of 0.10% or higher while operating a

motor vehicle (and, in some cases, a moped or bicycle). Other jurisdictions, including every province in Canada, set a lower BAC limit of 0.08%. BAC limits are normally much lower for commercial drivers and drivers under the minimum legal drinking age. You can also be charged with DUI if your ability to drive a vehicle is impaired by drugs or a combination of drugs and alcohol.

A DUI conviction can be financially devastating. Besides the fines assessed by a court, you may have to pay for the impoundment of your vehicle, attorney's fees, and a mandatory education program for DUI offenders. DUI convictions can also cause extreme expense and hardship for your family. In certain situations, your parents may even get sued for negligently supervising your behavior.

Figure 18–10 Depending on the jurisdiction, you may be charged with drunk driving if your BAC is 0.08% or 0.10%.

Figure 18–11 Just one DUI conviction can lead to jail time.

HOWARD E. ROLLINS, JR. _____

After a long career on the stage, actor Howard E. Rollins, Jr. (1950–1996), appeared in a number of critically acclaimed TV and feature film roles, including *A Soldier's Story* and *Ragtime,* for which he received an Oscar nomination for Best Supporting Actor in 1981. He was best known for his role as Detective Virgil Tibbs in the long-running series *In the Heat of the Night.* Rollins' promising career began to fall apart in 1988 when he was arrested near Baton Rouge, Louisiana, in March 1988 for DWI, speeding, and cocaine possession. Rollins was arrested three times in 1992 in Newton and Rockdale counties in Georgia, where the series was filmed, for DUI, speeding, and reckless driving. In 1993, he was arrested for speeding and driving with a suspended license. Despite numerous fines and time in jail, including one 5-week sentence for violating his probation, Rollins continued to get into trouble. In November 1993, three days before his license was to be reinstated, he was arrested yet again for DUI and other related traffic charges. This time he was fined $3,000, sentenced to six months in the Rockdale County Jail, and banned from the area for two years. Rollins, whose numerous run-ins with local authorities had brought unwanted publicity to the set of the police drama and caused awkward changes in the script, was released from the show. If you have a serious alcohol or drug problem, get help. Being a repeat DUI offender will ruin you financially and make your recovery that much harder.

DUI convictions may jeopardize your employment if you need to drive to perform your work. If you are convicted of a felony, you will likely be disqualified from most types of employment—a terrible hardship that could linger well after you have paid all your other debts to society.

Just one DUI conviction will tarnish your driving record for the future. Because you will be considered a high-risk driver, your car insurance will be *much* more expensive—if you can even find an insurance company that will accept you! Also, keep in mind that a growing number of insurance companies are excluding drunk-driving injuries from their health plans, meaning that if you sustain an injury in a collision in which you were convicted of DUI, you will have to pick up the tab for your own medical expenses even though you are insured.

Implied Consent

Every jurisdiction has an **implied consent law** for drivers. According to this law, any person driving a vehicle has given his consent to have his or her breath, blood, or urine tested for the presence of alcohol or drugs. This means that whenever or wherever you are driving a vehicle, you have already "agreed" beforehand to allow a chemical test of your BAC if requested by any peace officer who has "reasonable suspicion" to believe that you are operating a vehicle under the influence. A BAC test is usually mandatory if traffic fatalities or serious injuries are involved. In some United States jurisdictions, you have the right to choose which type of alcohol test you want to take. In Canada, a breath test is compulsory.

Tests for Intoxication

Tests for intoxication can be administered by the side of the road or at a police station. The **breath alcohol test** is the simplest and most commonly used. There are numerous types of breath-analyzing devices. The most commonly used is the intoxilizer. To take this test, you breathe into a tube and your BAC is measured using infrared light. Keep in mind that breath alcohol tests can give falsely high readings if alcohol residue is in your mouth, esophagus, or digestive system.

Another means for determining the level of intoxication is a **field sobriety test**, an "on the spot" roadside evaluation administered by law-enforcement officers. In many jurisdictions, DUI convictions can be based on field sobriety tests alone. By conducting a series of tests, an officer can detect physical or mental impairment from alcohol and/or other drugs. One such test, the "horizontal gaze nystagmus" test, requires the driver to follow a pen, small flashlight, or finger with his or her eyes as the officer slowly moves it from side to side. Most people impaired by alcohol and certain drugs have an exaggerated case of nystagmus, a natural condition in which the eyes involuntarily jerk as they change the direction of their gaze. They may also have trouble tracking the object.

Other field tests check for **divided attention impairment**, the inability to perform more than one task at once. These tests are often given to those suspected of DUI because both physical and mental tasks must be performed at the same time while you are driving a vehicle. They measure not only your ability to follow simple instructions but also your balance and cognitive skills. In the "walk-and-turn" test, for example, an officer might ask you to walk heel-to-toe along a straight line while counting off your steps aloud, turn on one foot, and return in the same way in the opposite direction. Other tests may require you to recite the alphabet, count backward, stand on one leg for 30 seconds, or perform various finger dexterity exercises.

Urine and blood tests are normally performed at the police station. A blood test must be administered by medical personnel and sometimes is performed at a hospital or medical clinic, whereas a urine test can be given by law-enforcement officials. A urine test is the least accurate way to measure BAC. The blood test is potentially the most accurate test. In most jurisdictions, you can re-

Figure 18–12 Always cooperate with law enforcement if you are pulled over.

quest a blood or urine test after taking a breath alcohol test.

A person who refuses to take a BAC or drug test can still be

DRIVING TIPS   *If You Are Pulled Over by the Police* _____

If you see a police car's flashing lights in your rearview mirror or hear a siren, slow down until you are sure that the officer is signaling to you. Pull over to the right side of the road or where the officer instructs you to park and stop as soon as it is safe to do so. Stay in your vehicle and follow the instructions that the officer gives you. Sit still, keep your hands on the wheel, and avoid sudden movements. Be prepared to show your driver's license, vehicle registration, and proof of insurance. Answer all questions honestly and courteously. If you need to reach into the glove compartment, under your seat, or into another area of the vehicle not in full view of the officer, tell the officer what you are about to do first. If he or she shines a flashlight in your face or otherwise acts in a way that you find intimidating, keep in mind that many police officers are killed in the line of duty during routine stops. Therefore, they are extremely cautious when approaching a vehicle, especially at night or if the windows are tinted and they cannot see inside.

charged with DUI based on erratic driving or other signs of intoxication observed by the police officer such as a staggering walk, thick-tongued speech, flushed face, red or puffy eyes, and the smell of liquor. Such evaluations may be admissible as evidence with or without test results.

Sobriety Checkpoints

Sobriety checkpoints are special roadside safety checks in which police officers stop drivers to determine whether any are impaired by drugs or alcohol. If DUI is suspected, officers can check for the presence of alcohol by placing a "preliminary breath-testing device" in front of the driver's mouth and nose. If alcohol or other controlled substances are detected and the person shows signs of intoxication, the officers may conduct field sobriety tests or send the driver to a special police van with a portable breath tester. Sobriety checkpoints have proven extremely effective in apprehending impaired drivers and in deterring other drivers from driving under the influence.

Open Container Laws

To discourage drinking and driving, many jurisdictions have **open container laws**, making it illegal to have any kind of open container of alcohol in a motor vehicle unless it is kept out of the immediate control of the occupants, such as in the trunk. Any alcoholic beverage transported in the passenger compartment of the vehicle, including the glove compartment, must normally be full, sealed, and unopened.

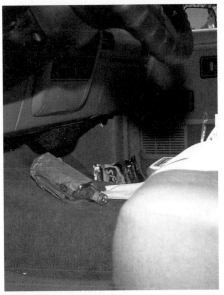

Figure 18–13 Having an open container of alcohol in your vehicle, even if it is empty, is illegal in many jurisdictions.

Administrative Per Se Laws

Most jurisdictions have what are known as **administrative per se laws**, commonly known as admin per se (pronounced "purr say") laws. Depending on local provisions, the arresting officer can suspend your license immediately if you are under the legal drinking age and have any alcohol in your blood, if you have been found to be driving with a BAC over the legal limit, or if you refuse to comply with a BAC or drug test. In some jurisdictions, refusing to take a test can have similar penalties to a DUI conviction even if you are not ultimately convicted of driving under the influence. In some cases, the arresting officer can also impound your vehicle. The length of the suspension varies by jurisdiction for first-time offenders, but on average lasts ninety days. Repeat offenders usually receive increasingly longer suspensions.

Penalties for DUI Convictions

The penalties for a DUI conviction depend on whether it is your first offense or you have had an earlier conviction for the same or a similar offense. In general, a first conviction involves a fine, license suspension or restriction, probation, mandatory attendance at a DUI education course, and possibly jail time. Subsequent convictions will usually result in higher fines and more time behind bars. Additional penalties may include the following:

- Revocation of your license
- Community service
- Installation of an **ignition interlock device** (These devices require that the driver breathe into them before the vehicle's ignition can be activated. The car will not start if the driver tests positive for alcohol.)
- Confiscation of your vehicle

Depending on the jurisdiction, you may also receive a **sentence enhancement** if you were excessively speeding, if your BAC was extremely high, if you refused a chemical test, if a child was riding in the car at the time, if there was property damage, or if certain other conditions existed. If injuries or death resulted from your actions, you can be charged with a

Figure 18–14 Interlock ignition devices are one of the high-tech weapons used in the war against drunk driving.

felony. Felonies are usually punishable by a heavy fine, an automatic jail term, and extended probation. If you are found responsible for causing the death of another person, you can be convicted of manslaughter or vehicular homicide. If you are sued in civil court and found liable for causing injury, death, or property damage, you could face drastic personal and financial consequences.

Some jurisdictions have **zero tolerance laws** for DUI offenses involving certain drug violations or underage drinkers. For example, although the BAC limit may be 0.08% for adult drivers, it may be 0.00% for drivers under the minimum legal drinking age. Zero tolerance means that offenses will be severely and immediately punished. Being charged with an offense in a jurisdiction governed by a zero tolerance law can lead to an immediate and lengthy suspension or revocation of a license, or a delay in a license being granted. In some cases, underage passengers found to be drinking in a vehicle are subject to the same penalties.

YOUR TURN

18–1 *Alcohol*

1. What determines a person's BAC?

2. What are the physiological effects of alcohol?

3. How does alcohol affect judgment?

4. What happens when alcohol and drugs are combined?

18–2 *Preventing Drunk Driving*

5. What is the role of peer pressure in driving under the influence?

6. How can you avoid drunk drivers on the road?

18 3 *DUI and the Law*

7. What does it mean to be charged with DUI or DWI?

8. What is the implied consent law?

9. What are administrative per se laws?

10. What are the possible penalties for a DUI conviction?

SELF-TEST

Multiple Choice

1. A synergistic effect may be triggered by alcohol if you:
   a. mix beer and hard liquor.
   b. eat before drinking.
   c. take drugs.
   d. take a cold shower.

2. If you experience tunnel vision, your field of vision is reduced by:
   a. 30%.
   b. 50%.
   c. 70%.
   d. 100%.

3. A person who refuses to take a BAC test:
   a. is free to continue driving.
   b. is exempt from any administrative per se laws.
   c. can be charged with driving under the influence.
   d. cannot be charged with driving under the influence.

4. According to the implied consent law, any peace officer can request a chemical test of your BAC if he or she:

   a. has reasonable suspicion that you are driving under the influence.

   b. has an intoxilizer.

   c. has your permission.

   d. sees an open container in your vehicle.

5. Penalties for a first-time offender convicted of DUI usually include:

   a. license suspension.

   b. license revocation.

   c. community service.

   d. installation of an interlock ignition device.

Sentence Completion

1. Your level of _____ is determined by your BAC.

2. Alcohol can cause _____, an uncontrollable rapid vibration of the eye.

3. A _____ is an "on the spot" roadside evaluation for intoxication.

4. The influence that others your own age have on you is called _____.

5. The best safeguard against drunk driving is to have a nondrinking friend volunteer to be a _____.

Matching

Match the concepts in Column A with examples of the concepts in Column B.

Column A	Column B
1. __ "Hard liquor"	**a.** Blood test
2. __ OTC drug	**b.** Aspirin
3. __ Breath tester	**c.** Intoxilizer
4. __ Most accurate measure of BAC	**d.** License suspension
5. __ Driver under drinking age	**e.** Urine test
6. __ Field sobriety test	**f.** Horizontal gaze nystagmus test
7. __ Administrative per se law	**g.** Vodka
8. __ Least accurate measure of BAC	**h.** Zero tolerance law

Short Answer

1. Why might an alcohol-impaired driver be willing to take more risks?

2. What are open container laws?

3. What are the possible financial costs of a DUI conviction?

4. When can a police officer request that you take a chemical test for the presence of alcohol or other drugs?

5. What is the purpose of sobriety checkpoints?

Critical Thinking

1. You are at a party, and the friend you came with has had several drinks. He appears to be sober and shows no symptoms of being even slightly impaired. He tells you that he has had a couple of cups of coffee and feels fine. You only live about 5 miles (8 km) away. What should you do?

2. You are driving a group of friends to a concert. One of your buddies has a case of beer he sneaked into the car with him. Even though you are all under the legal drinking age and there is an open container law where you live, he starts to open the beers and pass them around. What should you do?

PROJECTS

1. Visit your local drug store or supermarket and look at common OTC remedies. Read the labels and see which ones have side effects that might impair driving when taken with alcohol. Write down your results and share them with your class.

2. Contact the Department of Motor Vehicles or equivalent agency in your jurisdiction to find out what the DUI/DWI laws are. What is the illegal BAC level? Is it lower for youth? Is a BAC test required if fatalities or serious injuries are involved? What is the administrative per se BAC level? What is the mandatory length of license suspension or revocation for first, second, and third offenses? What are the penalties for refusing to take a chemical test? Is there an open container law?

Licensing and Vehicle Ownership

Many people think that owning a car is *the* ticket to freedom. Vehicle ownership, however, often involves obligations that are anything but liberating. You must be able to purchase, maintain, and insure a vehicle in addition to getting properly licensed to operate it. You must also budget for gasoline, citations, registration, inspections, and other operating costs. Both buying and selling a car take time and effort, as well as money.

CHAPTER OBJECTIVES

Upon completion of this chapter, you should be able to:

19–1 The Licensing Process

1. Understand the purpose of a driver's license.
2. Understand the purpose of a learner's permit.
3. Understand what graduated or provisional licensing is.

19–2 Insuring Your Vehicle

4. Understand what financial responsibility laws are.
5. Understand what a deductible is.
6. Describe the different types of insurance coverage.

19–3 Your Driving Record

7. Understand the purpose of the demerit point system.
8. Describe the difference between license suspension and revocation.

19–4 Buying and Selling a Vehicle

9. Describe the relative advantages of buying a new or used car.
10. Understand what precautions you should take before purchasing a used car.
11. Understand what factors you should consider when getting an auto loan.
12. Understand how you should prepare a vehicle for sale.

KEY TERMS

driver's license

restricted license

learner's permit

graduated (provisional)
  licensing

financial responsibility
  laws

policy

premium

claim

deductible

liability insurance

collision insurance

comprehensive insurance

no-fault insurance

exclusion

driving record

demerit point system

license suspension

license revocation

habitual offender

warranty

depreciation

list price

"sticker price"

rebate

invoice cost

wholesale price

purchase price

title

mileage (kilometer)
  allowance

trade-ins

19–1 THE LICENSING PROCESS

Not everyone can legally drive a car. Before you can get out on the road, you must go through a licensing process in which your knowledge of the rules of the road, your driving skills, and any physical limitations that may impact your driving are tested by the government.

The Driver's License

For teens, a **driver's license** represents one of the first steps to becoming a mature adult. Permission to operate a motor vehicle on public roadways allows more independence than most fifteen- or sixteen-year-old teens have ever had before. With freedom, however, comes responsibility. If you fail to fulfill your obligations to the community with whom you share the road, you can be denied a license or have it taken away. Always remember that *a driver's license is a privilege,* granted by the state or province in which you live, *not a right.*

A driver's license has many functions. It demonstrates proof of legal ability to drive a vehicle in the state or province in which it was issued in addition to all the other jurisdictions in the United States and Canada, and proof of identity for check cashing, credit card purchases, and other financial transactions. In addition, if you move to another jurisdiction or have to obtain a new license, holding a valid driver's license may entitle you to bypass certain requirements such as a driving test or written test.

The Department of Motor Vehicles

Every jurisdiction has a government agency that issues driver's licenses. Usually this agency is known as the Department of Motor Vehicles (DMV), but it may be called various other names, such as the Motor Vehicle Administration (MVA), the Bureau of Motor

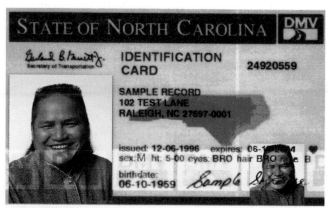

Figure 19–1 Your driver's license has many uses, including proof of identity.

ZSA ZSA GABOR

Zsa Zsa Gabor, actress and former Miss Hungary, has appeared in numerous films and television shows. On June 14, 1989, Gabor was pulled over by a Beverly Hills motorcycle police officer because the registration tags on her Rolls-Royce had expired. As the officer soon discovered, her driver's license had also expired. When he intercepted Gabor as she tried to drive away from the scene, she jumped out of the car and slapped him. Gabor was sentenced to three days in jail, nearly $13,000 dollars in fines, a psychiatric evaluation, and 120 days of community service for neglecting to obtain a valid driver's license and for striking an officer. If you want to drive a motor vehicle, you must comply with all licensing and registration procedures no matter how time-consuming or inconvenient you might find them. If you are "busted" for being negligent, do not attempt to flee or commit other violations that will add to your problems.

Vehicles (BMV), or any of several other names depending on the jurisdiction. You can own only one driver's license. When you move from one jurisdiction to another, you must surrender your old license to obtain a new one from the jurisdiction to which you have relocated.

The DMV may refuse to issue or renew a license to individuals who do not meet its requirements. The following are the most common reasons for refusal:

Figure 19–2 Driver's licenses are issued by an agency of the state or provincial government.

- Not being of legal age
- Having a history of irresponsible driving
- Not being a resident of the jurisdiction
- Having a physical or mental condition that would make it unsafe for you to drive
- Failing to pass the written test or road test
- Lying on your license application
- Failing to have paid an outstanding traffic fine
- Chronically abusing alcohol or drugs as determined by a court

- Failing to understand road signs
- Refusing to surrender a license from another jurisdiction in return for your new one
- Having had your license suspended or revoked in another jurisdiction

Age Restrictions

One of the most important restrictions on who can legally drive is age. The minimum age for holding a license varies by jurisdiction. Generally, you have to be between fifteen and sixteen years of age to begin learning how to drive, although some states and provinces make allowances for teenagers as young as fourteen to drive under special circumstances. The types of licenses you can obtain vary as well and include a learner's permit (also called a school permit or instructional permit), a minor's license, a provisional license, a license with parents' approval, a

license upon proof of independence, or a regular license.

Restricted Licenses

Sometimes the jurisdiction will issue you a **restricted license**, allowing you to drive only under certain conditions. A restricted license may permit you to drive only with corrective eyeglasses or lenses, during daylight hours, outside the limits of any city, or within a certain number of miles/kilometers of your home. You might also be restricted to a motor vehicle with an automatic transmission or with certain disabled-driver adaptations.

The Learner's Permit

A **learner's permit** is a special "pre–driver's license" that allows you to practice driving with a driver education instructor or another adult driver, usually for some months. *You may not drive alone with a learner's permit.* Not all jurisdictions offer learner's per-

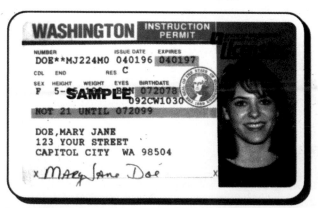

Figure 19–3 A learner's permit enables unlicensed drivers to practice driving with a supervising adult.

mits or require you to have been issued a learner's permit before obtaining a regular license. In most cases, jurisdictions that do not offer a learner's permit require you to wait until you are older to begin learning how to drive.

In jurisdictions that offer learner's permits, you may obtain one by completing an application with your state or provincial DMV. At that time, you will be required to prove your age and provide proof of your parents' consent. You will also have to pay an application fee and take both a vision test and a written test.

Once you have met all the requirements of your jurisdiction, you will be issued a permit. You must keep the permit with you when you drive. You must drive only during certain specified times (such as daylight hours), avoid certain specified locations (such as outside the jurisdiction), and be accompanied at all times by a properly licensed adult. Depending on the jurisdiction, this adult may have to be at least twenty-one years old or even older. Some jurisdictions also require that this adult sit in the right front passenger seat.

Graduated (Provisional) Licensing

Although only a few jurisdictions have a comprehensive **graduated (provisional) licensing** system, many states and provinces in North America have two or three stages of licensing or various components of this type of system. Graduated licensing imposes various restrictions on the young driver, including the following:

- A nighttime prohibition on driving (sometimes called curfew)
- "Zero tolerance" for drinking and driving
- Driving only when supervised by a parent or other licensed adult
- No collisions for the given period
- No traffic violations for the given period
- Mandatory safety belt use by all occupants
- Limits on the number of passengers able to be driven in the vehicle
- Restrictions on the types of roads that can be used
- Limits on speed

The goal of such programs is to ensure that no driver takes to the road without a long training period of low-risk driving under strict supervision. The young driver who has a good record is rewarded with progressively more independence and responsibility. Graduated licensing has proven to be very effective at reducing collision rates involving teenagers and is certain to become more common in the future.

Driver's License Testing

Driver's license testing involves multiple evaluations, including a written test, vision test, and road test. All of these tests are given by the DMV or by DMV-designated

factoid

Nighttime driving restrictions have been shown to reduce crashes by up to 60% during curfew hours.

Figure 19–4 The written test examines your understanding of basic traffic laws in your jurisdiction.

agents at local offices located throughout each jurisdiction.

The written test evaluates your knowledge of the fundamentals of driving, including signs, sig-nals, roadway markings, traffic laws, traffic maneuvers, and safe driving practices. All of the information you need to know should be in the driver's manual of your particular jurisdiction. Generally, if you fail this test you can take it again.

You must also undergo one or more eye exams that will determine whether you will be issued a normal license or a license requiring you to wear corrective glasses or contact lenses while driving. These tests may include a color vision test, a visual acuity test, a distance judgment test, and a field-of-vision test. The DMV usually also inquires about your hearing and any physical disabilities you may have. Failure to answer these questions honestly may result in the subsequent suspension or revocation of your license.

The most nerve-wracking test for most new drivers is the behind-the-wheel driving evaluation, commonly called the road

Figure 19–5 The "vision test" often includes a series of separate exams.

test. This test demonstrates how well you apply your knowledge of the items you have been tested on in the written examination to the real world of driving. Generally, if you fail, you can take the road test over again.

When preparing for the behind-the-wheel test, remember that you will need to demonstrate to the examiner that you have a clear knowledge of the rules of the road and that you have mastered basic driving skills. *Practice as much as you can.* While practicing, ask the driver supervising you to point out areas that need improvement. Spend extra time on difficult maneuvers such as parallel parking or three-point turns. If possible, practice in the vehicle in which you will be taking the test.

Figure 19–6 Where available, "satellite" driver's licensing offices may offer extended hours and shorter waiting times.

When you go to the DMV to take your test, bring all of the correct documents. The examiner often will ask for proof of insurance and registration before beginning the test. You may also need to prove that the vehicle you are using has passed an exhaust emissions test. Check the driver's manual of your jurisdiction to learn exactly what is required. Bring enough money to pay licensing fees, and do not forget other items you may need such as prescription glasses if you wear them.

Make sure that the vehicle you are using for the test is clean and in good working order and that you are comfortable with its special characteristics. Sometimes you will be able to take the test in the car you drove for your driver education class.

When you apply for your license, in some jurisdictions you may be asked whether you wish to be an organ donor. Your consent to have your organs donated for use in transplants or emergency surgery if you die in a collision will be indicated on your license.

After Receiving Your Driver's License

After receiving your license, it is a good idea to spend time driving with your parents or other responsible adult drivers to increase your confidence level and benefit from their tips and comments. Put off advanced driving challenges like long trips, left turns across multiple lanes of traffic, nighttime driving, parallel parking, dense commuter city traffic, and driving in bad weather. If you feel uncomfortable with a maneuver, practice it in a quiet area and do not attempt it on the road

REALITY CHECK *The Seven Driver's License "Nevers"*

1. Never allow anyone else to use your license.
2. Never use a fraudulent, copied, or fake license.
3. Never use a suspended, canceled, or revoked license.
4. Never use someone else's license as if it were your own.
5. Never drive a vehicle without your license.
6. Never let an unlicensed driver operate your vehicle.
7. Never refuse a police officer's request to see your license.

until you feel you can perform the maneuver easily and smoothly.

19–2 INSURING YOUR VEHICLE

Every jurisdiction has **financial responsibility laws**. These regulations make drivers responsible for any damage to property or any personal injury that they may cause while driving. To protect your safety and property, as well as the safety and property of others, you *must* purchase vehicle insurance. Insurance can make it possible to repair or replace your vehicle if it is damaged or stolen. It also covers some of the legal costs and damages that may arise if you injure another person or damage another person's property with your vehicle. Jurisdictions set severe fines and penalties for drivers who fail to purchase any insurance.

The provisions of your insurance are detailed in a **policy**, a written contract between the driver (also called the policyholder or insured) and the insurance company that outlines your

YOUR AUTO INSURANCE POLICY

A - Building - Any Town, State 00000

DECLARATIONS PAGE

ADDL INFO ON NEXT PAGE

PAGE 3
MAIL MCH-M-I

State			Veh Terr	POLICY NUMBER
	06	07		
TX	064	064		00000 00 000 0000 0

POLICY PERIOD: (12:01 A.M. standard time)
EFFECTIVE OCT 19 1995 TO APR 19 1996

Named Insured and Address

OTTO DRIVER
351 POLICY STREET
YOUR CITY, and STATE, USA

OPERATORS

01 OTTO DRIVER
02 KAREN DRIVER

Description of Vehicle(s)

VEH	YEAR	TRADE NAME	MODEL	BODY TYPE	ANNUAL MILEAGE	IDENTIFICATION NUMBER	VEH USE SYM		WORK/SCH Miles One Way
06	94	FORD	RANGER	PU	25000	HLS00000000	9	W	50
07	95	HONDA	PASSPORT	4DR	15000	0S0CG00VIS0000000	9	W	20

The Vehicles(s) described herin is principally garaged at the above address unless otherwise stated.

W/C = Work/School; B = Business; F = Farm; P = Pleasure

VEH 06 YOUR COUNTY, STATE and ZIP CODE
VEH 07 YOUR COUNTY, STATE and ZIP CODE

This policy provides those coverages for which a premium is shown below.

COVERAGES	LIMITS OF LIABILITY ("ACV" MEANS ACTUAL CASH VALUE)	VEH #6 D=DED AMOUNT	VEH #6 6-MONTH PREMIUM $	VEH #7 D=DED AMOUNT	VEH #7 6-MONTH PREMIUM $	VEH D=DED AMOUNT	VEH PREMIUM $	VEH D=DED AMOUNT	VEH PREMIUM $
PART A - LIABILITY									
BODILY INJURY	EA PER $ 100,000								
	EA ACC $ 200,000		107.00		107.00				
PROPERTY DAMAGE	EA ACC $ 50,000		35.00		35.00				
PART B2 - PERSONAL INJURY PROTECTION									
(OPTIONAL)	EA PER $ 5,000		21.00		21.00				
PART C - UM/UIM									
BODILY INJURY	EA PER $ 100,000								
	EA ACC $ 200,000		31.00		31.00				
PROPERTY DAMAGE	EA ACC $ 50,000	D 250	8.00	D 250	8.00				
PART D - DAMAGE TO YOUR AUTO									
OTHER THAN COLL LOSS	ACV LESS	D 50	63.00	D 50	108.00				
COLLISION LOSS	ACV LESS	D 200	89.00	D 50	111.00				
OTHER COVERAGES									
RENTAL REIMBURSEMENT			12.00		12.00				
TOWING AND LABOR $120 MAX			2.00		2.00				
ANTI-LOCK BRAKE DISCOUNT VEH 07									
VEHICLE TOTAL PREMIUM			368.00		435.00				

6 MONTH PREMIUM $988.00

LOSS PAYEE
VEH 07 YOUR BANK OR CREDIT UNION, YOUR CITY and STATE
ENDORSEMENTS: ADDED 04-19-95 - NONE
REMAIN IN EFFECT (REFER TO PREVIOUS POLICY) - 8513(01) 8523(02) 8524(01)
8551(01) 8500(02) 8573(01) 8593(01) 8530(02) *** 551A 25TX(01) 999TX(14)
22994(01) 703TX(03)
INFORMATION FORMS (NOT PART OF POLICY) - AACER 40TX(01) 200(02) 250(01)
41TX(09) 999TX(14)

VEH 06 1B 0 00 BN N VEH 07 1B 0 00 BN N VEH VEH

Figure 19–7 An insurance policy details the conditions of your coverage.

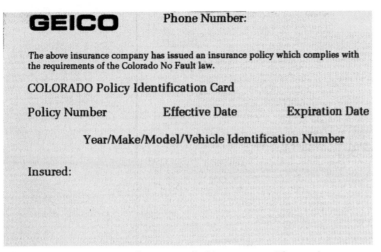

Figure 19–8 You must keep proof of insurance with you in your vehicle at all times while driving.

coverage and how much the insurance company is liable for. Insurance companies will normally issue you an insurance verification card or document that must be carried with you when you are driving at all times. If at any time you are pulled over by law enforcement, you must show proof of insurance.

Types of Vehicle Insurance

The type and minimum amount of coverage you are required to have varies by jurisdiction, and although in most jurisdictions private insurance companies compete for your business, in some Canadian provinces, the government or a semigovernmental agency is the only provider of insurance available. Requirements can be complicated in some states and provinces, and the costs of various plans can vary dramatically.

Insurance is acquired from an insurance company by paying a **premium**, a specified amount of money for a length of time, usually six months or a year. If your vehicle is damaged or stolen or if you are injured in a collision in your vehicle, you may make a **claim** against your insurance company to recover damages covered by the policy. If other persons are injured or their property damaged by your vehicle, they can make demands against your insurance company to recover their damages.

If the insurance company validates your claim or another person's demand, you must first pay a deductible. A **deductible** is the amount of money you must pay before the insurance company begins paying for you on a claim or demand. Deductibles can range up to $1,000 or more. Usually the higher the deductible for a given type of coverage, the lower the premium. Once the deductible is satisfied by your payment, the insurance company will then pay the balance of the damages arising from injuries to persons or damage to property up to the limits specified in the policy.

Liability insurance is mandatory in most jurisdictions. *Bodily injury liability* pays for the medical costs and the pain and suffering associated with injuries and death to other persons, including pedestrians, your passengers, and drivers or passengers in other vehicles when you are at fault in a collision. *Property damage liability* covers the repair or replacement of other people's property, or of public property such as road signs, telephone poles, or traffic lights, damaged by your vehicle. Bodily injury and property damage liability insurance also pay your legal defense fees and court costs in the event you are sued by another driver or pedestrian.

Collision insurance covers the cost of repairing or replacing your vehicle at its current market value when it is damaged after colliding with another vehicle or object. This coverage is also subject to a deductible and coverage limits. Collision insurance typically pays for damage even if you are responsible or if your car is damaged while parked in a lot or on the street. This type of coverage is generally required if you have an auto loan or are leasing your vehicle.

Comprehensive insurance protects you from the loss of your vehicle or accidental damages to your vehicle caused by anything except a collision. Comprehensive coverage pays for repair or for replacement costs up to the current market value of the vehicle, less the amount of deductible stated in the policy.

In many states and provinces, the insurance company of the driver at fault pays for costs arising from injuries and/or property damage to others. In some jurisdictions, however, the law requires that all drivers carry no-fault insurance. **No-fault insurance** provides that the insurer pays the owner and passengers for certain damages or personal injury claims regardless of who is at fault in a collision.

In some jurisdictions, drivers are required to carry uninsured/underinsured motorist coverage, which protects the insured driver and any passengers from damages resulting from a collision caused by a hit-and-run driver or by a driver who either does not have liability insurance or does not have enough to cover all losses for which he or she is held responsible.

Insurance Rates

Insurance companies charge a premium determined by statistics that indicate the likelihood that certain groups of people will be involved in a crash. Factors used to determine the cost can include driving record, age, miles/kilometers driven, gender, marital status, residence, and type of vehicle. However, there are ways to reduce the cost of insurance. Insurance discounts are often available for drivers who have no claims or moving violations for several

bumper sticker sightings

HIT ME . . .
I NEED THE MONEY

Wild Wheels

Figure 19–9 What was the name of this 1921 vehicle, assembled using sheets of solid copper and a rare form of ebony wood for trimwork, that would have cost even the best of drivers a sky-high automobile insurance premium?

years, have more than one vehicle insured by that company, have factory-installed air bags or automatic safety belts, have a car with an antitheft device, have successfully completed a driver education course, carpool, or are students maintaining at least a B average in school.

Exclusions

An **exclusion** in a vehicle insurance policy describes the conditions under which certain types of injury or damage are not covered. For example, a liability policy may exclude coverage if an injury or damage is caused intentionally or if an injury or damage is caused by another person who uses an insured vehicle without the insured owner's permission.

Filing a Claim

An insurance policy usually requires the policyholder to give "prompt notice" of any loss, damage, or collision. If the claim is for theft, property damage over a certain amount, injury, or death in a collision, the policyholder or his or her survivors must notify the police and file a report. If a report is not filed, the insurer will sometimes have a legal basis to either deny the claim or to not pay for the full amount of the claim.

19–3 YOUR DRIVING RECORD

Your **driving record** is a record maintained by the jurisdiction in which you live of all your motor vehicle violations that have oc-

curred in *all* jurisdictions. In some cases, a driver may have his or her license suspended or revoked in the state or province in which he or she currently lives even though the violation occurred in another jurisdiction. Communication exists between law-enforcement officials, the courts, and the DMVs across most jurisdictions, so each is aware of a driver's record at any particular moment. Police vehicles are often equipped with computers that can retrieve your driving record at the stroke of a key.

Figure 19–10 A police officer who pulls you over has complete access to your driving record.

The Demerit Point System

Most jurisdictions have a **demerit point system** in place to protect drivers against the dangers of sharing the roadways with those who cause collisions. Most crashes are caused by someone who breaks the law. The DMV is required to maintain a record of every individual who operates a motor vehicle. Under the demerit point system, the DMV puts points on a driver's record for each conviction of a moving-vehicle violation. These points remain a part of a driver's record for a specified period depending on the seriousness of the offense. The more severe the offense, the more points charged to your record. For example, the number of demerit points for speeding often depends on how many miles/kilometers per hour over the posted speed limit you were found to be driving.

In some jurisdictions, a specific number of points can be removed for each year of point-free driving and/or attendance at a court-approved or DMV-approved traffic violator's educational program. Jurisdictions with probationary driving systems usually allow drivers who have just received their licenses to accumulate far fewer demerit points than an experienced driver before their licenses are suspended. The hope is that by doing so new drivers will change their driving behavior before bad habits become established. Such drivers are considered on probation until a certain time has passed during which they do not accumulate any more demerit points. After that time, they then become subject to the general demerit point system.

License Suspension and Revocation

The state or province can suspend any driver's license for a speci-fied period. A **license suspension** leads to a temporary loss of the privilege to drive. A **license revocation** of a driver's license is more serious. In this case, the DMV cancels the legal permit given by the jurisdiction to drive a vehicle, denying the driver the privilege to drive. After the revocation period expires, the driver must apply for a new license. He or she may be investigated and required to file a document proving financial responsibility.

In general, jurisdictions specify how many offenses of various types the driver can accumulate in any given period before suspension or revocation occurs. Most jurisdictions entitle a driver to a hearing with the DMV before a license is suspended or revoked. A court often has the power to suspend the driver's license if he or she is convicted of certain violations, such as excessive speeding or reckless driving. A license can also be suspended if the driver fails to make a written report after a collision resulting in injury or in damage greater than a particular dollar amount.

Some jurisdictions allow drivers who have had their license suspended to take a defensive driving course to reinstate their suspended license. In Canada, such courses are often mandatory to reinstate one's license. Such courses should be seen as opportunities to make you a safer driver and one who understands the importance of observing the law.

Depending on the jurisdiction, some offenses may result in the mandatory revocation of a driver's license, including driving under the influence of alcohol or other drugs, being a hit-and-run driver in a collision that involves the death or injury of another person, and attempting to flee from a police officer after being told to stop.

Revocation of the license can be made permanent for offenders whose records demonstrate repeated serious traffic violations. Such a driver is called a **habitual offender**. If you are convicted of driving after your license has been suspended or revoked, some jurisdictions will send you to jail, charge you a fine, add more time to the period of suspension or revocation, and even impound your car.

Penalties for Traffic Convictions

The severity of the penalty for breaking traffic laws depends on the offense and the number of times you have been convicted. In most cases, you will receive a fine for parking offenses or for minor moving violations. You can usually pay the fine by mail and avoid going to court. Failure to pay the fine promptly results in further penalties that may significantly increase the original cost of the ticket. If you still fail to pay the fine, you could go to jail. For more serious offenses such as driving under the influence, you will have to go to court and may be subjected to fines, a jail sentence, probation, mandatory education, and suspension or revocation of your license.

19–4 BUYING AND SELLING A VEHICLE

Before you decide to buy a vehicle, weigh your options and think hard about your transportation requirements for the near future. Many types of vehicles are available, some of which are obviously not suitable for you whereas others could meet your needs very well.

Figure 19–11 The costs of owning a vehicle can add up quickly.

New or Used?

If you are ready to buy a car, you must first decide whether to purchase a new or used vehicle. A new vehicle will initially cost you more than a used car, but one of the biggest advantages of buying a new car is that you get a long-term warranty. A **warranty** is a written guarantee that the car

TIRES

The tires that come as original equipment on your new car are warranted separately by the tire manufacturers (including the compact spare tire). A separate warranty statement is included.

If a tire is damaged during the warranty coverage period because of a vehicle defect in factory-supplied materials or workmanship, the tire will be replaced by the ACME Motor Company.

ROADSIDE SERVICE

Your vehicle is eligible for the ACME Roadside Assistance Program. This Program is separate from the New Vehicle Limited Warranty, but the program period is concurrent with the Full Warranty period. Under this program ACME will cover towing, spare tire mounting, fuel delivery, jump-starts, and lockout problems. For more information call 1-800-555-ACME.

Towing necessitated by warrantable failure beyond the Full Warranty is covered under the applicable warranty.

For daily rental units that must be towed because a covered part has failed during the Full Warranty period. ACME will cover towing to the nearest dealership.

WARRANTY SUMMARY

New Vehicle Limited Warranty		Emissions Warranty	
Full Warranty	4/50,000	Emissions Performance Warranty	3/50,000
Safety Restraint System	4/50,000	Emissions Defect Warranty	4/50,000
Rust Perforation	5/Unlimited	Short Term	4/50,000
		Long Term	7/70,000
Years/Miles In Service			**Years/Miles In Service**

Figure 19–12 The warranty offered by a manufacturer or car dealer can be a major factor in your final choice of a vehicle.

manufacturer or dealer will repair or replace any defective parts or systems within a set amount of time or for a certain number of miles/kilometers driven. With such protection, you should spend less on maintenance in the first years of driving the vehicle. A new car is also more likely to hold up better under heavy use or long-distance traveling, and replacement parts are generally cheaper and easier to find.

On the other hand, a used car often has a lower purchase price. A good used car often represents a better dollar value because a previous owner has absorbed most of the cost of depreciation. **Depreciation** is the decline in a vehicle's resale value over time. It varies according to vehicle condition, age, mileage, and optional equipment. In most cases, used cars are also cheaper to insure.

Researching the Market

Once you have settled on a new or used car, you must decide what kind of car is right for you. Do you want something sporty, practical, or economical? How will

factoid

A new car can depreciate as much as 50% in value during the first year that you own it.

you be using the vehicle? How many passengers will you carry? Will you be towing a trailer or carrying heavy loads? How many miles/kilometers will you travel on average? Will you be going on long or short trips?

Once you settle on the type of vehicle that fits your needs, budget, and image, take the time to gather data on the various makes and models available. Bookstores, libraries, credit unions, banks, the Internet, insurance companies, mechanics, car dealers, and manufac-

Figure 19–14 Sports cars may be fun to drive, but they are generally less safe and more expensive both to maintain and insure.

turers are all good sources of up-to-date information. Narrow your choices by comparing prices, safety records, maintenance and insurance costs, fuel economy, available options, warranties, customer satisfaction, repair records, theft history, and other important factors.

Buying a New Car

If you are buying a new car, visit several auto dealerships to get a first-hand look at the vehicles you are interested in. Find out what is available, and determine what you are actually going to have to pay to drive one off the lot. Keep in mind that some car salespeople are paid by commission and tend to be aggressive in going after business. Ask to speak with the sales manager or fleet manager. Be

auto slang

"Corporate twins" are vehicles with the same body style and often the same engine sold under different names and sometimes at different prices.

Figure 19–13 Do as much research as you can before selecting a vehicle.

guess the vanity plate

Figure 19–15

REALITY CHECK *Do Not Rustproof Your Car* _____

Rustproofing, a common dealer-added extra, is generally not recommended by the manufacturer because most cars are adequately protected against corrosion. In fact, rustproofing may actually damage your paint and void the manufacturer's warranty.

DRIVING MYTHS *New Cars Do Not Have Zero Miles* _____

Just because you buy a new car does not mean that the odometer will read zero. New cars accumulate miles/kilometers during shipping from the manufacturer, parking at port facilities, and driving between dealerships.

auto slang

Rebates offered to car dealers by manufacturers for selling certain vehicles are called "holdbacks."

polite but firm when negotiating prices and options.

When shopping for a new car, compare dealer prices carefully. A new car's **list price**, or "retail price," is the manufacturer's suggested retail price (abbreviated MSRP) for the car and all factory-installed options. The **"sticker price"** is the list price plus destination charges and additional options and services provided by the dealer. The "destination charge" is the cost of shipping the vehicle from the manufacturer or, for foreign cars, from the point of entry, to the dealership. This charge may vary by location. Dealers often add a "preparation charge" to prepare a vehicle for sale by tun-

ing up the engine, checking the emissions, and performing other services. Because many manufacturers already pay dealers to "prep" a car, be wary of high preparation charges.

The actual selling price of a car is also affected by manufacturer or dealer incentives and the time of the year when you buy. Some manufacturers offer a **rebate**, a special payment to the customer, to boost sales on certain models. Dealers may also offer discounts at the end of the year to get rid of their inventory and make room for newer models.

When discussing prices with a salesperson, it is a good idea to know the **invoice cost**, the

Figure 19–16 Most car dealers will negotiate for a lower price.

amount the dealer paid for the car. You can get this information from various auto magazines, consumer groups, and pricing guides, but you may also want to consult an auto pricing service, which for a small fee can prepare an accurate report within a couple of days on a specific model's invoice cost.

Make sure that you also consider the warranty offered by various manufacturers and dealers, which are often negotiable. Car dealers are required to post a warranty statement in one of the windows of the vehicle (usually on the driver's side of the car) outlining which parts are guaranteed and for how long. Most new cars come with a standard warranty on major parts that lasts from three years or 36,000 miles (60,000 km) to five years or 60,000 miles (100,000 km). Dealers may also offer an "extended service contract" on all or part of the standard warranty.

Buying a Used Car

If you cannot afford a new vehicle, consider buying a used one from either a car dealer or a private seller. Selecting a used car is more time consuming and complicated than buying a new one because you have to do more detective work. Used cars can be great deals, but they can also be an endless source of regret if you find out too late that the vehicle you purchased was an auto-repair nightmare.

New-car dealers sell their best quality trade-ins and returned lease cars that have been reconditioned. These vehicles are generally in good condition, have low mileage, and include a limited warranty covered by the dealer's service department. On the downside, they are among the most expensive on the market. Most sell their vehicles "as is," and the risk of acquiring a car with serious mechanical problems or defects is greater. It is always a good idea to check the used-car dealership out with the Better Business Bureau before you make a purchase there.

Figure 19–17 Searching classified ads for used cars or special deals may cost you less, but it also carries risks.

You stand the best chance of finding a bargain if you purchase a used car from a private seller rather than a dealer, but you also take a bigger risk. Unless the seller can demonstrate that the vehicle has been properly maintained and serviced over the years, you will know nothing about its history. It

factoid

Car dealers typically make a bigger profit on a used car than on a new one.

auto slang

Car dealers often call an older car "preowned" instead of used.

Figure 19–18 Valuation guides are invaluable resources if you are buying a used car.

takes time to set up an interview with a person, and you are likely to come across many vehicles that do not live up to the glowing description you read in the newspaper classified advertisement. You must also handle all the registration paperwork by yourself.

The **wholesale price** is what a dealer is willing to pay for a used car. Wholesale prices for used cars vary depending on the model, year, mileage, and their general condition. Before buying a used car, you should consult several used-vehicle valuation guides on the market. These guides list the average used-car prices based on actual sales by dealers and wholesale auctions, average loan prices, and mileage tables used to adjust prices.

Once you have settled on a used car, thoroughly examine it. You can be sure that the previous owner or dealer will do all that he or she can to make the vehicle appear problem free. When inspecting a used car, go in the daytime when you can see well and wear old clothes that you do not mind getting dirt, grease, or rust on. It is also a good idea to take along a friend for a second opinion and to help you test drive it.

The only way to get the feel of a used car, just like a new car, is to test drive it. If possible, test drive the car on both highways and city

Figure 19–19 Thoroughly inspect a used car yourself before spending the money to have a mechanic look at it.

DRIVING TIPS *Avoiding "Lemons"* _____

Most jurisdictions have adopted what are commonly called lemon laws to protect consumers who buy or lease a vehicle. Lemon laws require manufacturers, not dealers, to either repair certain defects that impair a car's use, value, or safety or to refund the consumer's money. Laws vary by jurisdiction, but a "lemon" is usually defined as any vehicle that has been in the shop at least four times for the same problem or is out of service for thirty days or more in its first year.

streets, on hills, and on different road surfaces. Watch for any warning lights on the instrument panel. Test the brakes to see how hard you need to push the pedals to come to a complete stop or whether the car pulls to one side or the other. When you accelerate, the speed should gradually and smoothly increase.

Before you purchase a used car, always have a mechanic give it a thorough diagnostic check. For a moderate fee, a mechanic will provide you with a report listing the parts or systems that meet acceptable operating standards and those that fail inspection and need repairs. If you or your mechanic determine that repairs need to be made, either walk away from the deal or negotiate these costs into the final sale price.

Financing Your Vehicle

The **purchase price** of a vehicle is the amount of money that the dealer or owner is willing to accept. The least expensive way to buy a car is with cash because you will not have to add any interest cost to the final purchase price. If like most people you cannot pay cash for a car, your other options are to finance the purchase with a loan or to lease the vehicle.

Auto Loans

The total cost of a car loan depends on the interest rate, the total amount of money borrowed, and the length of time required for repayment. Car loans generally run from two to five years in duration. Shop around for the best interest rate (often called the annual percentage rate, or APR) available. Most car loans are limited to 90% of the purchase price,

factoid

The Ford Model T, the first mass-produced car, sold for less than $300.

Figure 19–20 A car advertised as having "low monthly payments" usually requires a large down payment.

but 100% financing is sometimes also available. Keep in mind, however, that the larger the down payment you can make, the less you will have to pay for the car in the long run.

When you finance a car, you must put up what is known as collateral in case the loan is unpaid. In most cases, the collateral is the vehicle itself. The lender will retain the certificate of title to the vehicle until the loan is fully paid. If you are a full-time student or lack a sufficient credit rating, the lender will require an adult to co-sign the loan. The adult who co-signs is responsible for the repayment of the loan.

Title and Registration

The **title** is a document that shows proof of ownership. When you purchase a vehicle, you need to apply for a title and pay the required fees that are set by each ju-

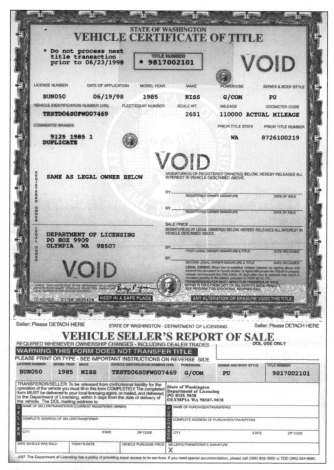

Figure 19–21 The title is your certificate of vehicle ownership.

risdiction. The title lists the owner, make, model, and vehicle identification number (VIN). The jurisdiction retains a copy and gives you a copy that must be carried in the vehicle at all times.

If you buy a car from a private owner, make sure that the seller owns the car and the title is in his or her name. If the lender still has the title, the seller and lender will have to transfer the title and any outstanding loan payments to the buyer. Refuse to buy the car if there are any problems transferring the title.

Motor vehicles must be registered each year with the DMV in your jurisdiction. As soon as you purchase a vehicle, you must also register your vehicle with the DMV. Annual fees for registration vary from one jurisdiction to another. In those with mandatory liability insurance, the name of the driver's insurance company must be provided at this time. After registering, you will receive license plates, a registration document, and license-plate tags or a windshield decal for the given year. Your registration may be canceled if your vehicle is determined to be

unsafe, lacks required equipment, is not in a proper state of repair, or is used for an unlawful purpose. In some jurisdictions, your registration can be canceled if you permit use of your vehicle by a person not entitled to use it.

Leasing a Car

Many people prefer to finance their car by leasing rather than purchasing it. *Leasing* is just a fancy word for renting. Instead of buying and owning the vehicle, you will be renting it. The main advantage of leasing is that monthly payments are up to 30% lower than payments on a car loan. Another advantage is that you often do not have to make a down payment. Leasing lets you avoid the risk of depreciation because you pay for the life of the car only while using it. Unlike buying a car, you are not stuck with it if it does not hold its resale value well.

Leases usually run from two to five years, with three years being the average term. The longer the term of the lease, the smaller your monthly payments will be but the higher the total cost of the

REALITY CHECK *Keep Your Tags Visible*

Among the most important required equipment on your vehicle is one (rear only) or two (front and rear) license plates. License plates, or "tags," normally must be illuminated at night with a white light, making them visible from 50 feet (15 m) away. This requirement helps law-enforcement officers and others identify vehicles in case of an emergency. In many jurisdictions, it is illegal to use products such as tinting, plastic coating, or any type of covering on license plates because they may hinder police officers' ability to read the number.

vehicle once interest is added. You can lease from either a new-car dealer or an independent leasing company. The fees and penalties of leases vary widely, so always remember to compare the total cost of the lease, not just the monthly payments.

One of the largest potential costs of leasing is exceeding your annual **mileage** or **kilometer allowance.** Most leases limit you to 12,000 to 15,000 miles (20,000 to 25,000 km) per year. If you drive more than the amount specified in your contract, you will have to pay a penalty for each mile/kilometer over that limit. Over the course of the lease, this can add up to thousands of dollars if you drive much more than you anticipated.

Selling Your Vehicle

Buying a car is an investment. One of the reasons it is important to take care of your vehicle is that you will want it to be worth something when it comes time to sell it or trade it in for a new car. There are many reasons why you might want to get rid of an older car. Costly repair bills or low gas mileage might make your vehicle too expensive to operate for your current needs. Replacement parts may be harder to find. It may need considerable body work or mechanical repairs you are not willing to pay for. Maybe you just want a change or can afford to upgrade. Whatever the reason, selling a car—just like buying a car—requires research, paperwork, and a little "elbow grease."

Thoroughly clean the car inside and out. If any major work needs to be done, determine whether you can get your money back when you sell the car or if it would be better to sell the car as is and deduct those costs from the final price. Organize your records on gas mileage and routine maintenance so that you can show them to potential buyers. This openness with buyers will go a long way to convincing them of the value of your car.

Check some of the used-car valuation guides for an estimate of what your car is worth based on its condition and mileage. Visit several dealers and compare what they would pay you for the car. Go through the classified ads to see what cars similar to yours are selling for. The price you can expect to get normally will be somewhere between the price charged by other private party sellers and the dealers' prices. Once you have a good idea of what you can expect, set your asking price and the minimum amount that you would be willing to accept as a compromise.

Advertise in the weekend editions of local newspapers when people will be more likely to shop for a car. Specialized auto classified ad publications, which usually pair photos with descriptions, are often the best way to show off your car. When advertising your vehicle, include the make, year, and model of the car. Describe selling points that will draw buyers such as "low mileage," "full maintenance history," or "original owner." If you advertise a firm price, you run the risk of scaring

71 VW KARMANN GHIA CONV.   **$6800**
New black top, glass rear window, new silver paint, rebuilt
engine, very clean, runs excellent.

Figure 19–22 When advertising your vehicle, include as many selling points as you can.

some people away. To increase your bargaining leverage, list a higher price than you are willing to settle for but say that it is negotiable. Providing a price range will spare you telephone calls from people who cannot afford the car.

Most people will want to test drive the car or have it inspected by a mechanic. Go with the potential buyer on the test drive not only to protect yourself against

---

DMV VEHICLE BILL OF SALE

DEPARTMENT OF TRANSPORTATION
DRIVER AND MOTOR VEHICLE SERVICES
1905 LANA AVE., NE SALEM OR 97314

VEHICLE DESCRIPTION

PLATE NUMBER	YEAR	MAKE

VEHICLE IDENTIFICATION NUMBER

I transfer all rights, title and interest in the above described vehicle to:

NAME OF BUYER (PRINT LAST, FIRST, MIDDLE)	DATE OF PURCHASE

BUYER'S ADDRESS

PRINTED NAME OF SELLER (BUSINESS NAME IF SELLER IS A BUSINESS)

SIGNATURE OF SELLER (AUTHORIZED REPRESENTATIVE OF BUSINESS)	DATE OF RELEASE
X	

PRINTED NAME OF SELLER

SIGNATURE OF SELLER	DATE OF RELEASE
X	

● BUYER ●

If you do not apply for a title within 30 days from the date of purchase, you may be subject to a late title transfer fee.

735 - 501 (7-94)

Figure 19–23 Inform the DMV as soon as you sell your vehicle.

theft but to answer any questions he or she may have while driving. Make sure that the person has a license, or you may be fined or have your own license suspended if you are pulled over by law enforcement.

Once you have a buyer, *it is recommended that payment be made by a cashier's or certified check made payable to the seller.* If the buyer insists on paying with a personal check, go with the buyer to his or her bank to cash the check. When you sell your vehicle, you must transfer the title to the new owner. *Never transfer the title until you are paid in full.* Make sure that all taxes are paid to the responsible government agency.

To protect yourself against being held liable for the new owner's traffic violations or collisions, immediately notify your jurisdiction's DMV and your insurance company. Whether or not you are required to submit specific forms on the terms of the sale, you should always give the new owner a receipt with his or her name and the purchase price, and keep a copy for yourself.

If you do not want to sell your car yourself you can trade it in for a new or used car at most dealers. In general, **trade-ins** are a bad value. You pay a heavy price for the convenience of having the person who sells you a new car to take your old one off your hands. If you are determined not to sell the car yourself, take the time to make the vehicle as presentable as possible and get offers from several dealers. Find out what the estimated trade-in value of your vehicle is through a reputable pricing guide. Most importantly, never negotiate a trade-in with a dealer until after you have settled on a purchase price for the new car. Otherwise, you have no idea whether you are getting a good value for your old car.

Y O U R   T U R N

19–1 *The Licensing Process*

1. What is the purpose of a driver's license?

2. What is the purpose of a learner's permit?

3. What is graduated or provisional licensing?

19–2 *Insuring Your Vehicle*

4. What are financial responsibility laws?

5. What is a deductible?

6. What are the different types of insurance coverage?

19–3 *Your Driving Record*

7. What is the purpose of the demerit point system?

8. What is the difference between license suspension and revocation?

19–4 *Buying and Selling a Vehicle*

9. What are the relative advantages of buying a new or used car?

10. What precautions should you take before purchasing a used car?

11. What factors should you consider when getting an auto loan?

12. How should you prepare a vehicle for sale?

SELF-TEST

Multiple Choice

1. Which of the following is *not* used by automobile insurance companies to determine rates?
   a. your driving record
   b. your marital status
   c. your driver license number
   d. your age

2. Which of the following is *not* a valid use of your driver's license?
   a. proof of your ability to operate a motor vehicle
   b. proof of your age
   c. proof of your residency
   d. proof that you have liability insurance

3. Loaning your driver's license to another person:
   a. may result in your license being suspended or revoked.
   b. will allow them to drive legally if they are already properly licensed.
   c. makes you a habitual offender.
   d. may affect your insurance rates.

4. A title is a document that shows:
   a. insurance coverage.
   b. driver's license restrictions.
   c. the interest rate of a car loan.
   d. proof of ownership.

5. Most standard warranties run from:
   a. one to two years.
   b. one to three years.
   c. three to five years.
   d. five to seven years.

Sentence Completion

1. The _____ is a special "pre–driver's license" that allows you to practice driving with an adult driver.

2. _____ is the decline in a vehicle's resale value over time.

3. A driver who continues to accumulate motor-vehicle violations and convictions may be considered a _____.

4. _____ are regulations that make drivers responsible for any damage to property or any personal injury that they may cause while driving.

5. Your _____ contains a history of all motor-vehicle violations you have committed.

Matching

Match the concepts in Column A with examples of the concepts in Column B.

Column A

1. __ Graduated licensing restriction
2. __ Standard warranty
3. __ Premium
4. __ Exclusion
5. __ Policy
6. __ Driver's license requirement
7. __ List price
8. __ Comprehensive insurance

Column B

a. MSRP
b. Protection from theft
c. Cost of a policy
d. Contract between policyholder and insurer
e. 36,000 miles (60,000 km)
f. Road test
g. Intentional damage
h. Curfew

Short Answer

1. What is the purpose of a road test?
2. What affects a car's depreciation?
3. How can you price a used car?
4. What is graduated licensing?
5. What is a diagnostic check?

Critical Thinking

1. You have accumulated several parking tickets while at school, but you are graduating later in the year and plan to return to your home in another jurisdiction. A friend tells you that the authorities in your home jurisdiction will never find out about the tickets when you reregister your car and apply for a new license. What should you do?

2. After visiting a few used car dealers and responding to several classified ads, you find two used vehicles of the same make and model that meet your requirements. One of the cars is for sale by a private seller. It needs some fixing up but it also has relatively low mileage. The other vehicle is for sale at a used-car dealer. It has 20,000 more miles (32,000 km) than the other car but comes with a limited 30-day warranty. The cost of the car at the dealer is $2,000 more than the one offered by the private seller. What should you do?

PROJECTS

1. *Call three different insurance companies for estimates of how much it would cost to insure your vehicle to meet the minimum liability requirements of your jurisdiction. Share the results with your class. Discuss how rates are affected by where you live, how far you drive, the market value of your vehicle, and other factors.*

2. *Go to the library and look up your vehicle in consumer magazines, valuation guides, or on the Internet to find out how it ranks in terms of safety, cost to insure, customer satisfaction, warranty coverage, and other indicators of value. Determine the same information for two other models from the same year that are similar in size and design but that are made by different manufacturers. Is your vehicle a good buy?*

20

Vehicle Maintenance, Equipment, and Security

A vehicle is much like your own body. Take good care of it, and it will serve you well for a long time to come. Maintenance is the key to keeping your vehicle running smoothly and reliably. What also contributes to greater road safety are special kinds of equipment and accessories. If you are a disabled driver, your vehicle can be outfitted with special equipment to adapt it for your use. You will also have to decide whether you want to obtain devices to protect your vehicle against the possibility of theft.

Upon completion of this chapter, you should be able to:

20–1 Preventive Maintenance

1. Understand what preventive maintenance is.
2. Describe how to check tires for inflation and wear.
3. Identify the fluids you should check as part of routine maintenance.
4. Understand the proper way to wash and wax a vehicle.

20–2 Selecting a Mechanic

5. Understand how to select a mechanic.
6. Understand how to avoid poor workmanship.

20–3 Vehicle Equipment and Accessories

7. Identify three types of safety-oriented equipment available.
8. Identify several of the devices used to adapt a regular vehicle for a disabled driver.

20–4 Vehicle Security

9. Describe three basic types of antitheft devices available.
10. Understand how a vehicle tracking device works.

KEY TERMS

preventive maintenance	hand controls	kill switches
fog lights	antitheft devices	tracking device
adaptive equipment	car alarms	

20-1 PREVENTIVE MAINTENANCE

The routine care you give your vehicle to avoid more serious repairs is called **preventive maintenance.** Preventive maintenance includes day-to-day care, such as changing the oil, filling the tires with air, and checking levels of key fluids, as well as routine servicing. Because vehicle requirements may vary greatly, you should always check your vehicle's owner's manual to determine the manufacturer's recommended schedule of preventive maintenance. Following the schedule will save you from paying expensive repair bills later. Ignoring the recommended service intervals may also void the manufacturer's warranty on your vehicle.

Tire Maintenance

Tires are one of the easiest parts of your vehicle to monitor. However, they often get overlooked. Keep in mind that it is easier and safer to change a tire at home than on a busy street with traffic whizzing by. Take the time to research the best tires for your vehicle when it comes time to replace them. Spending a little extra on better tires can often save you time and trouble in the long run.

Make sure that the tires on your vehicle are the proper size. If you are not sure that they are or if the tires do not "look right," check with the manufacturer's recommendations in the owner's manual. Never mix different types of tires. Your tires should be of equivalent size, quality, and tread design.

Inflation

Properly inflating the tires ensures that they will grip the road evenly and wear at the same rate. Tires without sufficient air grip the road only at their outer edges, which causes the tires to squeal, makes steering more difficult, leads to heat buildup, decreases fuel economy, and wears the tires out faster. Overinflating the tires allows only the center of the tires to grip the road, which leads to a harder ride, a reduction in the depth of the tires' print, and faster wear.

Check tire pressure at least once a month or when you stop to get gas. Make sure that you do so *only when the tires are cold.* The heat from friction with the road causes air in the tires to expand, so pressure readings taken right after driving are not accurate. When you check your regular tires, remember also to check the

Figure 20-1 Check tire pressure *before* you drive.

Driving on underinflated tires can reduce tread life by as much as 50%.

DRIVING TIPS *Tire Inflation in Cold Weather*

Tires need more air in cold weather. A tire that may have lost pressure during the summer and fall driving season could easily become underinflated on a freezing day. Pay special attention to air pressure in your tires during the winter!

spare. Station wagons and cars with engines in the rear may require higher pressure for rear tires than for the front, whereas some front-wheel drive cars require higher pressure for the front tires.

Wear

It is illegal, as well as dangerous, to drive on tires that are badly worn. Before getting into your vehicle, note the condition of all tires. "Bald" tires with little or no tread provide almost no traction and reduce directional control. They are also more likely to get punctured or go flat. Bald tires will also double the risk of skidding and hydroplaning on rain-slick surfaces. You should acquire a special gauge to measure the minimum depth of tread possible before the tire goes bald. Most tires have tread-wear indicators that tell you when they should be replaced. If your tires do not have tread-wear indicators, you should

Figure 20–2 Driving on bald tires increases the risk of getting a flat and skidding.

replace them when the tread wears down to no less than ⅛ inch (3 mm).

Look for bulges and embedded nails, glass, or metal. A frequent loss of pressure in a tire suggests a

AUTO ACCESSORIES *Tool Kit*

To help you perform routine maintenance on your car, invest in a standard automobile tool kit. These tools can be carried in your trunk or stored in your garage. Remember to purchase correctly sized tools— either "United States customary" for most North American vehicles or "metric" for some North American vehicles and almost all imports.

slow leak, which can cause an emergency when you drive. For equal wear, tires should be rotated on a regular basis, which means switching them from front to rear and from one side to the other. Check your owner's manual for the recommended guidelines for your tires. When rotating the tires, make sure that they are balanced so that the weight is evenly distributed as the wheels turn. This will provide better steering control, a smoother ride, and a longer tire life.

Fluid Levels

Fluids are the lifeblood of your vehicle, so do not take chances. Check your fluid levels regularly, and occasionally check under your vehicle for signs of leaking fluids. The color of any puddle on the pavement indicates the type of fluid leaking out. To make leaks easier to see, leave a large white sheet of paper under the vehicle overnight. Repair any leaking system before you have trouble.

Oil

If you have any reason to suspect a problem with your oil or if the oil gauge/indicator light is activated, stop the vehicle immediately! If you keep driving, you may irreparably damage your vehicle's engine. Running an engine without oil is a sure death sentence for the engine. Check the oil level at least once a month, more frequently on older cars, and change the oil at least twice a year, or every 3,000 miles (5,000 km). If you drive in hot weather or spend much of your time in rush-hour traffic, you should change it even more frequently.

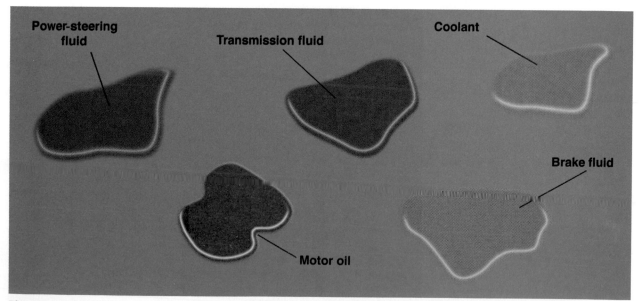

Figure 20–3 Learn to recognize what is leaking from your vehicle.

The oil level should be checked when the engine is cool and not running. To check the oil level, remove the dipstick and wipe it off. Reinsert it and remove it once more. If the oil level registers below the line, add the proper amount of oil. *Do not rely solely on your oil gauge to tell you when to change the oil.* By the time the warning light flashes, the engine has been without oil long enough to harm the machinery.

Transmission Fluid

Keep an eye on your transmission fluid level. Replacing or refilling transmission fluid is easy and can save you costly repairs in the future. The color of the fluid should be a bright, cherry red. Have a mechanic examine the transmission if the color is dark and has a burnt smell. Transmission oil should be changed every 25,000 to 35,000 miles (40,000 to 55,000 km) depending on the type of vehicle.

Brake Fluid

Have the fluid level in the dual master cylinder checked every time you have the oil changed and replace it at least once a year. Brake fluid attracts water from condensation and humidity in the air, causing corrosion in the master and wheel cylinders and shortening their lives.

Coolant

Check the level of coolant in the radiator overflow tank. Insufficient levels of coolant may result in overheating and damage to the engine. If the coolant level is low, start the engine and add more. *The engine should be running while the coolant is being added.* This prevents cracking of components from a sudden temperature change in the hot radiator. In warm weather, water alone can be used if antifreeze is unavailable.

Other Fluids

Make sure that you have the proper amount of battery fluid, if necessary, for your battery. Also be certain that you have enough windshield washer fluid. You do not want your wipers smearing mud or other foreign substances all over your windshield just because you forgot to refill the windshield washer fluid reservoir.

Belts, Hoses, and Wires

A loose belt in the engine may cause the electrical system to malfunction. Loose belts can also contribute to inefficient cooling of the engine and to problems with the power steering and air conditioning. Belts should feel tight when you push down on them. Tighten the belt if you can push it down more than ½ inch (1 cm). Replace frayed or cracked belts immediately. Check hoses and hose connections for leaks. Wires that are loose, broken, or disconnected, as well as cracked insulation on wires, should be repaired. Check to see that battery cables are tightly connected and terminals are free of corrosion.

Brake Pads

The braking system is obviously one of the most important features governing both your safety and the safety of others on the road. Pay strict attention to its maintenance. Test brakes by stepping on the brake pedal. You should feel firm resistance and the vehicle should come to a smooth, direct stop. Also, the pedal should stay well above the floor.

Let a mechanic know as soon as possible if you must depress the brake pedal very low to get it to work, if the vehicle pulls to one side when you brake, if one tire locks when braking, or if you detect a "spongy" feeling in the brake pedal. Other problems include grabbing or uneven brake action, accompanied by squealing or chattering noises. You may have completely worn the brake pads down, resulting in metal braking on metal. Also, let your mechanic know if you need to pump the brakes or push the brake harder than usual to stop the car.

The Engine

The quickest way to diagnose problems with your engine is from your exhaust. If your exhaust changes to a blue or smoky white color, you can assume engine damage is occurring or has already occurred. Turn the motor off immediately to prevent any further damage!

If you notice a foul, sulfuric odor like rotten eggs, your vehicle might have a damaged catalytic converter. Defects in the exhaust system create noise and increase the risk of carbon monoxide poisoning for the vehicle's occupants. The exhaust system should be replaced when a part rusts or becomes damaged in some other way. To protect your catalytic converter, use only unleaded gasoline.

Always pay attention to the temperature in your engine. Overheating can result from the breakdown of your water pump or from a malfunctioning thermostat. If you hear a suspicious knocking noise, stop and turn off the engine.

Steering and Suspension

Be alert to problems with your vehicle's steering system, such as vibration of the steering wheel, excessive "play" in the wheel, or difficulty in steering even though tires are properly inflated. You may also have a mechanical problem in your steering system if you

Figure 20–4

DRIVING TIPS *Improving Fuel Efficiency* _____

Improvements in design and performance have made modern cars more fuel efficient and more mechanically reliable than older vehicles. However, you can take the following additional steps to save money on gasoline:

- Avoid unnecessary lane changes.
- Drive the posted speed limit.
- Plan your route in advance.
- Avoid unnecessary braking and accelerating.
- Avoid "racing" the engine.
- Make sure that your engine's timing and idle are set properly.
- Keep your tires properly inflated.
- Perform routine maintenance as recommended in your vehicle's owner's manual.

feel a wobbling or if the vehicle pulls to one side under normal driving conditions. If you experience considerable sway or bounce when driving over a bump or turning corners, or if you detect rattling, your vehicle could have faulty shock absorbers. Be sure to report these problems to a mechanic as soon as you detect them.

Routine Maintenance Schedule

Based on recommendations in the owner's manual of your vehicle, set up a routine maintenance schedule. Keep a record of when and what type of service is done, and whether you do the work yourself or have a mechanic do it. Here is a typical routine maintenance schedule:

- *Every week:* Check the levels of the vehicle's oil, windshield washer fluid, and radiator coolant.

- *Every month:* Check the condition of the tires, belts, hoses, automatic-transmission fluid, brake fluid, and power-steering fluid. Clean dead bugs out of your radiator grille. Wax the car to protect the paint.

- *Every six months:* Check and clean the battery cables and terminals. Check the condition of the brakes.

- *Once a year:* Check the air conditioner refrigerant and shock absorbers. Replace the air filter and windshield wiper blades. Flush out the radiator and refill it with coolant. Hose down the undercarriage to remove dirt and salt after a cold driving season. Check the headlight alignment.

Your owner's manual will outline specific maintenance schedules for your vehicle based on the miles/kilometers that you drive.

7,500 miles (12,000 km) or at 6 months
☐ Change engine oil.
☐ Replace engine oil filter.

22,500 miles (36,000 km) or at 18 months
☐ Change engine oil.
☐ Replace engine oil filter.
☐ Inspect brake linings.

15,000 miles (24,000 km) or at 12 months
☐ Change engine oil.
☐ Replace engine oil filter.
☐ Lubricate steering linkage.

30,000 miles (48,000 km) or at 24 months
☐ Change engine oil.
☐ Replace engine oil filter.
☐ Replace air cleaner filter.
☐ Replace spark plugs.
☐ Inspect drive belt, adjust tension as needed.
☐ Lubricate steering linkage.
☐ Drain and refill automatic transmission fluid.
☐ Drain and refill transfer case fluid.

Figure 20–5 Each vehicle has its own recommended maintenance schedule.

Wild Wheels

Figure 20–6 What is the name of this car, introduced in 1972, that had most of its black Naugahyde upholstery on the *outside?*

In most cases, these procedures should be done by a certified mechanic.

Refueling

Pay close attention to your fuel gauge. You never want to let a vehicle run out of fuel because dirt left in the bottom of the tank will clog up the fuel filter. If the fuel filter becomes blocked, your engine will not receive the fuel it needs for combustion to take place in the cylinders. Always turn your engine off before refueling.

The types of fuel delivered at the fuel pump are indicated on the pump. If your vehicle requires unleaded or diesel fuel, a manufacturer's notice normally appears on the instrument panel near the fuel gauge, around the fuel cap, and in the owner's manual. The fuel octane rating necessary to prevent engine knocking or "pinging" during normal driving is also noted in the owner's man-

Figure 20–7 Always turn off your engine before refueling.

ual. The octane rating of any particular fuel is also displayed on the fuel pump.

Protecting the Exterior

If you want to preserve the value of your vehicle for resale or if you just want it to look as nice as possible for as long as you own it, you will want to protect it from the damaging effects of the environment, including acid rain, tree sap, bugs, and corrosion from road salt and dust. Wash your vehicle frequently, especially if you live in areas where salt is used to provide traction during snowstorms. You should also bear in mind that sunlight can prematurely damage a vehicle's exterior paint job, as well as fade and crack interiors exposed to sunlight through the windows.

If you wash your car by hand, wait until it is cool outside. Keep your vehicle out of direct sunlight as much as possible. Clean the tires and wheels first so that you will not splash water all over your newly cleaned vehicle. Spray the wheel wells and undercarriage to remove corrosive agents. Flood the car's surface with water before applying suds. This will remove the surface dirt and soil that may otherwise get rubbed into the body and cause scratches. Using a sponge, wash the car from the top down, in straight lines and using overlapping strokes. When drying your car, open up all the doors and lids to enable partially exposed areas to dry completely. You may want to use a chamois ("shammy"),

which is a piece of soft leather, to help dry the vehicle.

Wax your car at least six times a year, more often if it is exposed to salt air, road salt, or industrial air, or if you have to park it outside. If water does not bead up on the car's surface after a rain, waxing is needed. Always use real waxes that cannot harm the finish. Avoid products that promise to remove dirt, oxidized paint, or scratches.

Because hot metal surfaces can cause wax chemicals to damage the finish, do not wax your car in direct sunlight. If you choose to wax your car on a really humid day, the wax may streak. Never wax large areas of the car at one time. Apply the wax to small areas with a foam applicator. Remove it with a shining cloth, rubbing in a circular fashion.

No matter how often you wash and wax your vehicle, exposure to the elements will cause the

Figure 20–8 Use household detergents on your dishes and laundry, not your car.

driving tips

When washing your car, avoid household liquid soaps and laundry detergents, which can damage the luster and finish of the vehicle by stripping the protective wax coat.

bumper sticker sightings

DO NOT WASH— THIS VEHICLE IS A SCIENTIFIC EXPERIMENT

Figure 20–9 You should wax your car often to protect its finish.

may be performed elsewhere. After the warranty expires, you may have all services performed any place you choose, including at the dealership, at your local garage, or at a service station. You might also consider an independent mechanic. No matter who works on your vehicle, find someone you trust. Ask friends and relatives where they have had their vehicles serviced and if they were satisfied with the work.

Figure 20–10 Always get an estimate before authorizing repairs on your vehicle.

exterior paint to oxidize and fade in color. The color of the roof, hood, and trunk will often fade more rapidly than the color on the sides of the car. Long-term exposure to the sun's ultraviolet rays can cause paint to fade after one to two years, to crack after three to four years, and to lift and peel after five to six years. To minimize the effects of environmental damage to your car, keep it covered with a tarp or in a garage or carport if you are not going to drive it for a while.

20–2 SELECTING A MECHANIC

Sometimes new-car warranties require you to have certain services on the car performed by the dealer to enjoy the full protection of the warranty. Other services

Before you have any work done, *ask for an itemized estimate* of repair costs. The estimate should include separate descriptions of parts and labor. You should also inquire about whether the work will be protected by a warranty. *Inform the mechanic that no work should be done that is not specifically included in the estimate.* As an extra precaution against unnecessary repairs, ask that any parts that are replaced be returned to you for inspection.

There are many ways to protect yourself from poor workmanship at auto repair shops. One of the best ways to protect yourself is to shop around. Do not be content with merely one estimate from one mechanic regarding a repair. Get two or three estimates. And do not automatically fall for the lowest price. A golden rule of thumb is to eliminate the highest and lowest estimates. The mechanic with the highest estimate is probably charging too much, and the lowest may be cutting too many corners; may be tempted to use shoddy, used, or stolen replacement parts; and may even "create" some other problems with the car!

Check the shop's reputation before you agree to the estimate by calling your local consumer affairs agency and/or the Better Business Bureau. Once you get to the shop look for certification of the mechanics, either by the National Institute for Automotive Service Excellence (ASE) or by a manufacturer who provides training to mechanics that work on its vehicles. Show some interest in the job that the mechanic is doing on your vehicle. You may be surprised to find out how nice a mechanic is when he or she knows that you are paying attention.

If your best efforts to protect yourself from a bad mechanic fail, first return your car to the repair facility that did the work. Provide a written list of the problems, and keep a copy of the list. It is also a good idea to get a written statement from another mechanic defining the problem and outlining how it may be fixed. Give the repair facility a reasonable opportunity to fix your car. Speak directly to the service manager and have him or her test drive the car to observe the problem. You may be pleasantly surprised to discover that he or she will want to keep your business by pleasing you.

If you continue to have problems, report the facility to your local Better Business Bureau. Contact private consumer groups or local government agencies. A telephone call or letter from them

Figure 20–11 Let only certified mechanics work on your vehicle.

may persuade the mechanic to take action. If you charged the repairs, send a certified letter, return receipt requested, to the credit card company and a copy to the repair shop explaining the situation. The credit card company may assist you by deciding to not honor the charge. If all else fails, bring a lawsuit against the mechanic in small claims court. If the disputed charges are high, it may be worthwhile talking with an attorney.

Figure 20–12 Keep copies of all records related to repair work on your car.

No matter what your problems are with the car, keep accurate records. Copies of your service invoices, bills you have paid, letters you have written to the manufacturer or the repair facility owner,

and written repair estimates from an independent mechanic are essential in helping resolve your problems. Not only will these documents help you out legally, but they will also help lead to a quicker resolution of your complaint.

20–3 VEHICLE EQUIPMENT AND ACCESSORIES

Equipment and accessories exist to help you with emergencies, to assist disabled drivers, and to improve the comfort and appearance of your vehicle.

Safety-Oriented Equipment

Dozens of products are on the market that can make your vehicle safer or contribute to your becoming a safer driver. Some of the most important safety equipment that you can acquire are items that help the driver's ability to see. **Fog lights** can be mounted on the front of a vehicle to improve your visibility during fog and other bad weather. Most states and provinces usually limit you to placing a maximum of two on the front of a vehicle, and their use is often restricted to when the vehicle's low beams are on. In addition, up to two spotlights can also usually be mounted on the front of a vehicle to assist the driver's sight of the roadway in front of him or her. Interior, oversize rearview mirrors that are longer and larger than conventional rearview mirrors can be installed to provide the

Figure 20-13 Sometimes you can accessorize a car too much!

driver with a more extensive rear view.

To make your vehicle more visible, especially if your vehicle is an older model, consider installing daytime running lights, a

Figure 20-14 Fog lights can greatly increase your vision as a driver.

center high-mounted rear brake light, clearance lamps and cab lights, and extra reflectors or reflector strips.

Vehicle Accessories

When it comes to vehicle accessories, the list is almost infinite. Certain accessories can "expand" the cargo area of your vehicle, such as ski racks mounted on the vehicle's roof or side; luggage racks or bubble cases mounted on the roof or on the rear of the vehicle; bike racks; and bungee cords, which are stretchable ropes with hooks on the ends that work wonders when you have to tie down cargo.

Other accessories allow you to enhance the exterior appearance of your vehicle, adding value, increasing life span, and preventing costly repairs down the road. Mobile tents or car covers can protect your vehicle from the elements if you have no garage. Window vents and vent guards keep unwanted moisture from entering the passenger compartment. Exterior paint can be protected by installing mud flaps to the wheel wells and/or a car "bra," a leather or vinyl protector for the front hood and bumper; by regularly using paint protectant and sealer products; and by adding "cattle pusher" metal protective forks and/or rods mounted to the front and rear of a vehicle to protect the paint and body from direct impacts.

Some accessories, such as specialty wheel rims, airdams, air deflectors, flares, scoops, and spoilers

Figure 20–15 Bicycles are hard to stow in a vehicle without a specialized rack.

may make the vehicle more aerodynamic and/or stylish.

Some interior accessories contribute directly to driving safety, such as car sun visors, whereas other accessories merely add to your driving enjoyment and pride of ownership, such as car stereo systems and wood dashboard overlays.

Pickups, sport utility vehicles, and vans support additional ac-cessories that can enhance appearance, contribute to driver safety, and help make these vehicles even more practical than they already are. Winches mounted on the front of the vehicle use either tough wire cord or chain to pull other vehicles and objects out of the way or out of dangerous situations. Roll bars affixed to the chassis of pickups and sport utility vehicles add more structural support in the event of a rollover crash. Marker lights, which are small lights mounted along the sides of a vehicle, aid in making the vehicle more visible to other drivers.

Several different options are available when you want to either increase the cargo carrying capacity of your vehicle, protect the vehicle from cargo damage, or increase the amount of interior space. Exterior bed-mounted tool boxes for pickups are containers specially built to stow tools and other materials securely. Tonneaus cover the bed of a pickup, creating a secure, enclosed storage space.

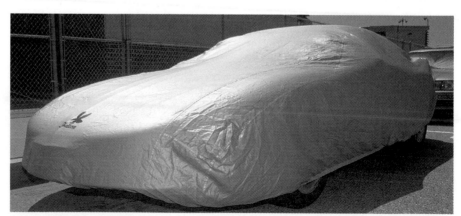

Figure 20–16 Keeping your car covered when not in use will protect the paint from the harsh effects of the environment.

Figure 20-17 Replacing your existing wheels can be a less expensive way to individualize your vehicle.

Cargo covers get around the problem in sport utility vehicles of not having a secure, locked trunk. These covers can be placed in the rear of a sport utility vehicle to hide stored items. Similarly, cargo vaults can be installed in pickup beds or in rear compartments of sport utility vehicles for safe and secure storage of belongings.

Pickup beds get a lot of rough treatment, and unsecured cargo tends to badly scratch and dent the bed. The best way to protect your bed is to purchase a tough plastic lining called a bedliner. In lieu of a bedliner or in addition to it, you may want to consider spider netting lift gates and flexible bed covers that "mold" to your cargo and keep it from jostling around. If you want to increase the interior space of a pickup, you can get a camper shell, which comes in a variety of shapes and sizes. This will create a large enclosed space out of your bed. If you want to increase the space on a van, look into getting a van top, which extends the roof vertically and allows for more headroom for passengers. Installing door steps and running boards on the undercarriage of high-profile vehicles will assist drivers and passengers to safely get into and out of these vehicles with a minimum of effort.

Equipment for Disabled Drivers

Just because you are physically disabled does not mean that you cannot or should not learn how to drive. Given the advances in automotive **adaptive equipment** technology in recent years, it has become possible for people with many types of physical disability, including cerebral palsy, spina bifida, amputations, muscular dystrophy, head and spinal cord injuries, and multiple sclerosis to drive.

If you are physically disabled and you find that learning to drive in a standard driver education course is impractical or not working out, there are many disabled driver education specialists in North America who can help you master the fundamentals of driving and work with you to obtain your license. Depending on your particular situation, it may even be possible to obtain financial help for this specialized training from your state or provincial government.

If you are a disabled driver, the process of adjusting a vehicle for your use centers around finding the appropriate mix of adaptations that will work specifically for your needs. Of course, not every disabled person is the same, and what works for one type of disability will often not work for another type of disability. Adaptive equipment is as unique as is the particular disability that it is being used to accommodate. Some of the more common devices used to assist with the steering function are spinner knobs, amputee spinners, foot steering mechanisms, and "tri-pins" that can be attached to the steering wheel to allow you to steer if you cannot grip the wheel. Adaptive devices for the various controls on the vehicle can be as varied as remote switches, extensions to existing controls, auto-

Figure 20–18 Installing a tonneau over the bed of the pickup creates a secure, enclosed cargo space.

matic clutches, pedal blocks, left foot accelerators, and **hand controls** that allow someone who cannot use their legs to control signals and pedals with their hands.

Although the cost of adapting a vehicle can sometimes be prohibitively expensive, many vehicle manufacturers have disability programs whose main purpose is to

Figure 20–19 A winch can be helpful in emergencies.

Figure 20–20 This accessory encloses the bed and greatly increases its size.

assist physically disabled individuals acquire a new car, either via lease or purchase. These manufacturers may even refund disabled drivers for some or most of the cost of the adaptive equipment necessary to make a new car drivable for their particular disability.

20–4 VEHICLE SECURITY

Unfortunately, we live in a day and age in which we all need to be concerned about the security of our vehicles. Because vehicles are valuable, mobile, and often parked in the open on public streets, it is no surprise that they are one of the most stolen possessions in society. More than 1.5 million vehicles— 1 of every 140 registered vehicles in the United States and 1 of every 100 registered vehicles in Canada—are stolen each year in North America.

When and Why Vehicles Are Stolen

A significant percentage of auto thefts are committed during the early morning when the owners are asleep and their vehicles are unattended. According to recent studies, about one-quarter of all stolen vehicles had the ignition key in them and in plain view of the thief when they were stolen! About 40% of stolen vehicles had at least one unlocked door at the time they were taken. Only about 10% of the stolen cars had any type of antitheft device installed.

Contrary to popular belief, the most targeted vehicles among thieves are not fancy luxury cars or sports cars. The average stolen vehicle is an ordinary family car that is a few years old whose spare parts value has risen. In other words, because the model is getting older, the availability of spare parts from the manufacturer and other suppliers is decreasing. This increases the value of the parts of that model and makes those vehicles still on the road a more attractive target for thieves. Some vehicles are actually worth two to three times their value on the black market when disassembled into parts!

factoid

A vehicle is stolen in the United States every 21 seconds.

Preventing Vehicle Theft

The typical car thief is an opportunist, looking for an "easy" car to steal. The more time that it will take to break into your vehicle, the less likely he or she will bother to steal your car. A completely unprotected car can be stolen in less than 30 seconds. The vehicle owner can become an active part of the solution to car theft by doing a variety of things to prevent his or her car from being stolen.

A large part of playing the antitheft game successfully is knowing where and how to park your vehicle. Always use the emergency brake when parking, even if you are on level ground, because this will delay a thief who intends to push your car away for a quick tow. Turning your wheels toward the curb when you park (which you should always do unless you are facing uphill) also makes it more difficult for a thief to tow the car. Make sure that you do this when the engine is still on because your steering column lock will prohibit you from fully turning the tires once the engine has been shut off.

Most thieves avoid doing their dirty deed in open view, so always park your car in well-lit areas with a lot of pedestrian traffic. If there is a parking lot security guard or attendant, try to park as close to where this person is stationed. If a secure garage or parking structure is available where the thief never even has a chance to see the vehicle in the first place, use it.

Before leaving your vehicle, always remember to take your keys out of the ignition, lock your car, and completely close the windows. Never leave your car running and unattended. Do not leave valuables in plain view to tempt thieves. Do not hide a spare key on the outside of the car because thieves can usually find these keys. Instead, keep a spare in your pocket or purse.

Do not let your guard down when leaving your vehicle with a mechanic for repair work. Investigate the mechanic before you entrust him or her with your vehicle. Remember to get a signed receipt from the repair shop that shows it has taken custody of your vehicle. Give a mechanic only your car keys, and clean out valuables from your vehicle before you drop it off.

Antitheft Devices and Systems

The next level of prevention is to install some type of antitheft device on your vehicle. **Antitheft devices** are any equipment installed on your vehicle that either deters, disrupts, or helps catch a car thief. Many automobile insurance companies will offer you a discount on your comprehensive insurance policy if your vehicle is equipped with one or more of these devices. There are three basic types of antitheft devices: warning devices, "shut off" devices, and tracking devices.

Warning devices usually emit either a sound signal or a visual cue intended to scare a would-be

auto slang

"Hot-wiring" a vehicle is slang for the method that auto thieves often use to start a vehicle by short circuiting its ignition system.

bumper sticker sightings

IF YOU LOVE YOUR LIFE
AS MUCH AS I LOVE MY CAR,
DON'T STEAL IT

car thief away. Audible **car alarms** are equipped with sensors that trigger a loud siren or a constant beeping of the vehicle's horn. Most people are so used to hearing these alarms go off by mistake, however, that they do not investigate when they hear them, and the owner is usually out of hearing range. "Silent" car alarms are normally more effective because they are inaudible to the thief but trigger an alarm with the owner or the police.

Steering wheel locks are metal bars with a hooking mechanism on both ends that are locked into place either on the steering wheel or between the steering wheel and the brake pedal. This makes it nearly impossible to steer or otherwise operate the vehicle, a major problem if you are a thief trying to make a quick getaway.

Steering column collars are metal collars that can be fitted around your steering column to prevent a thief from accessing the ignition or breaking into the ignition wires. They are particularly effective on older vehicles that are more easily hot-wired.

"Shut-off" devices operate on the principle that thieves will often bypass your ignition and attempt to hot-wire the car to get it to start. A variety of products defend against this. The two most commonly used are smart keys and kill switches.

Smart keys are ignition keys that are computer-coded or radio-controlled to signal your vehicle to start. Without this exact key, the vehicle's motor will remain "shut off," even if the thief has hot-wired it. **Kill switches** are sometimes called starter disablers, fuse cut-offs, ignition disablers, or fuel disablers. They are secondary ignition switches concealed in an unlikely location inside the vehicle that work by inhibiting the flow of electricity or fuel to the engine. To start the vehicle, you must restore that flow by

Figure 20–21 Using a high-voltage electrical shock, this steering wheel lock goes one step further than most to deter theft.

inserting a separate key or manually activating the switch. When a thief hot-wires a vehicle and it still does not start, he or she will suspect a kill switch is somewhere on the vehicle. Most thieves are too nervous to spend the time looking for the kill switch, especially if it is well concealed, so they will move on to another vehicle. A cheap alternative when you will be leaving the car parked for long periods is to remove the coil wire from the distributor cap. The vehicle will not start without this part.

You can also equip your vehicle with a **tracking device**. With this system, if your vehicle is stolen, you report its disappearance as soon as possible to a central response center. That center will then activate a tracking device hidden somewhere on the car that emits a signal to the police or to the central response center, allowing them to find the exact location of the vehicle. This system has proven to be very successful in recovering stolen vehicles quickly, sometimes even before they are stripped of parts.

YOUR TURN

20–1 Preventive Maintenance

1. What is preventive maintenance?

2. How do you check tires for inflation and wear?

3. What fluids should you check as part of routine maintenance?

4. What is the proper way to wash and wax a vehicle?

20–2 Selecting a Mechanic

5. How do you select a mechanic?

6. How can you avoid poor workmanship?

20–3 Vehicle Equipment and Accessories

7. What are three types of safety-oriented equipment?

8. What devices are used to adapt a regular vehicle for a disabled driver?

20–4 Vehicle Security

9. What are three basic types of antitheft devices available?

10. How does a vehicle tracking device work?

SELF-TEST

Multiple Choice

1. You should check tire pressure:
   - **a.** when the tires are cold.
   - **b.** when the tires are hot.
   - **c.** every time you change your oil.
   - **d.** when the tires are "bald."

2. What routine maintenance should be performed on your vehicle every month?
   - **a.** Replace the radiator cap.
   - **b.** Replace the fuel filter.
   - **c.** Check the exhaust system for leaks.
   - **d.** Check the power-steering fluid.

3. The paint on the _____ of your car will oxidize less rapidly than the other parts.
   - **a.** sides
   - **b.** hood
   - **c.** trunk
   - **d.** roof

4. If you were a disabled driver and wanted to obtain a refund for some adaptive equipment you wanted to place into a new car you just purchased, where would you seek the refund?
   - **a.** the Red Cross
   - **b.** a motor-vehicle manufacturer
   - **c.** your state or provincial government
   - **d.** your family physician

5. What is the typical type of motor vehicle stolen by car thieves?
   - **a.** ordinary family car
   - **b.** pickup
   - **c.** sports car
   - **d.** luxury four-door sedan

Sentence Completion

1. For equal wear, tires should be _____ on a regular basis.
2. The oil level in your car should always be checked when the engine is _____.
3. _____ lights on the sides of a vehicle greatly enhance its visibility.
4. A spinner knob is a common piece of _____ equipment used by disabled drivers.
5. Starter disablers and fuel disablers are two types of _____.

Matching

Match the concepts in Column A with examples of the concepts in Column B.

Column A	Column B
1. __ Preventive maintenance	**a.** Description of parts and labor
2. __ Exterior appearance accessory	**b.** Van top
3. __ "Pinging" engine	**c.** Car bra
4. __ Pedal block	**d.** Disabled driving adaptation
5. __ Tire rotation	**e.** Checking fluid levels
6. __ Increases interior space	**f.** Octane rating
7. __ Shut-off device	**g.** Front to rear
8. __ Itemized estimate	**h.** Ignition disabler

Short Answer

1. What documents should you have to help protect you in a dispute with a mechanic?

2. Why are bald tires dangerous?

3. What does a kill switch do?

4. Where can a disabled person turn to for financial assistance with private disabled driver education?

5. Why are so many vehicles stolen in the early morning?

Critical Thinking

1. After hearing your brakes make a grinding noise, you decide to take your car to a mechanic. You go to a garage that is offering a great deal on brake jobs. He writes you out an estimate to replace the brake pads, and you leave the car with him. When you return at the end of the day, he submits a bill to you that is four times the estimate. He explains that you needed new rotors, but he could not reach you at the telephone number you left him to discuss the problem. What should you do?

2. You just got a part-time job in a high-crime area of your city, and you must drive there every day. Your boss does not have enough parking spaces for all of the employees, so you are forced to find your own parking on the street, usually about two blocks away and out of hearing and viewing range. You are worried about the security of your vehicle but do not know which vehicle antitheft device is the appropriate one for you to purchase. What should you do?

PROJECTS

1. Call a local automobile repair shop and ask the owner or manager if you could spend a few hours observing what the mechanics do and how they do it. Ask to watch a "lube job," "brake job," tune-up, and other procedures. Take notes and share your experience with your class.

2. Go with a friend to a local automobile supply or accessory store and investigate all of the different antitheft devices available. Compare the prices, the claims of the manufacturers, and the warranties offered. Then go to the library or use the Internet at home to determine what the consumer press has said about each of these devices. How do they stack up against one another? Analyze all the information you have collected and come up with a recommendation for protecting your vehicle effectively and for a reasonable amount of money.

Driving Away
from Home

Whether you are going on a short overnight trip to the beach, lake, or mountains or a long vacation far from home, you must be prepared to deal with unfamiliar roads, customs, weather conditions, and driving regulations. If you are hauling a boat, towing a trailer, moving furniture to a new home, driving a recreational vehicle, or renting a car, you must familiarize yourself with different instruments, controls, and maneuvering capabilities.

Upon completion of this chapter, you should be able to:

21–1 Road Trips

1. Understand how to prepare for extended road trips.
2. Describe the basic features of a road map.
3. Understand how highways are numbered in North America.

21–2 Driving Unfamiliar Vehicles

4. Understand what precautions you should take when driving an RV or moving van.
5. Understand how to safely load and pull a trailer.
6. Understand what precautions you should take when driving an SUV.

KEY TERMS

scale	loop	sport utility vehicles
legend	spur	(SUVs)
mileage (distance) chart	recreational vehicles (RVs)	

21–1 ROAD TRIPS

Driving away from home can be fun and exciting, but without adequate preparation, your pleasant getaway could easily turn into a nightmare.

Planning Ahead

The key to enjoying any extended road trip away from home is to plan ahead. Most auto and travel clubs will provide you with maps, suggested routes, and travel guides at no extra charge. Some clubs can warn you about roads that are closed or under construction, tolls, and other potential problems you can expect to encounter on your route.

Maps and travel guides are also available from service stations; bookstores; local chambers of commerce; and state/provincial, regional, and city tourism bureaus. The Internet is a great resource for planning trips. Browse the World Wide Web for maps, directions, and detailed information on your destination. Computer software is available as well to help you plan trips.

Take seasonal weather conditions and traffic congestion into

Figure 21–1 There are many resources for planning road trips.

account when you plan the dates of your trip. Choose the simplest route that you can with the fewest number of hazards, even if it takes a little longer to get to your destination. Try to time your passage through cities and areas with heavy traffic at times other than rush hour. Nothing is more frustrating than spending your vacation stuck in the same traffic jams that you face on your way to work or school.

Organize your trip so that you do not have to drive too far in one day. Change drivers frequently. Allow plenty of time to relax and rest overnight along the way. If

ROAD WEIRDNESS *People Who Love to Drive* _____

Some people love to drive so much that they will go out of their way to "put on" extra miles. Members of the Extra Miler Club, whose motto is "the shortest distance between two points is no fun," take this mission seriously. One member met his ambitious goal of visiting every county in the United States by logging more than 500,000 miles (800,000 km) across the country, while others set more modest targets of visiting every state or province.

Figure 21–2 Vacations and other extended road trips require planning and advance preparation.

you are taking your trip during a peak travel season, reserve lodging ahead of time so you do not get stuck without a place to sleep. To break up the trip, plan to explore some of the tourist attractions along your route.

Figure 21–3 If you do not book lodging in advance, you may have difficulty finding a room.

Before You Leave

Before you begin a long road trip, always make sure that your vehicle is in the best possible working order. It is a good idea to have it serviced before leaving. If you are traveling far from home, especially through less populated areas, pack emergency supplies. Keep an extra set of car keys in your pocket or with a passenger. Do not forget to take your auto club membership card or a roadside service telephone number.

Figure out a budget that includes expenses for lodging (hotels, motels, hostels, or campsites), meals, entertainment, and fuel. Make sure that you include in your budget any additional expenses such as entrance fees, parking fees, equipment rental, ski-lift tickets, fishing permits, and souvenirs. Take along extra funds in case of an emergency or a vehicle breakdown. If possible, use traveler's checks and credit cards to cover your spending, and carry only a minimum of cash. In case they get lost or stolen, leave a copy of your traveler's check receipts and credit card information with a friend or relative. Put coins in a location accessible to the driver for toll roads, bridges, and tunnels.

Always tell a family member, friend, or neighbor what your intended route is and places where you can be reached along the way if necessary. If you are stuck in a remote area or are the victim of a crime, this information will make it easier for authorities to locate

Figure 21–4 Keep an assortment of coins in your car to pay tolls on road trips.

you. It is always a good idea to regularly check in with somebody during your trip to let him or her know all is well. If no one will be at home while you are away, arrange with someone to look after your pets and collect your mail. You should also postpone your newspaper subscriptions. Uncollected mail and newspapers are open invitations to thieves. Set timers to turn your home lights on and off so the house or apartment will not look empty while you are away.

Using Road Maps

Maps are invaluable to the traveler to find out where you are and how to get to your destination. Besides displaying the various roadways and ferry routes in a given area, they highlight points of interest, types of terrain, climate differences, time zones, and other useful information. The **scale** of the map determines its level of detail. State and provincial maps usually have an index of towns, cities, and recreation areas, as well as small inset maps of major cities and downtown areas. City maps generally have a street index to enable you to locate a particular address.

Of course, a map is useful only if you know how to read it. On most maps, the top border corresponds to the direction north. A compass or arrow marked somewhere on the map indicates the actual orientation. The letters and numbers that appear at intervals on the edges of the map correspond to the letter–number codes used in the index. For example, a city listed as "F-24" would be found within the space on the map where imaginary columns extending from "F" and "24" intersect.

The **legend** explains the colors and symbols used on the map to represent different types of roadways and common landmarks such as airports, rest areas, campgrounds, and ports of entry. On detailed city maps, the names of schools, shopping centers, parks, hospitals, places of worship, monuments, and other important sites usually appear on the map next to the symbol.

Many maps have a **mileage** or **distance chart**, a table that lists distances in miles/kilometers between key points on roadways. Depending on the scale, distances and approximate travel times may

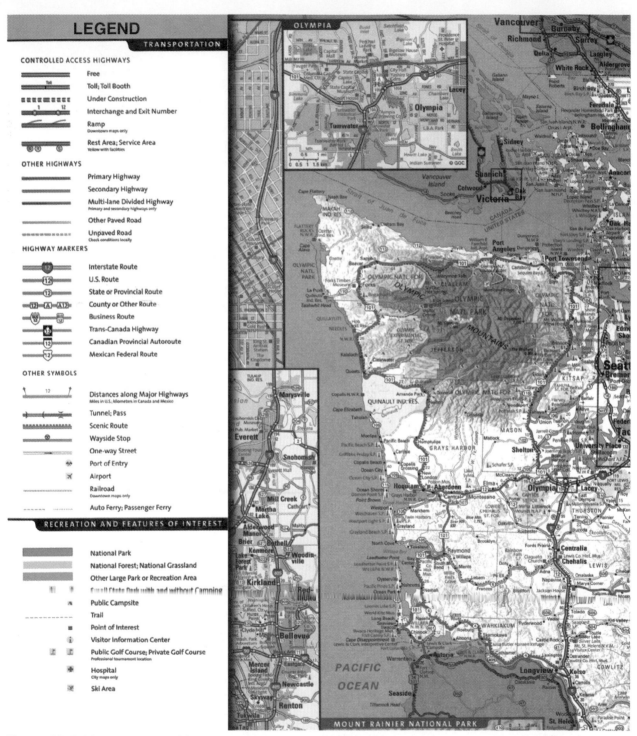

Figure 21–5 Maps are essential for any road trip to an unfamiliar area.

© GeoSystems Global Corporation

Maps Are Not Always Reliable _____

Just because a road or highway is on a map does not mean that you will be able to use it. Some maps clearly mark roads that are unpaved, under construction, or closed during certain times of the year, but the information may be inaccurate or out of date, depending on how old the map is. To determine the actual condition of a questionable roadway, contact local highway officials to make sure it is open and safe to use for the type of vehicle that you are driving.

also be indicated directly on the map next to the roadway, usually using a system of colored arrowheads.

Highway and Freeway Numbering

When you are traveling away from home, it is useful to know the numbering system for highways and freeways. These identification numbers are posted on signs at regular intervals along the roadway. On United States and Canadian freeways and highways, routes that run in a general north–south direction have odd numbers. Even numbers are assigned to routes running in a general east–west direction. In the United States, the greater the even number, the farther north the road is. The greater the odd number, the farther east the road is.

Most routes are one- and two-digit numbers. Alternative routes are generally designated with three-digit numbers, with the last two digits representing the main route. If the first digit is even, the alternative route is a **loop** that goes through or around a city. If the first digit is odd, the alternative route is a **spur** that leads di-

rectly into a city. Business loops and spurs that go to or around business sections of cities have the same one- or two-digit number as the main highway.

Crossing the United States–Canadian Border

Traveling between the United States and Canada is almost as easy as driving from one state or province to another. The primary difference is that Canada uses the metric system, whereas the United States does not. In several Canadian provinces, signs also appear in French or in both French and English.

If you are a citizen of either the United States or Canada, you need a valid driver's license, a passport or other proof of citizenship, and your vehicle's title certificate or registration to cross the border. You must keep these with you at all times while driving. If you plan to stay longer than six months in either country, contact immigration officials to determine whether you need a visa.

In general, DUI penalties, licensing requirements, and insurance laws are more strict in Canada than in the United States.

Figure 21–6 In which general direction does this route run?

Figure 21–7

 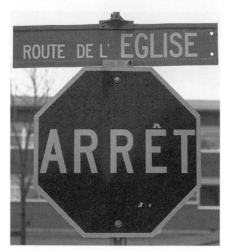

Figure 21–8 United States drivers in Canada must be prepared to tackle the metric system and, in some provinces, signage in French.

Each state and province has its own laws regarding when visitors must obtain a license and register their vehicle in that jurisdiction, but generally this applies only if you become a resident in that state or province. In most cases, exchange students are exempted from these requirements. Drivers are not required to show proof of insurance at the border, but they must have it if they are involved in a collision or are pulled over by the police.

21–2 DRIVING UNFAMILIAR VEHICLES

At one time or another, you may end up driving an unfamiliar vehicle such as a rental car, recreational vehicle, sport utility vehicle, or moving van, or you may have to tow a trailer. Before taking to the road, it is important for you to familiarize yourself with the limitations and capabilities of each of these vehicles.

Rental Cars

When renting a car, take a moment to learn how it differs from your own vehicle. Before you get in, walk around the vehicle to get a sense of how long and wide it is. Thoroughly inspect it for dents or scratches and report them to the rental agency. Make sure that the tires are properly inflated and that a flat tire kit and chains, if necessary, are stored in the trunk. Look at the layout of the dashboard. Note the location of warning lights, gauges, and hazard lights. Activate all switches, controls, and locks to make sure that everything works. Locate the emergency brake and adjust the seat and all mirrors. Take the car for a trial run so that you get used to the response of the steering wheel, brakes, gearshift, and accelerator. If you feel uncomfortable with the vehicle, request another one more similar to your own.

Most rental car companies require you to return the car with

Figure 21–9 Take time to inspect a rental car before you take it off the lot.

the same amount of fuel as when you picked it up. If you do not, they will charge you high rates to refill the tank themselves. Allow yourself plenty of extra time to stop and refuel before you are due to return the car.

Recreational Vehicles

Recreational vehicles, often called **RVs**, include motor homes, pickup campers, some kinds of vans, and trailer combinations of various types and sizes. They are generally much harder to handle than cars because of their size, weight distribution, and awkward shape. RVs share the same blind-spot problems as trucks, but they have less power and are less stable. Their high profile makes them vulnerable to gusting winds, and most lack the aerodynamic design and durable construction of commercial rigs. Many campers have heavy rear sections that are prone to veer from side to side. The high center of gravity of some RVs increases the risk of rollover on turns.

RVs accelerate, brake, and maneuver much more slowly than cars. Always maintain an extra-long following distance when driving an RV. When possible, try to avoid backing up because most RVs have very limited rear visibility. Instead, drive around the block and reach your destination head-on. If you have no other

factoid

The first rental car, the Hertz "Drivurself," was introduced in 1925.

DRIVING TIPS *Rental Car Insurance* _____

Rental car companies normally offer all renters extra insurance on their vehicles. Some of this coverage may duplicate the coverage of your own insurance policy. Although in many cases your insurance company will cover you in a rented car just as if you were driving your own vehicle, it often will not cover damages for revenue lost when a rental vehicle is being repaired. Before deciding whether to purchase additional insurance on a rental car, check with your insurer first.

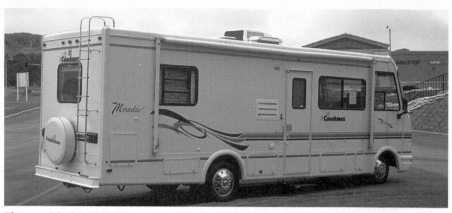

Figure 21-10 Driving a recreational vehicle is very different from driving a car.

choice, first get out and walk around the vehicle to check for any obstacles that you cannot see from the driver's seat. Have another person stand outside the RV to help guide you.

When driving in windy conditions, reduce your speed and keep a firm grip with both hands on the steering wheel. In extreme winds, stop in a sheltered area until things quiet down. Be prepared to feel the effects of wind gusts when driving out of a protected area such as a tunnel or when passing another large vehicle such as a tractor-trailer truck. Because driving an RV can be mentally and physically exhausting, plan frequent rest stops and switch drivers more often than you would in a car.

Being conscious of the large size of your RV will prevent you from hitting overhead objects such as overpasses or service station canopies. If your RV is rented, the total height of the vehicle may be marked on the outside, near the driver's door. If not, check with the rental agency or in the vehicle manual to find out

the correct height. As a reminder, it is a good idea to mark this height inside the vehicle within view of the driver. Most overpasses and tunnels will be marked with a clearance height. If your vehicle is too tall, or very close to the clearance height, or the passage seems very narrow, *do not proceed!* Turn off the roadway and find another route that can accommodate your vehicle such as a local truck route. Local regulations on extremely tall or wide vehicles may even restrict you to such a route.

Moving Vans

The challenges of driving a moving van are similar to those of an RV. Before passing under bridges or overpasses, know the van's height so that you can judge your clearance. Increase your following distance and give yourself additional time to speed up, brake, and stop. Make your turns slow and wide. When steering, compensate for wind gusts. Always load the heaviest items first, over the axles, and try to distribute the weight of the load evenly.

Wild Wheels

Figure 21-11 Which company, famous for making tractors and other kinds of farm equipment, built this early RV for use in African expeditions in the 1930s?

Figure 21–12 Make sure that the truck you rent is appropriate for the size and weight of the load you carry.

Most moving van rental agencies will inspect their trucks adequately before turning over the keys. However, you should still take a walk around the vehicle to check its condition. If you see any major damage, check that the rental agency has noted it in its records. Make sure that all lights and locks are working and that the tires have good tread and are properly inflated. When you leave the rental location, take a drive around the block to check that

the brakes feel and sound good. If you are not satisfied with the condition of the van, return to the agency and ask for another vehicle in better condition.

Towing a Trailer

Vehicles towing trailers are even less stable than RVs and moving vans. Most jurisdictions require towed trailers to be driven in the far-right lane of traffic except when passing, preparing to turn, entering or leaving a highway, and driving on a highway with four or more lanes in each direction, in which case you may use the two right-hand lanes.

Pulling a trailer puts a strain on your vehicle and its engine. If you are going to hitch a trailer to your vehicle, especially for long distances, study your owner's manual for specific procedures to prepare your vehicle. Besides checking engine fluid levels and filters, it is generally recommended that you increase the air pressure in your vehicle's rear tires to the maximum recommended limit. You will also

Figure 21–13 Be sure to properly connect the brake lights when attaching a trailer.

DRIVING TIPS *Towing at Night*

If you will be towing a trailer at night, check the alignment of your headlight beams *after* you have hooked up the trailer. The added weight of a trailer often tilts the headlights of a car or pickup truck upward into the eyes of oncoming drivers, which is dangerous and in most jurisdictions illegal.

need safety chains to connect the trailer to the car in case the hitch breaks, and special oversize rearview mirrors on both sides to allow you to see the full length of the trailer. Remember to remove these mirrors from your tow vehicle after you have unhitched the trailer. Because they project so far out, they are illegal in many jurisdictions.

Do not try to hook up a trailer by yourself if you have never done it before. If you are renting the trailer, have the rental agent show you how to hitch and unhitch it and to connect the brake lights so that other roadway users to the rear of the trailer will know that you are braking. Most vehicles with a trailer hitch are equipped with a special socket into which you can plug the brake-light cord extending from the trailer tongue. If your vehicle is not equipped with this socket, you can purchase special light bulbs that screw into your brake-light sockets and have electric cords extending from their sides that attach to the trailer brake lights. These light bulbs are available at trailer rental agencies and auto supply stores.

Always hitch the trailer to the tow vehicle *first,* and then load the trailer. When you are loading a trailer with loose cargo such as luggage, furniture, or camping equipment, always put the heaviest items in first over the trailer's axle. Try to distribute the weight of all other items evenly from left to right and front to back. Secure the load with a rope, net, or tarpaulin as necessary. *Never carry passengers in a trailer.* This is unsafe and is illegal in most jurisdictions. It is also illegal to tow more than one trailer or other vehicle at a time in a "trainlike" fashion.

Keep in mind that it takes much longer to stop, accelerate, and turn when towing a trailer. Increase your following distance, especially going downhill, and take your

Figure 21–14 Some roadways have lower speed limits posted for vehicles pulling trailers.

turns slow and wide. Because your vehicle is now much longer than it is without the trailer, keep passing and lane changes to an absolute minimum. Use lower gears on hills for added control and to reduce the load on your brakes. Keep an eye out for special posted trailer speed limits on highways, in urban areas, and on roads with steep inclines.

If you are towing something large and heavy, such as a boat or a camper, you will have to be prepared to adjust your steering to deal with gusting conditions and crosswinds created by vehicles as they pass you or as you pass them. If at any point your trailer starts to sway or fishtail, steer toward the center of your lane and gradually reduce your speed. If the trailer has a separate set of brakes, use them first while accelerating slightly. When the trailer stops swaying, use your vehicle's brakes carefully to slow down. If necessary, pull off the roadway to see if the load has shifted and whether it needs any adjustments.

Sport Utility Vehicles

Four-wheel drive vehicles, designed to operate both on- and off-road, are often called **sport utility vehicles (SUVs).** These vehicles differ from average cars in significant ways. They are usually taller, so you sit higher relative to the road. Because you can see traffic and the roadway ahead more easily, you may be tempted to follow the vehicle ahead of you too closely. Take care not to tailgate, a common bad habit of SUV drivers.

Because SUVs have a high center of gravity, they are more likely to "lean" as they go around a curve. They also have a rollover rate two to three times that of regular cars. Therefore, it is very important when driving an SUV to watch your speed and slow adequately for turns, curves, and even lane changes. *Never carry passengers in the open cargo area of an SUV.*

If you plan on doing frequent off-road driving in an SUV, you should have an experienced off-road driver show you some basic and advanced techniques. Off-road driving can be dangerous if you have little experience or understanding of how to maneuver a vehicle around difficult obstacles. Every off-road vehicle has different capabilities and limitations. Some general rules to follow when driving off-road are as follows:

- Drive directly up and down hills because traveling diagonally may result in a sideways slide.

- Cross ditches or logs at an angle so that one wheel at a time goes over the obstacle.

- Squeeze the accelerator gently to avoid spinning your wheels. If a spin does occur, back off the pedal to regain traction.

- Do not wrap your thumbs around the steering wheel. They could break if the wheel kicks around suddenly when it hits rocks or other obstacles.

factoid

SUVs have the highest occupant ejection rate of any vehicle.

uto slang

"Mud doggin'" means you are driving an SUV off the road for fun.

- Know your vehicle's performance potential.
- Vehicle speed should be reasonable, and not so fast as to endanger any passengers, pedestrians, or animals.
- Cross any two-way highways at a 90-degree angle.
- Drive in a manner that respects wildlife, land, and vegetation on public property. Stay in areas or on trails specially designated for off-road use.

In some areas of the United States and Canada, off-road vehicles must be registered, display special identification, and have special equipment mandated by law. As an off-road driver, you must comply with all the regulations and controls of the local jurisdiction.

YOUR TURN

21–1 Road Trips

1. How do you prepare for extended road trips?
2. What are the basic features of a road map?
3. How are highways numbered in North America?

21–2 Driving Unfamiliar Vehicles

4. What precautions should you take when driving an RV or moving van?
5. How do you safely load and pull a trailer?
6. What precautions should you take when driving an SUV?

SELF-TEST

Multiple Choice

1. Odd-numbered highways in North America:
   a. run in a general north–south direction.
   b. run in a general east–west direction.
   c. are loops.
   d. are spurs.
2. The legend of a map:
   a. explains what the colors and symbols mean.
   b. determines its level of detail.
   c. lists the distances between key points.
   d. displays the map coordinates of major cities.
3. The scale of a map:
   a. shows where you can find tourism information.
   b. lists the fees of tollways.
   c. determines its level of detail.
   d. gives you average seasonal temperatures in major cities.

4. When preparing to tow a trailer:
   a. load the trailer before attaching it to your vehicle.
   b. hitch the trailer to your vehicle before loading it.
   c. place the heaviest items in the front.
   d. decrease the tire pressure in your rear tires.

5. A spur route:
   a. starts with an odd number and leads directly into a city.
   b. starts with an even number and goes to rural areas.
   c. can be an even- or odd-numbered route.
   d. is always connected to loop routes.

Sentence Completion

1. The _____ is a table that lists distances in miles or kilometers between key points.
2. Carrying _____ in a trailer is unsafe and illegal in many jurisdictions.
3. Pickup campers and motor homes are examples of _____ vehicles.
4. A _____ goes through or around a city.
5. Alternate highways have _____ numbers.

Matching

Match the concepts in Column A with examples of the concepts in Column B.

Column A	Column B
1. __ Scale	**a.** Miles per inch
2. __ Trailer hitch	**b.** Travel time between cities
3. __ Legend	**c.** Airports, rest areas, parks
4. __ SUV	**d.** Interstate 5
5. __ Spur	**e.** Off-road vehicle
6. __ North–south roadway	**f.** Highway 179
7. __ Mileage chart	**g.** Interstate 40
8. __ East–west roadway	**h.** Safety chains

Short Answer

1. What should you bring with you if you plan to drive a vehicle across the United States–Canadian border?
2. What should you do before driving a rental car off the lot?
3. What are some of the hazards of driving a recreational vehicle?
4. What are some ways that you can prevent fatigue when driving on long trips?
5. What should you do to prepare your vehicle for an extended road trip?

Critical Thinking

1. You are towing a trailer up a mountain on a two-lane highway. Just as you exit a tunnel, a large gust of wind causes the trailer to sway toward the oncoming traffic lane. At the same time, you observe an oncoming big rig in the other lane. What should you do?

2. You have just arrived in your favorite city for a two-week vacation. You decide to go on a road trip to visit some of the outlying towns. You visit a rental car agency, and the agent sets you up with a car with a manual transmission. As you pull out of the lot onto a steep incline, your car stalls. A truck is right behind you, but you are having a hard time coordinating the gearshift and clutch to start the car and move up the hill. What should you do?

PROJECTS

1. Using a map of either Canada or the United States and a travel guide, plan a trip from one end of the country to the other. Make allowances for rest stops, tourist attractions, lodging, and places to eat along the way. Highlight your route on the map and indicate where you intend to stop. Calculate about how long it would take and how many miles or kilometers you would cover.

2. Call a few rental car companies and get a copy of their standard insurance agreements available to people who are renting a vehicle. Check with your own insurance company to find out what is and what is not covered in your policy. Determine what, if any, additional coverage you will need to rent a car.

Answers to Guess the Vanity Plate and Wild Wheels

Chapter	Guess the Vanity Plate	Wild Wheels
1	Ticket free (Figure 1–10)	Since 1936 (Figure 1–6)
2	Don't be too near (Figure 2–7)	Convair Model 118 (Figure 2–8)
3	Mad about you (Figure 3–8)	1907 Thomas Flyer (Figure 3–6)
4	Stop on a dime (Figure 4–14)	1911 Marmon Wasp (Figure 4–8)
5	Straighten up (Figure 5–9)	1903 Duryea (Figure 5–10)
6	Pump it up (Figure 6–12)	Chrysler Airflow (Figure 6–7)
7	Diamond driver (Figure 7–26)	
8	Yield to me (Figure 8–10)	26 feet (8 m) (Figure 8–6)
9	I hate lefts (Figure 9–6)	Roths' Beatnik Bandit (Figure 9–10)
10	Hate the city (Figure 10–9)	"Articulator" bus (Figure 10–4)
11	I'm so slow (Figure 11–11)	1913 "Stanley Steamer" 810 (Figure 11–13)
12	Double trouble (Figure 12–16)	Lamborghini Diablo Roadster (Figure 12–6)
13	Hog happy (Figure 13–13)	Unit Rig "Lectra Haul" (Figure 13–18)
14	Dimwit (Figure 14–5)	Hummer (Figure 14–7)
15	Gustbuster (Figure 15–10)	The Boeing Company (Figure 15–14)
16	I buckle up (Figure 16–12)	Isetta (Figure 16–10)
17	Skid row (Figure 17–11)	Reeves Octo-Auto (Figure 17–3)
18	Designated driver (Figure 18–7)	Grandpa Munster of *The Munsters* (Figure 18–9)
19	Too few miles per gallon (Figure 19–15)	1921 Rolls-Royce Silver Ghost (Figure 19–9)
20	Charge me (Figure 20–4)	Mohs Safarikar (Figure 20–6)
21	Southbound (Figure 21–7)	International Harvester Co. (Figure 21–11)

Glossary

A

ABS: *See* antilock braking system.

acceleration: the rate of change of an object's speed.

acceleration lane: a temporary freeway lane that is an extension of the on-ramp and is designed to allow entering vehicles to match freeway driving speeds before merging into traffic.

accelerator: the far-right foot pedal used to control the amount of fuel fed to the engine. Also called the gas pedal.

adaptive equipment: specialized equipment that adapts vehicle controls to allow a physically disabled person to drive.

administrative per se laws: laws that exist in most jurisdictions that permit an arresting police officer to immediately suspend a person's license for various types of offenses, such as driving with a BAC over the legal limit or refusing to comply with a BAC test.

air bags: cushions located in the steering wheel and, in some vehicles, the passenger-side dashboard that inflate in a front-end collision and distribute the force of impact over a wider surface of the torso. On some vehicles, air bags located to the sides of vehicle occupants deploy in side-impact collisions.

alternator: a generator that produces electricity to power a vehicle's electrical system

angled parking: parking in a space that's angled to the curb, usually about 30 degrees.

antilock braking system (ABS): a braking system in which sensors are used to adjust hydraulic pressure to each wheel of a motor vehicle to keep the wheels from locking, thus preventing the vehicle from skidding.

antitheft devices: equipment installed on a vehicle that deters, disrupts, or helps catch a car thief.

assess: to predict potential threats on the roadway before they happen by accurately anticipating what others are going to do in dangerous situations. Part of the SAFE method of defensive driving.

B

BAC: *See* blood alcohol concentration.

back-up lights: white or amber lights on the back of a vehicle that are activated when the transmission is set to REVERSE, indicating the driver's intention to back up.

banked road: a road that dips down in one direction, so that either the left or right side is higher than the other.

basic speed law: a law found in all jurisdictions that states that a driver should always operate his or her vehicle at a speed that is reasonable and prudent for existing conditions.

bicycle lane: a lane, usually on the far-right side of a roadway, designated for bicycles only.

blind spots: those areas not reflected in either the rearview or sideview mirrors of a motor vehicle.

blood alcohol concentration (BAC): a percentage measurement of the level of alcohol in one's bloodstream.

blowout: a sudden loss of air pressure in a tire.

Botts' dots: raised buttons or square-shaped reflectors placed on the roadway surface to help drivers stay within lanes.

brake fade: a condition in which brakes overheat after being applied continuously over time, such as when descending a long, steep mountain road.

"brake and hold": a reflex action to press the brake pedal and hold it down in an impending collision.

brake lights: red lights on the rear of a vehicle that are activated when the driver presses the brake pedal; designed to warn others that the vehicle is slowing down or stopping.

braking distance: the distance traveled by a vehicle from the time the brakes have been applied until it makes a complete stop.

braking skid: a skid caused by one or more of a vehicle's brakes locking up. It can occur only in vehicles without an antilock braking system.

breath alcohol test: the most common test for intoxication performed by law enforcement. It consists of having a person breathe into a tube on a device that uses chemical analysis to determine the BAC level.

bus lane: a lane designated for buses and right-turning traffic.

by-laws: local and municipal government regulations in Canada covering parking rules, certain speed limits, prohibited turns, and other traffic laws that act as a supplement to state or provincial vehicle codes.

C

car alarms: optional warning devices installed on vehicles that emit a sound, signal, or visual cue to deter car thieves.

car jackings: assaults on drivers to steal their cars.

carbon monoxide: a colorless, odorless, tasteless gas found in the exhaust fumes of gasoline engines that under certain circumstances can seep into a vehicle's passenger compartment.

carpool lane: a lane designated for buses, motorcycles, and vehicles carrying a minimum of two or three persons. Also called an HOV lane or diamond lane.

center of gravity: the point about which an object's weight is centered.

center turn lane: a lane in the center of a roadway marked by parallel solid and broken yellow lines designated for left turns only from either direction. Also called a two-way turn lane.

central vision: an area about 3 degrees wide directly ahead of a driver where everything can be seen clearly.

centrifugal force: the outward force or "pull" experienced when traveling in a circular path.

chain reaction: a series of collisions involving vehicles that impact one after another, usually front to rear.

child safety seat: a special seat for infants and young children that must be purchased separately and installed on top of the car seat.

choke: a device on older vehicles used to control the amount of air entering the carburetor while starting the engine.

claim: a report filed by an insured person against an insurance company to recover losses covered by his or her policy.

clutch: a pedal on manual-transmission vehicles located to the left of the brake pedal that the driver must press while shifting gears.

collision insurance: insurance that covers the cost of repairing or replacing an insured person's vehicle at its current market value.

color blindness: the inability to differentiate between certain colors, such as red and green. Color-blind drivers must interpret traffic controls by memorizing their shape and meaning.

color vision: the ability to see color. Color vision helps drivers determine the meaning of various signs and symbols.

commuter lane: a lane designed to allow increased traffic in one direction at a given time of day. It may be a permanent reversible lane or a special temporary lane created with orange cones or other dividers.

comprehensive insurance: insurance coverage that protects an insured person from accidental losses caused by anything except a collision, such as theft, vandalism, or fire.

construction sign: an orange sign that alerts you that you are in or about to enter a construction or work area.

controlled intersection: an intersection in which some form of sign, signal, or control device is used to direct the flow of traffic.

controlled railroad crossing: a railroad crossing with some combination of signs, warning lights, signals, roadway markings, and lowered crossing gates.

cornering skid: a skid caused by losing traction on a curve.

covering the brake: a way to be prepared to stop or slow suddenly that involves taking your right foot off the accelerator and holding it over the brake pedal as you cruise forward on your car's momentum.

crossbuck: a crossed white sign used to mark a railroad crossing.

crossover: a special area on a divided highway where vehicles can turn around to go in the opposite direction. Unpaved crossovers are generally restricted to emergency or law-enforcement vehicles.

crowned road: a road that is built higher in the center than on the sides.

cruise control: a device that allows you to regulate and maintain a vehicle's speed without using the accelerator.

curb parking: parking parallel to a curb with no surrounding vehicles.

D _____

deceleration lane: a temporary freeway lane that allows drivers exiting a freeway to adjust to slower-speed conditions without blocking traffic on the through lanes.

deductible: a specified amount of money that an insured person must pay before his or her insurance company begins paying for a claim.

defensive driving: a method of driving that emphasizes anticipating and avoiding danger on the roadway.

demerit point system: a system maintained by the Department of Motor Vehicles (or equivalent agency) in which a driver receives points for each moving-vehicle violation. These points remain on the driver's record for a specified period, and if a certain number are accumulated, may result in license suspension or other penalties.

depreciation: the decline in a vehicle's resale value over time.

depth perception: the ability to judge the distance between two objects.

designated driver: a nondrinking person who volunteers in advance to drive others who have been drinking alcohol.

distance chart: a table on a map that lists distances in kilometers between key points on a map.

divided attention impairment: the inability to perform more than one task at once.

divided highway: a multilane highway in which opposing directions of travel are separated by a fixed barrier or median strip.

double-merge lane: a lane at the end of an on-ramp in which drivers in adjoining lanes on the on-ramp must merge before they can merge onto the freeway.

double parking: parking parallel to another parked or stopped vehicle, blocking its movement as well as through traffic.

double vision: an uncontrollable rapid vibration of the eye that makes it virtually impossible to see.

downshift: to shift from higher to lower gears.

downshifting skid: a skid caused by downshifting too quickly.

driver education: instruction designed to help unlicensed drivers become familiar with the basics of vehicle control and rules of the road in order to pass the tests required to earn a driver's license.

driver's license: a permit issued by a jurisdiction that legally grants a person the privilege to operate a motor vehicle.

driving record: a record of a driver's motor vehicle violations in all jurisdictions that is maintained by the jurisdiction in which the driver currently resides.

driving under the influence (DUI): the crime of driving under the influence of alcohol or other drugs. In most jurisdictions, a person who has or exceeds a specified BAC is automatically charged with DUI. *See* driving while intoxicated.

driving while intoxicated (DWI): the crime of driving under the influence of alcohol. In most jurisdictions, DWI is equivalent to driving under the influence (DUI). *See* driving under the influence.

drop-offs: areas where the terrain literally drops off from the edge of the roadway without any shoulder.

DUI: *See* driving under the influence.

DWI: *See* driving while intoxicated.

E _____

exclusion: a statement in an insurance policy that describes the conditions under which certain types of losses are not covered.

execute: to carry out a decision to avoid an upcoming conflict on the roadway. Part of the SAFE method of defensive driving.

express lane: a special, sometimes reversible, freeway lane that goes into and out of cities.

F _____

fatigue: weariness or tiredness due to labor, boredom, eyestrain, and other factors that can severely affect a driver's reaction time and decision-making abilities.

field sobriety test: an "on the spot" roadside evaluation of a person's level of intoxication administered by a law-enforcement officer and consisting of a series of tests to detect physical or mental impairment caused by alcohol.

field of vision: the area that you can clearly see directly in front of you, and to the sides, when looking straight ahead.

financial responsibility laws: laws that exist in every jurisdiction that state that drivers must be responsible for any damage to property or any personal injury that they may cause while driving.

find: to identify an escape route or "out" that allows you the best means of avoiding a conflict on the roadway. Part of the SAFE method of defensive driving.

flooded engine: a condition that occurs when too much gasoline is in the engine. It is caused by depressing the accelerator too many times before starting the car.

fog lights: lights designed to be mounted on the front of a vehicle to improve visibility during fog and other bad weather.

following distance: the amount of space between your vehicle and the vehicle directly ahead of you.

force of impact: the force of a collision as determined by the magnitude of the kinetic energy of the objects that collide and the distance over which the kinetic energy is lost.

freeway: a divided roadway with at least two lanes going in each direction that has controlled and limited access. Also called an expressway, autoroute, beltway, and parkway depending on the location.

"fresh" green light: a traffic light that has just turned from red to green.

friction point: the position of the clutch at which the engine begins to engage the transmission.

fully protected turn: a protected turn in which you are permitted to turn only when you have a green arrow.

G _____

gauge: a scale with an indicator needle or numerical marker that keeps track of changing conditions like fuel level or speed.

gearshift: a device located on the console or right side of the steering column and attached to the transmission that allows the driver to change gears.

Good Samaritan law: a law existing in most jurisdictions that protects those who try to give first aid in emergency situations (such as a crash) from being liable for injuries or fatalities that they may cause or assist in causing due to the quality of first aid they administered.

graduated (provisional) licensing: a licensing process that places restrictions on young drivers. These restrictions are gradually relaxed in two or more stages as long as a good driving record is maintained.

gravity: an invisible force that objects exert on other objects.

gridlock: a situation in which traffic becomes so heavy that it comes to a virtual stop.

guide sign: a green sign that tells you where you are, where you are going, or how to get somewhere.

H

habitual offender: a driver who continues to accumulate violations and convictions on his or her driving record.

hand controls: adaptive equipment that allows a person to use his or her hands rather than legs to manipulate signals, pedals, and other vehicle controls.

hand-over-hand method: a method of steering in which one hand pushes the steering wheel around and down as the other crosses over to pull the wheel even further down.

hand signals: signals using hand and arm motions that communicate a motorist's or cyclist's intention to turn, stop, or slow down.

hazard lights: a signaling device that flashes all four turn signals at once to warn other drivers that a vehicle is moving slowly, stopped, or not functioning properly. Also called emergency flashers.

headlights: lights on the front of a vehicle that give off white light to help the driver see in conditions of low visibility. Headlights have both low-beam and high-beam settings.

head-on collision: a front-to-front collision between two vehicles.

highway: a main public roadway designed to carry traffic for long, uninterrupted periods at medium to high speeds.

highway hypnosis: an effect of open highway driving in which you literally become "hypnotized" by the road for several seconds and afterwards feel as if you just awakened from a dream.

Highway Transportation System (HTS): the network of roadways in North America designed to move people and goods in a safe, efficient, and timely manner across state, provincial, and international boundaries with a minimum of bother.

"hit and run": the felony crime of leaving the scene of a crash in which you are involved.

HTS: *See* Highway Transportation System.

hydroplaning: skating across a wet road after the tires lose contact with the road surface.

I

ignition: a switch, usually located on the right side of the steering column, activated by a key to start a vehicle's engine.

ignition interlock device: a special device installed on vehicles as a penalty for certain DUI convictions that requires you to breathe into a tube and test negative for alcohol before the ignition can be started.

implied consent law: a law that exists in every jurisdiction that states that any person driving a vehicle has already "given" his or her consent to have his or her breath, blood, or urine tested for the presence of alcohol or other drugs.

inertia: the tendency of an object at rest to remain at rest or an object in motion to continue in motion in a straight line until acted upon by a force.

inhibitions: the elements of your personality that stop you from behaving without regard to possible consequences.

interchange: an area where drivers can enter, exit, or cross roadways at different levels. Used on freeways instead of normal street intersections.

international sign: a sign designed to be understood with symbols instead of words.

intersection: a place where different roadways meet or cross.

intoxication: the condition of being affected by alcohol. The level of intoxication is determined by one's BAC reading.

invoice cost: the amount a car dealer pays the manufacturer for a vehicle.

J

jaywalking: crossing a street as a pedestrian without regard to traffic rules or signals.

jump-start: to recharge a car's battery by drawing electricity from another vehicle's battery using jumper cables.

K

kill switches: secondary ignition switches concealed inside vehicles to inhibit the flow of electricity or fuel to the engine.

kilometer allowance: the annual limit on the number of kilometers a person can drive a leased vehicle without paying a penalty.

kinetic energy: the energy that an object in motion has.

L _____

lane-use signals: signals mounted over re-versible lanes that indicate whether it is safe for you to use a given lane or whether it is open only to oncoming traffic.

law enforcement: agencies that enforce the vehicle codes and traffic laws governing the use of the HTS.

learner's permit: a "pre–driver's license" permit issued by a state or province that allows a person to practice driving for a certain period with a driver education instructor or another adult driver before receiving a regular license.

legend: a guide on a map that explains the colors and symbols used to represent different types of roadways and common landmarks.

liability insurance: insurance coverage, mandatory in most jurisdictions, that pays for bodily injury and/or property damage caused by an insured person who is found to be at fault.

license revocation: a cancellation of the legal permit to drive a motor vehicle.

license suspension: a temporary loss of the privilege to drive.

limit line: a wide white or yellow line painted across the roadway at an intersection behind which vehicles must stop. In intersections with only a crosswalk, the nearer crosswalk line serves as the limit line.

list price: the manufacturer's suggested retail price of a vehicle.

loading: adding weight to a vehicle's weight as measured when it is empty.

locking the brakes: an emergency braking technique in which the driver firmly presses and holds the brake pedal until the vehicle comes to a complete stop.

loop: an alternative route that goes through or around a city.

M _____

maximum speed: the maximum legal speed, based on considerations of safety and economy, as posted on a speed-limit sign.

median strip: an area of space that separates opposing directions of travel on a divided highway.

merging area: the space where an acceleration lane merges with the freeway.

mileage allowance: the annual limit on the number of miles a person can drive a leased vehicle without paying a penalty.

mileage chart: a table on a map that lists distances in miles between key points on roadways.

minimum speed: a minimum speed posted on some roads to prevent drivers from moving at such a slow speed as to impede or block the normal and reasonable movement of traffic.

moped: any two- or three-wheeled vehicle with pedals that has an automatic transmission and a motor that produces less than 2 horsepower and that is not capable of exceeding 30 miles per hour (50 km/h) on level ground.

motorcycle: any two- or three-wheeled motor vehicle having a seat or saddle for riders and weighing less than 1,500 pounds (3,300 kg) with at least 15 horsepower.

N _____

no-fault insurance: insurance coverage that requires the insurance companies of those involved in a collision to pay a set amount for damages or personal injury claims regardless of who was at fault.

"no-zones": the blind spots of large vehicles such as buses and tractor-trailer trucks.

O _____

odometer: a gauge that displays the total number of miles/kilometers that a vehicle has been driven since it was manufactured.

off-ramp: a one-way exit ramp from a freeway.

off-road vehicle: a specially equipped vehicle, such as a dune buggy or snowmobile, designed for driving off the roadway.

off-tracking: the tendency of truck drivers to swing wide on a turn, especially a right turn, to minimize interference with through traffic on the cross street.

one-way street: a roadway in which all lanes of traffic move in the same direction.

on-ramp: a one-way entrance ramp used to gain access to a freeway.

on-ramp meter: a special signal used to control traffic merging onto the freeway from an on-ramp.

open container laws: laws that exist in many jurisdictions that make it illegal to have any kind of open container of alcohol in a vehicle unless it is kept out of the immediate control of the occupants, such as in the trunk.

orderly visual search (OVS): a scanning technique developed in the 1950s by Howard L. Smith that requires using selective glances in a constantly repeating pattern to monitor all the different areas around one's vehicle.

overdriving your headlights: traveling at speeds that prevent you from stopping within the distance illuminated by your headlights.

oversteering: turning too sharply when making a turn or rounding a curve.

OVS: *See* orderly visual search.

oxidation: the process by which the liver rids the body of alcohol by turning it into oxygen and carbon dioxide.

P _____

parallel parking: parking alongside a curb between two parked vehicles.

parking brake: a manually set brake that keeps a vehicle in place when parked and serves as an emergency brake if the standard brakes fail.

parking lights: lights that are white or amber-colored on the front of the vehicle and red on the rear of the vehicle. They are normally activated by the first setting on the headlight switch and are designed to be used only when parking.

pass: to overtake a vehicle directly ahead by entering an adjoining lane, gaining a speed advantage, and re-entering the original lane in front of the other vehicle.

passive restraint: a passenger restraint, such as an air bag or shoulder belt on some vehicles, that operates automatically.

pedestrian: any person who uses or crosses a roadway on foot or by means of a self-propelled device other than a bicycle.

peer pressure: the influence that others of your own age have on you.

peripheral vision: the unfocused areas extending 180 degrees to the sides of your central vision.

perpendicular parking: parking at a 90-degree angle from the curb with the front or rear of the vehicle aligned with and parallel to the curb.

policy: a written contract between an insured driver and the insurance company that outlines the amount of coverage and how much both parties must pay on a claim.

power brakes: power-assisted brakes that require less foot pressure to operate than standard brakes.

power skid: a skid caused by accelerating too quickly, especially on a slick road surface.

premium: a specified amount of money a person pays for insurance coverage for a designated length of time.

preventive maintenance: day-to-day care and routine service given to a vehicle to avoid more serious repairs.

protected turn: a turn made from a turn lane posted with signs, road marked with arrows, and accompanied by a traffic signal arrow.

provisional licensing: *See* graduated licensing.

pumping the brakes: an emergency braking technique in which the driver alternately applies the brakes completely until they lock and then releases them in rapid succession.

purchase price: the amount of money that a car dealer or owner is willing to accept for a vehicle.

push-pull method: a method of steering in which one hand pushes the steering wheel up while the other pulls it down.

R

reaction distance: the distance traveled by your vehicle during the time it takes you to identify the need to stop and react to a braking situation.

rear-end collision: a collision in which one vehicle hits another from behind.

rearview mirror: a wide, rectangular mirror either suspended from the roof or attached to the windshield of a vehicle that allows a driver to see what's directly behind him or her.

rebate: a special payment to customers offered by vehicle manufacturers designed to increase sales of certain models.

recreational sign: a brown sign that tells you about nearby places of cultural interest and public recreation like historic sites, museums, and national parks.

recreational vehicles (RVs): vehicles, such as a motor homes, pickup campers, or trailer combinations, used for travel and recreational activities.

regulatory sign: a sign that tells you what you can or cannot do at certain times and places.

restricted license: a permit issued by a state or province permitting a person to drive only under certain conditions, such as while wearing eyeglasses, during daylight hours, or within a certain distance of a person's home.

reversible lane: a lane designed to allow traffic to go in one direction at certain times of the day and in the opposite direction at other times of the day. Used on high-density commuter roadways.

revoked license: *See* license revocation.

riding the brake: resting the right foot on the brake pedal while driving. Because this constantly activates the brake lights, it confuses drivers behind you as to your intentions.

right-hand rule: a general rule that at uncontrolled intersections, four-way stops, and intersections with flashing red or broken signal lights, drivers on the left should always give the right-of-way to drivers on the right.

right-of-way: the right to use a certain part of a roadway when two or more users of the roadway want to use it at the same time.

road rage: a term used to describe aggressive driving, including deliberate tailgating, yelling at other drivers, making obscene gestures, purposely blocking other drivers' paths, and in extreme cases, assault.

"rock out": a technique to get out of mud, deep sand, or snow by moving forward and backward in rapid succession until the stuck tire or tires are freed.

rollover: a result of a collision in which a vehicle is flipped upside down or literally rolls over one or more times.

rubbernecking: a term used to describe the common driver habit of slowing down to observe a crash site.

rumble strips: grooved or raised sections of the roadway used to alert drivers to slow down or let them know that they are straying out of their lane or off the road.

runaway vehicle ramps: short, steep uphill roads or pits, often with energy-absorbing material at the end, provided for vehicles that experience braking problems on long, steep downhill mountain grades.

running lights: lights located on the front of a vehicle that automatically illuminate when the engine is started. They may be a dimmer setting of the headlights or a separate set of lights located next to the headlights.

RVs: *See* recreational vehicles.

S

SAFE: a defensive-driving strategy to evade potential danger on the roadway. SAFE stands for *scan, assess, find,* and *execute.*

safety belts: automatic or manually fastened belts designed to restrain vehicle occupants in the event of a collision or quick braking action.

scale: the level of detail of a map, as indicated by a line representing a larger unit of measure (for example, 1 inch equals 1 mile).

scan: to look ahead down the road to gather information about the complete driving scene. Part of the SAFE method of defensive driving.

semicontrolled intersection: an intersection in which signs or signals are used to control one or several approaches, but not every approach.

semiprotected turn: a protected turn made from a turn lane but not accompanied by a traffic signal light that directs your turn with a green arrow or a special green light.

sentence enhancement: an additional penalty automatically applied to an existing sentence for certain types of criminal offenses, such as excessive speeding while driving under the influence of alcohol or other drugs.

service sign: a blue sign that informs you of nearby services such as hospitals, rest stops, and gasoline stations.

shoulder: a continuation of pavement or other stable surface that goes beyond the road boundary line.

side-impact collision: a side-to-side, side-to-front, or side-to-rear collision between two vehicles.

sideview mirrors: exterior mirrors mounted on the vehicle's doors that allow the driver to see along the sides of the car and neighboring lanes of traffic.

skid: a loss of directional control of a vehicle that occurs when a vehicle loses traction.

slow-moving vehicles (SMVs): vehicles not designed for high-speed travel, such as a wide-load trucks, bulldozers, or agricultural harvesters. Many slow-moving vehicles are required to have a special SMV sign attached to the rear.

sobriety checkpoints: special roadside safety checks in which police officers stop drivers to determine whether any are impaired by alcohol or other drugs.

soft shoulders: shoulders that slope downward or do not provide effective traction.

solo collision: a collision involving only one vehicle, such as with a tree or concrete barricade.

space cushion: an empty space between you and the cars and other objects on the roadway around you.

speed: the rate at which an object changes its position over time.

speed bump: a raised slab of pavement used to force drivers to slow to a near stop.

speedometer: a gauge that indicates how fast a vehicle is traveling in miles and/or kilometers per hour.

sport utility vehicles (SUVs): four-wheel-drive vehicles designed to operate both on and off the roadway.

spur: an alternative route that leads directly into a city.

"stale" green light: a traffic light that has been green for a long time or since you first noticed it.

steer: to control a vehicle's direction of travel.

steering wheel: a device that allows the driver to turn the front wheels of the vehicle. A "tilt wheel" is a steering wheel that can be adjusted for better comfort and control.

"sticker price": the list price of a vehicle plus destination charges and additional options and services provided by the dealer.

stopping distance: the total distance required to stop from the time you first recognize the need to brake to the time your vehicle is no longer moving. The sum of reaction distance and braking distance.

suspended license: *See* license suspension.

SUVs: *See* sport utility vehicles.

switchbacks: curves, typically found on mountain roads, that are so sharp that they reverse direction.

synergistic effect: the enhancement of a drug's side effects caused by mixing it with alcohol and certain other drugs.

T —————————————————————

tachometer: a gauge that measures an engine's revolutions per minute (rpm).

tailgate: to follow other cars too closely while driving.

taillights: red lights located on the rear of a vehicle that are illuminated when the headlights are turned on.

three-point turn: a way to reverse direction on a narrow street in which a driver turns sharply to the left and stops as close as possible to the opposite edge of the roadway, and then backs up before moving forward in the opposite direction.

3-second rule: a test to check your following distance during low-speed driving. It calls for picking a fixed object directly ahead of you and counting off three full seconds. If you reach the object before you reach the count of 3, you are driving too closely to the vehicle ahead.

threshold braking: an emergency braking technique in which the driver uses a full and firm application of the brake pedal up to the point where the brakes lock and cause the vehicle to enter a skid.

T-intersection: an intersection in which a side road joins a main road with through traffic at a right angle.

title: a document that shows proof of vehicle ownership. Also called a pink slip.

tollbooth: a booth located at an entrance or exit to a tollway where drivers pay a toll.

tollway: a controlled-access roadway that requires drivers to pay a fee or toll to use. Also called a turnpike, toll expressway, or toll road.

torque: the ability of a force to cause an object to rotate.

tracking: a method of steering that allows you to keep your vehicle on the intended path of travel by looking toward the center of the lane ahead and making only slight movements with the steering wheel.

tracking device: a system that uses a device hidden on a vehicle to emit a signal to the police or a central response center to locate the vehicle if it is stolen.

traction: the friction between a vehicle's wheels and the surface of the road that makes it possible for drivers to move, change direction, and stop.

trade-ins: vehicles that people sell to a dealers in exchange for credit on a new or another used vehicle.

traffic circles: circular roadways that allow traffic from many different directions to intersect.

traffic laws: state or provincial regulations covering the licensing of drivers, registering and titling of vehicles, financial responsibility of driv-

ers, minimum safety equipment of vehicles, the rules of the road, and infractions and penalties.

tunnel vision: a 70% reduction in one's field of vision, caused by blurred peripheral vision and fixation on a narrow field ahead.

turn lane: a lane added near an intersection to separate left- or right-turning traffic from through traffic.

turn-signal lights: flashing lights used to indicate right or left turns that are white or amber-colored on the front of the vehicle and red on the rear of the vehicle.

two-point turn: a way to reverse direction in which a driver either backs into a driveway or side street on the right side of the street and then drives forward in the opposite direction ("reverse, then forward") or turns into a driveway or side street on the opposite side of the street and then backs up into the street before moving forward in the opposite direction ("forward, then reverse").

U

uncontrolled intersection: an intersection without any form of traffic control device or roadway marking.

uncontrolled railroad crossing: a railroad crossing, typically found in rural areas, without signs, signals, or roadway markings.

understeering: turning insufficiently when making a turn or rounding a curve.

uniform speed zones: areas such as school zones, alleys, and open rural highways that have designated speed limits even if no signs are posted.

unprotected turn: a turn not made from a turn lane at an intersection and where there are no arrows—whether designated by a signpost or road markings, or signaled by a traffic control—to guide your turn.

U-turn: a way to reverse direction in which the driver traces a path in the shape of a large "U."

V

vapor lock: a condition in which gasoline in a vehicle's fuel system becomes so hot that it boils and turns to vapor, causing the engine to "lock," or stop running. It occurs only in older vehicles that have fuel pumps in the fuel tank rather than on the engine.

velocitation: an effect of open highway driving in which you unconsciously find yourself driving much faster than you intended.

visual acuity: the ability to see objects both near and far.

W

warning lights: red or yellow indicators on a vehicle's dashboard that indicate serious problems or safety concerns.

warning sign: a yellow sign that alerts you to hazards or possible hazards ahead.

warranty: a written guarantee that a car manufacturer or dealer will repair or replace any defec-tive parts or systems within a set amount of time or for a certain number of miles/kilometers driven.

"weave" lane: a shared acceleration and deceleration lane on a freeway in which vehicles entering and exiting the freeway share the right-of-way.

wholesale price: the amount of money a dealer is willing to pay for a used vehicle.

Y

Y-intersection: an intersection in which roads meet at unusual angles.

Z

zero tolerance laws: laws that exist in some jurisdictions that mandate severe and immediate punishment for DUI offenses involving certain drug violations or underage drinkers.

Index

Numbers in *italics* refer to figures.

Figure Credits

Map content provided by GeoSystems Global Corporation, publishers of the National Geographic Road Atlas, MapQuest, and other National Geographic map products.

To order your very own copy of the National Geographic Road Atlas, or to find thousands of other kinds of maps and atlases, visit **www.mapstore.com**

For door-to-door trip directions, visit **www.mapquest.com**